The Rise and Fall of the Broadway Musical

The Rise and Fall of the Broadway Musical

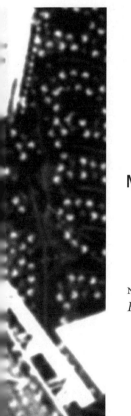

Mark N. Grant

NORTHEASTERN UNIVERSITY PRESS
Boston

Advisor in Music to Northeastern University Press
Gunther Schuller

Northeastern University Press
Copyright 2004 by Mark N. Grant

Library of Congress Cataloging-in-Publication Data
Grant, Mark N. [date]
The rise and fall of the Broadway musical / Mark N. Grant
p. cm.
Includes bibliographical references (p.   ) and index.
ISBN 1-55553-623-9 (cloth : alk. paper)
1. Musicals—New York (State)—New York—History and criticism.
I. Title.
ML1711.8.N3G727 2004
782.1′4′097471—dc22   2004014100

Composed in Minion by Graphic Composition, Inc., Athens, Georgia.
Printed and bound by Thomson-Shore, Inc., Dexter, Michigan. The paper is
Nature's Natural, an acid-free stock.

MANUFACTURED IN THE UNITED STATES OF AMERICA
08   07   06   05   04   5   4   3   2   1

To the memory of Philip Sterling (1922–1998)
Esteemed actor, fine musician, wonderful friend—
and the original Peter Ilyitch Boroff in Cole Porter's
Silk Stockings *(1955)*

ACKNOWLEDGMENTS

I would like to thank William Frohlich, the director of Northeastern University Press for twenty-seven years and a gentleman and friend, for commissioning this book and for chaperoning the project through some unforeseen straits. Thanks too to the ever-cheerful Sarah Rowley, who took over the reins on the project when Bill retired, to her well-organized assistant, Amy Roeder, to Ann Twombly, the ever-consummate production director, and to Jill Bahcall, the indomitable marketing director. A special thank-you to Gunther Schuller for his important words of praise at a critical juncture, and gratitude also for the supportive words of Jerry Bock, Philip Rose, and Eric Salzman.

Funds that helped make possible several years of research and writing on this book were furnished by the Furthermore program of the J. M. Kaplan Fund, the Harburg Foundation, and the DuBose and Dorothy Heyward Memorial Fund, to all of whom I am extremely grateful. Edith Hall-Friedheim has been a special champion of this project from the start. She generously offered her time and journalistic skills as a research assistant in the final laps of the writing, even while enduring a time of personal challenge in her own life. In addition, she and her late husband Eric Friedheim graciously helped fund my work on the book. I wish to express a special debt of gratitude to the Friedheims.

For their memories of Broadway, both recent and distant, my thanks to Aaron Frankel, Morton Gottlieb, Evans Haile, the late Al Hirschfeld, Jane Sherman Lehac, the late Bethel Leslie, John Mauceri, the late Mary Morse, Meg Mundy, the late Dana O'Connell, Trude Rittmann, Joan Roberts, Michael Starobin, Eric Stern, Frances Tannehill, the late Miles White, and the late Howard Whitfield.

Kudos to Jeremy Megraw and the other helpful librarians at the Performing Arts Library Research Division at Lincoln Center. For their friendly advice and good colleagueship, thanks are also in order to Janet Axelrod, Keith Brion, Neely Bruce, David Budries, David Chase, Jon Alan Conrad, David Cunard, Suzanne Eggleston, George J. Ferencz, Mary C. Henderson, George Izenour, Marty Jacobs, John Kenrick, Kim Kowalke, Miles Kreuger, Kean McDonald, Otts Munderloh, the late Bennett Oberstein, Arlene Anderson Skutch, Dave Stein, and Martha Swope. Eugene McBride did the superb music engraving, and Michael Kagan took his usual fine photographs.

Books were kindly loaned to me by Thomas P. Lewis and Cyrus Purdy, and recordings loaned by Seth Winner. Bench jockeying and moral support were unstintingly provided (sometimes late at night) by Joseph Mangiacotti, Daniel Baldwin, Glenn Cooper, and Nancy Giordano.

CONTENTS

CONTENTS

ILLUSTRATIONS

Where are the bards that pleasured me, . . .
Where are the rhymes of yesteryear? . . .
Alas, in Nashville, Tennessee,
Twanging their cliché hearts away. . . .
Woe to the culture that woos TV
Where sponsors flourish and songs decay,
Where clay is hailed as cloisonné
And catch-penny poet is sage and seer.

                                        —E. Y. "Yip" Harburg

Life is like a musical comedy . . .
Nobody seems to know just what it's about,
Yet ev'rybody's trying to figure it out.

                                        —George M. Cohan

CURTAIN RAISER

On March 28, 1954, General Foods sponsored a ninety-minute television program entitled "The Rodgers and Hammerstein Cavalcade" that was judged so important a media event that all four television networks (CBS, NBC, ABC, and Dumont) simulcast it. The program cost $500,000 to produce and was seen nationwide by an estimated 70 million people, at that time the largest entertainment audience in history. The performers included not only stars of the team's great musicals (Mary Martin, Ezio Pinza, John Raitt, Jan Clayton, Yul Brynner) but also Rosemary Clooney, Ed Sullivan, Jack Benny, Groucho Marx, and Edgar Bergen. "The Rodgers and Hammerstein Cavalcade" was aired by over 250 television stations, and newspapers across the country reviewed it as if it were a Broadway show opening. Musicals mattered to the country. Theater mattered.

In 1950s America, Richard Rodgers and Oscar Hammerstein II were megacelebrities, Broadway musicals cynosures from coast to coast. The television version of the musical *Peter Pan* with Mary Martin was broadcast almost every year, and hit Broadway musicals of the 1930s and 1940s were routinely given television productions with such stars as Bing Crosby and Mickey Rooney. In September 1953 New York's Mayor Vincent Impelliteri proclaimed the first week of that month Rodgers and Hammerstein Week in that city: four of their musicals were running simultaneously on Broadway (*The King and I, South Pacific, Me and Juliet,* and a revival of *Oklahoma!* at the City Center). Three years later, on March 31, 1957, CBS broadcast an original Rodgers and Hammerstein musical written for television, *Cinderella,* to an audience of an estimated 107 million.

Forty years later the advertising posters plastered on New York City's buses and subways for the hit musical *Rent* displayed the phrase "Don't you hate the

1

word 'musical'?" To sell a musical to a new audience, advertisers now had to pitch that it was "not" a musical. Time had passed the musical by as a commercial draw in the American marketplace. What happened?

On Friday evening, February 12, 1999, I was in the audience for a performance of Rodgers and Hart's 1937 *Babes in Arms* at New York's City Center. Semistaged versions of classic Broadway musicals have been presented in five-performance runs at City Center in the *Encores!* Great American Musicals in Concert series since February 1994. During the "Entr'acte" before act 2, when the orchestra reprised the tune of "Where or When," something occurred unique in my theatergoing experience. Audience members spontaneously broke out in a ghostly massed humming along with the melody. It sounded like campfire singing. It was a goosebump moment: a salute by theatrical cognoscenti not only to a marvelous song but to a cultural tradition's passing.

But how many people came to see *Encores!*'s *Babes in Arms*? Not millions. "Look at how many people are in City Center, and you multiply it by five, and you come up with a number, and that number is a shock," laments conductor John Mauceri, a champion for the cause of a national classic Broadway musical touring repertory company.[1] (Veteran *Playbill* writer Louis Botto told me that at the opening night of the original 1937 production of *Babes in Arms,* singer Mitzi Green was called back to do five encores of "The Lady Is a Tramp.")

Nostalgia can be overpowering for each generation. The Broadway director John Murray Anderson (1886–1954) as a boy saw Sir Henry Irving perform *The Merchant of Venice,* and at the end of his life Anderson wrote, "The play was illumined by gaslight, and presented many imaginative effects, which influenced and still linger in my mind, so much so that I aver to this day that no stage production since then, whether lighted by lime or electricity, has ever equalled in artistry those lit by gas."[2] As Hume Cronyn wrote in his memoirs, "Memory is a terrible liar." Nevertheless, there seems to be a consensus among theater professionals and audiences that the golden age of Broadway ended sometime in the 1960s. Says Harold Prince, "I've seen many productions of *A Streetcar Named Desire* but by far the best was the original Broadway production directed by Elia Kazan and starring Marlon Brando. I've seen many productions of *Guys and Dolls,* though none can compare with the Broadway original. Before economics killed it, Broadway was a magnet for all the best talents. It was a true theatrical elite."[3] Roger Angell wrote in the *New Yorker* on May 31, 1993:

> it is only lately that I have come to understand how deeply the New York stage
> suffused my mind and memory through my teens and twenties and thirties. . . .

Going to plays back then could be a complicated experience. Leaving the theatre in numbed silence after Mildred Dunnock's requiem lines in "Death of a Salesman," or, a dozen years earlier, aflame with a solidarity ignited in the union hall of "Waiting for Lefty," I felt at one with the strangers who had sat around me. "Oklahoma!" did the same thing, in happier fashion, because it made us feel so wonderful, there in the middle of the war. . . .

Everyone in those audiences felt the same way, of course, and these privately held and publicly shared experiences became a language of friendship and intimacy for my generation. Listening to a band work through a medley from "Pal Joey" (it was 1941, and I was in college), the girl I was dancing with and I absolutely knew that "I Could Write a Book" would segue on the next beat into "Bewitched, Bothered and Bewildered," and we had the choruses and the verses to both songs by heart; if the sets then moved on to "Our Little Den of Iniquity," which had not yet made the records or the radio, and my partner breathed that little "knock . . . on . . . wood" into my ear on the pause, it meant that she'd seen the show, too, and she and I became Vivienne Segal and Gene Kelly, just for a moment there on the shining floor.

Theatre is many things, and the Broadway of my youth, seen now, feels like a club, an acquired knowledge and language. . . . The theatre then seemed to have a breath and life of its own. . . . That Broadway has gone away. I went on attending plays into the sixties and after, though less often, and somewhere along in there it became a different experience. . . . Maybe it was the miking, maybe it was the new mechanics—sets that took wing or changed into something else; they took your breath away sometimes, and your belief as well.

Broadway and the theater formed a smaller world then, a more formal, elegant world, as Broadway costume designer Miles White recalled a few years back:

The whole world is different now. In those days, in a certain section in the balcony, people smoked during the performance. And the actors smoked onstage. Clifton Webb was always lighting up onstage. So did Noel Coward. People dressed for the theater much better than they do now. But at that time that wasn't considered formal. To us now, it seems formal. Ladies had special hats for the theater, theater hats, which were smaller, not big ones with a lot of stuff on them, and a veil. Some years before that, they wore hats this size with feathers up to here, so people behind you couldn't see unless you took your hat off. You dressed differently for the theater than you dressed to go out dancing. If you were going dancing you wore long dresses. You didn't *have* to wear long dresses to the theater.

Sometimes, if you were going to the theater, you could arrange, if you had dinner at Sardi's, to leave your topcoat in the checkroom there. They'd let you come back for it as long as you'd paid. The check girl, particularly at Sardi's, was a very influential person socially. You had to know her, be friendly with her. And she invested in shows.[4]

Dress codes may speak more about society than just about changing fashions; perhaps they evince a respect for art. Actress Bethel Leslie, who played Mary Tyrone to Jack Lemmon's James Tyrone in the 1986 Broadway and 1987 West End productions of *Long Day's Journey into Night,* told this story: at one London performance in 1987 Jack Lemmon noticed some people sitting in the front row wearing shorts and T-shirts; he got so rattled and angry that offstage between scenes he threw up.[5]

Yes, something intangible has changed in and about the legitimate theater. Even the photographs in *Theatre World,* the annual pictorial record of the Broadway theater since 1944, seem more vibrant and alive in the pre-1970 volumes than in the last three decades' annuals. "The entertainment business in the east up to about 1950 was theater and the road. You booked a show to play in New York and it toured. That was the whole deal in the 1930s and 1940s. Then television arose and took over,"[6] says Aaron Frankel, a onetime stage manager for the Lunts and the author of an excellent book on writing musicals. Thanks to road tours, this vanished Broadway was truly a national theater. Today, American regional theater lacks the national recognition enjoyed by Britain's regional theatre, or even that of professional sports here: sports fans in Boston know what teams in Denver are doing and vice versa. As Roger Angell recalled, the *Billboard* charts and *Hit Parade* used to ensure national distribution of Broadway show tunes. No more.

It was in the crucible of this now-vanished world that a unique popular art form reached its highest peak: the Broadway musical. What defines a musical? In 1950 critic Cecil Smith wrote:

In its basic form, musical comedy is not specifically American even now. The theatrical form in which speaking and action are alternated with musical set pieces and usually with dances, with some sort of plot as the chief unifying factor, is the form of singspiel, comic opera, operetta, opéra-bouffe, burlesque (in its historic aspect), and pantomime as well as of modern American musical comedy. It is, in short, the form of all musical works for the stage except revue, ballet, and through-composed opera.[7]

4

Then what is specifically American about the musical? This book argues that the American musical peaked as an art form during a forty-year golden age on Broadway that ended almost forty years ago. The best musicals of Broadway from about 1927 to 1966 coalesced and integrated the complementary theatrical arts—playwriting, music, design, dance, movement, truthful acting—in a way that differentiates them from and raises them above all other light music theater genres of the world, past and present: Spanish zarzuela, German singspiel, British Gaiety musicals, Viennese operetta, Parisian opéra-comique. The Broadway musical at its height was a vernacular version of Wagnerian *Gesamtkunstwerk:* a total art form for the masses. With its text-driven balletic element it even became a vulgate realization of Diaghilev's unification of dance, music, and drama. In 1949 the Berlin drama critic Friedrich Luft visited New York to guest-review several Broadway productions. Among the shows Luft saw was *Love Life,* a musical composed by Kurt Weill with book and lyrics by Alan Jay Lerner, directed by Elia Kazan, with dances by Michael Kidd and sets by Boris Aronson. He called it the "most beautiful and most powerful evening of theatre" he had seen while in New York. "Such a combination of music, lighting, dance, and wit could hardly be produced with such nonchalant precision by us at home, today or in the foreseeable future."[8]

In tracing the rise and fall of the musical, this book divides Broadway history into three eras: 1866 (*The Black Crook*) to 1927, 1927 (*Show Boat*) to 1966, and 1966 to the present, although the dates are used loosely. The central period of the Broadway musical that produced its peak I variously call the canonical period, the second age, the golden age, the high-water period, and the belle époque, a term freely borrowed from Alan Jay Lerner, one of our own belle époque's foremost practitioners (he in turn borrowed it from the nineteenth-century France of Offenbach). A few theater historians, such as Gerald Bordman and Richard Traubner, have argued for an earlier start to the American belle époque, but most concur with circa 1927; even the cultural historian Jacques Barzun agrees.[9] To understand why the second era is the golden one and why the third is not, it is necessary to delve back into our formative first era, to which our current, third era bears an alarming resemblance. Today theaters abroad revive neither pre-1927 Broadway hits like *The Pink Lady* or *Adonis* or *Irene,* nor post-1966 hits like *The Wiz, On the Twentieth Century, Big River,* or *City of Angels.* Rather, the opera houses of Vienna play our canonical era shows like *Kiss Me, Kate;* the revival houses of the West End play *Pal Joey.* To them our second-era shows are our significant literature, just as to us their *Merry Widow* or Gilbert and Sullivan is their significant literature.

Are musicals primarily fun or are they art? Why should people go to musicals to seek drama and catharsis, when they can go to Sophocles, or Shakespeare, or *A Streetcar Named Desire,* or *Tosca?* During the belle époque on Broadway some highbrow drama critics like George Jean Nathan thought that musicals should have rested content with being merely diverting. If musicals are only mindless and superficial, there can be no argument about a rise and fall. But the best musicals of the canonical era are dramatically challenging as well as tuneful and entertaining. On the other hand, if they were only fun, there would be little purpose to examining them from the perspective of art. Just as Wagner introduced to opera the idea of closely correlating text and music—before him set pieces were freestanding and the libretto was frequently preposterous—the belle époque Broadway musical achieved a higher level of expressive power when it started more tightly correlating text and music. But it didn't thereby cease to be entertaining. Great performers, great tunes, great dancing, and great sets were all part of Broadway musicals before 1927, but finely wrought lyrics and librettos consistently occurred only in the golden age. Interestingly, most of the song standards deriving from Broadway theater also were written during this same period.

Musicals in the high-water period were generative forms of cultural imagery. Whatever survives in the American cultural memory about showboats stems from the Kern-Hammerstein musical, not from the Edna Ferber novel. The 1950 musical *Guys and Dolls* fixes Damon Runyon characters in popular folklore; Frank Capra's Runyon-based 1933 film *Lady for a Day* and its 1961 remake *Pocketful of Miracles,* do not, nor have Runyon's stories lasted. Today's musicals are replicative rather than generative. They reflect and cannibalize other areas of pop culture—television, movies, techno special effects, rock music, music videos—and with few exceptions do so without developing any independent life as dramatic literature. They fix their advertising logos in memory, not their capacity to provoke the imagination. The commerce of Broadway musicals goes on as ever. The literature of the form seems to have stopped. And newer musicals have ceased to have any stature as art objects in pop culture. Charlie Rose fetes movies, not Broadway musicals.

Why don't they write the way they used to? Why did such composers as Rodgers, Gershwin, Porter, Arlen, Berlin, Schwartz, and Loesser all occur at once, and will their like ever come back again? In this book, musical analysis figures prominently in the search to find answers, but it is not the only road taken. Regarding the Broadway musical as a *Gesamtkunstwerk,* I have undertaken to investigate the progress of the form through all its parameters: music, words, dance, movement, sound. But everything comes back to the music. Almost all commentators seem to agree that the music of the golden period somehow has a heart, a conviction, a soul, a rootedness, that post-1966 theater music—the rock stuff; the traditional, nonrock stuff by Cy Coleman, Charles Strouse, and John Kander; and even the later works by golden-age writers such as Rodgers, Burton Lane, and Lerner—does not. Popular art before 1960 had the moral intensity of high art. As actor Carroll O'Connor, who as Archie Bunker lamented "The Good Old Days" in song, put it:

> Our pop music did not issue thunderous invitations to a semisensate flight from normality. Our music used to be played by skilled orchestras; intelligible singers rendered tunes about dancing in the dark while orchids bloomed in the moonlight and nightingales sang in Berkeley Square and stars fell on Alabama—silly sentiments, but carried along by intelligent melodic phraseology, and if the words were doggerel they were often wonderfully compelling. I know my comparison is cranky, but there it is.[10]

This book is not a year-by-year chronicle, a survey of the greatest shows or greatest songwriters, a plot summary digest, or an almanac or encyclopedia. There are already excellent books available that subscribe to those descriptions, many of which appear in the bibliography. Rather, this book is an inquest into what happened to raise an inconsequential entertainment genre to a level of popular art, and then to lower it back again to an inconsequential entertainment genre. Because I think some aspects of this mystery have gone unexamined in the literature on the Broadway musical, and need to be freshly investigated from angles other than the umpteenth recapitulation of the greatness of the iconic songwriters, I have sometimes taken a novel tack to shed light. Some well-known figures, for the purpose of illustrating a point, are given much more prominence here than other well-known figures, while some behind-the-scenes players in the theater come dramatically to the fore for the first time. An attempt has been made to rethink much of the received wisdom, and sometimes the conclusions arrived at are unusual (for example, *Hello, Dolly!,* not *Cats* or *Hair,* was the real death knell for the dramatically integrated musical, and Bing Crosby inadvertently helped destroy the high-water Broadway musical theater). To reassess why and how second-age Broadway music was theatrically superior, one chapter here reviews the 150-year history of Broadway vocal lines, singing voices, and the microphone, another the 150-year history of the rhythms, dance steps, and even instrumentation.

Some obvious questions about the art form never seem to get asked, much less answered, in the standard literature on the subject. What do the hours and hours of pre-1920 recordings of Broadway shows tell us about why singing styles evolved the way they did in the performance of musicals? When did song reprises start in musicals? When did overtures begin to be used? When did sound design begin, and why did its use escalate? How and when has the structure of investment had an impact on the quality of the artistic product? I tender no definitive proofs but do not shy from offering answers.

By the 1880s "Broadway" had come into use as a generic term for the large legitimate theaters that at that time clustered around 14th Street in New York City. By 1900 "Broadway" was considered the district from 14th Street to 45th; over the ensuing three decades "Broadway" migrated north to assume its present-day location. For the sake of convenience this book refers to any musical show produced after 1866 in Manhattan's larger theaters as a Broadway musical, whether it was an opera, operetta, musical comedy, musical play, revue, or other genre. The operative assumption is that patrons of theaters, whether in 1883 or 2003, who go to see an opera like *La bohème* or a ballet like *Swan Lake* at a Broadway theater understand that they have seen a "Broadway" production and not an opera house or ballet version. Venue is definitive of perception and reception.

If history is written by the victors, the victors on Broadway are the shows that get on at all, not those that run forever. Merely to open on Broadway is a triumph. Even shows that close the same night they open become history the way baseball players become major leaguers with a single plate appearance. This may be unfair to off-Broadway, off-off-Broadway, and to shows that close out of town, all of which rightly contribute to the history of the musical, but this book is the story of the musicals the main stem produced and what that tells us, for better or worse.

Deception about date of birth is a professional necessity for actors and other performers—even Beethoven during his lifetime claimed to be two years younger than he actually was. (Deception in entertainers' autobiographies is an ever-present hazard for theater historians.) Whenever possible, I have consulted Social Security Administration records to establish the true date of birth, so various dates given throughout this book may conflict with dates listed in other books. If uncertain, I append a question mark on the best guess, even if it differs from the usual date cited elsewhere. Broadway lyricist John La-touche, for example, was three years older than he claimed to be, and I have found only one other book among dozens that gives his correct birth year. The matter of George M. Cohan's birthday (either July 3 or 4, 1878) is still debated by scholars. One eminent theater historian privately told me that Helen Hayes was five years older than she claimed and was thus ninety-seven, not ninety-two, when she died, even though the Social Security Administration lists the later birth date.

Historian Oswald Spengler wrote that civilizations and great artistic forms germinate, flower, wither, and die. Can the greatness of musicals be reinvigo-rated, or are they doomed to recede into their historical moment? Are their writers and composers fated just to recapitulate the motions without remembering the substance? Can they survive the depredations of technology and still have a soul? Have music videos permanently displaced theater musicals? There are strong opinions on the pages that follow, but also strong reminders of a cultural heritage that gives every reason for hope and renewal.

ACT ONE

From Soaring Divas to Growling Rockers:
How Changes in Singing Forged and Felled the Show Tune

> New theatre music not only reprises what has
> been written before but, with few exceptions,
> does not do it half as well. . . . There is much to
> praise in the contemporary music scene, but it has
> not contributed any significant melodic material
> to the collective American unconscious.
>
> —Vocal coach David Craig[1]

Irving Berlin. Jerome Kern. Richard Rodgers. Cole Porter. George Gershwin. Harold Arlen. Arthur Schwartz. Burton Lane. Harry Warren. Frank Loesser. Harold Rome. Vincent Youmans. Pick your own list of the great standards these and other song composers of the golden age created for the Broadway musical. Yes, Mr. Craig, they indeed repose in the collective American unconscious in a way that the show music, and arguably the popular music, of forty or fifty years since does not.

That "they don't write them like they used to any more" is piety, an item of faith by now with commentators from radio's Jonathan Schwartz (son of the composer Arthur) to a long bookshelf of pop historians and cultural philosophers. (Schwartz himself has called Rodgers and Hammerstein's "Out of My Dreams" from *Oklahoma!* "a cathedral.")[2] Melodies by songwriters who wouldn't have known a tonic chord from a dominant seventh have in recent years been vivisected fearsomely by musicologists like Allen Forte, Geoffrey Block, and Joseph Swain, and elevated to classical folk art by Alec Wilder's seminal book *American Popular Song.* That a group of contemporary songwriters created something wonderful is not doubted. The question of why were they all born at roughly the same time—genetics? God? chance?—can hardly be argued.

But these composers' undeniable gifts do not alone explain exactly what it is that made the melodies of golden-age Broadway shows so instantly catchy and enduringly memorable. Something else has been overlooked: namely, how tune writing was driven by the types of voices that sang them. Our musical theater as it evolved from 1866 to 1927 gradually demanded a new kind of voice and a new kind of melody writing never heard in any nation's light opera before, not even in Gilbert and Sullivan. As librettos and lyrics improved in literacy and dramatic integration, what had been operatic in Broadway voices had to change to a more speech-based style. At the same time the songwriters couldn't "speechify" the music so much that melody was sacrificed.

The results peaked in Broadway's second age: melody that enabled the voice to make a lyric's content clear, and a new kind of singing voice that delivered both melody and lyric equally. The need to stay on the lyric forced composers to write melodies that were not only singable by the new kind of voice but that were also immediately grasped by the ear.

But today, while there are still marvelous belle époque–style singing voices on Broadway, the song idiom of Rodgers and Berlin is being elbowed into oblivion by a new vocal style on Broadway and elsewhere that has created a new composing style with an emphasis on the beat and the eardrum. We have gone from Tin Pan Alley to Tympan Alley.

The great Broadway tunesmiths of the second age all but invented three "golden means" of theater song composing: a golden mean between melodic soaring and melody riffing; another between the art voice and the vulgar voice; and a third between song primarily as speech and song primarily as music. All three occurred at a time when the microphone, though in use, had not yet taken over the legitimate stage. Since ancient Greece, theater music had been written to be sung in live performance, not in a recording studio. Then came the microphone, and these golden means all were sundered. The microphone and its practitioners ultimately engendered a complete redefinition of the art of singing in public entertainment. And public singing, which had originally come out of the theater and had existed unmediated for three thousand years, now ate its parent alive. The new upstart, microphone singing, came to regard the theater as a colony of its own empire. Ultimately, the microphone destroyed the very cultural paradigm that had made the golden age of live musical theater a paradigm to begin with. It made "live," which had been a defining property of the art of theater for a few thousand years, a misnomer. And it made obsolete the cultural hegemony of the Broadway melody.

Scene One. *Before the Microphone*

The Pre-1910 Musical: Busman's Holiday for Opera Singers

In America circa 2004 the accepted mainstream model of singing in public entertainment is the pop singer. When a vocalist is trotted out for the national anthem at a sporting event, more often than not that singer is a rock or country singer, not the Three Irish Tenors. It is difficult to imagine that only a little over a century ago the standard for such public singing performance was the operatic, or "legitimate," voice—not the untrained voice but the voice one cultivates by learning to "place" the voice using head resonance and the diaphragm. The lines between opera, operetta, and musical comedy singing were not then so distinct as they were later. In 1900–1920, the divas of the Metropolitan Opera were as celebrated as rock stars today. (Even into the 1930s, 1940s, and 1950s, well-known opera singers appeared in Hollywood movies.) Today, the word "diva" itself is more often heard in a rock context. But in 1900 the trained voice was the predominant style of performance in everything, including musical comedies on the legitimate stage, and stage songs no less than operatic arias were usually performed by such voices. As the conductor and musical theater authority Lehman Engel wrote:

Up to about 1920, a singer was a singer. That is, he was someone with a highly polished and sizable voice that gave evidence of having been "trained." In the big Victor Herbert successes, commencing about the turn of the present century, the leading singers were quite often borrowed from the Metropolitan Opera. In *Mlle. Modiste* there was Fritzi Scheff, who became a bigger star on Broadway singing "Kiss Me Again" than she had been at the Met as Musetta in *La Bohème*. Later, Herbert used Emma Trentini (coloratura) of the Manhattan Opera House and Orville Harrold (the Met's Parsifal) in *Naughty Marietta*. In a sense, the vocal requirements of Broadway were at the time nearly synonymous with those of opera.[3]

Even today, the term "legitimate" is generally understood to mean operatic singing in a nonoperatic context, with an emphasis on beauty of tone rather than on enunciating the syllables of the lyric (although great singers can do both). The singer in a legitimate style learns to manage the natural breaks in the voice so as to ensure continuity of sound between the head voice and the chest voice; when a singer breaks into a completely different timbre produced from the chest, she is said to be "belting." A legitimate voice has a larger range than an untrained voice, usually about two octaves (some legitimate singers have a three-octave range). Some pop and rock singers can and do sing "legitimate": Linda Ronstadt did so in the New York Public Theatre's 1981 production of *The Pirates of Penzance*, and currently the versatile singer-actress Audra McDonald sings both operatic arias and rock styles with equal aplomb.

The great-grandfathers of Broadway musicals were the late-nineteenth-century American operettas (or "light operas") that were performed on the legitimate stages in the district of Manhattan that by 1880 was coming to be known as Broadway (although it was farther downtown than the current Broadway of the West Forties). While Gilbert and Sullivan have endured, history has forgotten the composers of late-nineteenth-century Broadway, the most prominent of whom were Reginald De Koven (1859–1920), the British-born Julian Edwards (1855–1910), and the German-born Gustave Kerker (1857–1923); also among this group is John Philip Sousa (1854–1932), who wrote operettas as well as marches, and such stateside Europeans as Ivan Caryll from Belgium, Ludwig Englander from Vienna, and Lionel Monckton, Edward German, and Ivor Novello from England. De Koven led the pack with some two dozen shows, of which *Robin Hood* was his most successful and its "O Promise Me" his most famous song. Julian Edwards, an unjustly forgotten, very melodious composer,

14

played Frederick Loewe to De Koven's Richard Rodgers. Kerker wrote *The Belle of New York,* the era's musical most popular with European audiences.

The vocal style of these light operas was not that of *Guys and Dolls* (1950) or *Annie Get Your Gun* (1946), much less that of *Rent* (1996) or *Hairspray* (2002). It was more like Offenbach. For one thing, the overwhelming majority of musical numbers in these shows were choral. There were few solos and thus little material to enable a great singing actor or actress to emerge as a theater star like a Sarah Bernhardt. The scores consisted of one four-part soprano-alto-tenor-bass ensemble after another, with the elaborate vocal parts characteristic of opera or oratorio but rarely encountered in contemporary Broadway writing (exceptions: Bernstein's *Candide,* Sondheim's *A Little Night Music*). The hit songs, such as "Brown October Ale" in De Koven's *Robin Hood,* were usually sung in unison by large choruses. The SATB choruses and the vocal duets or trios were not sung in the close-harmony style of turn-of-the-century barbershop, much less that of the 1930s Boswell Sisters or the 1940s Andrews Sisters, but in chorale arrangements, a style still heard today in recent Broadway shows as various as *Phantom of the Opera, Ragtime,* and *Titanic* (but today heard certainly not as the *only* type of a musical's number). With large choruses onstage peopled with legitimate voices, audibility and projection were never issues, regardless of size of orchestra or theater. Yet despite all their choral singing, these shows were not through-sung; they had spoken dialogue, too, like opéra-comique.

Such operettas were at the time considered "musical shows." They were produced in legitimate theaters, not opera houses, and their tickets were sold to theatergoers, not to opera subscribers of the diamond horseshoe crowd. Even their comic relief numbers required legitimate singing chops: talkable patter numbers in works like *HMS Pinafore* and *The Mikado* sit cheek by jowl with full-fledged arias containing passages of vocalization on single syllables performable only by trained opera singers. And in the 1880s and 1890s even the comedic or farcical musicals on Broadway, like Charles Hoyt's *A Trip to Chinatown,* which had more solo singing, were usually performed in the legitimate voice.

The popular style and the legitimate style were thus nearly one and the same. How do we know? Because surviving pre-1900 recordings confirm this. Some fifteen to twenty hours of nineteenth- and early-twentieth-century musical theater recordings exist, which recently have been transferred from the hundred-year-old flat disc and vertical cylinder originals to contemporary compact discs. Thus, one can hear the Savoyard tenor H. Scott Russell (1868–1949) in his January 1899 Emile Berliner disc recording of the song "Saturnalia" from the

British West End musical of 1898 *A Greek Slave*, singing in an unmistakably legitimate, not a folk or music-hall, style. Even the songs of the nineteenth century we have come to regard as the pop songs of their time—those of Stephen Foster, for instance—are on early recordings sung in the legitimate style. Thus, in a 1904 recording of songs from the 1902 Civil War Broadway musical *When Johnny Comes Marching Home*, with added original music by Julian Edwards and words by Stanislaus Stange, Foster's "Swanee River" is rendered by William Thompson and Florence Quinn in an operatic duet style that could comport with a rendition of "Dite alla giovine" from *La traviata* or "O soave fanciulla" from *La bohème*. Yes, "Swanee River."

In elderly recording after recording, one musical theater performer of yore after another sings in the legitimate voice, even in light musical comedy. Edna May (1878–1948), perhaps the most famous ingenue of her time, star of the musical *The Belle of New York* (1897), in a 1900 recording sings two selections from that Gustave Kerker show in a pearly lyric soprano, negotiating unprepared leaps in the vocal line that would never happen in Rodgers and Hammerstein or Andrew Lloyd Webber. Marie Cahill (1870?–1933), a great comedienne and musical star of vaudeville, sings "Under the Bamboo Tree" in a 1917 recording of a song from the 1902 musical *Sally in Our Alley* in a legitimate lyric soprano, trilling her r's floridly but not otherwise making her consonants clear. And the most famous Broadway diva of the era, the buxom Lillian Russell (1861–1922), who epitomized the Gay Nineties and was mistress to Diamond Jim Brady, in her only recording, made in 1912, sings "Come Down, Ma Evening Star" from *Twirly-Whirly* (1902) in a light, flutey mezzo. On this antique recording one can clearly hear every gearshift of Russell's breath control, from inhalation to exhalation. This, despite the fact that Russell performed in the "illegitimate" music hall shows of Tony Pastor and Weber and Fields, and was widely regarded as a ballad singer (that is, what we mean now by "pop singer").

The earliest recordings of songs by original cast members reveal much the same type of singing. Cast members from De Koven's *Robin Hood* (1891) were recorded in the 1890s and 1900s. One, Eugene Cowles (1860–1948), a leading man of his time, sings "The Armorer's Song" in a 1906 recording with orchestra in a legitimate basso range from D above middle C all the way down to the D two octaves below that. By comparison, the operatic bass Ezio Pinza (1892–1957), who retired from the Met to go to Broadway, never sang such a two-octave range in songs from the musicals he starred in, *South Pacific* (1949) and *Fanny* (1954), nor ventured so low in pitch. In a 1906 recording of selections from Victor Herbert's *The Fortune Teller* (1898), all the singing is legitimate, and once again Cowles sings "Gypsy Love Song" in a bass voice, albeit this time a little higher, in a bass-baritone range. In the shows of the 1940s period, by contrast, the male romantic lead was almost always a baritone; true bass roles were rarely written, except for novelty numbers like the comic trio of suitors "Tom, Dick, or Harry" in Cole Porter's *Kiss Me, Kate* (1948).

Decades before Pinza left the Met to trot the Broadway boards, the famous contralto Ernestine Schumann-Heink (1861–1936) starred in a Broadway musical entitled *Love's Lottery* (1904), written for her by Julian Edwards and Stanislaus Stange. In a 1906 recording, Schumann-Heink sings "Sweet Thoughts of Home" from this musical, her only Broadway appearance, in an operatic voice replete with fioriture and vowel-biased diction that make no concession to the popular stage. *Love's Lottery* was a book musical, not a vaudeville bill with trained animal acts and bell ringers, but its creators didn't dumb down Schumann-Heink's vocal style as Rodgers and Hammerstein would for opera diva Helen Traubel a half-century later in *Pipe Dream* (1955), because back in 1905 it was normal for opera singers to sing musical comedy operatically. As late as *Show Boat* (1927), Jules Bledsoe, the original Joe (the part later more famously portrayed by Paul Robeson), performed "Ol' Man River" in a lieder-singing vocal style not so different from Schubert's "Erlkönig": in his 1931 recording he interpolates a penultimate leap of a fifth to a high G, extending the range of the song to two octaves, and occasionally distorts his consonants.

Such performers were singers first and foremost, actors a distant second. What was needed to mature our musical theater was a way of bringing the art of acting into the act of singing.

The Afro-Irish Invention of Musical Comedy Singing

The legitimate voice grew in legitimate venues: the theater, the opera stage. But a different singing style was emerging in other entertainment venues where comprehension of dialogue was essential, a singing that required more focus on consonants than vowels. The most popular such entertainment in the United States from the 1840s to the 1880s was the minstrel show, performed by white performers in blackface (toward the 1880s they were sometimes performed by blacks). The available evidence suggests that minstrel show singing was consonantal. Vaudeville was the direct descendant of the minstrel show, and the two forms overlapped by at least twenty years (there were minstrel shows as late as 1920).

Singers who in the nineteenth century performed in a vocal style closer to the Tin Pan Alley popular song or folk song—singing with more emphasis on consonants and the clarity of the lyrics than on vowels and tonal beauty—were at the time called ballad singers (a confusing term, because popular sentimental ballads of that day were often sung in the legitimate voice). The ballad singer style has been called talk-singing and even "nonsinging" by some authorities. Recordings from the 1890s reveal that ballad singing existed before 1900 on the legitimate stage, although it was the exception. For example, the great comedic stage star DeWolf Hopper (1858–1935) sings "You Can Always Explain Things Away," a song from the hit 1890 musical *Castles in the Air* composed by Gustave Kerker, in a style quite similar to Rex Harrison's talk-singing through the songs of Professor Henry Higgins in *My Fair Lady* (1956). Hopper's talk-singing style came out of the patter songs of the Gilbert and Sullivan operettas (in which Hopper performed extensively), but although patter songs may appear to have been deliberately designed for an untrained singer's voice, they actually were written in emulation of Leporello's "Catalogue" aria ("Madamina," in Mozart's *Don Giovanni*) and other "talking" arias that were written in the parlando style designed for opera singers. (Catalogue arias were famously parodied later on Broadway in the Weill–Ira Gershwin musical *Lady in the Dark* [1941] when Danny Kaye delivered the names of forty-nine Russian composers in thirty-nine seconds during his "Tschaikowsky" song.)

The patter song was not the only nonlegitimate style in turn-of-the-century showbiz: the untrained folksinger-type voice was popularized in vaudeville both in Britain and the United States by such singers as the Scottish music hall performer Harry Lauder (1870–1950), who sang "Roamin' in the Gloamin'" in an untrained voice. American vaudevillian Blanche Ring (1871–1961) was the first great practitioner of the audience sing-along with such favorites as "In the Good Old Summertime," and to lead an audience in a sing-along must have required an on-the-spot gearshift to untrained "folksinging," even though Ring's surviving recordings show her voice to have been a light legitimate lyric soprano with a delicate vibrato.

By 1900 the legitimate voice's primacy in musicals was being challenged by other British music hall and American vaudeville styles of nonsinging. Several selections from Victor Herbert's *The Serenade* (1897) were recorded in 1898, and although the legitimate style is the primary mode, some of the songs' verse sections are talk-sung. A woman's chorus in a 1902 recording from the British export hit musical *Florodora* displays a music hall ballad singing style.

Two chief influences brought the new ballad singing style onto the Broadway stage. One was Irish-American musical theater (excluding Victor Herbert, born in Ireland but trained in Germany). Edward "Ned" Harrigan (1844–1911) and Tony Hart (born Anthony Cannon, 1855–91), both second-generation Irish-Americans, teamed in the 1870s with British-born composer David Braham (1838–1905) to write Broadway musical shows about the Mulligan Guard. The Mulligan Guard was a parody of the local militias, peopled by lower-class ethnic groups, that in the Civil War's aftermath policed New York's Lower East Side. Harrigan had gotten his show business start as an Irish ballad singer, and both Hart and Braham had professional experience in minstrel shows. Braham thus based the vocal line for the Mulligan Guard shows on Irish ballad singing, instead of composing comic opera style, so that Harrigan's lyrics, written in the style of each character's ethnicity, could be clearly heard. Irish-American George M. Cohan (1878–1942) was Harrigan's artistic heir and not only emulated his songwriting and bookwriting style but paid him the ultimate compliment of writing a song about him ("H–a–double r–I–g–a–n spells Harrigan"). The many surviving recordings of Chauncey Olcott (1860–1932), the original "Irish tenor" (by style, not birth—Olcott was a native of Buffalo, New York), confirm the Harrigan-Cohan ballad as an Irish-American style. Olcott was a prolific musical comedy performer; "Mother Machree" and "When Irish Eyes Are Smiling" were two of his most famous numbers (he cowrote them). On his recordings Olcott sings with little vibrato in a light tenor that favors the consonants, perhaps because to achieve dramatic impact, the sentimental lyrics of the Irish songs had to be made clear. Rounded vowels and pear-shaped tones were not Olcott, Cohan, or Harrigan and Hart. Eventually this "Irish" singing style became universal and non-Irish; it was appropriated by the mainstream of musical theater and vaudeville, notably by Al Jolson, a "Jewish Irish" tenor. (In 1923 drama critic George Jean Nathan referred in print to Eddie Cantor, who performed in blackface in the *Ziegfeld Follies,* as a "Jewish Negro." Nathan himself was Jewish.)[4]

The other style of vocalism that eschewed rounded vowels was that of the black ballad singer. Its proximity to Irish-American singing is not surprising; Olcott himself had started his career in minstrel shows. During Olcott's heyday, the greatest black musical performer of the commercial theater was the Caribbean-born Bert Williams (1874–1922). He and his partner George Walker starred in the great African-American musical of its day, *In Dahomey* (1903)—a show that played both sides of the Atlantic. After Walker died, Williams went on to do solo star turns for years in the annual *Ziegfeld Follies*. Williams made recordings of several songs from a musical entitled *Son of Ham* (1902), and on these songs (with titles now offensive like "The Phrenologist Coon" and "My Little Zulu Babe") his diction and consonantal clarity far exceed those of any of the white legitimate singers of early musical theater recordings. The same can be said for the 1921 recording of Noble Sissle singing "Baltimore Buzz" from the Sissle and Blake musical *Shuffle Along*. Indeed, vocal historian Henry Pleasants has written that singing on consonants had long been a practice of black singers before white popular singers like Bing Crosby adopted it.[5] African-American scat singing is vocalise sung on consonants instead of vowels (in European music "vocalise" means to sing open vowels on a series of changing pitches); rather than singing and holding the same syllable through changing pitches, the scat singer improvises a different syllable on each pitch. ("Vocalese" is something else again: singing words, not syllables, to a well-known jazz instrumental tune.)

The consonantal vocalism of the black style is also found in recordings of the white singers known as coon shouters, who performed a genre of black dialect song said to have originated in minstrel shows. In 1907 May Irwin (1862–1938), a stout Scotch-Canadian blond coon shouter who would have looked at home in Wagner's operas, recorded her signature song, "The Bully" from *The Widow Jones* (1895). The lyrics of "The Bully," a rollicking comic number, include liberal use of the "n" word, which Irwin, in the style of her time, enunciates with unpleasant gusto; she also enunciates all the rest of the words equally clearly, even while in dialect. A versatile and gifted performer not limited to coon roles, Irwin recorded a number of Broadway musical hit numbers from the 1890s and 1900s in other vocal styles that look to the future; she renders "The Frog Song" from *The Swell Miss Fitzwell* in a voice that could easily be that of Celeste Holm singing Ado Annie in *Oklahoma!* forty years later, or even Bernadette Peters in the 1980s and 1990s. On the other hand, in "Moses Andrew Jackson, Goodbye," recorded in 1907, she sounds like Pearl Bailey. Other popular coon-shouting Broadway performers like Stella Mayhew sound on early recordings like the first belters. On a 1911 recording, Cohan's first wife, Ethel Levey (1881–1955), reprises a song she sang in her ex-husband's 1906 show *George Washington Jr.* called "I Was Born in Virginia"; she sings in a contralto range in a brassy chest voice that can only be described as belting.

In some of her recordings, May Irwin indulges in the talk-singing style of the patter song, with one difference. When she does so, one can hear traces of a quavery singsong delivery, characteristic also of DeWolf Hopper's recitation of "Casey at the Bat" (known to posterity from the sound film he made of it late in life). This "spoken tremolo" was widely popularized by Al Jolson's spoken interludes in his "Mammy" songs. The spoken tremolo is not exclusively Hebraic and cantorial in origin, as some commentators have claimed, because it clearly

20

occurred in the singing of performers of other ethnicities. Something like it is frequently heard in recordings of British and American poets such as William Butler Yeats and Robert Frost, who recite their own works with almost musical rises and falls in their voices. In classical music it was adopted by atonal composers of the Second Viennese School—primarily Arnold Schoenberg and Alban Berg—as a technique called *Sprechgesang* in which the singer performs from a written score that notates approximate pitches for the spoken syllables.

This singsong style of musicalized enunciation must have been popular in burlesque and vaudeville, because one can hear the vaudeville stripper Gypsy Rose Lee (1914–70) giving much the same delivery in the 1943 film *Stage Door Canteen,* and the exaggerated comic diction of W. C. Fields and Mae West, both ex-vaudevillians, also displays it. In Lee's delivery, she bestows an extra vowel after words ending in consonants as though she were Chico Marx. She was not, however, spoofing an Italian accent, but rather recreating the ornate delivery of vaudeville, with its comical oversyllabifying of every line as though it were iambic pentameter. Likewise, in Cohan's 1911 recordings of his own songs from *Little Johnny Jones* (1904), he performs them in their entirety in singsong talk. Cohan's vocal delivery on "I'm Mighty Glad I'm Living, That's All" and "Life's a Funny Proposition, After All" could well be described as iambic pentameter spoken with a musical lilt—Irish-American *Sprechgesang.*

But when used by early musical comedy singers like Cohan, vocalization without pitch wasn't just singsong; it was a style of musical speech that imitated musical instruments. In a 1911 recording, Cohan sings from *Mother Goose* (a 1903 show he did not write) "Hey There! May There!" in a nasal twang in which his voice ornaments some pitches by gliding between them like a trombone slide, falling off on other pitches like a brass instrument smear. Al Jolson, soon after Cohan, did much the same thing. They ornamented their singing or talk-singing by imitating instruments heard in vaudeville pit bands even before jazz, and long before Louis Armstrong, who is generally credited with the invention of this practice. The fact that Cohan used these vocal practices indicates that they were not unique to African-American styles; rather, there was an interactive melting pot of Irish and African-American that eventually brought us to modern nonlegitimate-voiced musical comedy singing.

Al Jolson: Emancipator of the Musical Comedy Voice

More than any other single performer, it was Al Jolson (1886?–1950) who liberated the musical comedy voice from the legitimate voice. (He also liberated it from physical beauty: he was not good-looking, and some notable musical comedy singing stars that followed him, like Fanny Brice and Gertrude Lawrence, were far from beautiful.) After starting in circus, vaudeville, and minstrel shows, he appeared in many Broadway musicals of the 1910s and 1920s. By the mid-1910s his presence would overwhelm the material of almost any book show or revue he was placed in.

Jolson was a one-man oxymoron of traditional legitimate singing and Irish/African-American talk-singing. Early on he sang with a light Irish tenor with a thin vibrato, then later with a somewhat lowered, enriched timbre and his trademark big vibrato—but early and late, he always sang with clear diction, always on the lyric. He pioneered the so-called Irish mordent, a vocal grace note on the last syllable of a line of lyrics (Crosby and Ethel Merman copied the mannerism). He improvised spoken asides in mid-song that stepped out of character (George Burns and Pearl Bailey copied this). He borrowed from Cohan the vocal falloff like a downward brass glissando, but unlike the talking-singing Cohan, Jolson did it while singing full out with vibrato. He took the "cuckoo-clock cadence"—starting the last syllable of a lyric on the note a major third above the written final note and then gliding on the same syllable to the final note—and made it his personal trademark, different from Eddie Cantor's and others' use of the device, by elongating the portamento (the glide) as though he were smiling and the sun were emerging from clouds. In singing "Chloe" from *Sinbad* (1918), the Irish-mordent–happy Jolson used an r-trilling brogue even though it was a black "mammy" song and he himself was Jewish—an ethnic trifecta that embraced the three peoples who most influenced the sound of modern musical comedy.

No matter what the situation onstage, Jolson played Jolson; as late as 1940 audiences waited for the moment when he would stop the show, come downstage, and proceed to deliver a mini-recital of his chestnuts ("California Here I Come," "Swanee," "April Showers," et al.). That he usually did not sing the lyrics in character does not alter the fact that, when he chose to, Jolson was capable of brilliant acting and could submerge his persona in the character and lyric. His 1928 recording of "Ol' Man River," transposed to his "baritenor" range, proves this: as sheer acting, and notwithstanding its racial stereotyping, his performance is as hair-raising and dramatic as Chaliapin singing Boris Godunov.

When Jolson emerged as a bigger star and gate draw than any of the previous male performers of musicals, his celebrated solos broke musical theater writing free from the undifferentiated, clumpy vocal ensembles of the turn of the century, free from their pseudomadrigal infantility. Because his singing was suffused with performer ego to a degree then unprecedented on the musical stage, Jol-

22

son inadvertently turned the theater song into a dramatic soliloquy that powerfully speaks the interior of a specific person or character. Ironically, this liberation of the solo musical number was a prerequisite for further dramatic and artistic development of the musical. The irony is that Jolson's egocentric style, while empowering the song, did nothing to promote a new kind of integrated book musical. But it did lay the groundwork for a new kind of melodic writing that *would* make possible the integrated book musical—the melody writing of Berlin, Kern, Gershwin, Porter, and Rodgers, even though they rarely wrote for him. Jolson was in this sense an artistic godfather of the show tune.

Continental Europe Strikes Back with the "Soaring" Broadway Melody

The advent of a superstar like Jolson did not make legitimate singing curl up and die on Broadway. De Koven, Sousa, and the other turn-of-the-century operettists were followed by the composers Victor Herbert (1859–1924), Rudolf Friml (1879–1972), and Sigmund Romberg (1887–1951), all European-born and classically trained. They wrote the kind of operettas later immortalized in Nelson Eddy–Jeanette MacDonald movies (Friml particularly), although Romberg was versatile enough to write songs for Al Jolson. They continued the tradition of writing elaborate melodies requiring legitimate voices, but unlike De Koven and Sousa, they adopted musical comedy's practice of writing solo songs, too. While Herbert, Romberg, and Friml have commonly been viewed as holdovers from the nineteenth century, they actually were keenly influenced by vaudeville and modern show business values in a way that Sousa, De Koven, Kerker, and Edwards never were.

Friml, though trained as a concert pianist and composer in Prague, failed to make it in classical music in America and found his way into the theater as a fallback. Romberg, although he studied serious music in Vienna, immediately entered theater and popular music upon his arrival in the United States and maintained a chameleon-like ability to write operettas, popular songs, or whatever else he was hired for. But it was Victor Herbert who was considered the titan; he was during his lifetime the leading figure in the country in both the classical and the pop fields, an achievement not duplicated even by Leonard Bernstein. Yet he is almost completely forgotten by popular culture today.

Herbert started his career as a cellist and composer of serious concert music and fully expected to stay in the concert hall. Though born in Ireland, he was brought up in Germany, where also he received his musical training. When his wife, the soprano Therese Förster, was given a contract at the Metropolitan Opera in 1886, the couple emigrated to America. But once in New York, Herbert was strongly drawn to popular entertainment. Like Sousa, he conducted military bands, succeeding the great Patrick Gilmore as bandmaster of the New York National Guard. (Gilmore [1829–92] is less well remembered than Sousa but in his day was just as famous; among the march tunes he wrote is "When Johnny Comes Marching Home.") About 1893 Herbert began composing the thirty-year string of some fifty scores for Broadway operettas and musicals that brought him lasting fame. Among Herbert's biggest successes were *Babes in Toyland* (1903), *The Red Mill* (1906), and *Naughty Marietta* (1910); among his most enduring songs, "March of the Toys," "Gypsy Love Song," "Kiss Me Again," and "A Woman Is Only a Woman, but a Good Cigar Is a Smoke." He was a tireless worker, often composing more than one show at a time, working on his feet at a stand-up desk (a feat of strength, as he was quite stout), and fortifying himself by imbibing fine wines as he composed (according to his publisher Isidore Witmark).[6] Herbert did almost all his own arrangements and orchestrations. He interrupted his Broadway career to conduct the Pittsburgh Symphony Orchestra for a few years, to compose two operas, to conduct what today would be called a pops orchestra during summer seasons, and to compose symphonic scores for silent films.

Herbert, Romberg, and Friml brought to their Broadway composing a deep grounding in the melody writing of European classical music and opera. Their tune writing gibes with what Nikolay Rimsky-Korsakov (1844–1908) wrote: "cantabile melody requires a fair number of long notes. . .'; "a good vocal melody should contain notes of at least three different rhythmic values"; "monotony in rhythmic construction is unsuited to vocal melody."[7] But not even Rimsky-Korsakov knew for sure what makes some melodies effective and memorable and others not. Melodies do have curves or arcs, and many musical analysts believe a good melodic curve contains one climactic note that deviates from the general direction of the curve. All melodies move in part by steps (a note moving to an adjacent note) and in part by jumps (skipping over adjacent notes), and the way steps and jumps are combined give a melody coherence to the ear. The ear, sensing the underlying melodic curve, generally wants to hear a big skip followed by a step in the opposite direction. A melodic curve with a sequence of jumps describes what is meant by "soaring"; the melodic curve ascends by jumping all at once to a long-held high note, then returns to earth as if in deference to a musical version of Newton's Third Law of Motion.

Can pop and folk tunes, then, be soaring? Usually they are not, because untrained voices cannot easily negotiate the large vocal leaps and the immediate turnarounds from the leaps that such grand melodic writing entails. Typical

24

melodies of Broadway musicals written during the 1875–1910 period (and many for some time after) have lots of jumps and skips negotiable only by a trained voice. De Koven's "O Promise Me" of 1890 has an unprepared jump of a seventh followed by a major third continuing in the same direction before its melodic curve arches back. By comparison, Richard Rodgers's tune "Bali Ha'i" from *South Pacific* (1949) begins with a jump of an octave (larger than a seventh, but easier for an untrained singer to hear and hit), then immediately steps down a half tone, and each succeeding statement contracts the interval to an easy-to-sing major sixth.

Melodies by Herbert, Friml, and Romberg usually have more chromatic steps than songs in later musical comedy. The verse to Friml's "Indian Love Call" from *Rose Marie* features a chromatic, helixlike vocal line at one point: down a diminished fourth, up a minor second, down an augmented fifth, up a major third. The famous chorus melody begins by upwardly arpeggiating the added sixth triad but then descends back into another chromatic corkscrew, all the while supported by relatively undaring chromatic alteration in the harmony. In the 1930s and after, as jazz harmony and the altered sevenths and ninths of Ravel began to infiltrate the pop idiom, similarly sinuous half-step melodies such as Cole Porter's "Night and Day" and David Raksin's "Laura" were supported by more chromatically altered chords than those used by Friml.

The tunes for *The Student Prince* (1924)—perhaps the most melodious of all American operettas—abound in halfsteps, and here as elsewhere composer Romberg used another favorite melodic device of the operettists: the chromatic appoggiatura, a nonharmonic tone that lands smack on a strong downbeat. Yet Romberg, like Herbert and Friml, often suddenly intersperses his chromatically filigreed melodies with a juicy but simple triadic or pentatonic melody (the added sixth being a staple of operettic "soaring" writing). Thus the lusty "Drinking Song" from *Student Prince*, like "Libiamo," the brindisi from Verdi's *La traviata*, is a triadic waltz, though more built on a hunting horn call than "Libiamo" and without Verdi's chromatic melodic steps. Romberg's "Drinking Song" creates excitement from a bridge section (the tune's "release") built on a circle of fifths, but its elemental excitement is made even more dramatic by being interleaved with the chromatic waltz tune and coloratura passages of Kathie the waitress.

The dramaturgical problem with soaring melodies of the Herbert-Romberg-Friml variety was that they could not support lyrics as equal partners. They focused audience attention on their musical beauty and thereby choked off the playwriting aspects of plot, character, and realism. Yet melody so theatrically compelling could not be wholly abandoned. A compromise was needed: something that would strike a balance between soaring tunes and intelligible drama and lyrics. Something had to change both in the construction of theater melody and in the very technique of theater singing.

A Songwriting Revolution: The Chorus Trades Places with the Verse

The first thing to change was the balance between the verse and the chorus of a song. After 1910 it was the tune of the chorus that became the tune identified with the song title; the verse was the song's cue, a mere intro. Before 1910, it had been just the opposite: the verses were long, independent, and self-contained, and their tunes were as important as or more important than the chorus tune. For quite a while, even as the tunes of song choruses began to grow simpler in the 1900–1920 period, the verse tunes remained long, florid, and operatic, especially in Herbert, Romberg, and Friml. The popular Herbert waltz tune "Kiss Me Again" from *Mlle. Modiste* (1905) is a case in point. The tune known by that title is actually the fourth in a back-to-back chain of ariettas in each of which the character Fifi sings of different types of stage roles she might play. Each arietta has coloratura elements. Finally she sings the main tune of the song, "Kiss Me Again," which is a slow waltz, free of vocal embellishment. Nevertheless, it has a range of an octave and a minor sixth (wider than the octave and a fifth range of "The Star-Spangled Banner," considered too hard for most untrained singers to sing), and on the penultimate words of the lyric—"Tenderly pressed close to your breast"—the vocal line suddenly swoops down a minor ninth, steps up a minor second, aerobatically leaps up a major seventh, and then repeats this whole sequence a minor third down—an example if there ever was one of soaring melody.

Somewhere between 1900 and 1920, such long melodic verses were replaced by short, simple tunes not requiring vocal agility. Once that happened, the verse became like a racetrack's starting gun at the gate, preparing the audience for a chorus tune they would latch onto and whistle on their way out of the theater. Once the verse ceded primacy to the chorus, the audience had only one tune to remember—the chorus's tune, front and center. That helped pave the way for the golden-age Broadway musical.

How Lowering the Vocal Compass Raised the Artistic Potential of Musicals

Another change that paved the way was in vocal compass; that is to say, the distance from highest to lowest note in a given song. Legitimate voices are trained to handle wide compasses; untrained voices may be great in other ways but are usually limited in compass (Billie Holiday could comfortably handle only

26

about an octave, or eight notes). Most of the arias in Gilbert and Sullivan's *The Pirates of Penzance* (1879) span a vocal compass from ten to twelve notes. In De Koven's *Robin Hood* (1890) the compass of the tunes varies from as little as an octave to two octaves, with many tunes spanning an eleventh or twelfth. By the time we get to Herbert's *Naughty Marietta* (1910) the compass is almost always at least an eleventh, with the title character's part extending almost two octaves. The vocal ranges in *Show Boat* (1927) are still demanding and require legitimate voices: an octave and a sixth (thirteen notes) for "Ol' Man River" and nearly similar ranges for most of the other songs (except "Bill"). On the other hand, the great songs of Rodgers and Hart's *Pal Joey* (1940) almost never range beyond the compass of an octave. Nor do those of Irving Berlin's *Annie Get Your Gun* (1946). A few of the songs in *Guys and Dolls* (1950) venture a few steps beyond an octave, but most do not. The song "On the Street Where You Live" from *My Fair Lady* (1956), considered its most soaring melodic line, has a compass of only a tenth, which sometime between 1920 and 1940 settled into the average maximum range allotted a musical comedy song. What was happening? As Broadway songwriters were moving toward the dramatically integrated musical, it became necessary to shrink the compass so that the singing actor *could act on the lyric.*

But shortening the vocal compass still wasn't enough. The vocal range (that is, the average height of the pitches) had to be lowered so that the singing could be still clearer on the lyric. To achieve this it was necessary not just to write in lower keys but also to lower the tessitura (the area where the greatest number of notes in a melody are sung). In musicals in the late 1800s and early 1900s, the tessitura was higher for both women's and men's roles than it became in the post-1930 golden age. When sopranos sing in a high compass and high tessitura, most of the consonants are less clearly audible and some of the vowel sounds of speech are slightly altered. In the pre-1930s, the male romantic lead was generally given to a tenor; later, that practice was abandoned as the lyrics' intelligibility became a more important value. In *Rose Marie* (1924) and *The Desert Song* (1926) the leading-man's tenor lines are written up to a¹;* in *Show*

---

*This note and other designated pitches mentioned in this discussion refer to the pitches in the published score. In recordings and other arrangements of the same songs, the original keys may have been transposed, and the pitches may differ by a semitone or whole tone (in rare cases, by more), but the tessitura remains generally about the same. The pitches are designated here by the prevailing international system of c¹ as middle C, c as an octave below that, C two octaves below middle C, c² as an octave above middle C, and so on.

Boat (1927) Gaylord Ravenal finds himself singing in that stratosphere in "You Are Love." After about 1930 the tenor roles in Broadway musicals were almost always comedic second bananas, the leading men almost always baritones. The only important exception is Billy Bigelow, a "baritenor" role singing up to g^1 (John Raitt used a crooning falsetto for some of the higher notes) in *Carousel* (1945). More typically, in *Oklahoma!* (1943) the "tenor" Will Parker is taken up only to f^1, a note most baritones can handle (the high-ended baritone Nelson Eddy reached the G above that with ease in his many movies). In *Guys and Dolls* (1950) only the comic character Nicely-Nicely Johnson takes a high tenor line, in the trio "Fugue for Tinhorns" and solo in "Sit Down, You're Rockin' the Boat."

The soprano lead in *Rose Marie* spans almost two octaves from b to a b^{b2}, and the tessitura is spread fairly evenly throughout that range. But in *Oklahoma!* (1943) both the soubrette, Ado Annie, and the lyric soprano lead, Laurey, stay below g^2 the whole time, and the tessitura is centered below c^2. An examination of Broadway scores after 1940 discloses that soprano line tessituras remain usually within the octave from c^1 to c^2 and that the melodic curve usually peaks in the area from c^2 to f^2. (The famous exception is the e^{b3} for Cunegonde in "Glitter and Be Gay" in Bernstein's *Candide* [1956].) As with the men's downward pitch trend, leading female romantic roles increasingly went during this period to mezzos or Broadway belters instead of sopranos.

These changes in "song altitude" were under way in musicals well before Rodgers and Hammerstein; certainly Fred Astaire in *Funny Face* (1927) sang in a lower tenor compass than Howard Marsh in *Show Boat* (1927), and even Nora Bayes (1880–1928), one of top stars of pre-1920 musicals, sang in a compass lower than typical for her era, judging from her recordings. Was the change in pitch compass and tessitura a conscious decision on the part of composers like Berlin, Rodgers, and Porter? No. It was instinctive. After all, Berlin could only compose his songs in one key, F-sharp major, so almost all his songs had to be transposed either up or down by one of his arrangers. The choice of key for a given song would have depended on the casting decision of the producer and the intuitive judgment of the creative team. A primitive composer like Berlin would know the vocal sound he wanted but not how to write for it specifically.

It is fair to say that composers, book writers, and lyricists from about 1915 to 1930 were gradually shifting to a new style of musical playwriting that demanded a more speechified presentation of song lyrics—which required a lower compass and a lower tessitura, however they were arrived at.

How Riffing Created the Catchy Show Tune

Still another change would come in the very conception of theater melody. While Herbert, Friml, and Romberg continued writing florid, chromatic melodies for Broadway well into the 1920s, George M. Cohan and Irving Berlin in the 1900s and 1910s were already pioneering an opposite style: diatonic (white-note) simplicity, free of melodic leaps and bounds, with few if any chromatic vocal steps. But these were already characteristics of nineteenth-century popular and folk song. What was new about Cohan, Berlin, and other Tin Pan Alley writers was that they built their songs on the direct repetition of short melodic motives ("Yes Sir, That's My Baby" is a good example), a style we might dub riff songwriting.

This style directly contradicts Rimsky-Korsakov's dictum that "monotony in rhythmic construction is unsuited to vocal melody." Berlin's "Alexander's Ragtime Band" (which never made it into a musical) is a classic example of the riff song: the initial four-note motive is repeated twice, then three times again at a higher pitch. Cohan's famous World War I anthem, "Over There," did the same thing: the bugle-call riff that is the initial motive is stated five times before any other pitches are sung. In the 1920s Vincent Youmans would make the riff song his personal signature: his "Tea for Two" is built on a four-note riff insistently repeated, while "I Want to Be Happy" is built on a longer riff that is repeated. In "I Wish I Were in Love Again" from the 1937 *Babes in Arms,* Rodgers brazenly opens the song with six statements of the same riff, harmonized with only two alternating chords: it is spared monotony thanks to Hart's spectacularly clever, caustic lyrics. The swing bands thrived on riff songs: the Glenn Miller perennial "In the Mood" is a classic example. Film scoring, too: the famous theme from *The Third Man* (1947) is a riff tune.

The melodies of the operettic musicals were through-composed; that is, they *don't* repeat melodic material, their tunes constantly go in new directions. The melodies sounded beautiful, but perhaps only highly musical people could whistle them back right away. Riff songs might almost be described as undercomposed. Their patterns are short and instantly repeated, which make them catchy to the ear. Cohan, who played the violin a little as a child but was essentially unlettered as a composer, had an intuitive knack for writing riff songs. "You're a Grand Old Flag" was another example. Victor Herbert, despite his protestations that Cohan's shows were "vaudeville musical atrocities," absorbed some of this style and began to simplify his melodies. The choppy, catchy 1906 song "Every Day Is Ladies' Day with Me" is a perfect example. Herbert's "Gypsy Love Song" from *The Fortune Teller* (1898) has a vocally complex verse, but its chorus is written in a folk song style: basically a simple lullaby, it packs a dramatic wallop by unexpectedly conjuring up the sentimentality of Stephen Foster within the context of the show's gypsy exoticism, and by confounding the listener's expectations after the more operatic vocal line of the song's verse. Herbert may not quite have written riffs, but he was perhaps American history's original crossover composer.

Berlin, Kern, Rodgers, and Gershwin would later take a cue from Herbert's attempt to simplify the melody and carry the process further by marrying the operettic to the riff. Thus the melody to Irving Berlin's "Cheek to Cheek" starts with a riff (itself borrowed from Chopin's A-flat-major Polonaise), repeats the riff, and then climbs by twists like a Herbert or Romberg melody to "soar." Gershwin's "Mine" is pure riff, but it contains chromatic intervals characteristic of operettic melody. Rodgers's "Johnny One Note" is pure riff interspersed with gradually larger vocal jumps.

Berlin (1888–1989), like Cohan, was a master of both the riff song ("Putting on the Ritz," "There's No Business Like Show Business") and the simple ballad written in nonchromatic style ("The Girl That I Marry"). In "You're Just in Love" from *Call Me Madam* (1950) he even managed to write a riffed ballad, in "Always," a riffed waltz. Unlike Cohan, Berlin added chromatic steps (blue notes) to his songs. Sometimes the rhythmic riff underlying the melody holds a Berlin tune together ("Blue Skies," "What'll I Do"); other times his intuitive ear enabled him to sustain melodies on the operettic soaring model with chromatic stepwise motion, like "A Pretty Girl Is Like a Melody" or "Say It with Music."

The problem with riff tunes is that what they gain in catchiness they can lose in power and emotionality. Legitimate voices can't open up on them. There are seldom long-held notes à la Rimsky-Korsakov in a riff tune (exception: the high note Ethel Merman sustained for sixteen bars in "I Got Rhythm"). But if riffs and long soaring lines could be melded, singing actors could be heard and understood projecting melody *and* at the same time projecting no less the sense of lyrics and character. That achievement was the collective accomplishment of many songwriters, but the person first and most responsible was Jerome Kern (1885–1945), composer of the Princess Theatre musicals and *Show Boat* (1927).

Three Ways in Which Jerome Kern Invented the Modern Musical

The Jerome Kern–P. G. Wodehouse–Guy Bolton musicals of the 1910s for the Princess Theatre have been celebrated by most authorities as the first body of integrated book musicals. The books were well-plotted, realistic drawing-room comedies, and the lead-ins to the songs were cued by dramatic situation rather than by extraneous costumes or comedians. (The 299-seat Princess at 104 West 39th Street, at the time considered a Broadway house, would by size and location now qualify only for off-Broadway status. It was demolished in 1955.) Kern's songs for these shows are not riff tunes, and they are not soaring operettic melodies. Rather they are the first successful amalgamation of the two. Instead of insistently repeating the same riff (though he did so sometimes in a ragtime number like "The Siren's Song"), Kern would spin out a chain of melodic phrases of different length—eight bars, four bars, two bars—within the thirty-two-bar AABA chorus, usually altering rather than repeating the pitches of the previous phrase, building a sense of drama within the chorus's symmetrical confines. In songs like "Till the Clouds Roll By," "Whip-poor-will," or "Sunny," he would mix his punches, alternating long-held notes and sudden skips in the vocal line with a quick succession of stepwise, rifflike patterns. Kern's melodies always seem to be going somewhere, moving toward a payoff, as if the whole song were like a giant melodic curve headed toward a climactic point: "Bill," built on talk-singing stepwise patterns until the dramatic jumps of its final four bars, offers a classic example. But unlike most of Herbert's melodic lines, Kern's never tax a singer's chops to the point of slurring consonants into unintelligibility and losing the lyric.

Kern's melodies—attractive enough to soar yet earthbound enough to be effectively sung on lyric—once tethered to dramatically logical scripts, helped invent the modern book musical. He also invented the book show tune as a melody that contains its own song plug. Kern had begun his career in the London theater as a pianist; the producer Charles Frohman hired him to improvise songs for the audience before the curtain went up. Kern learned early from this and other experiences as a song interpolator that he had to grab the ear quickly. His melodies are constructed so as to sell the listener on a melodic hook, so the first-time listener can leave the theater humming a part of the tune. With Herbert and Friml often still writing through-composed arialike melodies that ran beyond the bounds of the thirty-two-bar chorus, there wasn't always so simple a melody to whistle. Kern usually gave the listener a musical mnemonic, embedding it somewhere in the strophic, periodic structure of the AABA thirty-two-bar chorus: it could be either a riff like the dah-dah, dah-DAH of "Ol' Man River" or a twist-and-turn mini-soar pattern like the first five syllables of "Smoke Gets in Your Eyes." Usually Kern repeats these mnemonic hooks in the course of developing his melody, which helps cement the whole song in the listener's memory. It's as if Kern is reprising the tune within itself. He was not the only songwriter to do this, but he did it earlier, more consistently, and more effectively with book musicals than Irving Berlin, who was primarily a revue songwriter until late in his career.

The third Kern innovation was the institutionalization of the song reprise to help bind and unify the book, a practice extended by musicals of the Rodgers and Hammerstein era. Before Kern (and even after, for a while) musicals reprised their tunes much less frequently, sometimes hardly at all. *Florodora* (1899), the great hit of its day on both sides of the Atlantic, has only one tune reprise, a brief occurrence in the "Finaletto" to act 1. In *Irene* (1919), the longest-running book musical (670 performances) before *Oklahoma!*, only two tunes are reprised; even the show's finale is a brand-new tune. In the original score for *No, No, Nanette* (1925), "Tea for Two" is played only once, although in performance it may have been encored. Romberg's *The Desert Song* (1926) hardly repeats any material. Kern's scores, however, are notable for their frequent reprises. He seems to have regarded them both as another means of plugging his tunes and as a vernacular adaptation of Wagnerian leitmotifs, the latter particularly in *Show Boat* and his post–*Show Boat* scores where Kern pioneers the underscored reprise. (Kern's arranger-orchestrator Robert Russell Bennett said Kern "was actually the composer of a great deal of the background music behind scenes.")[8]

Perhaps as a reflection of his obsession with tune plugging (only Andrew Lloyd Webber tops Kern as a shameless tune plugger), Kern's shows are also among the first consistently to have overtures that are medleys of the show's tunes. As with song reprises, such overtures were a sometime thing in the early days of musicals; *Florodora, Irene,* and *No, No, Nanette* all did without them, instead opening with a chorus line number. In opera there is the Verdi model of an overture that previews the opera's arias and the Puccini model of starting with a few orchestral chords. Kern subscribed to the Verdi model and helped make it a fixture of the book musical, a device that uses the tunes to conjure up the book situation and characters for the listener. He also seems to have been the first composer of musicals to reprise riffs from songs in a reworked form and implant them elsewhere in the show: "Ol' Man River"'s first four notes are the first four notes of the show's opening number, "Cotton Blossom," run backward. Thirty years later, Meredith Willson in *The Music Man* disguised the melody of "Seventy-six Trombones" as the melody of "Goodnight My Someone" simply by changing meter and pace from a fast 6/8 to a slow 3/4.

Reprising material can be a labor-saving device in the musical theater: you can fill out time more easily by simply repeating the same tunes. Kern was known to recycle material frequently; such self-plagiarism is far more wide-spread than most theatergoers are aware. Sousa was an early tune recycler; many of his still-remembered marches come from his forgotten operettas. Even a legitimate theater composer like Kurt Weill did it. Weill first used the tune to "September Song" in his 1935 operetta, *Der Kuhhandel.* From his 1945 Broad-way flop, *The Firebrand of Florence,* he rescued the tune to "There was life, there was love, there was laughter" and used it intact in *Street Scene* (1947) as "Ain't it awful, the heat, ain't it awful." Jule Styne recycled an entire song from *Fade Out Fade In* (1964), fitting it to a different lyric in *Hallelujah Baby!* (1967). When Richard Rodgers consciously quoted his own 1925 tune "Mountain Greenery" as source material in a flashback scene in *Allegro* (1947), the critic Richard Watts Jr. (unfairly) let him have it. But when he practically rewrote the title tune of *Babes in Arms* (1937) as "Do, a Deer" for *The Sound of Music* (1959), nobody noticed. Max Steiner, who had been a Broadway conductor in the 1920s, lifted a tune he wrote for the 1939 film score of *They Made Me a Crimi-nal* and used it later the same year as the "Tara" theme in *Gone with the Wind.*

The line between influence and theft is a thin one; Rodgers's *South Pacific* tune "Bali H'ai" sounds suspiciously similar to Franz Waxman's theme for *The Bride of Frankenstein* (1935), and the third four-bar period of the chorus from Irving Berlin's "Cheek to Cheek" is extremely similar to the third four-bar period in Kern's "Make Believe" from *Show Boat.* For *Pipe Dream* (1955), Rodgers cribbed *Carousel*'s "Mr. Snow" and *South Pacific*'s "There Is Nothing Like a Dame"; for *Allegro,* "One Foot, Other Foot" is a rewrite of *Carousel*'s "The Highest Judge of All." Andrew Lloyd Webber's opening minor-key descending riff in the title tune of *Phantom of the Opera* is stolen from Vaughan Williams's *London Symphony.*

Kern's innovations ended with *Show Boat,* and even there the score reverts to a surprising extent to operettic singing and melody. "Ol' Man River" has a vocal compass of almost two octaves; "You Are Love" throws off the thirty-two-bar chorus and returns to a Victor Herbert–like open-ended aria form with a lengthy multisection verse preceding it. Kern had never written up-tempo rhythm numbers like those of Cohan, Berlin, and Gershwin to begin with, and in his 1930s shows he curiously went backward in melody writing toward the operettic; even his harmony became more chromatic in a mittel-European style. Kern was not a fan of jazz, and his later tunes began to assume a more Continental character just as every other composer for musicals was striving for a resolutely American sound. He also began to overuse the reprise.

He left Broadway for good in 1939, but he had by then long since invented the modern musical.

Yet already by 1920 the riff school, not the operettic school, was the herald of the future of musical theater song. Shortly thereafter, several watersheds occurred. First, trained singers altered their vocal techniques to conform to the new vocal style. Second, as the microphone and loudspeaker made their debuts, the very notion of what constitutes singing slowly but inexorably changed to the practices of untrained singers. And last, Broadway melodies themselves changed with the new trends in the singing voice—at first artfully and constructively, then, much later in the 1960s, for the worse.

Scene Two. *After the Microphone*

The Four Horsemen of the Singing Apocalypse: "Nonsinging," Legitimate Belt, Radio Croon, and Rock Growl

The up-tempo number pioneered by Cohan, Berlin, Youmans, and Gershwin (and by the mid-1920s used by DeSylva, Brown, and Henderson and by early Rodgers and Hart) gradually drove legitimate singing from its near monopoly into being merely a competing style. Operettic singing continued on Broadway in such 1920s hits as *Rose Marie, The Student Prince, Blossom Time, The Desert Song, The New Moon,* and even *Show Boat.* But now legitimate singers who had always made a living on Broadway had to retool their vocal chops if they wanted to continue to be employable, just as a few years later silent film stars had to produce credible speaking voices in order to survive the transition to talking films. Greta Garbo's silent-film leading man, John Gilbert, failed the transition because his lightweight and casual speaking voice was laughably at odds with his image as a passionate lover. Likewise, Ernestine Schumann-Heink, operatic Broadway star of 1905, could not have been cast in a Broadway musical by the 1920s. But other full-voiced performers like Vivienne Segal and Howard Marsh did successfully negotiate the transition to the new style, as described by Lehman Engel:

By the mid-twenties . . . the new roles created by the younger generation did not need opera singers, neither their techniques nor ranges, and almost certainly without meaning to do so, these young writers were vaguely envisioning another kind of vocal style. . . . For want of a better label, let's call this then-new style "non-singing." Anyone who sang "I Want to Be Happy" or "I Get a Kick Out of You" or "I'm Bidin' My Time" like "Musetta's Waltz" from *La Bohème* was definitely way-out wrong.[9]

Yet as we have seen, "nonsinging" had been well under way for some thirty years, borne along by Irish and African-American influences until it reached the mainstream and was given an extra push by Al Jolson. The "nonsinging" Engel is describing here is a little closer to legitimate singing than talk-singing:

> And this raises the question of vocal technique. If Mary Martin, Ethel Merman, and Alfred Drake had not known how to use their voices, they would have lost them long ago. What they had to do was "place" their voices differently—in a lower, "belting" register—and (to put it as simply as possible) to make them fat and loud without making them round. They sang more on words than on pure vocal lines.[10]

It was the development of this kind of singing actor that made possible a musical theater quintessentially different from opera: a theater in which the verbal arts of the stage contributed as much to the final result as the music. It made possible Broadway's canonical golden age of musicals with their better librettos, better lyrics, and more artistically ambitious dancing and concepts at no sacrifice to melodic charm. The nonsinging style Engel describes also embraced a second phenomenon new in the 1920s and virtually the invention of a single performer, Ethel Merman: the legitimization of the belt voice.

But a third new vocal style was also just around the corner, thanks to the introduction of the microphone about 1925: the radio croon. And in the course of another thirty years, this same microphone, abetted by newer musical influences, would grandfather a fourth vocal style, the rock growl, that would deconstruct theater music and remove Tin Pan Alley–style theater music from America's collective unconscious.

The four horsemen of the legitimate singing apocalypse—nonsinging, legitimate belt, radio croon, and rock growl—spelled armageddon for legitimate singing as the default style of American musical culture. So far-reaching were the consequences that American popular musical history overall, not just the history of the Broadway musical, could plausibly be divided into "Before the Microphone" and "After the Microphone."

Ethel Merman and the Legitimization of Belt

In the half-century of musicals on Broadway before the 1920s, the leading lady was almost always a genteel legitimate soprano. There were no Carmens or Kundrys in the pre-1920 musical theater, much less contraltos (notwithstanding Mme. Schumann-Heink's appearance). Nonlegitimate low female voices were principally to be found in folk forms like blues singing or Appalachian hog calling. The first female Broadway performers who used the belt voice, the white coon shouters of the early 1900s, likely had heard African-American singing to have imitated it in that manner; but the recorded history of female blues singers starts only in the 1920s with such vocalists as Gertrude "Ma" Rainey (1886–1939) and Bessie Smith (1894–1937), the former of whom doesn't shout, so coon shout antecedents must go back well into the nineteenth century. It is possible that forms of nonlegitimate belt singing by women of other races also occurred onstage before 1900.

The female vocal range divides into a lower "chest" voice and a higher "head" voice. The vocal cords are thick and fat for the former, stretched thin for the latter. Most of the range of the legitimate female voice lies in head voice. In nonlegitimate singing styles, women expand their chest ranges upward and do not try to mix them with the sound of their head voices, as do legitimate singers. Belting is a form of chest voice in which the singer "pushes" her volume and lung capacity to achieve a timbre distinct from the lighter sound of the head voice (the head voice timbre is created by using the resonating passages in the head). The larynx is higher in belting, and the vowels are more speechlike than in legitimate singing. The male voice is mostly chest to begin with, so male belting has more to do with the timbre and volume of tone projected. Was Cohan a belter? Not timbrally, but he certainly was heard in the back of the theater: just listen to his recording of "Life's a Funny Proposition After All" to hear the "built-in" microphone of his voice.

Though May Irwin, Stella Mayhew, Ethel Levey, Sophie Tucker, and other vaudeville and Broadway performers used the belt before 1920, they did so only in roles stereotyping black women. For white female singers, the counterpart to the blues was the torch song; but white torch song singers before 1930 did not belt. Fanny Brice sings "My Man" from the *Ziegfeld Follies of 1921* on her recording of the same year in a talkish light alto with an Edith Piaf–like vibrato (Brice's parents were Hungarian and French). Libby Holman, the torch singer and acquitted alleged murderess, sings Cole Porter's "Love for Sale" in her 1931 recording in a light contralto similar to the range and vocal style of Brice, Marlene Dietrich, or Lotte Lenya. Helen Morgan, the original Julie in *Show Boat*, sang "Bill" and all her similar torch numbers in a light, flutey soprano. In *Show Boat*, "Can't Help Lovin' Dat Man of Mine" was sung by Morgan, playing the mixed-race Julie, wholly in her lyric soprano. But Tess Gardella, the mammy-impersonator white actress known by the stage name of Aunt Jemima, who played Queenie, recorded the same song in 1928 with a belt voice. In short, prior to 1930, belting was used only for blacks or for whites who imitated blacks. Belting was only for character roles; there were no leading-lady belters.

Enter Ethel Agnes Zimmermann (1908–84), who on October 14, 1930, debuted as Ethel Merman at the Alvin Theatre in Gershwin's *Girl Crazy*. Sustaining the C above middle C with her chest voice for sixteen bars of the second chorus of "I've Got Rhythm," she was heard without amplification over a pit orchestra that combined the celebrated Joseph Smith strings and the Red Nichols jazz band, which included Nichols and Charlie Teagarden on trumpet, Glenn Miller on trombone, Benny Goodman on reeds, and Gene Krupa on drums. Overnight Merman made the belt voice legitimate. Quickly thereafter she assumed a series of leading-lady roles in *Take a Chance* (1932), *Anything Goes* (1934), and twenty-five ensuing years of musicals (principally by Cole Porter and Irving Berlin), and made them safe for belting. She single-handedly liberated a vocal style and made it mainstream and theatrically viable. (Irene Castle recalled that Blossom Seeley [1891–1974] sang like Merman before Merman, but Seeley was a character type, not a leading lady.)

Merman's chest voice was highly unusual in not being dusky but rather bright and almost a spinto soprano in timbre—in a word, brassy. Actually, what she did with her chest voice can't be described solely by the term belt. Belting has come to mean a certain deformation of the voice, and Merman was able to belt without modifying her vowels or her consonants or the speech of the lyric. Almost uniquely among musical theater singers past and present, male and female, Merman spoke while she sang; unlike a Rex Harrison, Robert Preston, or Noël Coward, her singing sounded like speech yet was carried by well-shaped, clearly intoned pitches, especially early in her career when her vibrato had not yet veered out of control. That she could softly croon and had a superbly modulated sense of phrasing is evident from her early recordings and rare film appearances, such as *Alexander's Ragtime Band*. When she chose to, she could sing on the lyric and interpret it in a Sinatra-like style, as one can clearly hear in her 1934 recording of "I Get a Kick Out of You." She could sing softly and yet project without the microphone. She could whisper like Crosby but ultimately got typecast for belting. She also has an unacknowledged debt to Jolson, freely using Jolson-style grace notes and appoggiaturas as late as "You'll Never Get Away from Me" in *Gypsy* (1959).

Merman's success in musical comedy might arguably be ascribed as much to her larger-than-life stage presence as to her voice. But Merman, unlike her tomboyish predecessor Blossom Seeley, could and did play seductive, feminine, and sexy. And it's her voice that advanced the writing of musicals. She proved that the chest voice could be used in a way to make the lyrics be more clearly heard; that paved the way for other nonlegit or lower-ranged singers like Mary Martin to act as much as sing, so that the dramatic values of the lyric could come through. Patti LuPone's singing in *Evita* directly descends from Merman's innovation; if *Evita* had been written in the 1920s, the title role would have been sung by Norma Terriss or Vivienne Segal entirely in a head-voice soprano, completely changing the character of the role.

The downside of Merman's example is that eventually the use of the belt devolved into a raucous exploitation of its vocal timbre instead of a means to make lyrics clearer and enhance the throughline of the character. Such a use of belt for its timbre alone can be dramatically motivated and funny, as in Joan Diener's singing in the original cast album of *Kismet* (1953). But lately it has been indulged for no dramatic purpose other than to artificially pump up excitement, much the way sound amplification itself would be used on Broadway in later years. Eventually the Merman belt descended into the rock belt, which after *Hair* (1968) permeated the Broadway singing even of child performers in nonrock musicals, such as Andrea McArdle in *Annie* (1977).

Bing Crosby, Unheralded Revolutionary of the Microphone and Great-Grandfather of Modern Sound Design

> A case could be made that every singer since Crosby has "crooned."
>
> —Max Morath[11]

If Jolson was the greatest nonlegitimate live male voice ever in American musicals, Merman was the greatest nonlegit live female voice. The key word is "live." Earlier in the year Merman debuted in *Girl Crazy*, Harry Lillis "Bing" Crosby (1903–77), who had achieved a modest name as a vocalist with the Paul Whiteman band, was singing at the Cocoanut Grove ballroom at the Ambassador Hotel in Los Angeles—live, but with a microphone. Crosby made his network radio debut on CBS September 2, 1931, and boo-boo-booed his way into history. "Crooning" may now be passé but the revolution of the microphone was born, a revolution whose far reaches are still endlessly unfolding in the 2000s.

Microphones were introduced sometime around 1924; that year President Coolidge demonstrated the new device by broadcasting a live address to Congress over the radio. The next year microphones and the electrical recording process replaced the acoustic horn that had been used to make phonograph recordings since 1877. Before Crosby the term "crooning" had been used to describe mothers singing lullabies to their babies in the cradle, and sometimes applied to very light, high-pitched Irish tenors singing pianissimo. "Whispering" Jack Smith was perhaps radio's first so-called crooner in 1925, followed by Rudy Vallee in 1928.

But Crosby did far more than co-opt the moniker of crooner; he made the use of the microphone arguably the single most important innovation in audible entertainment since the ancient Greek amphitheater. The microphone meant that an untrained singer could project as far as amplification allowed. Traditional voice training was no longer necessary. The microphone was like a close-up camera of the voice, and in the hands of a master like Crosby it was a new musical instrument, making audible nuances of vocal expression heretofore impossible. But in the hands of a lesser mortal, it is a karaoke appliance.

More than any other single performer, Crosby invented singing for the microphone, expanding the term crooning to encompass an undreamt-of expressive palette, singing softly but not only softly. Every pop singer after Crosby, in every style and genre (even folk, eventually) has been a microphone singer, from Sinatra to Presley to Dylan to Jagger to Springsteen to Celine Dion. But the standing of legitimate singing as the model and premise for all other singing was dealt the fatal blow. And though it would take decades for the damage to register, live singing in the Broadway theater, and some essential aspects of the theater experience as a whole, would eventually be one of the prime casualties.

As a young man Crosby had been much influenced by the ultimate in live, unrehearsed entertainment, vaudeville. He did not invent boo-boo-boo-ing; he may well have gotten it from a Broadway musical star he saw in vaudeville and admired, Blanche Ring. Ring had done it first, syllabifying the last word of "I'd Leave My Happy Home for You" into "oo-oo-oo-oo" back in 1899.[12] In 1940 Crosby helped get the aging Ring (and her husband, Charles Winninger, the original Cap'n Andy of *Show Boat*) cast in his musical film *If I Had My Way*. In 1899 Ring had done her oo-oo-oo-oo for what was then termed a "novelty coon" song. As the jazz-influenced Crosby practiced it, boo-boo-booing was a kind of fragment of scat singing.

Jolson (who was Crosby's idol) was the singer who enlivened show music's capacity to be dramatic art; Crosby put the voice in a box, and his rock descendants of microphone singing eventually took his invention to extremes, using the device not to amplify whispering but rather to amplify what is already loud. The biggest development after Crosby was the invention of the wireless microphone, abolishing the tether of the cable that, in its very physical restriction, had forced singers to be more projective. Today Madonna, Whitney Houston, Mariah Carey, Bjork, Sheryl Crow, and other singers of apparently differing styles are united by their inability to be their public entertainer selves without a cylindrical metal appliance practically inserted in their mouths.

Jolson's sound was a live sound; Crosby's sound was alive, but not live. Except in the opera house, the human singing voice has ever after been a processed phenomenon. Fifty years after Crosby first sang "Where the Blue of the Night Meets the Gold of the Day" on the radio, audiences at performances of live musicals in Broadway theaters no longer would hear even a single performer onstage unmiked and unamplified. Everyone onstage, even the trained legitimate singers, had become Bing Crosby.

Robert Johnson and the Tradition of Vocal Deformation

The fourth revolution in singing, although it entered the mainstream only in the 1950s, can best be explained by describing how the style got started back in the 1920s and 1930s. If Merman is the godmother of Patti LuPone and Bernadette Peters and Crosby the godfather of body-miked nonsingers on Broadway, then Robert Johnson (1911–38), the legendary Mississippi delta blues singer, is the godfather of the rock growl, a style that ultimately had a profound impact on the Broadway musical .

Johnson lived his entire short life working on a plantation in Robinsonville, Mississippi. He made twenty-nine recordings in 1936 and 1937 in San Antonio and Dallas, Texas. Though marketed as "race records" in the South, they reached the enlightened jazz producer John Hammond in New York. Hammond thought Johnson the greatest country blues singer ever, greater than Leadbelly or Blind Lemon Jefferson, and attempted to bring him to New York for the famous "Spirituals to Swing" Carnegie Hall concert in 1938. But Johnson by then had already died, poisoned by a jealous girlfriend. Johnson's recordings were not generally available until a 1961 LP reissue that reestablished his legend; a 1990 CD rerelease became a worldwide best-seller in the crossover market, appealing to heavy metal fans as well as jazz and alternative rock fans. Johnson is now a deity in pop music history's pantheon.

The emphatic difference between Johnson's singing and that of city blues singers like Bessie Smith and Billie Holiday is that Johnson deforms both his consonants *and* his vowels. Rainey, Smith, Holiday, Ethel Waters, and others sang clearly and consonantally, enacting the lyrics as words, just as Bert Williams had done around 1910 and Noble Sissle around 1920. Johnson's crystalline guitar playing contrasts mightily with his vocal utterance: a kind of primitive, primeval choked sound, sometimes howled, sometimes moaned, often nasalized, always intoned from a tightened throat. His singing has great emotional power, but it is a style based on distorting the very ground materials of songwriting: the melody line and the lyric. Bob Dylan's sound comes right out of Robert Johnson. So does Mick Jagger, Janis Joplin, and Led Zeppelin. Eventually this style found its way into the mainstream of rock. Even Randy Newman owes a debt to Johnson.

When such a powerful style achieves worldwide popularity (Johnson was not the only progenitor of it, but he is clearly regarded as a central starting point) and a whole generation is brought up with its vocabulary, it cannot help penetrating all entertainment forms. Inevitably, this style of singing has been imported into the Broadway musical, even though it would seem to contradict every precept of musical theater. The scores and singing of *Hair, Grease, Tommy, Dreamgirls, Rent, The Lion King,* and *Aida,* and the anointing of Elton John as a leading Broadway composer, have all descended from a tradition of vocal deformation and lyric unclarity traceable to Robert Johnson in 1937.

The Great Theater Singers and the Great Song Stylists: Dual Golden Ages in Entente Cordiale

The four horsemen of the singing apocalypse did not put legitimate singers on Broadway out of business. High-tessitura sopranos continued to appear, but they were no longer de rigueur. Hollace Shaw, sister of the choral conductor Robert Shaw, was the star of Jerome Kern's last musical, *Very Warm for May* (1939); rather than use her chest register, she sang up to a high F in "All the Things You Are" and stayed relatively high in every chorus. In the 1947 original Broadway production of *Brigadoon,* Marion Bell, as Fiona, sang in high keys and tessitura, as did Jo Sullivan and Barbara Cook in musicals of the 1950s. When he set out to re-create Rodgers and Hart musicals on records in the 1950s, Lehman Engel hired Portia Nelson (1920–2001), a songwriter, comedienne, and actress who was a popular cabaret singer. But Nelson also had a strong legitimate soprano, and it is the head voice, not the chest, that she uses on Engel's *The Boys from Syracuse* studio re-creation. In the 1997 *Encores!* production of *The Boys from Syracuse* at New York's City Center, Rebecca Luker, one of the fine soprano voices singing in musicals today, sang "Falling in Love with Love" less operatically than Nelson does on the 1953 recording (also less so than Ellen Hanley on the 1963 Theatre Four cast recording). It isn't that Luker lacks the vocal chops, but that styles have evolved so much in forty years that audiences today won't buy a high head voice in that song.

The belle époque from about 1927 to about 1966 was the heyday of our musical theater's greatest singing actors: Ethel Merman, Vivienne Segal, Dennis King, Mary Martin, Angela Lansbury, Alfred Drake, John Raitt, Todd Duncan, Barbara Cook, Julie Andrews, Helen Gallagher, Nanette Fabray, Celeste Holm, Robert Preston, Richard Kiley, Jack Cassidy, Judy Holliday, and others. These performers balanced a combination (the exact balance varying from performer to performer) of acting values, musical values, singing on lyric, and a personal charisma tempered by deference to the role (unlike Jolson). They were the original stars of the canonical musicals, and today's best Broadway performers— Brian Stokes Mitchell, Mandy Patinkin, Audra McDonald, Donna Murphy, Betty Buckley, Bernadette Peters, and others—echo their style. Prior to these performers, people came to musicals to see clowns like Fanny Brice or Bert Lahr make them laugh, to hear Jolson or Ruth Etting sing, to look at sumptuous Ziegfeldian production values, or to bask in operettic melody sung by legitimate voices. A musical was a polymorphous entertainment not requiring the skills of a gifted actor like Drake or Lansbury.

Coincidentally, the 1927–1966 golden theater era was roughly the same as that of the great signature pop song stylists: Sinatra, Crosby, Peggy Lee, Ella Fitzgerald, Tony Bennett, Rosemary Clooney, Judy Garland, Mel Tormé, Sarah Vaughan, Carmen MacRae, et al. In this period of dual golden ages, big bands and their vocalists helped spread Broadway theater music to the nationwide public over the radio and phonograph. Cole Porter's 108-bar "Begin the Beguine" from *Jubilee* (1935) became a standard when the 1938 Artie Shaw band version made it the number-one recording in the country. Other songs from Porter shows that made the Top Ten in the 1930s and 1940s include "You're the Top," "Love for Sale," "Night and Day" (in Fred Astaire's rendition), and "In the Still of the Night." The notion that the more integrated book show of the 1940s left less fodder for pop cover versions isn't entirely true: songs from Porter's *Kiss Me, Kate* were recorded by Dinah Washington, Sinatra, Mabel Mercer, Fitzgerald, Julie London, Tormé, and Lee.

In the 1950s original cast albums were often in the national Top Ten charts of popular music. Dinah Shore recorded "Whatever Lola Wants" as a promo for the opening of *Damn Yankees* (1955). The year before, Rosemary Clooney had a chart hit with her version of "Hey There" from *The Pajama Game*. Columbia recorded an LP of various songs from *Guys and Dolls* in renditions by Frankie Laine, Jerry Vale, Jo Stafford, and Clooney. The pop/Broadway entente extended into the early 1960s, with Bobby Darin scoring hits with "Mack the Knife" and "Artificial Flowers" from Bock and Harnick's 1960 musical *Tenderloin*, and Louis Armstrong hitting number one with "Hello, Dolly!" even as the Beatles were taking command. Diana Ross and the Supremes did an album of the complete *Funny Girl* at the time of the release of the movie (1968). By the 1970s, however, the pop/Broadway recording link was fading out. Judy Collins and Sinatra recorded Sondheim's song "Send in the Clowns" from *A Little Night Music*, and Barbra Streisand occasionally weighed in on Lloyd Webber. But the long entente was over.

Theater songwriting in the belle époque supported jazz improvisation and song styling in a way that rock-influenced theater songwriting does not. Today popular vocalists who bridge the worlds of 1940s Broadway and rock are unusual. Among the exceptions are rocker Joe Jackson, who has performed versions of songs from Kurt Weill's *One Touch of Venus*, and the aging ex-rock diva Petula Clark, who recorded a song from *Rent*, music from *Tommy*, Sondheim, and songs from *Kismet* and *Finian's Rainbow* (she appeared in the 1968 film version) on one album. In pre-1925 Broadway, opera singers and theater singers were almost the same performer pool. In the belle époque of circa 1930–65 great theater singers were good actors and, frequently, so were pop vocalists, but the two breeds were as distinct as theater stars and movie stars. In the current Age of Disney on Broadway, pop vocalists and theater singers have all too often become as fused at the hip as opera singers and theater singers were one hundred years ago.

The Tao of Rock Crooning: Vulgate Bel Canto and Vocalized Electric Guitar

Alfred Drake did not imitate Bing Crosby. Although Broadway musicals and big band music shared certain dance rhythms and similarities of style in vocal line, there was a tacit understanding that the two worlds were separate. But the ethos of contemporary pop does not respect such boundaries. In a pop-dominated world, musical theater sounds like pop music and singers in it sound like pop singers, unless they are performing revivals of classic musicals. Phrasing is not important in rock singing; rawness of vocal utterance is. The great song stylists of the big band era sang on the text without deviating too far into pitch deformation. Certainly, there were some subtle rhythmic alterations of the vocal

44

line and a tasteful embellishment here and there (what Sinatra meant when *he* used the term "bel canto"), but the integrity of the song as written was preserved. Since 1960 many rock singers have adopted Presley's closely held miking but abandoned his clarity of diction (Presley was a protean singer who could do many things well, among them singing in a theater baritone). Because contemporary pop vocalists are generally not lyric interpreters and are more interested in using the song to exploit their voice boxes in the style pioneered by Robert Johnson, Broadway musical singing today has curiously reverted in some aspects to that pre-1930 paradigm, vaudeville. Like vaudeville singers, today's rock voices in the theater stand apart from the show and communally relate with the audience even while nominally playing a role. The show becomes more of a concert than a play, no matter how scripted its libretto.

Whereas American teens of the 1930s and 1940s absorbed big band singing styles by osmosis, the youth of the 1950s, 1960s, and later absorbed the new lingua franca of rock, country, and pop. The Broadway musical theater in the last thirty years has thus become a warehouse for almost every pop music style on the market: Europop, Motown, country and western, neo–big band, neo–early jazz, hip-hop, and even smaller niches. The styles are often presented frankly as revues (*Mamma Mia* is the music of Abba, *Movin' Out* is Billy Joel, *The Look of Love* is Burt Bacharach), which in many cases could have been more justifiably presented as concerts than theater. In the past forty years, while pop singers have frequently appeared on the Broadway musical stage (Sting, Adam Pascal), virtually no opera singers have, although many opera singers have indeed appeared on recordings of elaborate restorations of classic musicals, rendering the lightest-voiced musical comedies in legitimate head voice—a style now dignified as crossover.

Vaudeville singers like Jolson, Cohan, Blanche Ring, and others freely ornamented the vocal line with grace notes, mordents, and even the imitation of musical instruments. Later singing stars like Merman (Ella Logan, too) perpetuated some of these vocal ornamentations in book musical comedy. The rock singing style embraces much more extensive distortions of the vocal line: grace notes, whoops and swoops, sliding up to a note, and even a different way of sitting on a sustained tone, emulating the twang of an electric guitar string. The voice placement itself frequently emulates a sustained electronic twang. Vaudeville (and later, jazz) singers emulated the sounds of brass instruments; rock singers emulate the sounds of electronic instruments, including electric pitch bends.

The bel canto of early-nineteenth-century opera involved a style of virtuoso vocal ornamentation for the sake of display, not for the sake of text exposition. Rock singing, with its free use of ornaments, is a kind of modern vulgate bel canto. It calls attention to itself, not the plot, just as legitimate bel canto does. Broad brushstroke emotions can be delivered by this technique, as in *Rent*. But psychological complexity of character and situation, as in Sondheim, requires that the singer subordinate his style to the lyric and vocal line, not vice versa. Rock crooning would be no more suitable to Sondheim than Alpine yodeling. While Jolson and his merry vocal embellishments focused on himself, he also interpreted the song and sang the lyrics. Most rock singers, however, keep the focus on the embellishments. Even fine singing actors with legitimate trained voices now routinely inflect and bend the pitch in a rock style in Broadway musicals. Two excellent performers, Brent Carver and Carolee Carmello, fluently blended theater singing with rock grace notes and other ornamentation in *Parade* (1998). When Carver did it in his last song, "All the Wasted Time" (because it was written that way), a stylistic levity was injected that was alien to the high drama of the moment.

At its extreme, the melismatic ornamentation of a Whitney Houston or Mariah Carey can become a kind of faux coloratura. But that style doesn't work in the theater because it draws attention to the vocalist and away from the character she is playing. Yet that is exactly how Heather Headley sings in the hugely popular Disney show *Aida* (2000). It's not character illuminating or lyric illuminating any more than the fioriture of Bellini's opera *Norma* are. And curiously, despite the fact that Elton John's music seems to portray raw emotion well, it also tends to superimpose a prefabricated emotion, taking the specificity out of dramaturgy. The net result is the homogeneity of operetta without the beauty of its melody. Andrew Lloyd Webber is a better theater composer than Elton John because he is resourceful enough to marry pseudo-Friml, long-lined melodic curves with a contemporary pop style including a drum machine track (Frank Wildhorn of *Jekyll and Hyde* and Claude-Michel Schönberg of *Les Miz* have also essayed this approach).

"The Song Is Ended"

With composers other than Lloyd Webber, rock tunes tend to return to riff patterns without good melodic curves. Rimsky-Korsakov was right: you do need the long-held notes to offset the short, and you do need a well-distributed mix of the two to ensure tune catchiness and memorability. Instead of unified, coherent melodic curves, rock tunes are most frequently constructed of chains of minimelodic curves that correspond to the improvised melismas of rock's vulgate bel canto. Melisma is improvisatory and mutable. Melody must have something stable and immutable to imprint itself on the ear and the memory. With melodically unstable tunes born of the singing style of rock melisma, the ear has nothing to hang on, no Jerome Kern–style hook to take out of the theater and into one's subconscious. With no initial earhold, and no gateway to the inner melodic grammar of the brain, this music, when used in the musical theater, cannot enter our collective unconscious.

There can be little perceptible difference between rock melisma and singsong. In opera, recitatives trace no melodic curves; rather they mark time (while furthering the plot line) in between arias that do. Recitatives are opera's singsong, not designed to catch the ear. Operatic arias are built on melodic curves but are usually not strophic like Tin Pan Alley songs or show tunes; in other words, arias are not built in regular symmetrical phrases like the thirty-two-bar AABA pattern. Rock tunes are frequently neither strophic nor built on melodic curves, and thus start off the bat with a two-strike count against effectiveness as theater music. In recent years Sondheim sometimes (*Passion*) writes pseudoarias that are nonstrophic and built on recitative-like melodic lines accompanied by ostinato vamps. In his earlier shows Sondheim, a fine tune writer, more frequently wrote in traditional strophic song. When one attempts to base either opera arias or theater songs on melodic material that is recitative-like, the ear forgets fast.

The instability of rock melody is also largely why such songs support jazz improvisation less well than song standards of the golden era. It's hard to ring changes on a moving target. Rock tunes also lack the dynamic, functional, chromatic harmony of the Tin Pan Alley/Broadway theater song. Rock songs have a different kind of harmony, more static, more blocklike. With the functional harmony of classic song standards, improvisers can make chord substitutions that seem to recast the tunes on the spot with a rainbow of new colors. The chord changes in such songs as Porter's "Night and Day" (*Gay Divorce,* 1932), Kern's "All the Things That You Are" (*Very Warm for May,* 1939), and Weill's "This Is New" (*Lady in the Dark,* 1941) seem on first hearing harmonically enriched, as if they were already improvised substitutes, and yet they have an inner logic and stability that permit jazz variations and song stylings. Broadway musicals have seldom yielded similarly harmonically surprising songs in the last thirty years. One exception, no longer recent, is Marvin Hamlisch's "One" from *A Chorus Line;* its dramatic buildup stems not from its insistent vamp beat but rather from the piquant and unexpected chord changes Hamlisch introduces to increase the tension. A more recent example is Stephen

Flaherty's title tune from *Ragtime,* with its cleverly accelerating melodic pinwheels and peekaboo chord changes. Sondheim seldom does this, and neither have most other composers on Broadway in the last twenty years. (When Lloyd Webber tries to throw in surprising chord progressions, even his most unanticipated chords remind one of others'.)

Rapture or Rap-sure? Welcome to Tympan Alley

> No matter the extent of one's affection for the
> rock scene, this music is not intended for the
> stage.... Mainstream songs are written for voices
> with no vocal training.... the songs betray a
> melodic-harmonic inanity.
>
> —David Craig[13]

On April 24, 2003, *Da Boyz,* the first hip-hop version of a classic Broadway musical—Rodgers and Hart's *The Boys from Syracuse* (1938), itself based on Shakespeare's *The Comedy of Errors*—opened at London's fringe Theatre Royal. The show opened with break dancing. According to the *New York Times:*

> A booming sound system and two large video screens have been installed onstage, the strutting singers all carry hand microphones, the doors stay open to let people wander and the seats have been removed from the ground floor level so the audience can do some swaying of its own to the insistent rhythms of rap. The end effect is a club outing . . . with throngs of youths, most of whom have never seen a live theatre production before. . . . [DJ Excalibah] stands on a perch high above the stage in sweats and a baseball cap, bouncing to the rhythms and scratching rasps and growls from the vinyl discs on two turntables. . . . DJ Excalibah said he got the idea of interspersing filmed scenes with live ones from rock show DVD's. The Rodgers score has been remixed to allow for garage, R & B, hip-hop and Jamaican bashment. . . . Some recognizable melodies disappear behind declamatory rapping.[14]

Nowhere in the *Times* article is there any mention of how well the songs are sung. It's become irrelevant.

The typewriter and the word processor did not change how fiction was written or how words were put together. But the microphone did change how singers produce their voices. It also killed liveness as a viable commercial concept. For centuries theater has been based on an intimate, immediate liveness. At the same time it has also been based on a paradoxically impenetrable wall between stage and audience. Inserting microphones, displaying video screens, and allowing the free ingress and egress of patrons results in a club experience, not multimedia theater. And it is foolish to hide behind the cutting edge and pretend otherwise.

Are long-line melodies obsolete today, in an era when the sounds of hip-hop and heavy metal have crossed the threshold into the theater? Clearly not. The human ear and collective unconscious still respond to them; if that were not so, Madison Avenue and Hollywood wouldn't use such tunes as Puccini's "O mio babbino caro" and "Nessun dorma" or Leoncavallo's "Vesti la giubba" for subliminal enhancement of film scores and television commercials. Lloyd Webber wouldn't have cloned them. The innate human response to these materials has not been dislodged by the newer idioms.

It is thanks to the microphone that so much of the singing and melody of our theater's past has been preserved. Can a way be found not to use it as a mortician's tool to embalm our musical theater before it has even died?

ACT TWO

How Mavericks, Highbrows, and Enlightened Collectivism
Invented the Book and Lyrics and Tweaked the Music

The theatre is a collective art in which the
strongest man rules
                —Boris Aronson, scenic designer[1]

I think a large part of musicals coming together is
the will of the group, not the individual talent. The
field is really not about talent. It's about collaboration. It's not like writing a novel.
                —Ira Weitzman, Lincoln Center
                    Theater associate producer[2]

Can the collaborative art of musical theatre contain a single creator's vision? The very concept of
an autonomous artist's solitary vision is drawn
from "high art." How far is it compatible with
commodity-mindedness?
                —Bernard Rosenberg and Ernest Harburg[3]

Jokes about creating something by committee are so legion in our culture that
they are too numerous to repeat. Yet Broadway musicals *are* created by committee. Rare instances in which a single person wrote the book, music, and
lyrics are exceptions that prove the rule. Perhaps only George M. Cohan starred,
directed, coproduced, choreographed, and wrote the book, lyrics, and tunes.
Nevertheless, wherever the Broadway musical is celebrated, the celebration
always first extols the singular voices of individual artists and writers—composers, lyricists—as if they hadn't at all times been working by committee. The
dynamic tension between creation by committee and expression of personal
voice is exactly what brought the Broadway musical up from a frivolous enter-

51

tainment to a high popular art. Somehow, personal voice triumphed. When personal voice began to lose the battle, to lose distinction, so did the Broadway musical.

Indeed, as a collaborative art, the Broadway musical is a throwback to the collective, communal art forms of ancient and medieval times. Before the Renaissance, art in the Western and non-Western worlds was collaboratively and communally produced, expressions of the whole culture more than of an individual creator. When works of art were executed by individuals, like paintings and sculptures, they were anonymous and expressive of communal belief or iconography; this could be said even of great epic poems like *Beowulf* or the *Bhagavad-Gita,* or of medieval morality plays like *Everyman.* Team-executed works of art, such as the oriental rugs of Persia or the architecture of the cathedral at Chartres, were collective both in creation and expression. Since at least the Renaissance, however, Western art increasingly has become the province of personal expression. With Beethoven, Byron, and nineteenth-century romanticism, personal expression and one-man manufacture became the dominant mode.

Curiously, the art of musical theater prior to the existence of Broadway was an exception to this historical pattern of collective creation:

> Twentieth-century American musicals differ above all in one respect from musical theatre of the past. While always a fusion of several art forms, earlier musical theatre was not created through continuous collaboration or give and take among artists and artisans. In ancient Greece it was almost a one-man show. Much later, in European opera, a playwright would complete a libretto (dialogue and song lyrics), then a composer would set it; they would not work back and forth, but separately. Thus, in the past, a composer would literally "score the action" a playwright gave him, setting music to the text or story and lyrics to the music. . . . "Scoring the action" in an American Broadway musical, on the other hand, . . . [is] a group skill. . . . from the collaborative creation of several primary artists, each skilled in different crafts, emerges the first written draft of a musical (script and score) that is then transformed into live theatre by being rehearsed many times on a stage before an audience.[4]

Rarely is a show mounted as a Broadway musical without some of this collaborative, on-the-spot, step-by-step authorship. When Lehman Engel was hired as musical director of *The Consul* (1950), an opera for which Gian Carlo Menotti wrote the libretto, the music, and the orchestration and which he directed, Engel was amazed that it was being produced on Broadway. "There were never any trial-and-error things in *The Consul,* unique in my experience. No music was ever changed or deleted, nor any words. . . . In the end, he [Menotti] made only small choreographic and light alterations."[5]

Of course, individual voices do emerge out of the collaborative process; sometimes one voice does dominate, and sometimes there is synergy—a metavoice, the collaborative chemistry greater than the sum of its parts. But the only sure road for an individual to attain guaranteed personal expression in the Broadway musical is to first achieve enormous commercial success in the collaborative mode. That way, one gets power and becomes the "muscle." The Theatre Guild produced *Oklahoma!,* but the show was such a wild success that Rodgers and Hammerstein quickly were able to become their own de facto producers. Playwrights, directors, composers, and choreographers in non-profit venues don't run this gauntlet—they can be auteurs from square one; opera composers and librettists can too. Collective give-and-take and daily evolution of the material through rehearsal doesn't occur in opera.

Musicals in the pre-1920 era were collaborative, but the communal model prevailed: very few voices identifiable as personally expressive emerged (Ned Harrigan and Cohan come to mind). Call it an age of casual collectivism. There was no tradition; ways of doing things evolved without a guiding intelligence; shows were thrown together in slapdash fashion. In the next era, the golden age of circa 1927–66, the form was still collaborative and commercial but a benign tolerance of personal expression occurred: call it the age of enlightened collectivism. In the third era there has been a return to aspects of the first era: personal expression is either muted or far less original, and the collaborative process, instead of enlightened, is now bottom-line obsessed—resulting in commodified product, prepackaged or recycled, all too often bereft of the auteurist qualities that made high-water Broadway unique.

Mavericks and highbrows are to be found among our choreographers and directors, but the maverick writers and composers came earlier and were the true instigators of the classic integrated musical that raised song and dance to an artfulness vaudeville and revue never approached. The musical stage before 1920 had been lowbrow. The high-end practitioners of the ensuing era of enlightened collectivism were culturally upward middlebrows, even as lowbrow shows for the "baldheads" (later known as tired-businessman specials) persisted. Today the product on Broadway seems to regard the audience as all baldheads, even if some of them are female flight attendants from Asia who don't speak English.

Sometimes in Broadway's formative years there was a whole herd of mavericks, like the 1920s lyricists who read Franklin P. Adams's column "The Conning Tower," worshiped W. S. Gilbert, and fraternized. Sometimes the maverick was an individual who didn't seem like a maverick, such as Oscar Hammerstein II. Sometimes the highbrow element was a subtle general influence, and sometimes there were active highbrow practitioners, such as playwright-turned-lyricist Maxwell Anderson or composers Kurt Weill, Marc Blitzstein, Leonard Bernstein, and Jerome Moross. The pantheonic songwriters—Porter, Gershwin, Berlin, Rodgers, et al.—were a gift of history, but they were not all necessarily mavericks. But the books and lyrics that define our great musicals were invented by mavericks. Indifferent lyrics and scripts of course had always existed, but not the lyrics and scripts that raised the form to artistry.

The ex-wunderkind Sondheim, a classic maverick, is still around, but the fecundity of a herd of mavericks is gone from the commercial theater. A body of distinct creative voices no longer exists. The production costs are now so overwhelming that commodified creation has co-opted inspiration. Ziegfeld did not create *Show Boat* by commodifying it; Kern and Hammerstein went ahead with writing *Show Boat* before they had a producer. Producers did often initiate the writing of shows in those days, but enlightened collectivism ensured that personal expression untempered by marketing came through.

If certain writers and groups of writers had never assumed in the first place that musicals were worthy of artistic development, the musical would never have progressed beyond the realm of amusements into the art of theater. It would have stayed arrested in development along with circuses, Wild West shows, vaudeville, burlesque, and the other staged entertainments it coexisted with a hundred years ago, none of which are today considered art forms any more than musicals were a hundred years ago. But the golden age did emerge because writers and composers considered themselves creative authors, in spite of the straitjacket of creation by committee.

The conscious effort to push beyond entertainment is what made the Broadway musical art. The triumph of individual will in a collaborative medium roused the latent art within it, like the irritation in the oyster that yields the pearl.

Scene One. *The Book*

When the Script Wasn't Yet a Libretto: The Infantile Dadaism of Early Musical Books

> Once, in an interview, Jerry Bock . . . and I were
> asked the inevitable question: "What comes first,
> the words or the music?" Jerry's unexpected an-
> swer was, "The book.". . . I have heard of situations
> in which a whole score was written and then a li-
> brettist hired to weave a book around the score . . .
> but it would be difficult for me to believe that
> they were the "homogeneous" kinds of shows that
> I admire myself.
>
> —Sheldon Harnick, lyricist[6]

> Although the major point of a musical is still sheer
> enjoyment, the story, or "book," has become more
> literate over the years. . . . A song that doesn't
> work in one spot may work in another. But the
> story is vital; it is the necklace on which all the
> beads are strung. A good story for a musical is one
> of the most difficult things to achieve.
>
> —Cheryl Crawford, producer[7]

Pace Harnick and Crawford, once upon a time musicals had no book. The notion of a book as a well-constructed drama is itself the single greatest innovation in the history of the Broadway musical. Most early musicals either had no plots at all or only very loosely conceived ones. Charles Hoyt's "book" for the 1891 musical *A Trip to Chinatown* is a case in point, according to the scholar Douglas L. Hunt:

> Hoyt's method of workmanship was a combination of sloppiness and careful technique. He made notes at odd times on bits of paper, putting down witty remarks he heard or conceived, remembering strange names or peculiar people. Later he assembled his scrambled notes and made from them a working script of the play. After a piece was put in rehearsal it was constantly being altered. . . . *A Trip to Chinatown* is printed as supplied to me in a copy of the play sent me by Mr. George W. Poultney of San Francisco, Calif., a gentleman who appeared in at least one of the Hoyt companies playing on the Pacific coast. He assures me that it is the form of the play in which he acted. It differs radically from the copy in the bound volume in New York, so much so, in fact, that I have printed the entire last act of both versions. . . . Mr. Poultney could not tell me at exactly what point and in what order the songs were to be introduced into the play. I have placed them where they seemed most logically to belong. . . . As a matter of fact, there is ample evidence that the plays differed so vastly as presented that it is not at all certain that even Hoyt's own songs were always sung in the same spots or that the same songs were sung all through the long run and by the many road companies presenting the piece.[8]

The Harrigan and Hart Mulligan Guard shows, whose scripts were written somewhat like modern television situation comedies, and some of the operettas (*Robin Hood*) were exceptions in the prevailing scene of book chaos. When dramatically credible books began to mesh with entertainment in *The Pink Lady* in 1912 or the 1910 Princess Theatre musicals (even if today they play like cutesy sitcoms), the ground for a mature musical theater was broken. From *The Black Crook* in 1866 to *Show Boat* in 1927, the book was not a unifying structure binding the songs and dances. The script of a musical with rare exceptions was instead improvised around the stars, the sets, and the songs. Even though the dialogue could be highflown at times, there was little attempt at dramatic continuity. Musical playwriting operated on the principle of free association long before Freud got a hold of it.

> DeWolf Hopper stated that although the staged story and the music were often "unfriendly," promising songs always took precedence over the plot's logic. To ac-

commodate the music, the story might leap from a Louisiana cane field to the ice of Greenland to exotic India, then to a "Montana ranch by way of the Bowery." It was not unusual to see central European peasants and soldiers sing a rollicking drinking song then suddenly reappear "as cotton pickers cakewalking to the strains of 'Georgia Camp Meeting.'"[9]

The book and lyrics to *Evangeline* (1874), a musical burlesque of Longfellow's poem, were written by J. Cheever Goodwin (1850?–1912), called by Gerald Bordman "the first professional librettist to leave his mark on the American Musical Theatre." Goodwin's real contribution to literary history was his invention of the costumed cow, with one man operating the front legs and the other the hind legs; that was the gate draw in *Evangeline.* The musical historian Cecil Smith commented, "The plot was the least of its attractions. The book bore astoundingly little relation to Longfellow's poem, or, for that matter, to anything coherent at all." There were special-effect whales, a balloon trip to Arizona, and scenes in Africa, none of which occurred in the original poem and which were introduced onstage for no logical reason. Although *Evangeline* was, next to *The Black Crook,* the most frequently revived musical of the late nineteenth century, it is no coincidence that none of the musicals of this era are revived, nor do the names of their once-renowned librettists such as Goodwin or C. M. S. McLellan, survive. Nor did they have a life as international imports, whereas Viennese operettas, Gilbert and Sullivan, and Offenbach were all exported to Broadway during the same years and had an enormous impact.

The first man to make a lasting career as a librettist and lyricist on Broadway was Harry Bache Smith (1860–1936), who claimed to have written the books for three hundred shows and lyrics for six thousand songs in the half-century from the late 1870s to the early 1930s. Stagestruck from the time at age nine he saw the burlesque performer Lydia Thompson in Chicago, Smith dropped out of high school to plunge headfirst into the Chicago theater scene, first as an actor, then as a Gilbert and Sullivan singer. At the age of only eighteen he cowrote an English adaptation of von Suppé's operetta *Fatinitza* that opened on Broadway. In his twenties he tried newspaper reporting, then music and drama reviewing, and went from theater critic directly to playwright and librettist (one could do that in those days; the great impresario Augustin Daly started as a drama critic). Smith teamed up in 1887 with Chicago composer Reginald De Koven to write operettas; their *Robin Hood* (opening in New York in 1891) was so successful that it made Smith the first millionaire lyricist/librettist of Broadway (in modern adjusted dollars), permitting him to retire from journalism.

He then settled in New York City to work ceaselessly on Broadway shows for forty years.

For all his prodigious output, and despite becoming considerably self-educated about books and the world's literature, Harry B. Smith was the incarnation of the literary hack. He was available for hire to one and all, writing books for musicals, revues (including the *Ziegfeld Follies*), operettas, and operas, indifferent to partner chemistry, working with virtually every composer of every style of his era from De Koven to Sousa, Herbert, Berlin, Kern, Romberg, Franz Lehár, and Imre [Emmerich] Kálmán and giving them a one-size-fits-all style of writing. He worked at factory speed, cranking out scripts for as many as four shows in a month. He wrote most of his lyrics in a generic florid style, faux Keats and Wordsworth, the way Lloyd Webber's tunes are faux Puccini and Vaughan Williams. A typical Smith song lyric is thoroughly unvernacular, full of poetic apostrophizing and "thees" and "thous." His lyrics can be idiotic: "and even the cows are idyllic kine," warbles the ensemble in one Smith–De Koven song chorus. "Gypsy Love Song" from Herbert's *The Fortune Teller* (1898) is one decent Smith lyric that has survived. Smith's torrent of words never produced phrases that entered the permanent American vernacular like "Ol' Man River" or "I'm a Yankee Doodle Dandy."

Smith was the leading practitioner of the pre-1930 style of American musical theater in which the book had no integrity: it was accepted by theater professionals that the script would be a slapdash, jerry-built mess, that it "was almost never finished before the cast began to work; when *Sunny* went into rehearsal [1920], the dialogue and numbers for the first act weren't set, and the second act didn't materialize until the run-through before the opening out-of-town. . . . George M. Cohan said that it was much better not to write a second act beforehand because after you heard the cast read the first act, you got to know them better and could write a better second act for them!"[10] As a one-man industry, Harry B. Smith not only helped perpetuate this ad-lib method of writing but also contributed more than any other writer to institutionalizing the high-flown drivel of operetta dramaturgy: the idiotically coincidental plotting; the cardboard cutout characterization; the fairy tale gauze covering everything.

Where did he come up with ideas for three hundred scripts, most of which were presented as original and not adaptations? Like a Tin Pan Shakespeare, Smith stole from established texts and recobbled them for a given production. Often Smith pirated European texts: "With his encyclopedic knowledge of ancient plays, many of which could be recycled for current consumption. . . .

much of his work consisted of loosely adapting long-forgotten scripts by others."[11] He was said to boost his writing speed by improvising short stories and then adding dialogue, like a quick-sketch artist. For *Watch Your Step!*, the 1914 Irving Berlin musical with Vernon and Irene Castle, his playbill credit was printed as "Book (if any) by Harry B. Smith." "With a lack of logic so characteristic of Smith's scenarios," *Watch Your Step!*, after opening in a law office, "suddenly shifted to a stage door, a change of scene that served as an excuse for the entire production to turn into a backstage musical."[12] Posterity has completely forgotten this all-time champion word-spinner and one-man script factory.

Omitting Cohan (whose scripts were panned by the drama critics of his time), the first author to write well-constructed scripts for musicals was P. G. Wodehouse (1881–1975), creator of the famous Wooster and Jeeves novels. Wodehouse wrote the books for the Princess Theatre shows of Kern, and a few Gershwin shows (*Oh, Kay!*), and cowrote Cole Porter's *Anything Goes*. His books for musicals were drawing-room divertissements, a higher breed of his era's theater of fun, but not drama. The man esteemed by both Oscar Hammerstein and Alan Jay Lerner as the important pioneer of the musical play was not Wodehouse but Otto Harbach (born Hauerbach, 1873–1963). The son of Danish immigrants who settled in Utah, Harbach was a college English professor who came to New York to study at Columbia. He worked for newspapers and ad agencies, met the composer Karl Hoschna, and started writing songs with him. By 1908 he was writing for Broadway. Oscar Hammerstein remembered that "the field of libretto writing was filled with hacks and gagmen. . . . There were, on the other hand, a few patient authors who kept on writing well-constructed musical plays. . . . Otto was the best play analyst I ever met. . . . He taught me never to stop work on anything if you could think of one small improvement to make."[13] Indeed, according to Alan Jay Lerner, Harbach, wheelchair-bound in his late eighties, was still kept awake at night trying to figure out what was wrong with his 1934 lyric to "Smoke Gets in Your Eyes."

Like Victor Herbert, Harbach was a mover and shaker now forgotten. According to John Murray Anderson, Harbach was the Broadway theater's leading play doctor of the 1920s, not just for musicals but for straight plays. Incredibly, in 1925 Harbach's annual income was almost twice that of Irving Berlin. He was the principal librettist for Friml's operettas and for Kern's shows of the 1930s, but he also wrote the words for "Just a Love Nest / Cozy and Warm," which later became the theme song for George Burns and Gracie Allen in radio and television. But the antique, quaint language of his lyrics and an old-fashioned if warm-hearted European sensibility in his books have dated his work to the point of unrevivability. *Sic transit gloria mundi.*

The books of Wodehouse and Harbach, even while superior to those of most of their contemporaries, tended to stock characters and formulaic situations, and lacked depth and verisimilitude. They reflected the legitimate plays of the Broadway of their time, an age of superficiality marked by the comedies of Clyde Fitch and the potboilers of David Belasco, Ned Sheldon, Owen Davis, and Avery Hopwood. Until Eugene O'Neill, Elmer Rice, Sidney Howard, and Maxwell Anderson hit their stride in the 1920s, American playwriting had no one who aspired to or remotely bore comparison with Shaw, Ibsen, Wilde, Strindberg, Galsworthy, or other Europeans.

Though *Show Boat* (1927) is usually cited as the first dramatically mature book for a musical, a year earlier a similarly semioperatic Broadway musical with an equally mature book called *Deep River* opened to the acclaim of drama critics Burns Mantle, Brooks Atkinson, and others. Perhaps earlier than any other advanced musical—*Show Boat, Porgy and Bess,* the Kurt Weill musicals, or *West Side Story*—*Deep River* coalesced highbrow elements in an artistically enlightened collaboration. The writer of the book and lyrics was Laurence Stallings (1894–1968), a Georgia-born literary critic, novelist, and *New York World* journalist who, as a marine captain in World War I, had lost a leg in the Battle of Belleau Wood. With Maxwell Anderson he had coauthored three plays, including the antiwar play *What Price Glory?* (1924), perhaps the first on Broadway to use gutter language extensively. Like *Show Boat,* Stallings's libretto for *Deep River* had a colorful historical southern setting (an 1835 New Orleans ball), white and black characters, interracial romances (between Creoles and quadroons), and melodrama; unlike *Show Boat,* it had a tragic ending and no showbiz hoofing.

Did Hammerstein see *Deep River*? The coincidences are suggestive. He and Kern first began to work on *Show Boat* during the fall of 1926; *Deep River* opened October 4, 1926, and ran only a month. *Deep River* had an important supporting role played by Jules Bledsoe (the 1927 *Show Boat*'s singer of "Ol' Man River"). Bledsoe (1897–1943) has been so overshadowed by Paul Robeson that his own accomplishments have been forgotten. Born in Waco, Texas, he originally came to New York to attend medical school at Columbia but dropped out to concentrate on becoming a professional singer. He studied music in Paris and Rome, sang opera around the world, and also became an accomplished composer; Willem Mengelberg conducted the Amsterdam Concertgebouw Orchestra in Bledsoe's song cycle *African Suite.* He even appeared in a few movies.

The composer of *Deep River*, W. Franke Harling (1887–1958), had possibly the most checkered résumé of any Broadway composer. Born in London, raised in the United States, and trained as a violinist, Harling seems to have begun his musical career as a church organist; he was once the chapel organist and choirmaster at West Point and composed a hymn, "The Corps," that to this day is sung there. He also composed operas and symphonies; at about the same time he was composing *Deep River* he was commissioned by the impresario S. L. "Roxy" Rothafel to compose an *American Choral Symphony*, a three-movement work for 110 orchestral musicians, an onstage jazz band, and chorus; the work was performed at the palatial Roxy Theatre on May 14, 1927. But Harling also wrote the song standard "Beyond the Blue Horizon" and about one hundred other popular songs, plus music for a great many films, including the Flash Gordon serials and *Stagecoach*.

Deep River was mounted by the most enlightened producer on Broadway, Arthur Hopkins, who allowed Harling a thirty-piece orchestra. Given its innovation, ambition, and talented creative team, there is a good possibility that *Deep River* is an unheralded missing link in the trend toward higher artistry on Broadway.

Undeterred by *Deep River*'s box-office failure, Stallings next collaborated on a book and lyrics with none other than Oscar Hammerstein. The show, *Rainbow* (1928), with music by Vincent Youmans, choreography by Busby Berkeley, and musical direction by Max Steiner, was a grand attempt to emulate both *Deep River* and *Show Boat* and create the Great American Musical. This time the canvas of the California gold rush provided the story. Libby Holman became a star singing the torch song "I Want a Man." Again, critical praise; again, a box-office flop, partly because the show never recovered from a series of opening-night staging mishaps. *Rainbow*, like *Deep River*, may well be a forgotten harbinger of the dramatically integrated musical of the 1940s. Although his dramaturgy may have been uneven, all the evidence suggests that Stallings was one of the very first book writers to handle the task as if he were a legitimate playwright, not a hack.

The Hidden Paradoxes of Oscar Hammerstein II, Guiding Genie of the Musical Play

Whether or not Hammerstein saw *Deep River*, he certainly attended many of the probing dramas that were finally competing with the traditional fluff on Broadway in the 1920s. The usually curmudgeonly critic George Jean Nathan was then tub-thumping for the causes of Sean O'Casey and the young Eugene O'Neill. Challenging plays by Paul Green, DuBose Heyward, Elmer Rice, Sidney Howard, and Robert Sherwood were being produced, along with imported European drama by Ferenc Molnár, and the Moscow Art Theatre was touring New York.

Oscar Hammerstein II (1895–1960), born and bred into the Broadway theater, could hardly have avoided exposure to these new currents. His grandfather Oscar Hammerstein I (1847–1919) had been the impresario of the Manhattan Opera Company, at one time the Met's great rival. His father, William (1870?–1914), was the manager of the sumptuous Victoria Theatre, and his uncle Arthur (1872–1955) was a leading Broadway producer of musical comedies. Young Oscar graduated from Columbia and entered law school, but in August 1917 he abandoned the law, sneaking into show business as an assistant stage manager for Uncle Arthur. (He first met Richard Rodgers in 1916, when Rodgers was only fourteen; they collaborated on two songs in 1919 before Rodgers teamed up with Lorenz Hart.) Oscar's first play, *The Light,* opened and closed out of town in May 1919. His first Broadway lyrics were written for *Always You,* which opened in January 1920 (the composer was Herbert Stothart). He then cowrote the book and lyrics (usually with Otto Harbach) for several operettas and musical comedies in the early 1920s by a potpourri of composers: Stothart, Youmans, Romberg, Friml, and even Gershwin.

From his earliest collaborations Hammerstein was seized with the notion of rescuing libretto writing from what he later called the "hacks and gagmen who extended the tradition of ignominy attached to musical comedy books." When his early hit *Rose Marie* (1924) went on tour, Hammerstein brashly circulated a warning to the drama critics in all the cities the show was traveling to, informing them they were not qualified to review musicals because "the critics' problem is that they do not recognize what a good libretto is, and do not realize that a good musical comedy must not necessarily be a good play." Not until his eleventh Broadway musical did he pair up with Jerome Kern for *Sunny,* a hit which opened in September 1925. Kern then wrote three utterly forgotten musicals with other writers before reteaming with Hammerstein (who in the meantime had also worked on three shows) for the legendary *Show Boat* in 1927.

What was so innovative about *Show Boat*? In the words of Cecil Smith, *Show Boat* was and is by consensus the first American musical "to achieve a dramatic verisimilitude that seemed comparable to that of the speaking stage."[14] It was Hammerstein's invention more than Kern's. First, before Hammerstein, musicals had almost never been adapted from novels (Edna Ferber, author of the novel, was incredulous that Kern and Hammerstein wanted to write a musical based on her book). The librettos more often than not were originals, not adaptations, stitched together ad hoc or cribbed like Harry B. Smith's from forgotten plays. To use a four hundred-page novel as the basis for a musical's libretto was to raise unprecedented dramatic demands not just on the book writer but on the songwriters. The very idea of using a realistic novel (as opposed to a fantasy novella like *The Wizard of Oz* or *A Connecticut Yankee*) enlarged the musical's vocabulary.

Second, prior to *Show Boat*, librettos dispensed not only with the classical unities of time, place, and action, but with playwriting itself: logic, coherence, and narrative were optional. In adapting Ferber's book Hammerstein *had* to observe theatrical protocol, but he did retain musical's charming illusion of immunity to the three unities. By deliberately not adapting the story to a restricted time frame, he adopted the chronological technique of Shakespeare and suggested a depth never before hinted in a musical, jump-cutting across the characters' histories in "a series of coincidences [that] persuades us that these people aren't just bumping into, but *revising,* each other, playing out a mutual destiny," writes Ethan Mordden.[15] As an anchor to hold *Show Boat*'s chronologically far-flung action together, Hammerstein (not Kern) ingeniously came up with "Ol' Man River" to create time unity (asserting the timelessness of the river) while also expressing the oppression of racism and the metaphysical oppression of all human fate.

Yet the fifteen years (and eleven musicals) that followed *Show Boat* found Hammerstein oddly floundering, unable to further his artistic advance. The paradox of Oscar Hammerstein, peerless advocate of structure in musical books, was that he himself had difficulty with structure when he had to create the story whole, as the orchestrator Robert Russell Bennett noted: "He told me more than once that he hated plots. Give him an outline of what happened and he was dynamite."[16] Most of the Broadway librettos Hammerstein wrote from 1928 to 1943 were originals rather than adaptations; none of these shows survive as repertory. He went to Hollywood during the 1930s but was unhappy as a movie lyricist. He wrote the lyrics to some song standards in the 1930s, but also wrote lyrics for *Hellzapoppin'.* Then in 1942 came the fortuitous pairing with Richard Rodgers after Lorenz Hart declined to work on the adaptation of the Lynn Riggs play *Green Grow the Lilacs.* The rest is history—*Oklahoma!* and Rodgers and Hammerstein—and a spectacular rebuff to F. Scott Fitzgerald's dictum that "there are no second acts in American life." Hammerstein was truly the maverick prime mover in the book-driven musical, an even more important person in our theater than he is usually credited to have been.

Hammerstein ("Ockie" only to his intimates) was a class act in a world of sharks, regarded with love by many he worked with. The film director Fred Zinnemann said, "I never remember him saying anything ugly or nasty about anybody or anything. I felt very strongly about him, and he was one of the very important people in my life." The blacklisted actor Hy Kraft, whom Hammerstein hired when no one else would, said, "I liked the world a lot better when he lived in it." The real-life Maria von Trapp of *The Sound of Music* said, "I am Catholic, and I would say that he was a living saint. That means that a person is as close to perfection as one can get and still be alive. It just emanated from him, and I'm sure he didn't know it himself." (Hammerstein was a "mischling": his father was Jewish, his mother Episcopalian; he was baptized and brought up Christian.) Russell Bennett, who once described Hammerstein as his "closest and dearest friend in show business," believed the sensitive Oscar had missed his true calling: poet. In the 1930s Hammerstein told Bennett that he and his wife Dorothy were going to live in France for a time so he could write poetry, not lyrics. Bennett told him, "You have great poems in you. But if you always stay in show business, where I've been, it'll never come out."

> He said, "Well, it's going to come out now. This is it." Then, a little bit later, along came *Carmen Jones* and then *Oklahoma!* and that was the end of Oscar as a poet. After that, he didn't much care about writing a great poem any longer. He was satisfied to write those lyrics, which he made into works of art. But they have it all . . . they all sound as if it's a poet trying to talk.[17]

In contrast with Harry B. Smith, Hammerstein wrote book and lyrics with agonizing deliberation. "When Oscar finished writing his lyrics," Rodgers said, "he was drained. He had to lie down."[18] Hammerstein's fellow book writers of the early golden age—Howard Lindsay and Russel Crouse, Guy Bolton and P. G. Wodehouse, Herbert Fields, even George S. Kaufman and Moss Hart—wrote divertissement books for musicals, requiring less excogitation. Hammerstein aimed higher, at the expressive level of a serious dramatist. He did not always succeed. *Allegro,* his most ambitious original libretto, lacks the power to elicit empathy so abundant in his shows based on existing plays, yet it fathered the "concept" musicals of Sondheim (by Sondheim's own admission: "I realize that I am trying to recreate *Allegro* all the time," he told the biographer Meryle Secrest).[19]

A seamless continuum between book and lyrics is also Hammerstein's invention. Song cues before Hammerstein were shoehorned in regardless of context. The lyrics of "The Surrey with the Fringe on Top" or "Soliloquy" are not just poetry, they are part of the play. They speak the story and the characters as much as the dialogue does. With Hammerstein the lyrics and dialogue alike are driven by the characters' superobjectives (in the Stanislavsky sense). This Stanislavskyan fusion of libretto and lyric existed nowhere before him, not even in W. S. Gilbert.

Handsome as a young man, Hammerstein grew craggy and Lincolnesque as he aged. He has become an almost mythic icon of Broadway, often seen as sweetness and light personified, but he embodied many contradictions. Usually considered an apostle of conformity, he actually was a genteel maverick in his profession. He was a champion of playwriting for the musical, but he was technically limited as an original playwright. He was a saint to Baroness von Trapp but to Arthur Laurents "hard as nails," and not someone to buck in a business deal, according to Elia Kazan. Kern was his buddy, but Rodgers never did learn whether Oscar liked him. He was offended by Tennessee Williams's seaminess, yet his own adaptations of plays and novels do not shy away from many lurid moments, whether it's Billy Bigelow beating his wife or the King of Siam beating a concubine.

Show Boat and his best shows with Rodgers are emotionally powerful because of their paradoxical yoking of romantic escapism with realism. Romantic escapism based on pastoral retreats was the whole cloth of operetta librettos, as Hammerstein too well knew: he had written them himself early in his career. Their dramaturgy was strictly Cinderella legend and Prince Valiant comic strip. As Hammerstein matured as a dramatist, he transcended this genre into verisimilitude, but he had the shrewdness not to throw the baby out with the bathwater: he retained elements of pastoral escapism and put them to higher ends. Hammerstein's pastoral retreat is like the forest of Arden in *As You Like It,* an idyll that is rudely and untidily interrupted by "man's ingratitude." Meryle Secrest has called the Rodgers and Hammerstein shows fairy tales for adults. But it's the 1920s Hammerstein operettas that are fairy tales for adults. If the Rodgers and Hammerstein musicals are fairy tales for adults, then so are Frank Capra's movies and perhaps most of the Hollywood studio-era films. But Hammerstein, unlike Capra, consistently embodied the social concerns of the Playwrights Company and the Group Theatre in his librettos with Rodgers—slightly sweetened, yes—but surely embedded in "You've Got to Be Carefully Taught."

It has been widely observed that Hammerstein's musicals with Rodgers were more successful when he adapted his books from other properties, less so when he wrote original books. His counterpart on the other great team of the 1940s and 1950s, Alan Jay Lerner (1918–86), said that in the beginning of his own career, "I was determined to write musicals with original stories, that is to say not based on other plays, novels or short stories, and in doing so doubled the pitfalls."[20] Though later on he worked from adaptations, Lerner did come up with one strikingly original libretto for *Brigadoon* (1947), a fantasy about two blasé Manhattan men who stumble upon a magical Scottish town that appears only once every hundred years and decide to disappear into it and out of time. Although Lerner wrote it, *Brigadoon's* mélange of New York angst and fairy-tale romantic escape was echt Hammerstein. While a few cynics dismissed it as hokum, *Brigadoon* is actually one of the few original Broadway musicals that dared to explore a potent imaginative conceit worthy of magic realist fiction. Even the tough critic George Jean Nathan picked up on its metaphysical resonances, liking the show but accusing Lerner of plagiarizing the story from a German folk tale. After *Brigadoon,* Lerner again followed Hammerstein by taking a cue from *Allegro* and writing a protoconcept show, *Love Life* (1948), in which he structured the libretto as a vaudeville show following a married couple through several imagined generations of American history. The music was by Kurt Weill, who in 1942 had written several songs with Hammerstein.

In 1959 Hammerstein thought he had an ulcer. It turned out to be cancer. He battled his way through the writing and production of *The Sound of Music* before becoming too sick to complete a newly urgent undertaking, his autobiography. When he passed away the world lost not only the balm of Oscar Hammerstein to help it weather the upheavals of the 1960s but also what would undoubtedly have been an indispensable theater memoir. Always the excruciatingly careful writer, he had finished only a few pages before he died.

Yip Harburg and Kurt Weill: Unsung Heroes of the Libretto

Like many opera composers, Broadway's operetta composers had often managed to write inspired tunes without the support of cogent librettos. And the ambitious dramaturgy of *Deep River, Show Boat,* and *Rainbow* did not immediately ignite further advances in book writing. Hammerstein himself faltered for years. The baldheads still wanted to bring on the dancing girls, and to some extent this kind of musical would persist forever. But after *Show Boat, Of Thee I Sing,* and *Porgy and Bess,* "the standard musical comedy began to look blowzy. It had an increasingly hackneyed appearance," wrote Brooks Atkinson.[21] In the period between *Show Boat* and *Oklahoma!* there were isolated instances of dramatically ambitious books, plays embedded within musicals: Kaufman and Ryskind's political satires for the Gershwin brothers' musicals *Strike Up the Band* (1930), *Of Thee I Sing* (1931), and *Let 'Em Eat Cake* (1933),

DuBose Heyward's libretto for *Porgy and Bess* (1935), and the novelist John O'Hara's remarkable play-within-a-musical book for Rodgers and Hart's *Pal Joey* (1940).

Book writers had with few exceptions always received a smaller percentage of royalties than composers or lyricists. They always had been the play carpenters who had to structure the script so as to leave space for the dances, the songs, and so on. (Both of these statements are still true today.) What they hadn't done, and still too often don't, was to combine this necessity of carpentry with the independent expression of a playwright working within the medium of the musical. The idea of a play embedded within a musical had really started with Hammerstein. Its spark was further kindled in the 1930s and 1940s by two unlikely brethren: a German émigré opera composer fleeing Hitler, and a lyricist best known in the early 1930s for the words to "Brother, Can You Spare a Dime?" Kurt Weill (1900–1950) and E. Y. "Yip" Harburg (1896–1981) were both mavericks and, like Hammerstein, could only have succeeded during Broadway's era of enlightened collectivism.

Harburg is probably the least familiar name in the pantheon of golden-age lyricists, although he penned some of the best-known lyrics of all time— "Brother, Can You Spare a Dime?" "April in Paris," "It's Only a Paper Moon," "Somewhere over the Rainbow," "How Are Things in Glocca Morra?" Born Irwin Hochberg to Russian-Jewish immigrants who worked in the sweatshops on the Lower East Side of New York City, he was dubbed "Yipsl" (Yiddish for "squirrel") by both family and kids in the neighborhood. (He changed his name to Edgar Y. Harburg when he married for the first time in 1923 but was forever "Yip" Harburg.) From his schoolboy years he was a tough kid with a propensity for learning and fine literature. At Townsend Harris High School he befriended a classmate named Ira Gershwin; soon they were swapping Gilbert and Sullivan records. At City College in the 1910s they cowrote a campus newspaper column, signing it "Yip and Gersh." In the 1920s, married and a father, Harburg worked prosperously in the electrical appliance business, confining his lyric writing to his spare time. When the stock market crash ruined his fortunes, he bravely decided to junk the business world and commit himself full-time to lyric writing. Soon enough he was placing lyrics with radio programs, Broadway revues, and talking films; when his "Brother, Can You Spare a Dime?" (to music of Jay Gorney) became the boffo number of a 1932 revue entitled *Americana*, he had his first song hit and the beginning of show business solvency.

Unlike most golden-age lyricists, Harburg worked with many different composers (he called himself a "chameleon"), but his best partners were Vernon Duke ("April in Paris"), Harold Arlen (with whom he wrote *The Wizard of Oz*), and Burton Lane (*Finian's Rainbow*). A lifelong political liberal but never a Communist party member (and at no time a Stalin sympathizer), he was blacklisted in 1950 while in the middle of production on an Arthur Freed–unit MGM musical and promptly fired from the set. Ironically, the first of the perennial television broadcasts of *The Wizard of Oz* occurred while he was still blacklisted (1956). But his royalty and investment income was solid enough that he could weather the storm, and he continued to work on Broadway—show business's only blacklist-free zone—through the 1950s and later.

Harburg entered the Broadway ranks of songwriters through revues in the early 1930s (*Americana, Life Begins at 8:40, The Ziegfeld Follies of 1934, The Show Is On*), but with the book show *Hooray for What!* (1937)—conceived and written by Harburg if rewritten by Howard Lindsay and Russel Crouse—he began to inject his distinctive worldview into the post–*Show Boat* crucible of high libretto writing. What was that worldview? In 1961 Harburg wrote, "Eugene O'Neill took five hours to say in *The Iceman Cometh* that man cannot live without illusions. My own belief is that man cannot live *with* them." But in his actual theater writing Yip sweetened that bitter pill somewhat: his musicals embody the view that "cock-eyed optimism" (Hammerstein's lyric)—in other words, belief—while "only a paper moon" (Harburg's lyric)—is still in some measure necessary for human survival. A farcical antiwar musical that anticipates Chaplin's 1940 film, *The Great Dictator, Hooray for What!* depicts a weapon of mass destruction falling into the hands of fascists, only to turn into laughing gas; Hitler, Hirohito, and Mussolini laugh themselves to death. Harburg emerged in *Hooray for What!* not as a journeyman scriptwriter but as a thoughtful poet and thinker who just happened to work in the musical theater.

Harburg's latent ambitions as a librettist had been stimulated by the success of the sharp political satire in the Gershwin musicals *Strike Up the Band!* (1930), *Of Thee I Sing* (1931), and *Let 'Em Eat Cake* (1933) with scripts written by George S. Kaufman and Morrie Ryskind. But Harburg was different from Kaufman, Ryskind, or the Gershwins in that he was the prime auteur: "it is Harburg who first gets the idea and then finds collaborators he believes will be best suited to a particular project."[22] Furthermore, Harburg's real innovation in libretto writing wasn't his injection of a progressive point of view: rather, it was his disregard of the tradition of the jerry-built musical book. Yes, sometimes he had to write to order what the producer asked him to write, and here and there he adapted elements from existing properties, but overall he conceived his original librettos prior to production. He took the task of writing the musical book as an independent feat of playwriting—the librettist-playwright was to be the chief voice of the evening, to be assisted and not upstaged by the songs and dances. The genre of musical fairy tale as political allegory, pioneered by W. S. Gilbert and retooled by Gershwin and Ryskind, was carried quite a bit further by Yip Harburg. He took the whimsical, helter-skelter fantasies that had characterized musical comedy books before *Show Boat* and tweaked them into flying missiles that delivered social messages, but with such charm and poetry, and with such improved dramatic construction that audiences could only be delighted.

In his three most important book musicals—*Bloomer Girl* (1944), *Finian's Rainbow* (1947), and *Flahooley* (1951)—Harburg made sure no performer would upstage his contribution. More even than Hammerstein, he made himself by sheer orneriness Broadway's first and perhaps only "muscle" librettist, a commanding auteur like the post–Jerome Robbins choreographer-directors of later decades but with the verbal intelligence, thematic consistency, and playwriting skills they conspicuously lacked. *Bloomer Girl,* which Harburg conceived, drawing on a treatment by screenwriters Dan and Lilith James (he supervised the actual script, cowritten by Sid Herzig and Fred Saidy), appeared on the surface to be an entertaining, folklorish Civil War–period operetta in the style of *Oklahoma!:* a story of the woman who invented the garment that replaced hoopskirts. But as Harburg and his colibrettists framed it, *Bloomer Girl* was almost subversive toward the bourgeois sentiments of the Broadway audience of the 1940s: under the guise of its Harold Arlen tunes and Currier and Ives period charm, it flaunted antiwar sentiment during the Second World War and overt feminism and civil rights advocacy years before the agitation of the 1960s. Yet it became a hit.

If Oscar Hammerstein brought realism to the musical play in *Show Boat,* Yip Harburg, in his best-known and most successful show—*Finian's Rainbow* (1947, with music by Burton Lane)—brought magic realism to the musical play. In fact, Harburg based some of his libretto for *Finian* on a story from *The Crock of Gold* by James Stephens (1882–1950), a 1912 book written in the style of magic realism before the term was applied to Borges and García Márquez. (The metamorphosis of Senator Billboard Rawkins in *Finian* also owes something to *A Midsummer Night's Dream,* and Og the leprechaun to Puck and Bottom.) In *Finian,* Harburg took the anarchic disconnects of nineteenth-century musicals and breathed new life into them. An Irish immigrant plants a crock of gold he has stolen from a leprechaun in the ground at Fort Knox; the leprechaun grants a wish that mistakenly turns a racist Mississippi senator black; black and white sharecroppers dance together onstage led by a labor organizer named Woody (after Woody Guthrie). Looked at one way, the libretto appears an artless hodgepodge, and yet it is impossible to watch this show and not be aware that the librettist is not merely ambitious, but that he is challenging the very notion that a musical's libretto is not supposed to be noticed or taken seriously. The recent musical *Urinetown* affects a similar pose, but at its core its idea cupboard is bare. Yet *Finian's Rainbow* is built on ideas: it can be interpreted as a serious socialist critique of capitalism, notwithstanding the fact that it ran 725 performances on capital-driven Broadway. That its *Wizard of Oz*–like unmasking of illusion does not abandon all sentiment (one writer called *Finian's Rainbow* "an act of demystification that celebrates belief") may explain its appeal to apolitical audiences.

Ironically, *Finian's Rainbow* is regarded as unrevivable today; society has changed so vastly that what seemed a cutting-edge attitude toward race in 1947 now appears patronizing. But to rewrite Harburg's script would gut the piece. (A 2000 Broadway revival was up and running but scratched before it made it to the gate. A well-received concert adaptation at off-Broadway's Irish Repertory Theater in 2004 abridged the script.) Somehow racial issues have not impeded revivals of *Show Boat* and *Porgy and Bess*. Why is Harburg considered uniquely dated? The revelation in 2003 that Strom Thurmond fathered a child with a black woman is like life imitating *Finian's Rainbow*'s supposedly too-old-fashioned scene of Senator Rawkins suddenly turning black.

Though Bretaigne Windust was *Finian's* nominal director, Lee Sabinson and William Katzell the producers, and Michael Kidd the choreographer, "Yip was the one in control," flatly stated the show's composer, Burton Lane (who declined to work again with Harburg precisely because he resented being relegated to second banana). "Because of his deep concern with every phase of production, Harburg was able to make his musicals more totally an expression of his own personality and point-of-view than were the composers with whom he worked. Rather than merely setting words to melodies or blocking out the rudiments of a story to hold the songs together, more often than not he was the motivating force behind each production," wrote the music theater historian Stanley Green.[23]

The third of Harburg's high-libretto trilogy—*Flahooley* (1951)—was neither a commercial success (forty performances) nor a good show, but rather a fascinating failure: an attempt to use a Broadway musical to lash back at McCarthyism. *Flahooley,* outrageous even by Harburg's standards, is perhaps the

most politically outspoken musical ever produced on Broadway. A toy manufacturer invents a Christmas season doll called a Flahooley that laughs instead
of cries. He finds himself sought out by various meanies: the State Department,
a group of Arabs who want him to fix a broken magic lamp (whose genie is
"Abou Ben Atom"), a small-town phalanx of paranoid McCarthyite Babbitts,
and a competitor toy manufacturer. Communist witch hunts, loyalty oaths,
wiretaps, the atom bomb, big business conspiracies to fix prices and demand
for goods, the CIA, FBI, HUAC, and F.A.O. Schwartz all make cameo appearances (real or allegorical) in *Flahooley*. Adding to the show's overall effect of a
"Macy's Thanksgiving Parade" (in Brooks Atkinson's words) were the Bil Baird
marionettes, "Professor" Irwin Corey, and the four-octave trick vocalist Yma
Sumac. A very young Barbara Cook made her Broadway debut in this strange
duck of a show, which could have been dubbed "Buffalo Bob and Howdy
Doody meet Lenny Bruce." In the out-of-town tryouts, the Flahooley doll, instead of laughing, cried "Dirty Red!"; that line was scrapped before Broadway
and the cast album, but reinstated in a 1998 off-off-Broadway revival that also
reinstated a Yipsterized Christmas carol deleted from the 1951 production:

> *Sing the merry Christmas spirit*
> *Sing the joys of brotherhood*
> *In the ivy-covered walls of*
> *Saks Fifth Ave. and Bergdorf Good. . . .*
> *Ring out the old, ring, Maestros, please*
> *Ring in the new from Tiffany's*
> *Ring in the bells that gaily peal*
> *Dividends from Bethlehem and U.S. Steel . . .*
> *Sing the cashbox*
> *Sing inflation*
> *Sing the gadget overpriced*
> *And for Christ's sake*
> *May this nation*
> *Soon give Christmas back to Christ!*

Flahooley is more notable for Harburg's daring, if not hubris, than for its
artistic qualities. The librettist hectored rather than bemused his audience, the
characters were cartoon cutouts, the tunes were unmemorable, the imaginative excursions too elaborate to be assimilated. *Flahooley* desperately needed
Finian's charm to work; as its producer, Cheryl Crawford, later noted, "the
writers had been unable to mix properly their delightful fancy with their seri-

ous intent." Sammy Fain's music was generic and untheatrical, far below the level of Vernon Duke, Harold Arlen, or Burton Lane. Years later, television's *Saturday Night Live* would make Flahooleyan satire both mainstream and supportable by corporate advertising, but in 1951 the pamphlet "Red Channels" made Harburg unemployable on television. Harburg was trying to say not just that he thought McCarthy was the unAmerican one, but that the musical play was an artistic form that could legitimately express something grand and unfrivolous. It is doubtful that any other Broadway musical librettist in the fifty years since has gone so far or with such skill to prove the latter point. Harburg's next two librettos, *Jamaica* (1957) and *The Happiest Girl in the World* (1961), also essayed political commentary, but the former was rewritten as a star vehicle for Lena Horne, and the latter, an adaptation of *Lysistrata* to music by Offenbach, lacked the punch of his earlier shows.

It's not his politics in themselves that define Yip Harburg's contribution to musical theater but rather his view of the expressive possibility of the form. For all the madcap woolliness of his books, he dignified the musical theater with the outrageous aspiration that a musical's librettist could be Henrik Ibsen and W. S. Gilbert rolled into one. Since Harburg, career musical book writers have sunk into ever greater anonymity. Playwrights known to be artistically unfettered in their dramas (Arthur Kopit, Terrence McNally) become tame journeymen in their books for musicals. They or the changing commercial climate has opted for safe harbor; no longer do librettists dare to push the envelope (although Kopit's book for Maury Yeston's *Phantom of the Opera* is more interesting than Richard Stilgoe's for Lloyd Webber's version). There are exceptions to this boilerplate anonymity: the book written by Derek Walcott for Paul Simon's self-financed musical *The Capeman* (1998), perhaps not successful, but certainly not dramatically timorous, and David Henry Hwang's rethought book for the 2002 revival of *Flower Drum Song*. There are certainly recent musical librettists who have written their books like good plays: Peter Stone, Arthur Laurents. And highbrow playwrights do not, of course, foreordain success in musical librettos: Robert Sherwood (*Miss Liberty*, 1949), Truman Capote (*House of Flowers*, 1954), and Lillian Hellman (*Candide*, 1956) all faltered.

The problem today lies not with the writers themselves but with the theater's change from enlightened to bottom-line collectivism: the producers are interested only in packaging a commodity; the directors exert absolute control over the construction of the book; and the book writer today, no matter who he is, has only the feckless, expendable clout of a Hollywood screenwriter,

Dramatists Guild contract or not. A poetic book in a commercial musical is a virtual impossibility today.

The third of the golden-age triumvirate to establish the libretto as the fulcrum of a musical wasn't a librettist, a lyricist, or even a writer. He was Kurt Weill—after Victor Herbert the only legitimate composer to sustain a full-time career writing musicals for Broadway. His legacy to Broadway is twofold: not just the creation of much enduring music, but the enhancement of the role of the playwright/librettist.

Weill was born in 1900 in Dessau, Germany, the son of a cantor who was also a composer and took Kurt to the opera at an early age. At twelve he was composing, and at fifteen he was already working as an accompanist for opera singers. At eighteen he went to Berlin to study with composer Engelbert Humperdinck (*Hänsel und Gretel*) but left after a year to conduct the orchestra of a provincial opera company. At twenty Weill entered the composition master class of the pianist-composer Ferruccio Busoni (1866–1924) and continued to work with him and his assistant, Philipp Jarnach, for three years. When the young composer made it known to Busoni the kind of musical theater he wanted to write, Busoni sarcastically replied, "So you want to be a Verdi for the poor?" Weill was to actualize Busoni's characterization more than twenty years later, when, while musically adapting for Broadway Elmer Rice's drama of tenement life, *Street Scene,* he carefully studied Verdi's adaptations of Shakespeare.

Though Weill composed orchestral and chamber works in his early twenties, almost immediately he also began writing for the theater and opera house. The 1926 Dresden production of his first opera, the one-act *Der Protagonist,* to a libretto by the playwright George Kaiser, brought him immediate acclaim and commissions. That same year he married Karoline Blamauer, a sometime prostitute and sometime dancer-actress to become better known by her stage name, Lotte Lenya. Popular music and jazz infiltrated Weill's theater scores from the start, even before his famous collaboration with Bertolt Brecht. The Brecht-Weill partnership lasted only three years but yielded the immortal *Die Dreigroschenoper* (*The Threepenny Opera*), the musical *Happy End,* and the opera *The Rise and Fall of the City of Mahagonny,* an expansion of their earlier half-hour *Mahagonny Songspiel.* The 1928 *Dreigroschenoper,* freely adapted by Brecht from the eighteenth-century British ballad opera *The Beggar's Opera* by John Gay, was performed some ten thousand times all over Europe in the five years after its opening, was filmed, and freed Weill permanently from having to teach to supplement his commission fees. However, a 1933 Broadway production lasted only twelve performances (in the cast was a young Burgess Meredith, who later became a friend and neighbor of Weill in New City, New York).

When Hitler came to power in 1933, Weill emigrated from Germany, spent two years in Paris, and then settled permanently in the United States. The immediate reason for the journey was a commission from the director Max Reinhardt to write the music for the New York production of the biblical pageant *The Eternal Road* (1937). Once in America, Weill faced new dilemmas. He had freed himself from totalitarian control of expression and Nazi persecution. But had also cut himself loose from the benign European system of state subsidy of opera, and he could not hope to make a living writing for opera houses in America as he had in Europe. By 1930 the usual path European émigré composers took to making a living in the States was to write for the movies, as did Erich Wolfgang Korngold and Max Steiner. No symphonically trained composer had made a career of writing Broadway musicals since Victor Herbert had died in 1924. Weill briefly tried Hollywood, but it didn't work for him. Instead, he decided to stick with an American version of what he had done in Europe: seek out the best playwrights of the legitimate theater and persuade them to create librettos for artistic musicals producible on Broadway. Weill's closest friend in America was the esteemed playwright Maxwell Anderson; he collaborated with Anderson on *Knickerbocker Holiday* (1938) and *Lost in the Stars* (1949). Weill worked only with such dramatists; he never teamed with lightweight journeyman book writers like Herbert Fields or Guy Bolton. Despite genuine commercial success on Broadway, Weill was never quite accepted by the Broadway community. During a break in rehearsals for *One Touch of Venus* (1943), the rehearsal pianist Trude Rittmann recalled, "I took a sandwich and went onstage to my piano and started playing Schubert. Kurt stood around the piano and was practically crying. He was never absolutely certain of his role in America."[24]

Weill sought out highbrow collaborators because he believed that "only when artists of different fields set out to combine their efforts in the creation of a 'mixed' art form can we speak of an active relationship between the arts. This true amalgamation of the arts takes place in the theatre." As a result, Weill collaborated not only with Anderson but also with Paul Green, S. J. Perelman, Elmer Rice, Franz Werfel, Ben Hecht, and Arnold Sundgaard. He sought out similarly literary lyricists: Anderson, Ogden Nash, Langston Hughes. The list of illustrious playwrights he began collaborations with that didn't result in produced musicals is equally long: Clifford Odets, Marc Connelly, William

Saroyan, Bella Spewack, Philip Barry, Paul Osborn, S. N. Behrman. He even contemplated adapting George Bernard Shaw (Shaw was still alive). Weill was elected to the Playwrights Company, the producing organization formed by playwrights Robert Sherwood, Rice, Behrman, Sidney Howard, and Anderson—the only composer ever so honored.

As he settled into American life, Weill tried almost to erase his previous self. He would not speak German except with Lenya; he once wrote a letter to *Life* magazine rebuking them for referring to him as a "German composer." He pronounced his name "Weill" instead of "Veill." He told the press that his favorite location in the world was the drugstore in his adopted hometown of New City, New York. He permitted no performances of his German works while in America and composed no concert music here. Asked why he didn't set recitative in his American works (as even Gershwin had done in *Porgy and Bess*), he replied, "I address myself to Americans, and I don't think they want 'Do you want another cup of coffee?' to be sung."

Weill was anything but a snob toward Broadway; Ira Gershwin was his lyricist twice, and the Weill–Gershwin–Moss Hart *Lady in the Dark* (1941) was "a high point in the history of the American musical stage," according to Cecil Smith. "It proves that a musical show can be both engrossing and magnificently entertaining without sacrificing high imagination, acute intelligence, superbly unified and thoroughly artistic production, and an underlying sense of purpose." Weill bragged to Ira Gershwin that songs from *Lady in the Dark* were outselling the songs from Rodgers and Hart's *Pal Joey,* and that big bands such as Benny Goodman and Eddy Duchin were recording his tunes. His next show after *Lady in the Dark, One Touch of Venus,* was more commercial in tone and an even bigger hit. With a book by the humorist S. J. Perelman loosely based on the Pygmalion-Galatea theme, and lyrics by Ogden Nash, *One Touch of Venus* gave Mary Martin her first starring role, featured ballets by Agnes de Mille, and had the compelling beguine tune "Speak Low."

In some ways, *Street Scene* (1947) apotheosized the whole direction of Weill's career since his days of writing opera in Germany. "Starting out as a composer of grand opera at the age of twenty-five," he wrote shortly before *Street Scene* opened,

I soon discovered the limitations of a form of entertainment in which almost all of the other demands of the theatre had to be sacrificed to the music. . . . The special brand of musical entertainment in which I have been interested from the start is a sort of "dramatic musical," a simple, strong story told in musical terms, interweaving the spoken word and the sung word so that the singing takes over naturally whenever the emotion of the spoken word reaches a point where music can "speak" with greater effect.[25]

"All art should return to its roots and become popular again," he added. "Traditional opera, represented in this country by the Metropolitan Opera, has rejected these roots by catering only to a narrow public." By so stating he was implicitly rejecting the criticism of his American work from some quarters that he had sold out and, in effect, dumbed down his musical idiom.

Sometimes, of course, even the strong-willed Weill had to yield to the contrary wishes of his collaborators. There he remained a paradox: an ardent practicing advocate of collaborative theater who was also a "control freak." Trude Rittmann told me in 1998 that Weill "didn't want anybody touching his music." Elia Kazan writes in his autobiography that at times Weill usurped his direction of *One Touch of Venus,* leaving Kazan little more than an "overpaid stage manager." Like Wagner, Weill was a hands-on theater man, involved in every aspect of his shows' productions, not just the music. A memo he wrote to *Street Scene* producer Dwight Deere Wiman, book writer Elmer Rice, lyricist Langston Hughes, and director Charles Friedman while the show was in tryouts in Philadelphia amply illustrates how concerned he was with the libretto:

> But in some parts, specially [*sic*] in the first act, we have not succeeded yet in blending the elements of the show. In some places we try to be too legitimate, in other places, too musical comedy. We are definitely using too much the number technique of musical comedy instead of the flowing technique we had in mind. There are far too many stops for applauses. . . . So here are some suggestions:
> *Heat Number:* Cut musical tag at end and start music of Willie's entrance on last note of Heat chorus.
> *1st Gossip Number:* Make all movements of the women more natural, less deliberate, take out whispering into ear, replace by stronger expression of gossiping women. Take out pose for applause at the end. . . .
> *Sam's entrance:* Give Sam a few more serious lines to build up his character. . . .
> *Opening 2nd Act:* There could be a little more life and activity of the waking house. There are long pauses between entrances which should be filled in. Since we have taken out the relief material of the 2nd act, we should do a little more with the opening, which is full of possibilities.[26]

Kazan, who directed both *One Touch of Venus* and *Love Life,* wrote later of Weill, "I found him always swinging to whoever had the most power. . . . but I did admire his ability . . . to adapt himself to the requirements of our musical theatre. If, when he left Germany, he'd landed in Java instead of the United States, within a year he'd have been writing Javanese temple music and receiving praise from their high priests. If he'd been dumped on an African savannah, he'd quickly have mastered the tribal drum!"[27] Conductor John Mauceri believes that if Weill were alive and writing for the Broadway musical today, he would be using rock grooves, minimalism, or even rap in his composing.[28]

But what a time-transported Weill wouldn't change is his practice of working with serious dramatists and meaningful librettos. Could a Kurt Weill still play that role on a Broadway that touts *Hairspray* with thirteen Tony nominations and eight awards?

The Gospel of the Good Book According to Lehman Engel

The notion that something artistically unique was taking place during the decades of the golden age of the Broadway musical took shape only retrospectively. The composers, lyricists, book writers, choreographers, and other creators of the period were too busy creating their works to be able to stand back and beatify them. But one collaborator who had been there with them in the trenches (literally—in the orchestra pit) saw the forest for the trees sooner than most. This man, the Mississippi-born composer Lehman Engel (1910–82), who between 1936 and 1965 conducted more than a hundred musicals and fifty recorded albums of musicals, became the first important champion and historical preservationist of the golden age of Broadway musicals. He was the first Broadway working professional to attempt an analysis of what made golden-age Broadway musicals tick. He was also the first to re-create lost golden-age scores on recordings (for composer-producer Goddard Lieberson on Columbia Records in the 1950s) and the first to found a school for aspiring musical theater writers (the BMI Musical Theatre Workshop, started in 1961).

Beginning in the mid-1960s Engel also wrote a series of books elaborating on the fruits of his long professional experience. What, indeed, made the golden-age Broadway musicals uniquely great, wondered this conductor, who by his own estimate had, in performing eight times a week for thirty years, entertained eight million people? What was it something hummable in the tunes? Tappable in the beat? The éclat of the dancing or sets? The dash of the lyrics? The chemistry among collaborators? The swift pace of the stage direction? The charisma of star performers?

Nope. It was . . . the script. The book. How did an orchestra pit conductor arrive at this stunning aperçu?

Engel grew up Jewish and gay in Jackson, Mississippi (he remained a life-long close friend of the novelist Eudora Welty, a neighbor), briefly attended the Cincinnati Conservatory of Music, and in 1929 went to New York City to study music composition with Rubin Goldmark (one of Aaron Copland's teachers) and Roger Sessions. He had social as well as artistic talent and met many important young people in the theater and related arts, including Copland, Orson Welles, and Martha Graham, for whom he composed several ballet scores in the 1930s. He conducted madrigal choruses, wrote music criticism, was invited by Melvyn Douglas to compose incidental music for a Sean O'Casey play, and soon found himself making a living conducting musicals. (Engel was one of the long list of legitimately trained composers—Robert Russell Bennett, Trude Rittmann, Albert Szirmai, Hershy Kay, and others—who make a living by servicing Broadway musicals but rarely write them.) He also composed many concert works in his spare time but eventually abandoned the attempt to make a career as a serious composer, although he wrote incidental music for dozens of Broadway plays. The one musical Engel wrote, a WPA production entitled *A Hero Is Born* (1937), was a flop by his own admission: "My music, written without conviction, was a horrible confusion of innocuous operetta-like ditties and inexperienced jazz."[29]

Well-read and endowed with an intellectual's broad culture, Engel was as knowledgeable about opera, drama, and poetry as about musicals. Is it really such an irony that the musician who conducted and witnessed more Broadway performances than perhaps anyone else in history became the leading proselytizer for the librettist, the most anonymous of the triumvirate of book, music, and lyrics? Who better would know what works before a live audience? "I have long felt that our musical theatre has thus far produced few librettists," Engel wrote in his autobiography. "The success of our best shows is due first to the effectiveness of their books," he wrote in 1967. In book after book he flogged this refrain: "In musicals—strange to say—the quality of music and lyrics has little to do with the total result. These help or hinder, make memorable or are bypassed as a negligible contribution to the end product, but the libretto must carry the prime responsibility for success or failure precisely as in a non-musical. It is the workability of the play that accounts for the end results."[30]

Engel was no slavish idolater of sacred cows. Of *Show Boat's* book he wrote, "The characters are two-dimensional, the proportions are outrageous, the plot development is predictable and corny, and the ending is unbearably sweet. . . . Not a single detail departs from formula. . . . The element of coincidence in the book is not only silly, but sloppy, for the action could have been motivated without resorting to nonsense."[31] But he believed that the well-constructed books of the best post-1927 shows by Rodgers and Hammerstein, Porter, Loesser, Lerner and Loewe, Bernstein, Bock and Harnick, and others were what made them superior to earlier shows, which sported only "collections of songs (they were not 'scores,' since their relationships to characters, situations, and to each other were peripheral)." Engel believed the golden-age shows were a higher art form not because of their music and lyrics but because their books engendered "three-dimensional characters, and scores that characterize the singers, further the plot, and in themselves help to form a coherent entity." He was the first to recognize that while most musicals produced were still tired-businessman specials, the musicals that achieved the greatest public success had narrative and depth, and even at times produced what Aristotle had claimed great drama always achieved: catharsis through pity and terror. By "feeling," a word that recurs throughout his books as a term describing how the best musicals play in the theater with an audience, Engel clearly meant catharsis in the classical sense.

Engel was not only an evangelist for the golden age, he was a Cassandra who foresaw its impending demise. He quit the business in 1969 after a frustrating experience with an egomaniacal director. He lamented the popularity already in the late 1960s of "a kind of kinetic non-musical which threatens to destroy and to a large extent discourage more serious, better based creativity."[32] He predicted faux concept musicals: "a musical minus all of the elements of story, premise, characters, conflict, development would wind up as a revue, but the non-plot shows are *not* revues. There is no recognizable start or stop to the 'happening' as a whole, no well-defined units, no sketches, no dance, no connecting thread. What is it then that such a theatrical 'happening' has left?"[33] He predicted the nonspecific, nonsituational songwriting approaches of rock-based shows where the songs "lack the all-important theatrical ingredient of having been born of some recognizable theatrical situation and made for a specific identifiable character reacting in it. Without such motivations, the songs become generalized, will not arouse audience empathy, will occur in unconnected and therefore meaningless sequence. The audience may as well arrive and/or depart at will without having missed anything." And he predicted the triumph of loud volume and production glitz over dramaturgy and nuance: "the audience is cheated of any experiencing and are given in its place some 'sensing.' The first of these words suggests feeling, encounter, undergoing, actual living through an event, while the latter connects with sensuous perception, instinctive reactions, and many other things the precise effects of which cannot be calculated and require neither art, knowledge, discipline, or experience."[34]

But much of his advice has fallen on deaf ears. The songwriting style of John Kander and Fred Ebb is a rebuke to Lehman Engel. In almost every Kander and Ebb show virtually every song is some variant of camped-up neo-Jolson razzmatazz, no matter what the specifics of character or situation. In defiance of Engel's wisdom, they have written revue songs for book shows, they have deconstructed the golden-age writing style, and they have been one of the consistently successful teams of the last quarter century.

Engel invented the idea that Broadway had an equivalent of what classical music has referred to as a "common-practice period." The classical music common-practice period of masterpieces runs roughly from Mozart to Brahms (definitions vary). For Engel the Broadway common-practice period was from *Pal Joey* (1940) to *Fiddler on the Roof* (1964). The problem is that people in classical music today don't write exactly like common-practice period composers, and neither should writers of new musicals. Engel's BMI Musical Theatre Workshop devolved into codifying and recipe-izing the construction of common-practice period musicals of the 1940s and 1950s: write a "charm song" here; put an "I want" song there. Inspiration cannot be manufactured. The flowering that was Broadway's golden age came about through seat-of-the-pants practical experience, instinct, and spontaneous combustion, not through classroom workshops. Craft is necessary, certainly, and can be a liberation for the truly gifted, but for the uninspired, creation by imitating craft is a recipe for staleness and nonrenewal.

Engel also was fond of pointing out that as adaptations were used more frequently after *Show Boat* as the basis for librettos, the musical theater improved artistically. Indeed, the books of the early musicals were mostly both original and inept in the blowzy pre-golden age. But Engel failed to see the repercussions of his advice about adaptations: it licensed vulgar and unenlightened producers to option properties and use poor artistic judgment in turning them into mediocre musicals written by indifferent talent for the sake of commodifying a sellable show. This is essentially what has happened on the Broadway of the last twenty years, an era in which retreads have largely replaced inspiration.

Today's producing organizations—Shubert, Jujamcyn, Nederlander, Hyperion, Dodger—have paid no heed to Engel's advice about the book and have supplanted nuanced libretto writing with packaging. The spectacle replaces the text. Or the choreographer-director orchestrates the book. Or the book is subliterary: the property it is adapted from is a dramatically vacuous movie or television show.

Certainly the books of great musical shows are not invariably great play structures. And merely to have ideas does not make a great play, much less a good musical; there are many bad plays brimful of ideas. Nevertheless, the notion that a strong book drives a musical has been abandoned by Broadway. Musical books of the 1980s, 1990s, and beyond have reverted to the dramatically simple stories of the 1920s and earlier. In the 1910s and 1920s, Cinderella fantasies were popular grist for Broadway musicals; today's most popular fantasy is the unmasked secret self; it's in *Phantom of the Opera, Jekyll and Hyde, Beauty and the Beast, Side Show,* even Sondheim's *Passion.* Signor Puccini has been pillaged repeatedly: *Madama Butterfly* is in *Miss Saigon, La bohème* in *Rent* (to say nothing of *La bohème* in *La bohème*).

Cantata musicals like *Cats, Les Miz,* and *Rent* do not run on play dramaturgy, although they can evoke the "feeling" that Engel so frequently cited as essential for audience communication. But the mixture of spoken dialogue and song is what gave the traditional Broadway musical a flexibility both to evoke this emotional power and to involve the brain and the critical faculty. That mixture was the quintessence of the strength of the genre, made possible by a book that is *not* a sung-through libretto. Unlike in opera, sung-through librettos in musicals attenuate, rather than enhance, dramatic momentum.

With the BMI workshops, Engel acted as a behind-the-scenes power broker, quietly pushing some talents into real-life opportunities. He generally favored men over women, but not always. After Engel's death the BMI Musical Theatre Workshop was carried on by the composer Maury Yeston. Engel was immortalized as a character in *A Class Act,* the 2001 musical about his BMI workshop disciple Ed Kleban (the lyricist of *A Chorus Line*). On April 2, 2001, at New York's Merkin Hall, BMI presented "Lehman's Children: The Legacy of Broadway's Greatest Teacher." The most discomfiting aspect of this heartfelt tribute was that its opening number, a two-piano arrangement of Leonard Bernstein's "Wrong Note Rag" from *Wonderful Town* (which Engel had conducted on Broadway in 1953), seemed to eclipse the rest of the evening, making almost every ensuing song by "Lehman's children" feel like an anticlimax—living proof that the golden age could not be resurrected?

Lehman Engel unfortunately got it right: when the book was deconstructed, so was the musical.

Scene Two. *The Lyrics*

The Ups and Downs of Lyrics: From Brushstrokes to Dance Partner to Irrelevance

> Lonely women watch are keeping,
> Hearts are sighing, eyes are weeping.
> Just a year we have been waiting,
> Much too long I don't mind stating.
> For a kiss I'm nearly dying,
> Oh, this waiting is most trying.
> Would there were some mischief brewing,
> But there's really nothing doing.
> —"What Can We Do without a Man"
> lyrics by Stanislaus Stange
> from *The Chocolate Soldier* (1909)

Those moronic words by Stanislaus Stange, one of the busiest and most successful Broadway lyricists and librettists of the pre-golden age, are archetypal of the theater of their time. In songs before about 1910, "in almost all instances, the music is far superior to the lyric," writes the music historian Nicholas Tawa. "Indeed, one senses that most lyrics exist only for the sake of the music, not the other way around."[35] Notwithstanding England's great exemplar W. S. Gilbert, the Broadway lyricist, when not one and the same as the composer, was a hired appendage, not an independent artist. A typical lyricist was paid a flat fee of five dollars for a song lyric before the founding of ASCAP in 1914; then and only then did lyricists acquire royalty rights and an artistic parity with the song composer.[36]

In Broadway's early era, as Tawa notes, most songs' lyrics treaded water and marked time for the melody. It's as if they were dummy lyrics used in a kind of scat singing with actual words. To the extent they had any content, the lyrics would dress the tunes with generic sentiments in broad brushstrokes, like bad light verse or greeting-card doggerel. "Until the third decade of the twentieth century, lyrics by the main line writers were not only cliché-ridden, but also stodgy, awkward, pretentious, stentorian, and grandiloquent," wrote Lehman Engel.[37] Against this precedent, the post-1920 golden age of Lorenz Hart, Cole Porter, Ira Gershwin, Yip Harburg, Oscar Hammerstein, and their confreres was a revolution. They elevated the function of the song lyric to a kind of subtle, sensuous dance partner with the tune—the words dipped while the tune pivoted and then vice versa, over and over again. These canonical lyricists eliminated the vague verbiage and made specific images deliver universal truths.

What has happened to lyrics in the Broadway musical of recent vintage? There are certainly preservationists of the high-water style (Stephen Sondheim, Betty Comden and Adolph Green, a handful of newer writers). But in most cases the world has turned backward: lyrics again dress the music in broad brushstrokes, again retreat from the specific to the general and thereby lose the universal. It is no coincidence that today's revived operettas or rock poperettas (Andrew Lloyd Webber, Alain Boublil and Claude-Michel Schönberg, Frank Wildhorn) have revived the subliterate lyrics of yore.

The revolutionariness of the notion of making word and tune "dance partners" can be demonstrated by quoting the one kind of pre–golden-age lyric that was specific in word imagery: the narrative patter ballad, which was so prominent a feature of vaudeville as well as early Broadway musicals. Here's an example from the 1901 Klaw and Erlanger production of *The Sleeping Beauty and the Beast,* "Rip Van Winkle Was a Lucky Man," with lyric by William Jerome:

> *He never had to ride around in overcrowded cars*
> *Or smoke those generously good infantile Child cigars*

Eat Dennett's cakes, or buckwheat flakes,
He never had to listen to those ragtime organs play,
Or read about two hundred thousand extras every day,
Omega oil is very good for shoes.
He saw the Catskill mountains and he saw the Catskill rats,
But he never had to live in any stingy Harlem flats,
Four rooms and bath, just room to laugh,
Those narrow chested dining rooms that really are too small,
That every time you want to eat, they serve you in the hall:
It serves you wrong, but still it serves you right.
He didn't have to chop the wood or carry in the coal,
Or walk upon his heels all day, to try and save his sole.

Unfortunately, the tune for this clever lyric makes no attempt to partner with it; like George M. Cohan's "Life's a Funny Proposition After All," the lyric can just as sensibly be talked over its accompaniment as sung to it (indeed, Cohan did talk such lyrics rather than sing them). The effect is that of a musical comedy recitative and the opposite of Tawa's description: the melody is an afterthought to the words.

The relatively late arrival of artful song lyrics on the American stage is surprising in view of the facts that the lyceum movement had popularized verse readings by literary celebrities already by mid-nineteenth century, that Gilbert and Sullivan played Broadway from the late 1870s, and that until the dawn of radio "the popular arts were oral—the singer, the minstrel show, the theatre, the evangelist, the Chautauqua lecturer," in the words of *7 Lively Arts* author Gilbert Seldes. By the 1910s fine light verse itself had become what Seldes meant by a lively art. Schools and colleges in the 1900s and 1910s "still stressed a rigorous training in classical poetic forms—forms that appeared daily in the most widely read columns in New York."[38] Yip Harburg, who grew up in New York City's Lower East Side like fellow golden-age lyricists Ira Gershwin and Irving Berlin, later recalled the high level of literacy he and his colleagues aspired to:

> We were well-versed in all French forms. . . . the ballad, the triolet, the rondo, the villanelle, the sonnet. . . . We were never permitted to use . . . a tonal rhyme like *home* and *tone.* . . . My roots are Shakespeare, Wordsworth, Shelley, Shaw: the English language. If you want to write songs and you don't know A. E. Houseman, if you don't know Dorothy Parker, Frank Adams . . . you cannot be a good lyric writer.[39]

Harburg and Gershwin also studied what was then known as society verse—witty, light conversational poems by the seventeenth-century Cavalier poets Robert Herrick and Richard Lovelace and the nineteenth-century poets Ernest Dowson and Lewis Carroll, who were arguably the aesthetic ancestors of Broadway golden-age lyricists, as Philip Furia explains:

> Yip Harburg and Ira Gershwin were not alone in their youthful admiration of society verse. Along with Howard Dietz, Dorothy Fields, and many other lyricists, they began their writing careers as writers of "smarty verse," their highest aspiration to place a poem in magazines like *The Smart Set, Vanity Fair,* or that pinnacle of verbal wit, Franklin Pierce Adams' (F. P. A.'s) column, the "Conning Tower," in the *New York World.* When these aspiring poets turned to the more lucrative art of songwriting, their lyrics still were rooted in *vers de société.*[40]

When broadcast radio was born in 1920, the high oral tradition of American pop culture was only enhanced. Without a visual element, the writer for radio (whether of dramatic scripts, comedy routines, or song lyrics) had to use words imaginatively, and the listener had to focus on the words and fill in an imagined visual correlate. During the heyday of radio (1920–50), jokes, even for a mass audience, were more literate, and the radio audience's response to the verbal timing of on-air performers was hair-trigger. Abbott and Costello's "Who's on first?" routine is far quicker and far more verbally sophisticated in their radio version than in their later movie version. Is it entirely a coincidence that the best years of Broadway songwriting mostly coincide with the golden age of radio?

Lyricists were a social fraternity in those years; no BMI workshops were needed. As Harburg recalled,

> I write for my peers. In fact, our tribe of songsmiths always wrote for our peers. We were very much ashamed of ourselves if we wrote anything clichéd, if we took an idea from another person. By "our tribe," I'm talking about Cole Porter, Ira Gershwin, Hart, Dietz, all those people who got together every week, usually at George Gershwin's house, and we would more or less compare the things we were working on.

> All the songwriters got together regularly at the Gershwins in the twenties and thirties. Something like Fleet Street in Samuel Johnson's time—an artistic community where people took fire from each other. We'd hang around George's piano, playing our latest songs to see how they went over with the boys. We were

all interested in what the other fellas were up to; we criticized and helped each other. . . . You wouldn't dare write a bad rhyme or a clichéd phrase or an unoriginal or remotely plagiarized tune, because you were afraid of being ripped apart by your peers.[41]

Can there be any doubt what Harburg's elitely self-educated "tribe of songsmiths" would have thought of the inept mixed metaphor contained in Lynn Ahrens's lyric "he will ride on the wheels of a dream" in *Ragtime* (1998)? It appears that the creators of *Ragtime* were unaware of their verbal faux pas. A Harburg or Hart would have used a mixed metaphor only with a knowing self-referential wink at the listener, both to make clear he knew the error and to convey an additional innuendo through it.

Lorenz Hart, Cole Porter, Ira Gershwin, Irving Berlin, Oscar Hammerstein, E. Y. Harburg, Howard Dietz, Dorothy Fields, Irving Caesar, Frank Loesser, Alan Jay Lerner—the corpus of their work for the Broadway theater embodies a common practice that defines the high tradition of lyric writing in the golden age. The defining characteristics include:

- using specifics to evoke universals (or as Harburg said, "the aim of a song is to make a specific thing general, to give a thing a universal quality rather than a specific quality"[42]);
- playwriting the human condition in miniature, rather than writing lyrics about casually observed trivia;
- writing dramaturgically even when the lyrics were interpolated into revues and thus not book-driven;
- using the emotional power of poetic language freely and without embarrassment while also using vernacular language with maximum cleverness;
- achieving complete expressive freedom while abiding by the technical constraints of versification;
- interacting dialectically with the song's melody and the composer's personality;
- subsuming expression to elegance, which meant that off-color material could get expressed but was filtered through oblique wordplay;
- and, above all, being sincere—that is, believing in what they were writing, not just going through the motions.

So many of the song standards written by the golden-age lyricists can be distilled to a statement about the human condition. Lorenz Hart's "Spring Is Here" (from Rodgers and Hart's 1938 *I Married an Angel*), a lament of vernal lovelessness, says much the same thing Edna St. Vincent Millay expressed in her poem "Spring" when she wrote:

> *To what purpose, April, do you return again?*
> *Beauty is not enough. . . .*
> *Life in itself*
> *Is nothing,*
> *An empty cup, a flight of uncarpeted stairs.*
> *It is not enough that yearly, down this hill,*
> *April*
> *Comes like an idiot, babbling and strewing flowers.*

When Hammerstein wrote "I Whistle a Happy Tune" for Anna Leonowens in *The King and I,* he had her express not only her character at that specific dramatic moment, but a universal truism for human beings at all times and seasons: make yourself believe you aren't afraid and maybe you'll believe it (Hammerstein borrowed the sentiment from French psychologist Emile Coué). When Yip Harburg gave Og the leprechaun the lyric "When I'm Not Near the Girl I Love / I Love the Girl I'm Near" in *Finian's Rainbow,* he was both driving the throughline of the show's book and addressing the inescapability of compromise in life. When Maxwell Anderson had Peter Stuyvesant sing "September Song" to Tina Tienhoven in *Knickerbocker Holiday,* he made Stuyvesant speak for a time in all men's lives. Conversely, there is not a single lyric in *Sunset Boulevard* (1994) that rises above a one-dimensional interpretation of the character and story of Norma Desmond, or that poetically extrapolates from her situation to extend to the general human condition.

It is typical in golden-age musicals for multiple songs to step out of the action and address human universals. In *Babes in Arms,* "Where or When," "I Wish I Were in Love Again," and "My Funny Valentine" all do so. In *South Pacific,* the songs "A Cock-eyed Optimist," "Some Enchanted Evening," "Carefully Taught," "This Nearly Was Mine," and arguably others resonate beyond the immediate dramatic situation. In *Fiorello!* (1959), even "Politics and Poker" and "A Little Tin Box" rise above Mayor La Guardia's New York City to etch Tammanyism for all cultures over the entire planet. How do recent musicals' lyrics compare? In *Kiss of the Spider Woman* (1992), a musical supposedly addressing the problem of human illusion, there is only one song lyric out of twenty-three—"Where You Are"—that even attempts a larger resonance. "Ol' Man River" is a scene-setter that portrays the force of timelessness in human events; Tim Rice's opening number for *The Lion King* gauchely attempts to do the same with an Earth Day cliché, "The Circle of Life." *Side Show* (1997), about Daisy and Violet Hilton, real-life Siamese twins who played vaudeville, purports to tell us that freaks are just like you and me, yet it does not contain a single song lyric that illustrates how general human predicaments may have commonalities with the freaks' condition.

Sir Tim Rice (b. 1944, knighted in 1994) is as nearly single-handedly responsible for a paradigm shift in musical books as Hammerstein was earlier, but his approach is to dispense with the well-constructed spoken script and replace it with the all-sung libretto of opera, transmuted into rock/pop idioms. Starting with *Joseph and the Amazing Technicolor Dreamcoat* (1968), Rice and Lloyd Webber "returned to a cantata form, a sung-through text with no intervening dialogue."[43] The result for thirty years has been both the ongoing artistic deconstruction of the book musical and the commercial redefinition of what constitutes marketable material as a Broadway musical. The lyrics *are* the book in a Rice musical, which would seem to redouble the need for careful workmanship. But Rice "liked to exhibit a relaxed attitude to his craft. He wrote lyrics off the top of his head," reports one Lloyd Webber biographer.[44] He apparently took no heed of Alexander Pope's famous couplet, "True ease in writing comes from art, not chance, / As those move easiest who have learned to dance." As Hammerstein might have said, lyrics have got to be carefully wrought, and Rice's are not. Recently Rice has turned to collaborating with the composer Reginald Kenneth Dwight (b. 1947), also known as Sir Elton John (*The Lion King, Aida*).

The failings of modern theater lyrics do not lie in the question of whether Tim Rice writes the words before Lloyd Webber composes tunes or vice versa. Gilbert wrote his words before Sullivan composed his tunes; Kern wrote his music first for P. G. Wodehouse and Hammerstein, but Hammerstein wrote his words first for Rodgers. Rodgers wrote music first for Hart but not for Hammerstein. Ira Gershwin set words to his brother's already written tunes— "mosaically," in Ira's famous phrase. In actuality, "which came first" is rarely clear-cut. For the title song from *Oklahoma!,* according to the show's vocal arranger and orchestrator Robert Russell Bennett, "Richard Rodgers and Oscar Hammerstein 2d worked out the words and music together, part of it words first and part the other way 'round."[45] It's not about "which came first" because both methods have provided great results musically and lyrically. The problem today is that there is no longer any dialectic between the lyric's content and the way the lyric is presented musically; there is no "dance partnering" going on between Rice's words and Lloyd Webber's or Elton John's music, or between Alain Boublil and Claude-Michel Schönberg, or between Frank Wildhorn and his lyricists, or between Stephen Flaherty and Lynn Ahrens. In what songwriting team today can one find the dialectical tension between the cheerful up-tempo tunes of Rodgers and the melancholy of Hart? Where do we find the modern counterpart to George Gershwin's gentle foxtrot tune turned into acid by his brother Ira's lyric that spoofs all lyrics:

> *Blah blah blah blah, moon*
> *Blah blah blah, above*
> *Blah blah blah blah, croon*
> *Blah blah blah blah, love*

Where can we find today Ira Gershwin's gift for adept self-parody of the lyricist, not just in "Blah Blah Blah Blah" but also in "Jenny and her saga / proves that you are gaga" from *Lady in the Dark,* or his Gertrude Stein–like "You Have to Do What You Do Do" from *The Firebrand of Florence*? Where today can we find a coexistence of opposites like Harburg's borderline socialist ballads set to courtly gavotte tunes by Burton Lane in *Finian's Rainbow*? Or the recitative-like excursion into fantasy of Sondheim's "I Had a Dream" leitmotif (from *Gypsy*) improbably set to Jule Styne's unremittingly driving brass tune? Since modern pop theater music is either all irony or all broad brushstrokes, there's nothing either in the lyric or in the tune to push off against. (Susan Birkenhead's lyrics for *Jelly's Last Jam* [1992] do stay on character—especially the title character—*and* partner with the tunes.)

The sexual and other social revolutions of the 1960s certainly liberated a great many things for the better, and a new frankness of theater lyrics has been one of its byproducts. But in theatre lyrics the baby was thrown out with the bathwater. Poetic diction—and great song lyrics are a form of poetic diction—is not expository prose; it is indirect, yet elevates expression by the artfulness of its indirection. Thus, something of verbal craft, and of expressive power itself, is lost when there are no taboos for the lyricist to circumvent. The eye-winking artful obliquity of Porter, Hart, and others is a lost art today. Porter's lyric to "Too Darn Hot," a production number from *Kiss Me, Kate,* though written in short lines and full of code and double entendres, nevertheless conveys the gritty physical act of sex with astounding realism; Michael John LaChiusa's lyrics for his show *Hello Again* (1994), based on Schnitzler's *La Ronde,* while purporting to describe the sex act or the fantasy thereof, use frank and uncoded but flat and one-dimensional language, never remotely approaching Porter's achievement of palpable heat; the conveyance of actual sexiness was left to the show's costume designer.

Since Edward Kleban's famous "Tits and Ass" lyric for *A Chorus Line* (1975), profanity has abounded in Broadway show lyrics. Kleban's was a case of artful, dramatically justifiable usage. In *The Full Monty* (2000), the lyrics by David Yazbek for the show's cast of blue-collar males are freely written in "testosteronese." One song about dissuading someone from suicide is entitled "Big Ass Rock"; the title refers to the object a friend would use to assist the suicide. The songs do subscribe to the Hammerstein model insofar as they are written in character. But because they stay entirely at the let-it-all-hang-out level, they lose the power of poetic suggestion. *The Full Monty* has a funny topical number, "Michael Jordan's Ball," which could be summed up thus: you can only persuade macho men to let themselves be directed by a choreographer by getting them to pretend they're Michael Jordan on the basketball court. But again Yazbek stays literal: there's no poetic investigation of the initial image. Compare Frank Loesser's lyrics for *Guys and Dolls* (1950), a show that like *Full Monty* not only depicted the macho types of its time ("Gotta have the game or we'll die from shame"), but was replete with topical references comparable to Michael Jordan's ball (hollanderizing mink coats, Bromo Fizz, Vitalis, and Barbasol). But *Guys and Dolls* also has gangster Sky Masterson come up with this poetic image while singing "My Time of Day": "the smell of the rain-washed pavement comes up clean and fresh and cold." Very rarely do rock-era lyrics yield such concrete yet poetically observed details.

The musical theater no less than other venues has been affected by the devaluation of ornate language pervasive in contemporary America's visually oriented culture. It was eminently clear to anyone attending the 1999 revival of *Kiss Me, Kate* that the audience did not understand or appreciate the multiple puns in Porter's lyric for one of the show's funniest numbers, "Brush Up Your Shakespeare." But neither did the director help; the tempos for this and other songs throughout the production tended to run too fast for clear enunciation and expression of the lyric, amplification or not. Moreover, the actors playing Fred Graham/Petruchio and Lilli Vanessi/Katharine were not directed to center their performances in the subtle verbal battle of the sexes intended by Porter and librettists Sam and Bella Spewack, but rather on crude physical comedy— mugging. Farce was substituted for wit in this wittiest of all Broadway shows, based on the real-life Alfred Lunt and Lynn Fontanne's productions of *The Taming of the Shrew*. In *Bring in 'Da Noise, Bring in 'Da Funk* (1996), a speech full of references to Oscar Micheaux, Countee Cullen, and other literary figures of the Harlem Renaissance was so quickly rushed, so poorly enunciated, and so poorly sound designed that only the most alert of listeners would have heard the names Micheaux and Cullen mentioned at all, let alone what was said about them. By contrast, the superfast patter of "Rock Island," the opening number in Meredith Willson's *The Music Man* (1957) ("Waddaya talk waddaya talk / But he doesn't know the territory") is by its very indiscernability integral to the characterization of the tribe of salesmen to which Harold Hill belongs.

Another way in which theater lyrics today don't dance or dovetail with the music they set stems from a certain rock songwriting practice. Rock songwriters freely ignore the unwritten one-note-one-syllable rule of the belle époque. Rather than change the rhythm or otherwise work to conform a lyric syllable to a single musical note, they will keep a song's rhythmic groove intact and write a vocalise pattern of several musical notes—a melisma—to cover one syllable. This style originates in gospel and blues and was widely adopted by white songwriters starting in the late 1950s: from Carole King and Gerry Goffin (in their 1961 song "Will You Love Me Tomorrow?" recorded by the Shirelles) to the Bob Crewe–Bob Gaudio songs for the Four Seasons ("Big Girls Don't Cry-y-y") to folk song writers like Pete Seeger (the last line of "If I Had a Hammer") to many John Lennon and Paul McCartney songs ("Help," for instance). The same pop melismatic writing is all over the scores of young Broadway musical writers of the 1990s and 2000s—Stephen Flaherty, Jason Robert Brown, Jonathan Larson, Michael John LaChiusa. It doesn't exist in Kern, Porter, Rodgers, Berlin, Loewe, or even Harold Arlen, and appears in Gershwin solely in *Porgy and Bess.* When a character in opera sings legitimate vocalise, there can be a heightening of the drama. When a character in a serious dramatic musical sings a song with a melody written in pop vocalise, there can be a certain dignity gap between the musical style and the dramatic situation.

According to the composer-lyricist Elizabeth Swados (*Runaways, Doonesbury*), "The joy of noise . . . is a crucial element of rock feeling. This often eliminates the need for precisely understanding lyrics. . . . songs written to be complete in themselves can't develop a narrative, character, or theme."[46] Swados's characterization applies to the communal, celebratory quality of successful modern rock lyrics. But it also equally describes the lyrics of *Ragtime,* which, while pretending an homage to the Lehman Engel school of character writing, really depict only stereotyped cut-out characters with generic language. The show's best song, musically as well as lyrically, is the opening title number, perhaps because it spared the lyricist and composer the pretense of rendering character or situation.

One could almost spell out a formulary of postmodern Broadway lyrics that would reverse almost point for point the practices of golden-age lyricists:

- Instead of adapting to the technical constraints of versification, theater lyricists today tend to use free verse. With rare exceptions, they are indifferent to the nuanced construction of good light verse. Unfortunately, with few exceptions they are also indifferent to how rich poetic language can be used when free verse is employed, as by Maxwell Anderson in his unrhymed lyrics for Weill's *Lost in the Stars* (1949) or by DuBose Heyward for *Porgy and Bess* (1935). (Stephen Sondheim believes that Heyward's lyrics for *Porgy and Bess* are the finest ever written for the musical theater, although Ira Gershwin wrote about half of the show's lyrics.)[47]
- Instead of leading from the specific to the general, they either stay marooned in specifics or wallow in vague generalities. The lyrics by Charles Hart for *Phantom of the Opera* offer a classic example of the latter; they paint vague, characterless emotional impastos no less than did the lyrics one hundred years ago of Harry B. Smith. Examples of lyrics not rising above the level of the specific—truly a failure of the imagination of contemporary writers—abound in almost every recent contemporary Broadway musical except for Sondheim's.
- Instead of putting elegance above expression, they put expression before elegance, although it might be more correct to say that elegance itself has become obsolete as a value in lyric writing.
- Instead of respecting the interaction between lyric and music, they "nonchalant" this interaction. The rhythmic imperatives of rock music rebuff storytelling, development, and verbal logic, defeating the very purpose of good theater lyrics, which is to interact with the music in an ongoing dialectic. A few of Jason Robert Brown's lyrics to his own rock-based tunes in *Parade* (1998) bravely try to be exceptions to this rule.
- Instead of dramaturgically constructing songs and lyrics, they indulge a kind of vulgate dadaism, which arguably started in the 1960s with the charming (LSD-inspired?) nonsense and gibberish of Beatles songs like "I Am the Walrus." Vulgate dadaism has devolved into Tim Rice's lyrics for *Aida* (2000), which eschew sequence, construction, coherent imagery, and common sense. Such lyrics as "Every Story Is a Love Story," "The Past Is Another Land," and "My Strongest Suit ('I Am What I Wear')" violate almost every precept of traditional theater lyric writing, but splendidly exemplify vulgate dadaism.
- Instead of offering sincerity, they write from insincerity and lack of emotional commitment. Oscar Hammerstein said the most important

quality of lyrics is sincerity. Today's lyrics are largely pose, clichéd language, and retread emotions. Rice's lyrics apostrophize vague, meaningless entities and feign a pseudouniversal dimension. Because the zeitgeist doesn't believe in the musical play medium anymore, its writers can't invest belief in the words. Only Sondheim's lyrics, sincere in their very sardonicism, have not lost power.

The watershed (or Waterloo) for lyrics was *Cats* (1982), a musical set to the words of one of the twentieth century's greatest poets, T. S. Eliot. It marked the definitive separation in the modern musical theater of word from meaning: with *Cats*, the words might as well be scat syllables. The spectacle was more important than the sense, and a phenomenon was born: the "scattification" of lyrics. With *Cats*, theater lyrics turned full circle back to pre-1900 days. Harry B. Smith, Stanislaus Stange, and Sir Tim have become the functional equals of T. S. Eliot. Explaining the Rice-Webber writing style, Alan Jay Lerner wrote, "As a clue to Webber's fundamental concept, he said to me one day that what interested him when he wrote was less the plot and more a visually exciting effect."[48]

The Auteurs Are the Writers, Not the Directors

> Is the director of a musical show an *auteur*, as he (or occasionally she) is widely assumed to be in motion pictures? Is such a person the visionary who contributes most to a Broadway show's overall artistic and commercial success? That question, which in one guise or another keeps coming up, is as debatable for musicals as it is for films. . . . But the question bears repeating: how can one person's ideas control an essentially collaborative form?
> —Bernard Rosenberg and Ernest Harburg[49]

Sometimes one person creates so much of the finished piece that the result can be said to be controlled by a single intelligence: Cohan. Noël Coward. Gian Carlo Menotti. Perhaps Meredith Willson in *The Music Man* or Leonard Bernstein when he wrote and composed *Trouble in Tahiti*. In opera, Wagner, of course. But the more frequent question in a collaborative musical is, whose point of view gets delivered, and how?

The idea that high art can be found in mass-produced entertainment forms may have started with the American critic Gilbert Seldes in the 1920s, but it took a great leap forward with the auteur theory devised by French film critics writing for the magazine *Cahiers du cinéma* in the 1950s. Although the idea that certain film directors brought a personal style to their work predates the 1950s—the "Lubitsch touch" was proverbial during Ernst Lubitsch's film-directing career in the 1930s—the French auteur theory suggested that even a director's studio hack work could secretly disclose a creative intelligence like that of a great literary writer or painter. The *Cahiers du cinéma* critics applied their idea not to art films, but to commercial movies manufactured by the Hollywood studios in the 1930s and 1940s, claiming that it was the directors—not the screenwriters or producers—that endowed lowbrow movies with a personal voice and raised them to the level of art. Sometimes auteurist critics would ascribe recurrent themes and creative characteristics to the most unlikely of directors, but even at its most absurd the theory held a kernel of truth.

The auteur theory can be adapted to the Broadway musical to explain how musicals can generate statements about the human condition even as they operate superficially as mere entertainments. However, if an auteur is defined as a subliminal authorial voice that emerges from a collaborative mass medium to elevate the medium to art, then the real auteurs of the Broadway musical are Herbert, Cohan, Kern, Berlin, the Gershwins, Rodgers, Hart, Hammerstein, et al.—writers and composers, not directors, choreographers, designers, producers, star performers, or other role players in the collaborative process. What made the golden-era Broadway musical play different as a theatrical form from the light musical theater of other countries was a strongly individualized writing absent from the popular musical theater of other nations (W. S. Gilbert excepted).

In the adolescent years (ca. 1890–1925) of the Broadway musical, the marquee draws were the star performers and the star producers. The public came to see singers like Lillian Russell, Nora Bayes, Elsie Janis, Blanche Ring, Blossom Seeley, Chauncey Olcott, Al Jolson, and Fanny Brice, or comedians like Montgomery and Stone, Weber and Fields, Clark and McCullough, and Bert Williams. These great performers provided entertainment, not an authorial view of the world. Nor were the producers—Ziegfeld, Arthur Hammerstein, the Shuberts, Charles Dillingham, Charles Frohman, Klaw and Erlanger—auteurs. Rather, they simply provided compelling packaging: glitzy production values. What eventually came along circa 1925 to raise an entertainment medium to a dramatic medium was a paradigm shift: the writers gradually became the gate draw. It was at that juncture that art merged with entertainment.

The great writers of the Broadway canon were indeed artists with a consistent point of view sustained through a body of work. Such Broadway auteurs started back in the nineteenth century with Ned Harrigan, whose worldview was that ethnic stereotypes are funny, that the burlesquing of them tends to bring people to their common humanity, that the local color of city life binds audiences together. George M. Cohan's worldview was a red, white, and blue merger of Rudyard Kipling with Horatio Alger. Cole Porter apotheosized the swank and soigné that could be admired by average Joes. Lorenz Hart was the verbal virtuoso of unrequited love. Oscar Hammerstein stood for the necessity of dream and the reality of sentiment in a violated, postlapsarian world. Yip Harburg represented the poetic cynic unable to rebuff what Hammerstein stood for. Irving Berlin was Everyman for the average American. Alan Jay Lerner's point of view was that Everyman can be found, too, in the aristocracy. Stephen Sondheim is the cosmic bard of approach/avoidance. Comden and Green are the poets laureate of New York. For Kander and Ebb, life is a cabaret. These writers have a consistent stamp, a signature, a sensibility. Can one speak of an auteurial sensibility in the work of Maury Yeston?

Hammerstein wrote "Make Believe" for *Show Boat* and then rewrote it as "If I Loved You" for *Carousel;* the very self-plagiarism bespeaks an obsession with both songs' theme. Harburg wrote "Over the Rainbow" for the movie *The Wizard of Oz* and then rewrote it as "Look to the Rainbow" for *Finian's Rainbow* for the same reason; he was reworking the same creative issue the way great painters repaint the same scene. Harburg put the word "rainbow" in *The Wizard of Oz:* the original L. Frank Baum book nowhere contains it. (For a tough guy who didn't believe in a "Barnum and Bailey world," Harburg was big on rainbows.) Hammerstein transformed Molnár's play *Liliom* by transporting the heaven scene into the starkeeper scene in *Carousel,* an inspired bit of concept tweaking only he could have dreamed up. There's a dark undercurrent in *Oklahoma!, Carousel, South Pacific,* and *The King and I* that gives them a depth and darkness that balance their heliotropic tendencies. It's the same vague hint of unspoken terrors of the unconscious found in Grimm's fairy tales or in Alfred Hitchcock's suspense films. These traits are in the shows because they were in Hammerstein's personality, and he put his personality into his adaptations.

Auteurial point of view is precisely what's missing from most Broadway musical theater of the last thirty years. Where once we had great proprietary lines of auteurship—Rodgers and Hammerstein, Porter, the Gershwins—we now have generic Broadway "products": the boilerplate Disney style; the boilerplate Europoperetta style; the boilerplate rock style. There may be felicities, but are there philosophies in the lyrics of David Black, David Zippel, Lynn

Ahrens, or Richard Maltby Jr.? The nearest thing recently to lyricists with discernible philosophies and signatures were the rock and folk bards of the 1970s and 1980s: James Taylor, Patti Smith, Bruce Springsteen. The commercial musicals of the post-1965 era, with a few exceptions (*A Chorus Line,* the Sondheim shows), are corporatized collaborations that admit of no individualistic voice. *Finian's Rainbow* was collaborative but reflected Harburg's sensibility. *West Side Story* was collaborative but reflected Jerome Robbins's sensibility. Even the MGM movie musicals reflected the sensibility of the producer Arthur Freed, who also wrote lyrics. But *Ragtime* reflects market research more than the sensibilities of its adaptor Terrence McNally or the author of the original novel, E. L. Doctorow. Describing *Ragtime*'s producer, Garth Drabinsky, Michiko Kakutani wrote in the *New York Times:*

> A 20-year veteran of the movie business, Drabinsky is methodically transferring Hollywood practices to the stage. He insists that a show's prospective book writer submit an initial treatment to insure that the writer is not "going off on a tangent and doing something that is incongruous to the philosophy or ideas of the producer." For *Ragtime* he hired a polling firm to help calibrate audience reactions. The show's book eventually went through some 20 drafts.[50]

There are no hidden signatures in today's studio-system Broadway. Because book writers are now usually called upon to serve a visual rather than a verbal or dramatic concept, the process requires them to be faceless, just as they were prior to 1927.

Also responsible for the vanishing strong book in today's musical is the disrespectful view of art and literature that underlies much contemporary popular culture. In the 1920s, 1930s, and 1940s an appreciation of both popular culture and high culture could exist in the unlikeliest places. The great film producers Harry Cohn and Louis B. Mayer, crude as they were, understood high culture better than the media moguls of today. Yip Harburg said his idol was George Bernard Shaw; in the 1920s Harburg frequently attended "all the exceptional imports—Ibsen, Shaw, Chekhov, Molnár. Plus Americans like O'Neill. I depended on the theatre for my spiritual life. I attended every show I could get into."[51] Lorenz Hart said his life's ambition was to write lyrics that would transcend what he termed "the brutally cretin aspects of our culture."[52] Lawrence Langner, cohead of the Theatre Guild in the 1940s, remarked that Oscar Hammerstein "had read extensively. . . . his knowledge of philosophy, economics, and world affairs was greater than that of almost any other man that he had met in the theatre."[53] Elsewhere in this book I have noted Hammerstein's frequent veiled borrowings from Shakespeare. Gary Giddins has pointed out that Hammerstein's lyric "tired of livin' and scared of dyin'" from "Ol' Man River" is a paraphrase of a sentence from *The Confessions of St. Augustine:* "I was at the same time thoroughly tired of living and extremely frightened of dying." On the other hand, in a 1999 *New York Times* article Michael John LaChiusa, the composer-lyricist of *Marie Christine,* an adaptation of the Medea legend presented as a high-concept musical at Lincoln Center Theater that year, stated that television sitcoms are "one of our great artistic contributions to the world."[54]

The Martyrdom of Saint Stephen

Amid the depredations of the visigoths on Broadway has stood one great continuator of the past glories of well-written musical theater. Stephen Sondheim (b. 1930) appears to be the last of a genealogic line, the last inheritor of the golden-age tradition. There is no arguing that his shows and lyrics as a body of work embody extraordinary high-end writing for the musical; there is no question that he is in a class by himself as a lyricist and that his is as auteurial a sensibility as has ever managed to survive in the commercial shark waters of the Great White Way. Although he does not write his librettos, the gravitational pull of his style and lyrics is so strong that they seem to guide the action of his shows, and even to direct the director. No higher compliment could be paid to the originality of a writer for the theater. Perhaps the only unobserved fact about the thoroughly studied Sondheim career is that his musicals are the only ones of recent decades to feature consistently strong books. This is not a coincidence, but rather an object lesson in the rightness of Lehman Engel's aesthetics.

Sondheim is celebrated not just for what he has done but for what he represents, and therein lies some mischief. He is probably the last writer for Broadway who will ever become a celebrity strictly by writing for Broadway, and that very fact stings and embarrasses the mainstream theatrical establishment. His work is perceived rightly as an elegy for the great musical theater of the past, and he himself has become a one-man metaphor for the glories of that lost past, ironically self-incarnating his own show *Follies.* Intellectuals (and, alas, pseudointellectuals) obsess and fuss over Sondheim to a degree undreamt of by songwriters of the Irving Berlin era. (Has any living playwright, never mind composer or lyricist, ever had a quarterly journal solely devoted to him equivalent to *The Sondheim Review*?) He is the object of serial hagiography by such arbiters of taste as the "Arts and Leisure" section of the *New York Times.* He has become an institution, a brand name, a talisman that enables Broadway to say, we can tolerate the dumbing down of the musical theater as long as we continue bearing offerings to the cult of Sondheim. The result has been a fulsome beatification of an artist within his working lifetime, and a curious unwillingness to entertain further development of the artistic possibilities of the musical, as if American musical theater history ends with Sondheim, or as if Sondheim worship somehow purges Broadway of its larger creative failure.

Sondheim has written marvelous songs, but his mystique is such that he is usually regarded as a composer rather than a mere songwriter. Yet he does not and never has orchestrated his music, and thus does not entirely "compose" his scores; arrangers such as Jonathan Tunick and Michael Starobin add essential colors no less than Robert Russell Bennett did for Kern, Berlin, and Rodgers. In *A Little Night Music* (1973), Sondheim achieved a parity between extraordinarily dense lyrics and equally dense polyphony and polyrhythm in ensembles. *Night Music*'s melodies soar and yet slither in symbiosis with its verbal ingenuity, and the harmony is striking. He has never since quite equaled *A Little Night Music*'s achievement of balancing a melodious if baroque musical design with dense lyric writing; *Passion* (1994), an estimable piece, is built on recitative and arioso and lacks the striking melodic part writing of *Night Music.* The music of *Sweeney Todd* (1979), which has been accepted into the repertory of opera houses, has little of the harmonic pungency, urgency, and originality of the other "Broadway operas"—*Porgy and Bess, Street Scene, Candide,* and *Regina*—with which it clearly seeks comparison.

Sondheim should be praised and thanked for eschewing rock groove–driven writing, but he has overused another kind of groove and suffered an attenuation of melody as a result. From *Pacific Overtures* (1976) onward, Sondheim has frequently written extended musical vamps and ostinatos not just as incidental accompaniments (a vamp is usually used only to lead into a song), but as the essential tissue of his musical material. Lehman Engel once defined recitative style as "many words on a single note";[55] Sondheim, a good tune writer, has increasingly created his scores as recitatives built on rifflike repetitions of vamps. The words are as clever as ever, but the ear begins to hear an undifferentiated singsong instead of melodies. At times Sondheim appears to have grown indifferent or even lazy toward compositional device; he will settle for hyperextended grooves under his words instead of "dance partnering" his words with an independently conceived melodic line. Sondheim's lyrics also have grown increasingly fragmented and pointillistic in form; free verse rather than closed forms and short poetic feet are his latter-day signatures.

Unfortunately, Sondheim hagiolatry being so pervasive and enthusiasts so eager to emulate him, many young composers have mimicked both Sondheim's vamp-your-way-through music and his fragmented lines. These "Sondheimistas" imitate his manner without being able to duplicate his substance. The results can be poorly constructed melodies (or no melodies) or a lack of logically sequenced musical material. The Sondheimistas tend to use vamps to support overly fragmented lyrics, as if they were layering recording tracks and the lyrics were one track layered on a music track. Spasmodic gasps of words are favored over clauses or even intact phrases. The faux-Sondheim effect is observable in writers as diverse as Jonathan Larson, Michael John LaChiusa, Bill Russell (lyricist of *Side Show*), and even the English adapters of *Miss Saigon*. It's as if the entire musical theater community is paying court to Sondheim. Imitation is the sincerest form of flattery, but it is also a sign of creative desiccation that would-be musical theater creators can find only one model to imitate.

Sondheim remains indispensable, but the cult threatens to overwhelm the reality. This living icon, who is considered an apostle of the cryptogram and whose mystique as a wordsmith is nonpareil, told Frank Rich in 2000 that he has hardly ever read a complete book since college.[56]

Scene Three. *The Music*

Highbrow Composers on Broadway: Also Pushing the Envelope

After about 1925, legitimate composers abandoned Broadway; some went to Hollywood to write movie music. When Richard Rodgers started work on *The King and I,* the film composer Bernard Herrmann, who had composed the score for the 1946 movie *Anna and the King of Siam,* in a friendly gesture volunteered to Rodgers his film preproduction research on authentic Siamese music. Rodgers brushed off Herrmann's materials. Herrmann later had nothing but contempt for Rodgers.[57] In later years some legitimate composers who tried Broadway got confused about how to write "down" for it. When he was writing for the 1950 musical *Arms and the Girl,* Morton Gould recalled of his lyricist, Dorothy Fields, "I would start to write a tune, and she would say, 'no no no, that's not commercial, keep it simple.'. . . I should have given it a little more imagination."[58]

But other composers such as Kurt Weill and Leonard Bernstein have successfully bridged the gap, and legitimate composers and "art musicals" played as much a role in setting the stage for what mainstream musicals later achieved as did the maverick book writers and lyricists. As early as 1922, thirteen years before the completion of *Porgy and Bess,* George Gershwin was already writing opera;

his twenty-minute jazz opera, *Blue Monday* (orchestrated by the black composer Will Vodery), opened the second act of *George White's Scandals of 1922.*

Victor Herbert had been the first composer to establish practices and precedents in writing musicals that would benefit all suceeding composers, from lowbrow Berlin to highbrow Bernstein. For his first light opera commission, *Prince Ananias* (1894), Herbert insisted on a contractual clause stipulating that no changes be made in his music (or in the libretto, for that matter) without his consent. This marked the beginning of the end for song interpolation and songwriter anonymity. Herbert thereby brought to the American musical the modus operandi of writing opera: one composer, one score. Perhaps most important, he was the guiding force in founding the American Society of Composers, Authors, and Publishers (ASCAP) in 1914, thus elevating the songwriter to the status of legally protected author and intellectual property holder and making both a song's composer and lyricist creatively the equal of a dramatic playwright. Producers continued mixing songwriters in revues, but the practice of song interpolation in book shows gradually came to a halt.

ASCAP's elevation of the songwriter to dramatist also had the effect of galvanizing songwriters to sustain a mood or style to match the libretto. In this they were also indebted to Herbert, who altered his musical fancy and characterized his scores to suit each libretto's different exotic locale, whereas Reginald De Koven before him had applied a one-size-fits-all color scheme to his scores (even Arthur Sullivan can be accused of this). Nor did Jerome Kern vary his musical vocabulary to fit the scene of the libretto (certainly not before *Show Boat,* and only occasionally afterward). But for *Mlle. Modiste,* a Parisian Cinderella-like romance, Herbert composed "Kiss Me Again," a chromatic mittel-European waltz. For the children's fantasy *Babes in Toyland,* he composed a rickety tin soldier march in a minor key (with a major-key trio), "March of the Toys." For the colonial New Orleans setting and Neapolitan characters of *Naughty Marietta,* his musicalization changed according to the character or setting but maintained an exoticism. Not only did Sigmund Romberg and Rudolf Friml follow suit, but decades later, Frederick Loewe wrote "Scottish" music for *Brigadoon* (1947), Burton Lane wrote "Irish" music for *Finian's Rainbow* (1947), Richard Rodgers wrote "Siamese" music for *The King and I* (1951), and Frank Loesser wrote "Italian" music for *The Most Happy Fella* (1956)—all unconsciously emulating Victor Herbert (who, of course, in this practice was himself emulating Bizet and other opera composers).

Marc Blitzstein: Unheralded Innovator

Lehman Engel, who met him in the 1930s, wrote that even then he was "bent on self-destruction or failure."[59] Trude Rittmann, who worked with him on *Juno* (1959) and had known him since 1934, said he made no attempt to hide his contempt for Broadway. Late in life he became well known for the long-running off-Broadway English adaptation of Weill and Brecht's *The Threepenny Opera.* Yet Marc Blitzstein (1905–64), a thoroughly schooled modernistic classical composer who was a political radical, left a definite mark on Broadway, mentoring Bernstein, influencing Loesser, and anticipating Sondheim and even some of Rodgers and Hammerstein and Lerner and Loewe.

Blitzstein began writing theater material for Broadway even as he was making his way in avant-garde classical circles. His fifteen-minute dadaistic musical farce *Triple Sec* was interpolated into the third and last edition (1930) of the Theatre Guild revue *Garrick Gaieties,* cheek by jowl with the songs of Rodgers and Hart. In 1935 musical sketches he wrote and composed were again interpolated on Broadway, this time into the politically daring satirical revue *Parade* (known on the street as the "Red Revue"), also produced by the Theatre Guild. That year he composed the words and music to a ballad about a prostitute, "Nickel under the Foot." He played it at a party in New York for Bertolt Brecht, who at once suggested, "Why don't you write a piece about all kinds of prostitution—the press, the church, the courts, the arts, the whole system?" The next year, after the sudden death of his wife, Blitzstein found creative renewal and release from grief in the white-heat composition over five weeks of the book, music, and lyrics of a full-length "play in music" based on Brecht's suggestion, *The Cradle Will Rock.*

Taking place in the imaginary "Steeltown, USA" and ingeniously using archetypes for characters as in morality plays, *The Cradle Will Rock* parodies not only capitalist robber barons but also art patrons, newspaper editors, and even artists themselves (the violinist "Yasher" and the painter "Dauber"). When its production by the WPA Theatre Project (directed by Orson Welles) was canceled at the Maxine Elliot Theatre for political reasons on June 16, 1937, the entire cast marched twenty blocks uptown to the Venice Theatre, sat down inside, and performed the show seated from the audience, with Blitzstein singing and accompanying at the piano. (The event is dramatized in the 1999 film *Cradle Will Rock.*) The next year there was a short Broadway run.

Somewhat neglected in the brouhaha over radical politics were *Cradle's* many musical theater innovations. Blitzstein took the talking/nonsinging style of song-and-dance man George M. Cohan and served it up as a singing style equal to high dramatic demands, years before it was adopted for conventional Broadway musicals (Yul Brynner in *The King and I*, Rex Harrison *in My Fair Lady*, Robert Preston in *The Music Man*). He also pioneered the through-underscoring of stage dialogue, not just as song lead-ins or scene change accompaniment but in the way film soundtracks underscore film dialogue. Even *Show Boat* had not had such underscoring. Aaron Copland wrote that "the musical sections, instead of being formally set with definite beginnings and endings, seem to start and finish casually, so that one is rarely conscious of where the music begins and the dialogue leaves off, or vice versa. . . . One of the most striking characteristics of *The Cradle* is the extent to which every moment in the piece seems controlled. Nothing is left to chance."[60]

Blitzstein said that he regarded his companion piece to *Cradle*, *No for an Answer* (1940), as "an extended study of all forms of musical theatre from earliest to most recent times." The score alternates between musical comedy and choral passages. "Francie," a two-part counterpoint, anticipates Emile de Becque and Nellie Forbush's parallel monologue song, "Wonder How It Feels," in Rodgers and Hammerstein's *South Pacific*. "Penny Candy," a narrative song about a panhandler outfoxing a rich lady, is a veritable five-minute singspiel and anticipates Billy Bigelow's "Soliloquy" from *Carousel*. Blitzstein's musical portrait of a singing Dead End Kid predates Sondheim's "Gee, Officer Krupke" for *West Side Story* by more than fifteen years. The British musicologist Wilfrid Mellers wrote of *No*, "the song-tune tends to merge into a wonderfully sensitive treatment of speech inflection—a kind of 'American recitative' in which Blitzstein reveals the roots of some features of jazz in American dialect. . . . this vocal line provides a link between musically accompanied speech and song: the transitions are so subtle that 'real life' dialogue dissolves into music."[61]

The young Leonard Bernstein, thirteen years Blitzstein's junior, conducted an undergraduate Harvard performance of *The Cradle Will Rock* in 1939 and became Blitzstein's lifelong friend. The through-composed underscoring of Bernstein's *On the Town, Candide*, and *West Side Story* comes directly from Blitzstein. So do some melodies: the tune of "Maria" in *West Side Story* is all but lifted whole from an underscoring melody early in the first act of Blitzstein's opera *Regina* (1949). *Regina* was Blitzstein's surprisingly Chekhovian adaptation of the Lillian Hellman play *The Little Foxes*; it ran on Broadway for fifty-six performances and later became an opera house staple. The score has soaring melodies and catchy ditties, nineteenth-century polkas and old black spirituals, arias and ragtime. Frank Loesser, then working on *Guys and Dolls*

(1950), came to see *Regina* repeatedly; when Blitzstein caught him in the audience for the fourth time and asked him why, the songwriter replied, "I'm
studying."[62] Loesser's pseudo-operatic musical *The Most Happy Fella* (1956)
was undoubtedly influenced by his study. Loesser later wrote of *Regina*, "Beyond delivering neat musical capsules that conveniently paraphrase steps in
the narrative, Blitzstein gives a special magic illumination to the whole thing,
making the already enormous emotion of the story even more wonderfully
memorable than before."[63]

Vladimir Dukelsky, a.k.a. Vernon Duke: The Jekyll and Hyde of Broadway

The composer Vladimir Alexandrovich Dukelsky (1903–69) led a double life: as
Vernon Duke he wrote "April in Paris" and about a dozen Broadway musicals. As
Dukelsky he prolifically composed symphonies, sonatas, and chamber music,
and, like Stravinsky, wrote ballets on commission for Diaghilev. Once he hosted
"a party given by Mr. Vernon Duke to meet Mr. Vladimir Dukelsky. My pride
was hurt when most of my guests wanted to know who in hell Dukelsky was;
two or three of the Dukelskyites present professed complete ignorance of Duke's
identity, but they were in a distinct minority and, after listening to some bla-
tant boogiewoogie, caught on fast and left in a hurry."[64] Oscar Levant quipped,
"For a man who's destined for obscurity, why do you need two names?"[65]

Duke seems to be the only Broadway composer to have also composed musicals for both the London and the Paris stages. In addition to being a composer, he was regarded as a significant poet in his original language, Russian.
Possessing ample abilities as a versifier in several languages (he made several
translations of difficult modern American poetry into Russian), he wrote English lyrics well enough to have been his own lyricist—which he was on a few
occasions (such as the song "Autumn in New York"), although he mostly
worked with the leading lyricists of his time: Yip Harburg, John Latouche, Ogden Nash, Ira Gershwin, and Howard Dietz.

Born into Russian nobility, Dukelsky was a musical prodigy. His family fled
the country during the Bolshevik Revolution of 1917, taking refuge in Con-
stantinople, Turkey, where the young composer played his first American pop
tunes as a café pianist. In the early 1920s he composed a piano concerto for his
friend Artur Rubinstein. In 1921 he sailed to New York, where he soon met the
young George Gershwin, who was so impressed with his modernistic music
that he hired Dukelsky as a kind of ghostwriter. Dukelsky made piano arrangements of some of Gershwin's songs, composed some incidental dance music
for Gershwin shows, and arranged the piano solo version of *Rhapsody in Blue*.

Gershwin also persuaded Dukelsky to anglicize his name to Vernon Duke, and for most of the rest of his life, Dukelsky pursued a career as a symphonic composer as Dukelsky and a career as a popular composer as Vernon Duke (he finally settled on "Vernon Duke" for both roles in 1955).

Prokofiev and Dukelsky were also good friends, and the extensive correspondence between the two has recently been published. They had similar idioms as composers, but, according to Nicolas Slonimsky, Prokofiev "was disgusted with Dukelsky's plunge into the lucrative field of popular music. 'You have become a prostitute,' he wrote to him. 'When you are paid enough money you spread your legs and invite a client to enter.'"[66] (In lighter moments Prokofiev would write Duke and inquire of his Broadway music, "How's 'tra-la-la'?")[67]

For 1930s revues Duke wrote such standards as "April in Paris," "Autumn in New York," and "I Can't Get Started," but his greatest success came with the Broadway musical *Cabin in the Sky* (1940), choreographed by George Balanchine and performed by an all-black cast. The script, by the Hollywood scenarist Lynn Root, was the kind of whimsical, primitive fantasy about black people that had been made popular by Marc Connelly's 1930 play *The Green Pastures,* but it differed from Connelly in its complexity and piquant hints of the Faust legend and *Paradise Lost.* But after *Cabin,* Duke entered a protracted phase of flops and near misses. The theater caricaturist Al Hirschfeld (1903–2003) recalled working with Duke on the 1946 musical *The Sweet Bye and Bye,* which had a book by S. J. Perelman and Hirschfeld, lyrics by Ogden Nash, and music by Duke, and which closed out of town:

> The book—I just reread it recently—is still a very funny book. It was about the future. . . . Boris Aronson did marvelous sets, based on kind of Braque or Matisse arbitrary shapes like a jigsaw puzzle. The opening curtain, and the thing spreads apart, up and down, and you're taken into the future. Aronson had a marvelous conception. I don't think Vernon really understood what we were up to. I remember one evening—he had had dinner with some people the night before—he said he had told them about the script. And he said to them, "And they say it's a satire of advertising and of the future. Have you ever heard of anything so stupid?" Sid and I looked at each other and realized, we're in trouble! Because he didn't really get what we were trying to do. He didn't have a satirical point of view on it.[68]

Royalties from his handful of immortal songs kept him going, yet Duke's second and more sourball volume of memoirs, *Listen Here!* (1963), suggests that he was irked in his riper years by the fact that he was more famous for light music than for serious composition, notwithstanding that most of his theater ventures had been failures. He was jealous of his friend Prokofiev's success, and he wrote a notorious article sarcastically blasting Stravinsky and his ascension to the role of "greatest living composer."

While his shows have retreated into history, Duke's best songs are so good that he will never die. His rhapsodic ballads come closer to art song than the songs of any other Broadway composer. But where Herbert, Gershwin, Weill, Bernstein, and other highbrows succeeded with musicals, Duke failed on Broadway for two reasons. First, he had the misfortune or misjudgment to work on several projects with poor books. But more important, unlike Herbert, Gershwin, Weill, Bernstein, and the others, he did not write "to the book." For all his literary and musical gifts, he somehow misunderstood the composer's function in the Broadway musical to write to character and situation. The Hirschfeld anecdote about Duke's misunderstanding the book of *The Sweet Bye and Bye* is emblematic. Duke did not take a cue from Lehman Engel or Oscar Hammerstein (or Weill, Blitzstein, or Bernstein) and compose dramaturgically. Had he done so, we might have had another *Porgy and Bess.*

John Latouche and Jerome Moross: The Forgotten "A Team" of the Art Musical

Duke's most frequent lyricist was a boyish southerner whose face Duke described as that of a "precocious infant." Short and pudgy, John Treville Latouche (1914–56) was likened in appearance by others to a pint-sized bullfrog. He was a meteor who in his brief life and seventeen-year career was Broadway's nearest thing to a "preface to Sondheim," as the composer Ned Rorem has said of him. He wrote lyrics and librettos for musicals composed not only by Vernon Duke but also by Duke Ellington and Bernstein. He also wrote the libretto to the 1956 Douglas Stuart Moore opera, *The Ballad of Baby Doe,* and was adapting it into a Broadway musical for producer Michael Myerberg when he suddenly died on August 7, 1956.

Like Duke, Latouche led a creative double life. Upon his death the *New York Times* reported that Latouche "was regarded by his associates as a poet rather than a lyricist because of his sensitive and evocative style of writing." His librettos are indeed imaginative and literate, but in spite of his poetic mystique a surprising number of his lyrics for musicals now seem pedestrian. His lyrics for risqué supper-club entertainers, however, brought back to life in the 2000 off-Broadway revue *Taking a Chance on Love,* are wickedly clever, daring, and verbally virtuosic, a match for the best of Hart, Porter, and Sondheim. It appears he couldn't always express his full gifts in the commercial theater of his time, yet he was esteemed nonetheless as a highbrow working in a middlebrow medium.

Latouche's first real fame came when he adapted a long poem he had written, "Ballad for Uncle Sam," for the WPA revue *Sing for Your Supper,* which opened on Broadway in the spring of 1939. When Paul Robeson sang the piece under the title "Ballad for Americans" over national CBS radio in November 1939, the radio studio was so flooded with calls that regular programming couldn't be resumed for twenty minutes. Robeson repeated the song on the radio many times and recorded it with the Philadelphia Orchestra, and opera artists and amateur groups alike performed it around the country. Soon after, Latouche wrote the lyrics for Duke's *Cabin in the Sky.*

Six years later, he became the first white lyricist-librettist to write a Broadway musical with a black composer, Duke Ellington: *Beggar's Holiday.* Latouche created a modern adaptation of the eighteenth-century British ballad opera *The Beggar's Opera*—the same work Brecht and Weill had adapted as *Die Dreigroschenoper*—in which Macheath became a contemporary gangster, played by Alfred Drake. *Beggar's Holiday* (1946) featured the first fully integrated casting in Broadway musical history, going one up on *Show Boat's* miscegenation scene by romantically pairing the white Drake with the black Muriel Smith. Other performers in the cast included Libby Holman (fired before the opening), Zero Mostel, Herbert Ross, and Marge Champion. The show went through three directors (John Houseman, Nicholas Ray, and George Abbott) and was accorded a mixed reception: the critic and musical comedy historian Cecil Smith wrote, "Everyone wanted *Beggar's Holiday* to succeed, but it could not, because it was too chaotic." The young Stephen Sondheim liked it, but Alan Jay Lerner wrote in the 1980s that "despite brilliant moments, [it] was far from perfect." Ellington believed that it failed simply because of the racial intermixing onstage; only two months before *Beggar's Holiday,* a revival of *The Duchess of Malfi* had opened with the black actor Canada Lee playing in whiteface makeup opposite Elisabeth Bergner.

Though Latouche also wrote lyrics for Bernstein's *Candide,* his most original work and his most influential collaboration was with Jerome Moross (1913–83). Moross is the great forgotten composer of Broadway—a thoroughly melodious composer, more American than Weill, less acrid than Blitzstein, more folklorish than Bernstein, and yet like Bernstein a composer at his best writing strong dance music. He is the least credited source from whom Andrew Lloyd Webber steals tunes: "All I Ask of You" from *Phantom of the Opera* is arguably a direct steal from Moross's great 1958 film score, *The Big Country.*

Born in Brooklyn, New York, Moross was a prodigy: he began piano at five and composing at eight and skipped four grades, graduating from New York University at eighteen. He spent a year or so at Juilliard and then became a free-lance composer and pianist, writing orchestral works, working with various ballet groups, and writing music for CBS radio. He was the pit pianist for the 1936 tour of Gershwin's *Porgy and Bess* and again for its West Coast revival in 1938. His music first appeared on Broadway in 1935 in *Parade*, the leftist revue to which Marc Blitzstein also contributed.

From the beginning, the folklorish musical idioms of Americana fired Moross's imagination. Critics have called his style "cowboy jazz." He wrote the ballet *Paul Bunyan* in 1934, and in 1938 his *Frankie and Johnny*, a ballet based on that familiar American folk tune, was produced by the Chicago Federal Theatre. To make a stable living, however, Moross went to Hollywood in 1940 to work as an orchestrator and, eventually, a film composer. Meanwhile, he kept up his concert composing on the side; Sir Thomas Beecham premiered his first symphony in Seattle in 1943. Later he also composed for television, notably the theme from *Wagon Train*.

Latouche and Moross met in 1938 and began an on-again-off-again ten-year collaboration, inventing a unique genre of "dance opera" that was not destined for commercial success in its time but prophetically heralded the sea change in musicals around 1980. A backer's audition of the first dance opera they completed, *Susannah and the Elders* (a Southern Gothic adaptation of the biblical tale), so impressed the Broadway producer Michael Todd that he commissioned three others. *Willie the Weeper* was the elaborate jazz-driven marijuana dream of a chimney sweep, including a "Cocaine Lil" episode; *The Eccentricities of Davy Crockett* was "a musical portrait of the popular American hero who fishes a mercurial mermaid out of the Tennessee River, catches Halley's Comet by the tail, goes to Congress, and returns to Texas to suffer martyrdom in the Alamo massacre."[69] *Riding Hood Revisited* was a parody of the fairy tale that included the Good Humor man as a dance character. All four works were written and composed to be performed without spoken dialogue—through-sung and also through-danced. Moross later said that their "idea was to so mix the singing and dancing that you didn't know where the singers began or where the dancers ended." (John Murray Anderson later claimed he had done the same thing earlier in *The Greenwich Village Follies* in the 1920s, but that music had been previously composed, not written specifically for the shows.)

All but *Riding Hood Revisited* were presented on May 9, 1948, at the ANTA Theatre as an evening of *Ballet Ballads;* musical accompaniment was limited to piano (Moross had orchestrated them all), but the lighting and staging were imaginative. Each piece featured singers and dancers and was choreographed by a different choreographer. The critical reception was favorable, and the show moved almost immediately to the Music Box Theatre but did not survive the summer box-office lull. Emboldened by their succès d'estime, Latouche and Moross set to work on a full-length ballet ballad, based on a Latouche conceit that retold Homer's *Iliad* (act 1) and *Odyssey* (act 2) as a fey, whimsical evocation of turn-of-the-century small-town America in the aftermath of the Spanish-American War. It took several years to find a producer, and even then the show was first mounted off-Broadway. When *The Golden Apple* finally opened in March 1954, it garnered enough critical acclaim to be moved uptown to Broadway's Alvin Theatre, where it folded over the summer.

Like *Ballet Ballads, The Golden Apple* was dialogue-less, through-sung, and substantially told by its choreography (the choreographer Hanya Holm, who had choreographed *Davy Crockett* in 1948, took over the direction). It had several wonderful tunes; one, "Lazy Afternoon," proved extractable enough to become a modest pop hit. *The Golden Apple* is a high-quality problem child. Despite its distinctive atmosphere and wonderful music, it never overcomes a certain preciousness. It is dramatically inert, lacking narrative urgency and characterizations the audience can empathize with. Ironically, in a shorter piece such as *Willie the Weeper,* Latouche's dramaturgical construction was much tighter and more persuasive. *Golden Apple* is charming but diffuse. Brooks Atkinson of the *Times* wrote, "*The Golden Apple* is more like a faculty joke than a sharp musical satire with an explicit theme," and in the *Herald Tribune,* Walter Kerr agreed.

The producers who brought the show uptown altered the ending. Off-Broadway the show had concluded with the reunion of Ulysses and Penelope, expressed in a "duet of middle-aged hope," "We've Just Begun." The producers installed a reprise of the big ballad tune, "Coming Home Together." According to the theater scholar Erik Haagensen, "Moross and Latouche so disliked the Broadway ending that they removed it from the licensed performance version of the show."

However problematic *Ballet Ballads* and *The Golden Apple* are as theater, Latouche and Moross laid out in embryo the future course of the megacommodified Broadway musical. In their refusal to follow the music-dialogue-lyrics pattern practiced by Rodgers and Hammerstein–style Broadway, and in their substituting a totally sung libretto animated by narrative dancing, every element of the commercial musical of later decades can be found: the through-sung cantatas of Lloyd Webber and others; the director-choreographer shows; the "dansicals" such as Bob Fosse's *Big Deal,* Susan Stroman's *Contact,* and Twyla Tharp's *Movin' Out.* However, there is an all-important difference: Latouche and Moross, both highly educated, cultivated sensibilities, created and controlled the concepts. They—not the director, the choreographer, or the producer—were the authors of their shows (even if the producers did change the ending of *The Golden Apple* for Broadway). Their innovation of through-sung, through-danced musicals has been vulgarized and miscarried by post-1980 Broadway.

In his last years Moross retired from Hollywood and returned to New York to concentrate on writing classical music; his later efforts at writing muscals never made it even to off-Broadway. His film scores brim over with melody, as if they were operettas in search of a libretto. A great deal of Hollywood movie music of the 1990s and 2000s is watered-down Moross. The irony is that as a film composer, he was commercial; as a theater composer, he was not. Moross's love affair with musical theater remained unrequited, although he told an interviewer in 1979, "I'm not going to complain about the royalties I've received for 'The Big Country Theme'" (which at that time was being used for a Taylor Wine television commercial).

Like Duke, Moross found working with Latouche exasperating at times. Latouche never had a big hit that kept him in money and comfort for a sustained period. He lived a bohemian, hand-to-mouth life, sometimes crashing on a friend's spare bed; he was sought after for high-toned parties as a manic conversationalist and wit. He was openly gay, although briefly married in the early 1940s to a lesbian and for a time in the 1950s the kept lover of a friend's mother. Fragile in health (he was hospitalized after a series of illnesses in his twenties), he was both a heavy drinker and a chronic abuser of uppers and downers. Then he was blacklisted and could not work in television. His pill popping, or perhaps a pill-booze mixture, is thought by some to have contributed to, if not induced, his death at forty-one, allegedly of a heart attack. His one-time collaborator Dawn Powell elegized him, and much else about commercial Broadway, in her diary:

> Talentless but shrewd users pursued him always—he was *driven:* harnesses and bridles and wagons were always being rushed up to him to use this endless gold. I have seen him so harried by the users he burst into tears. Contracts, advances, deals, love offers were all around—trying to get him in a corner room, lock him

up and get out the gold when he wanted only to talk all day and all night. He never could sleep—lights on all night—so there were sleeping pills and for the grim collaborators demanding the real work, he must have Benzedrine, Miltown tranquilizers, Nembutal, dex. I'm sure this was a desperate, hysterical escape from Lillian Hellman and others waiting for his output to finish up "Candide." Like George Gershwin—a natural gusher that grim syndicates tried to harness for the stock exchange. Ending up now an incorrigibly sweet, indestructible little ghost.[70]

Exeunt Maverick and Highbrow Composers and Writers

Before 1910, legitimate composers had written much of Broadway's music. After popular dance music redefined the musical comedy song, and the rhythm section was introduced to the theater orchestra in the 1920s, the legitimate composer was an endangered species on Broadway. It became increasingly difficult to produce operettas unless they incorporated hot dance episodes, as did Friml's *Rose Marie* (1924). So the composer either went to Hollywood (like Max Steiner), stayed on in Broadway as an orchestrator or arranger, or, after about 1930, went underground and became the avant-garde (Blitzstein, Moross, Weill).

In the period from about 1945 to 1955, as a result of the success of the integrated musical, there was a vogue on Broadway for a kind of opera that would play like a musical, stressing dramatic rather than vocal values. The most successful composer of these was Gian Carlo Menotti (b. 1911), whose works *The Telephone, The Medium, The Consul,* and *The Saint of Bleecker Street* all had short but successful runs as Broadway shows; all had intensely suspenseful librettos (written in English by Menotti). Weill's *Street Scene* (1947), Bernstein's *Trouble in Tahiti* (1952), and Blitzstein's *Regina* (1949) were all also built on solid librettos and have lasted; *Magdalena* (1948), which Robert Wright and George Forrest adapted to music by the great Brazilian composer Heitor Villa-Lobos, was not, and has not survived, despite some striking music.

During these postwar years the notion of an artistic Broadway musical, of the musical as a *Gesamtkunstwerk,* reached a zenith and exerted an attraction for serious composers it would never regain. Bernstein, who composed *On the Town* in 1944, wrote *Wonderful Town* (1953) in six weeks when the producers called upon him to replace Leroy Anderson's score. His *Candide* (1956) and *West Side Story* (1957), written almost simultaneously, have never been excelled as American theater music. Other legitimate composers tried the medium but were less successful than Bernstein: Morton Gould's *Billion Dollar Baby* (1945) and *Arms and the Girl* (1950) have faded, but they at least played Broadway. The most successful American classical composer of the 1940s, Aaron Copland, was offered a $2,000 advance to write a musical in 1946; that was about $18,500 in 2004 dollars and less than he could earn from Hollywood at the time, but he proceeded to do it. The show, *Tragic Ground,* was to have been adapted by Lynn Riggs, author of *Oklahoma!*'s source play, *Green Grow the Lilacs,* from a novel by Erskine Caldwell, author of Broadway's long-running *Tobacco Road;* Agnes de Mille signed for the choreography. The show was never finished or produced; Copland later used two of the unused songs in other works.

Even the symphonic composer William Schuman and the avant-garde serialist Milton Babbitt took stabs at writing for Broadway musicals during this enlightened period. During these same years, it was common for novelists such as William Faulkner, Irwin Shaw, and James Agee to write scripts for Hollywood films for purely mercenary reasons. They didn't mind if their scripts were altered beyond recognition, because the money bought them time for other projects. But while the highbrow writers and composers who toiled in Broadway musicals certainly hoped to make money, they also wanted the artistic cachet that they could not obtain from Hollywood screenwriting. The fact that they thought there were legitimate creative challenges in writing for the musical stage seems remarkable to us today in the theatrical Age of Disney.

After the enlightened Broadway of the Truman years passed, the few composers who had the chops to write more operatic musicals opted to write in the existing commercial idioms. It is not well known that Meredith Willson (born Robert Meredith Reiniger, 1902–84) composed two symphonies in the 1930s. He was a skilled composer, conducted symphony orchestras, and was a dance band arranger for radio in the 1940s (especially for the Burns and Allen Show). He was so gifted a flutist that at age seventeen he was engaged by John Philip Sousa for a nationwide tour with the Sousa Band, and at age twenty-three he joined the flute section of the New York Philharmonic, playing for Toscanini and other conductors. Later he composed film scores such as *The Little Foxes* (1941). Willson's *The Music Man* (1957), despite its cornpone setting, is, in its internal construction, one of Broadway's most sophisticated scores and also one of its most underrated books (written by Willson). But Willson stayed commercial for his next shows, as did another legitimately trained composer, Charles Strouse. Today, even in cases where it would make artistic sense to engage legitimate composers to provide through-composed scores, pop composers are inevitably used. While a superbly tuneful folkloristic composer like

Moross would have been eminently appropriate for a musical based on Huck Finn, the producers of *Big River* in 1985, looking for a rural Americana sound, commissioned Roger Miller, a country music entertainer who had never written a musical, to compose the score.

Legitimate composers from Herbert to Bernstein took the strophic song forms and the harmonic limitations of popular music and gave them a dramatic power derived from opera and symphony. They were able to do so because they were technically equipped to conceptualize beyond the level of "tune." Without Herbert, Gershwin, Weill, Blitzstein, Moross, and Bernstein composing Broadway musicals, and without legitimately trained composers like Robert Russell Bennett and Hans Spialek assisting Broadway's untutored songwriters, the art form would never have risen above its crude nineteenth-century antecedents in minstrel show, vaudeville, and burlesque. The sung-through, pseudo-operatic aspects of contemporary poperas like *Miss Saigon* have nothing to do with the genuine musical continuity of Gershwin's *Porgy and Bess,* or of Bernstein's *Candide,* or of Herbert, Blitzstein, Duke, or Moross. The music in these ambitious works supplies the emotional information missing from the text. Poperettas do not do this; they simply string together a daisy chain of all-sung segments and glue them together with an undeviating rock groove. That is not the same thing as psychologically developed through-composition.

Highbrow book writers of musicals like Truman Capote or John O'Hara or composers like Aaron Copland were rarely bankable, but in the old days some of their efforts were produced. In today's Broadway it would be impossible. When literary writers like Joyce Carol Oates write librettos today, they collaborate with opera composers, not with composers of musicals. There are no Weills or Blitzsteins today for such writers to work with in the Broadway theater. Bernstein said many times in later life that he had fully expected the Broadway community to pick up from *West Side Story* a new model for how to artistically develop the musical. He was abidingly perplexed when it never happened.[71] For the next forty years the Broadway musical mostly continued to seek its lowest common denominator of expression. Highbrows need not apply. Broadway's view of a maverick composer today is Elton John.

Conversely, if there were an equivalent to Kurt Weill on Broadway (or even off-Broadway) today, would he seek out Edward Albee or Athol Fugard to write the book to his music, or adapt a novel by John Updike or Don DeLillo without Drabinskyizing it? That is exactly the kind of thing Weill did on Broadway routinely during his lifetime. One can hope that playwright Tony Kushner's writing the book and lyrics for a *Caroline or Change* (2003) heralds a trend. But don't bet on it.

What has broken down is the element of personal expression that Broadway's brief but glorious era of enlightened collectivism permitted to surface, an element that enriched the artistic possibilities of what had been an inconsequential form of light entertainment.

When there are no mavericks allowed, there can be no new directions for the herd.

The Hippodrome's souvenir book every year gave top billing to the conceptual superdirector Arthur Voegtlin. The stage directors, choreographer, and composer were second bananas.
(Billy Rose Theatre Collection, New York Public Library for the Performing Arts, Astor, Lenox, and Tilden Foundations)

CARROLL FLEMING
General Stage Director
of the
New York Hippodrome

MANUEL KLEIN
Musical Director
of the
New York Hippodrome

ARTHUR VOEGTLIN

WM. J. WILSON
Stage Director
of the
New York Hippodrome

VINCENZO ROMEO
Ballet Master
of the
New York Hippodrome

The comedian-singer-hoofer Harry Fox, whose accidental invention, the foxtrot, helped spawn the modern show tune and Broadway's golden age.
(Photo by Apeda. Billy Rose Theatre Collection, New York Public Library for the Performing Arts, Astor, Lenox, and Tilden Foundations)

Above: ASCAP's lineup in 1920 included the leading musical comedy creators at the cusp of Broadway's second age: lyricist Gene Buck, composer Victor Herbert, composer John Philip Sousa, librettist/lyricist Harry B. Smith, composers Jerome Kern, Irving Berlin, George M. Meyer, Irving Bibo, and lyricist/librettist Otto Harbach. *(Photo by Al Aumuller. Library of Congress)*

Below: Ned Wayburn at his dance studio routining two Broadway hoofers in precision formation. Wayburn used mathematics to achieve geometrical patterns onstage; Busby Berkeley imitated him. *(Photo by White Studio. Billy Rose Theatre Collection, New York Public Library for the Performing Arts, Astor, Lenox, and Tilden Foundations)*

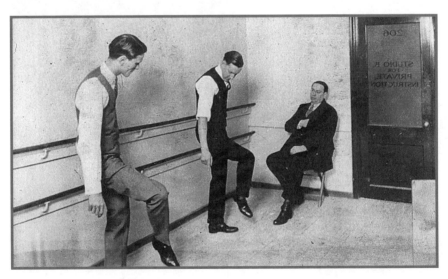

Ethel Merman as Reno Sweeney belts to the rafters during an actual performance of Cole Porter's *Anything Goes*, at the Alvin Theatre, 1934, when microphones were not yet used in the theater. *(Billy Rose Theatre Collection, New York
Public Library for the Performing Arts, Astor, Lenox, and Tilden Foundations)*

Above: Jerome Kern, Paul Robeson, and Oscar Hammerstein II. Robeson played Joe in the 1928 London production and 1932 Broadway revival of *Show Boat* and was forever identified with "Ol' Man River," although Jules Bledsoe created the role in 1927. *(Billy Rose Theatre Collection, New York Public Library for the Performing Arts, Astor, Lenox, and Tilden Foundations)*

Below: George Abbott, who lived to be 107, directing June Havoc, Gene Kelly, and Leila Ernst in Rodgers and Hart's *Pal Joey*, 1940. At 95, Abbott was still directing Broadway musicals. *(Theatre Collection, Museum of the City of New York)*

Above: John Raitt as the carousel barker Billy Bigelow in the greatest musical pantomime in the American theater—the waltz prologue to *Carousel* (1945). *(Theatre Collection of the City of New York)*

Left: Rouben Mamoulian directs Jan Clayton and John Raitt in *Carousel*, 1945. Rodgers and Hammerstein felt Mamoulian took too much credit in the press for their shows' success. *(Theatre Collection, Museum of the City of New York)*

Alfred Drake, the golden age's leading man par excellence, a consummate actor as well as baritone, in his dressing room backstage at *Kismet* (1953). *(Photo by Rothschild. Billy Rose Theatre Collection, New York Public Library for the Performing Arts, Astor, Lenox, and Tilden Foundations)*

Todd Duncan, who was the original Porgy in *Porgy and Bess* (1935), with the composer Kurt Weill at the piano rehearsing *Lost in the Stars* (1949). *(Photo by George Karger. Billy Rose Theatre Collection, New York Public Library for the Performing Arts, Astor, Lenox, and Tilden Foundations)*

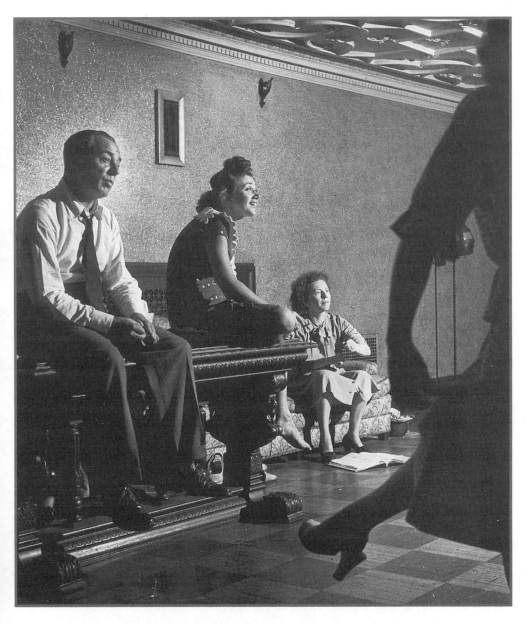

From right to left: Agnes de Mille, de Mille's assistant, Dania Krupska, and Richard Rodgers at a rehearsal for *Allegro* (1947), the first musical with a combined director/choreographer—de Mille. *(Billy Rose Theatre Collection, New York Public Library for the Performing Arts, Astor, Lenox, and Tilden Foundations)*

The director-choreographer Jerome Robbins, sadistic genius, and Mary Martin, incandescent star, between scenes in the 1955 television version of *Peter Pan* (1954). *(Photo by Sy Friedman, Library of Congress)*

Harold Lang as the title character in Robert Alton's dream ballet at the end of the first act of *Pal Joey* (1952 revival). "Joey Looks into the Future," arguably the first character-driven dream ballet, was the brainchild of the original 1940 production's set designer, Jo Mielziner. *(Theatre Collection, Museum of the City of New York)*

Richard Rodgers going over the score of *Victory at Sea* (1952) with the arranger/orchestrator Robert Russell Bennett. Though Rodgers furnished Bennett with less than thirty minutes of tunes for the eleven hours of music, Rodgers, not Bennett, was credited as the composer.
(Courtesy of the Rodgers and Hammerstein Organization)

Above: This photograph of *Beggar's Holiday* (1946) shows a simple painted backdrop still typical of Broadway musical scenic design in the 1940s and early 1950s. *(Theatre Collection, Museum of the City of New York)*

Below: The men's chorus during an actual performance of *Paint Your Wagon* (1951). Note the absence of foot mikes and the trombone slide projecting from the orchestra pit. Today the pits are either lower or covered, necessitating amplification of the orchestra through loudspeakers all over the theater. *(Theatre Collection, Museum of the City of New York)*

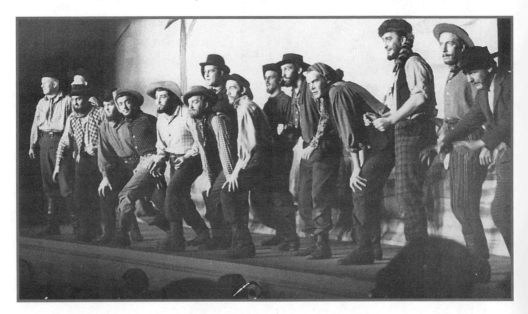

Above: By the 1990s, shows like *City of Angels* (1989) used movable objects, platforms, and scrims, which removed the stable sound board previously provided by unit sets, so that every performer was forced to use wireless microphones. *(Martha Swope)*

Below: Lehman Engel, singer John Reardon, composer Jule Styne, producer David Merrick, and RCA Victor's George Marek in preparation for recording the original-cast album of *Do Re Mi* (1960). Engel founded the BMI Musical Theatre Workshop. Most observers believe its alumni have fallen short of creating a second golden age on Broadway. *(MSS 39, Lehman Engel Papers, Irving S. Gilmore Music Library, Yale University)*

The sound console operator at the rear of the theater for *The Boy from Oz*, Imperial Theatre, 2003, must follow the script (in the looseleaf binder), read video monitors, and run board switches simultaneously. *(Michael Kagan)*

In the basement underneath the Imperial Theatre stage, all the performers' wireless transmitters are plugged into a rack of audio receivers next to another console. *(Michael Kagan)*

ACT THREE

*Revolutions in Broadway Rhythm: How the Rock Groove
Decomposed the Musical and Dismantled the Fourth Wall*

> Broad-way rhy-thm Broad-way rhy-thm . . . every-
> body dance!
> —"Broadway Rhythm" lyric by Arthur Freed,
> from the film *Broadway Melody* of 1936

The classic cliché about the happy theatergoer's leaving the theater humming
the tunes doesn't mention the beat or rhythm of the tunes being hummed. It
assumes that the tune itself is the whole ball of wax. After all, anyone can sing
"There's No Business Like Show Business" a cappella, without a rhythm section, and be immediately understood. But what musical ingredient makes a
tune a show tune, as distinct from a folk song, a religious hymn, a patriotic anthem, or an operatic aria?

The answer is danceable rhythm—even if the tune isn't actually choreographed onstage. A show tune is dancified song. Hummable melody plus palpable beat equals show music. And while danceable rhythm can occur in folk
songs ("Turkey in the Straw"), religious hymns (the Shaker hymn "The Gift to
Be Simple"), patriotic anthems ("Yankee Doodle"), and arias (Carmen's "Ha-
banera"), it is intrinsic to Broadway show tunes. An aria in opera is not rhythmically regular and periodic (unless it's a nineteenth-century cabaletta). A
show tune almost always is. Broadway show music is an incitement to movement in a way that folk songs and even patriotic anthems are not. It is no coincidence that when Hollywood made the first film musical glorifying the
Broadway sound—MGM's 1929 *Broadway Melody*—the title song was not a
ballad or a torch song but a foxtrot with a tap-dance chorus. (The incomparably

echt-Broadway composer of "Broadway Melody" and "Broadway Rhythm," Nacio Herb Brown [1896–1964], was a California haberdasher turned real estate investor turned vaudeville pianist who didn't even attempt a Broadway musical until after he wrote "Broadway Melody.")

No less than the director George Abbott noted that lively rhythms periodically erupt in musical comedy like a heartbeat reminding you that you're alive. The through-line of audience foot taps that exists in musicals, which doesn't exist either in straight plays or in operas, is like a spine of joy. A musical's promise of periodic irruptions of foot-tapping song beats heightens the drama, quickens the pace, and creates most of the sheer fun of the entertainment. The cat-and-mouse game of the audience's not knowing where or when the dialogue is going to break into foot-tapping song is where a musical derives much of its suspense: the sheer unpredictability of the alternation between straight dialogue and music, which even opéra comique does not afford, and which through-sung poperettas utterly lack.

We have already examined how the singing voice, and historical changes in singing styles, played a role in the evolution and devolution of the Broadway musical. Could historical changes in popular dance rhythms also help account for the rise and fall of the Broadway musical?

A Short Course in "Top" Rhythm and "Bottom" Rhythm

There are two different kinds of "Broadway rhythm." The first kind sits on the top of the musical texture and grabs the ear immediately; the second kind infiltrates the musical texture from the bottom up like subliminal advertising.

The first kind, called melodic rhythm by music theorists, is the rhythmic pattern of the melody's notes, the pattern that endows the tune with catchiness. The melodic rhythm can reside either in the pace of the overall melody or in the relative lengths of the individual notes of the tune. A famous example of altering the melody's pace occurred in 1926, when George and Ira Gershwin were writing the songs for their musical *Oh, Kay!* In Ira's words, "George wrote a rather exciting tune which he played at a brisk tempo. . . . Then one day, for no particular reason and hardly aware of what he was at, George played the dance tune in a comparatively slow tempo. The melody hadn't reached the halfway mark when both of us had the same reaction."[1] Their reaction was that the tune hadn't really been given birth until it had been slowed. The slowed version of the same notes—catchy when slow, forgettable when fast—became the great standard "Someone to Watch Over Me."

Another famous example: when Hoagy Carmichael wrote a fast ragtime piano solo for bandleader Isham Jones in the early 1920s, it met with only modest success. In 1930 an arranger advised Carmichael to try slowing the tune and fitting it to words, and when lyricist Mitchell Parish provided a text in 1931, the enduring result was the twentieth century's twenty-third most-performed song (in ASCAP's ranking), "Stardust."

Changing the pace of an already completed melody, however, is the less typical way of altering rhythm to enhance a tune's catchiness. More frequently, the songwriter tweaks the note lengths and the rhythmic values between the notes and arrives by instinct or design at the best combination. One can demonstrate this by altering the familiar riff pattern of "Tea for Two," the song from the 1922 Vincent Youmans–Irving Caesar musical *No, No, Nanette* that is ranked the second most-performed song of the twentieth century by ASCAP ("Happy Birthday to You" is first).

Riff pattern from "Tea for Two." © 1924 (renewed) Irving Caesar Music Corp. (ASCAP) and WB Music Corp. (ASCAP). All rights administered by WB Music Corp. All Rights Reserved. Used by permission.

An altered rhythmic pattern based on "Tea for Two"

The altered (or shall we say fractured) version, though employing the same pitches in the same order as the original, is melodically incoherent and ludicrous; the ear retains no memory of this "Tea for Two." But then how can we account for the success of jazz improvisers' melodic alterations of songs? Jazz musicians are able to fracture the rhythmic values of song standards precisely because the listener's ear has long before imprinted the rhythmic pattern of the original tune and participates in a kind of silent conspiracy of memory with the jazz player. The piquancy of the jazz transformation depends on the listener's familiarity with the unaltered original. A good jazz takeoff is thus paradoxically a litmus test of a tune's memorability.

Nobody leaves the theater humming or whistling the rhythm—just try humming "dah . . . di-dah . . . dah-dah . . . di-dah" without mentally hearing the melody notes of "Tea for Two." Still, the soft-shoe step of "Tea for Two," the ragtime syncopation of Joseph Howard and Ida Emerson's 1899 "Hello Ma Baby," and the beguine tempo of the Bernstein-Sondheim *West Side Story* song "Tonight," though not "hummable," are nonetheless *felt,* just as pianissimo bass drum strokes are not heard so much as felt in symphonic music in the concert hall. This felt-but-not-heard subliminal beat exists even in a slow ballad like the Gershwins' "Someone to Watch Over Me," in which the ear knows the rhythm's there, though the toe is not necessarily tapping to it.

The second kind of rhythm, the "bottom" rhythm, provides the fundamental beat. As important as melodic rhythm—the tune pattern or foreground kind of danceable rhythm—has been to the creation of memorable songs and the canon of great musicals, it is the bottom rhythm—the accompanimental background of danceable rhythm, the beat—that has more fatefully charted the rise and fall of the musical as an art form. Regardless of tune pattern, the songs of the musicals that defined Broadway's golden age are almost always beat-driven: they are marked by strong downbeats and regular rhythms. Whenever commentators try to tease out the difference between opera and musical comedy as art forms, they usually overlook the obvious element of beat: most operatic set pieces do not have regular downbeats and do not occupy symmetrical musical periods (i.e., sixteen-bar verses, thirty-two-bar choruses, and so on), whereas musical comedy numbers almost always have both.

After about 1960, as rock began its global takeover of popular music forms, the traditional beat of theater song, popular song, hot jazz, and swing was supplanted by a new rhythm: the rock groove. And while the rock groove is also a form of beat, it has entirely different characteristics from its dance-beat predecessor, as we shall explore later in this chapter. Inevitably, the music of Broadway musicals gradually began to incorporate the rock groove, until by the 1990s entire Broadway and off-Broadway show scores by the new generation of writers were groove-driven.

The proposition that rock music killed the show tune is not novel. But the suggestion that the intrinsic rhythmic structure of the rock groove is partly responsible for killing off the Broadway musical as an art form is.

Scene One. *Era of the March*

The Afro-Celtic Origins of Broadway's Bottom Rhythm:
Nineteenth-Century Jigs and "Rhythm Violin"

Many commentators have described the Broadway musical as a marriage of vaudeville and operetta; others, as a miscegenation of African and European musical influences. But rarely have the rhythmic patterns of the music of vaudeville and operetta been analyzed, or of the nineteenth-century African and European musics that were the ancestors of twentieth-century popular music. To understand the evolution of Broadway rhythm into the rock groove, one must delve back to the instrumentation used in nineteenth-century bands and orchestras, including the bands that accompanied vernacular forms of musical theater.

Most European classical music written for the orchestra during the nineteenth century was composed without regard to the regular, symmetrical phrase lengths of dance forms. The sense of beat is relatively free and unfettered in most traditional classical music and opera; for the most part you don't stomp your foot listening to a Beethoven symphony or a Wagner opera, though you may do so listening to a Minkus ballet or Verdi's "Anvil Chorus." In classical symphonic music the downbeat (first beat of a measure of music) is a convention for the composer to order his musical thoughts and for the conductor to mark the beginning of each baton pattern so the players stay together. The untutored listener feels the downbeat as a distinct pulse only in dance music—minuets, gavottes, polkas, mazurkas, polonaises, waltzes, and so on—and in marches. There are also some classical works built on a relentlessly repeated, unvarying rhythmic pattern, such as Ravel's *Boléro*. Music theorists refer to such a pattern as an ostinato. Ostinatos tend to move the underlying rhythm from the background to the foreground of the listener's awareness.

The symphony orchestra is composed of separate instrumental choirs—the strings, the woodwinds, the brass, the percussion—blended together. None of these choirs functioned as a "rhythm section" for the nineteenth-century orchestra, not even the percussion. The drums of indefinite pitch used in the orchestra—the snare drum and the bass drum—do not mark the beat in the nonstop manner of an ostinato, except in brief march episodes (such as those in many Verdi operas). Rather, they offer tone color, fill out the texture, add force to accented notes, underline the articulation of other groups of instruments, or help build crescendos and climaxes. Furthermore, the drums that are pitched—the timpani—do not continuously double the bass line of the cellos and double basses; instead, they speak only at moments of color or climax. The pulse of symphonic music is thus distributed equally and evenly among all the instrumental choirs—strings, wind, brass, and percussion. The pizzicati of the strings and the repeated staccato notes of the winds support the rhythm in the symphony orchestra as much as or more than do the drums, pitched or nonpitched.

The symphonic approach of using all instrumental choirs about equally in carrying the rhythm, even in especially rhythmic music, was adopted not only by all European and American opera composers of the nineteenth century but by all the operetta composers: Sir Arthur Sullivan, Jacques Offenbach, Franz von Suppé, Johann Strauss, et al., as well as the Americans John Philip Sousa and Reginald De Koven. In *The Mikado,* for example, the rhythm of the song "We Are Gentlemen of Japan" is accompanied by repeated string pizzicati and staccato woodwind notes playing eighth-note backbeats; no strong downbeats here. In "A Wandering Minstrel" a tonic-dominant bass line is gently outlined in the cellos and basses; no "oom-pah" there. The treatment of repeated accompaniment notes is similar in "Three Little Maids from School": every instrument in Sullivan's orchestra syllabifies the prosody of Gilbert's patterish lyrics, rather than laying down a beat for dancing. The cymbal, bass drum, and triangle merely mark and punctuate; timpani rolls are used sparingly.

Sullivan's instrumentation of rhythm and beat, though presented to a "light opera" audience, is not substantially different from that of Rossini's *Barber of Seville* or Mozart's *The Magic Flute.* The audience at a Gilbert and Sullivan operetta heard phrases, not a danceable beat, and the same can be said for much of the music of the other operetta composers, excepting their specialty dance numbers, such as the can-cans of Offenbach, the galops of von Suppé (e.g., the "Light Cavalry" overture), and the waltzes and Viennese polkas (e.g., the "Tritsch-Tratsch") of Johann Strauss Jr.

Much of the popular songwriting of early-nineteenth-century America conformed to this European symphonic model of keeping the beat in the background. The first great popular song hit in an American theatrical production, Henry Bishop's "Home, Sweet Home" (in the 1823 New York production of *Clari*), was a rhythmically flaccid sentimental ballad. Most Stephen Foster songs fall into the category of sentimental ballad ("Jeannie with the Light Brown Hair," "Beautiful Dreamer") and do not have any kind of strongly marked beat ("Oh! Susanna" and "Camptown Races" being exceptions). Nevertheless, by the middle of the nineteenth century, vernacular forms of light music emerged in America to introduce a more foregrounded kind of rhythm. Chief among these was the music for minstrel shows and the Celtic-influenced folk music played by country fiddlers.

Minstrel shows—for most of the nineteenth century enacted by whites in blackface—were the first widespread American form of nonoperatic song and dance show. Popular from the 1840s, they presented song numbers interspersed with dialogues and comedy routines based on stereotypes of African-American life. The band for the typical 1840s–1860s minstrel show comprised four minstrel performers doubling as musicians playing the violin, banjo, tambourine, and bones (a castanet-like clapper). This primitive band, instead of warbling sweet, sentimental songs of the "Home, Sweet Home" variety, played choppy tunes with an ostinato beat. The minstrel-show violin was a rhythm instrument, not a melody instrument; it was played in a country fiddling manner with the bow arm employed in rapid, vigorous sawing motions, playing repeated arpeggiated patterns of four notes that allowed for little vibrato. Not surprisingly, the earliest precursors of beat-driven songs emerged in minstrel shows: Daniel Decatur Emmett's "Dixie" and "Jimmy Crack Corn" (attributed to Emmett), for example, and Foster's "Camptown Races" and "Oh! Susanna" were premiered in minstrel shows. The literally off-beat twang of banjo playing inevitably filtered into song composition itself.

Minstrel shows were a white man's secondhand copy or imagined evocation of the rhythms of black slaves' music; the first reported minstrel performers were two African-Americans known in the late 1820s around New Orleans as "Old Corn Meal" and Picayune Butler. One could argue that minstrel music was not an authentic representation of African rhythmic patterns. The minstrel-show fiddling style borrowed equally from the Anglo-Celtic folk dance music of jigs, reels, and hornpipes. But the banjo itself was imported from West Africa, and there is some evidence of a true mingling of African and European styles.

At about the time that minstrel shows seized the public's imagination, there were dance exhibitions in New York City's slum Five Points by the African-American dancer William Henry Lane (1825?–52), known to history as "Master Juba," and John Diamond, an Irish immigrant who was an 1840s version of the Irish step dancers of today's *Riverdance*. The public paid to watch dancing contests in which Lane and Diamond each tried to outdo the other—an equivalent, perhaps, of the break-dancing exhibitions of the 1980s. Each would tend to incorporate aspects of the other's style; according to one historian, "In Juba's case, he adopted some of the high-stepping, foot-stomping style of the jig into his own footwork. It was from this interaction between African-Americans dancing the shuffle and the Irish dancing the jig that tap dancing developed."[2] (Other writers have credited the early *Ziegfeld Follies* choreographer Ned Wayburn [1874–1942] as the developer of the modern tap dance. He was certainly the developer of the ensemble tap dance used in the *Follies* and later made famous in movie musicals such as *42nd Street,* and he was apparently the earliest person to use the term "tap dancing" [around 1902], although metal plates did not come into general use until 1910.)

Early Show Music Rhythm Grooves: Two-Steps, Boom-chucks, and Bowery Waltzes

Ostinato rhythms are native to the dance and folk music of many nations and races, and one continent's folk ostinato is often surprisingly similar to another's. The true ancestor of tap, clog dancing—a British folk dance in which the dancers tap heavy shoes—predates both "Master Juba" Lane and John Diamond by at least a century (and is enjoying a rebirth of popularity today). When Lane made a tour of London in 1848, British authorities on clog dancing were called upon to judge him; they marveled at the innovations of his steps. There are also similarities between the dance steps of white hillbilly hoedown, Spanish flamenco dance, and African-American buck and wing, and it's hard to say which came first or who influenced whom. A heavily downbeat-accented, foot-stomping two-step pattern of DAH-dit DAH-dit DAH-dit DAH-dit is common to Irish jigs, Hungarian gypsy music, Jewish klezmer bands, Cajun zydeco, African-American ragtime and stride piano, and the reels of Appalachian square dance.

This two-step DAH-dit accent pattern is also the metrical foot called the trochee in English verse, the reverse of the more familiar metrical foot called the iamb (dit-DAH) that was the basic verse unit for Shakespeare and much of English poetry for centuries. Musical ostinatos built on trochees are common in light music before the twentieth century. Some are based on an accented beat that is subdivided into four quick notes (jigs and reels); others subdivide the accented beat into two notes (Sousa's "The Stars and Stripes Forever," Henry Clay Work's "Kingdom Coming," Scott Joplin's "Maple Leaf Rag," and, arguably, James P. Johnson's early stride song "Carolina Shout"). Some trochaic ostinatos are written in 2/4, others in 4/4. Most are folk derivations of march rhythms. The csárdás of the Hungarians, for example, was derived from the verbunkos, a frenzied march dance that was at one time used by the Hungarian army to "drum up" recruits. Liszt adapted the csárdás into the fast 2/4 sections of his Hungarian Rhapsodies called "friskas" that have sometimes been vulgarized for use as circus music.

An alternative to the trochee also popularized by minstrel shows for fast rhythmic songs was the boom-chuck pattern, suggestive of the banjo. The boom-chuck differed from the DAH-dit by placing a secondary accent on the backbeats; the first (or first and third) beats still bore the primary accents, but the second (or second and fourth) beats were also marked with a lighter accent. Many minstrel shows featured cakewalks that popularized this pattern; the cakewalk was later a frequent rhythm for songs by the composer David Braham and lyricist Edward Harrigan for the Harrigan and Hart musical comedies of the 1870s and 1880s. "Dixie" can be performed with the boom-chuck pattern; so can Septimus Winner's "Listen to the Mockingbird" (a tune that Winner stole from an African-American barber named Richard Milburn in Philadelphia).[3] The boom-chuck later became the rhythmic template for ragtime songs. The songs "Hello, Dolly!" and *Cabaret's* "Willkommen" (in its slowed-down chorus) are modern show tunes written in a cakewalk rhythm with implied high kicks on the "dits."

When nineteenth-century light opera composers were confronted with the challenge of setting metrically complex verse like the lyrics of W. S. Gilbert and his operetta imitators, a trochaic DAH-dit or boom-chuck pattern didn't fit the words. Most of Gilbert's lyrics were iambic (dit-DAH), with the stress opposite to that of the trochaic beat. As a solution, the 6/8 march rhythm typified by

Sousa's "Washington Post" and the Patrick Gilmore–attributed "When Johnny Comes Marching Home" was adopted by Sir Arthur Sullivan and also by Americans David Braham, Reginald De Koven, and Sousa himself. Although Sullivan used the 6/8 rhythm for Gilbert's anapestic verse (dit-dit-DAH, dit-dit-DAH, as in "The flowers that bloom in the spring, tra la"), the Americans used it for iambic verse: the 6/8 rhythm is conducted in a beat of two, like a march or trochee, but the beat's subdivision into three rather than two notes yields an extra verbal lick and musical lilt that stretch out iambic verse and in effect endow it with a false downbeat. Marches composed in 6/8 time tend to suggest the trotting gait of horses, and this meter was the most frequently employed in up-tempo theater music prior to 1910 and could still be heard in the 1960s in cheerful, up-tempo musical comedy numbers such as the Cy Coleman–Carolyn Leigh "Hey, Look Me Over" from *Wildcat* or Lionel Bart's "Consider Yourself" from *Oliver!* The songs of George Gershwin, Jerome Kern, and Richard Rodgers are rarely written in this peppy 6/8 rhythm; they were predominantly foxtrot writers (more on that later).

Also commonly used for fast rhythmic songs was a 3/4 meter with a lively, Americanized beat; examples of these so-called bowery waltzes (named for the song "The Bowery" from the 1891 Broadway musical show *A Trip to Chinatown*) include "In the Good Old Summertime" (heard on Broadway in the 1902 musical show *The Defender*) and the title song from Cohan's 1906 musical, *Forty-five Minutes from Broadway,* as well as "Take Me Out to the Ballgame" and "The Sidewalks of New York," which did not originate on Broadway. For slower songs before 1910, the most typical rhythm was an ambling four-beat meter that was itself a slowed-down march, such as Henry Clay Work's popular song "Grandfather Clock" or David Braham's theater song "Slavery Days." Even some sentimental ballads adopted this slowed-down march rhythm: Victor Herbert's Puccini-esque "Ah! Sweet Mystery of Life" (from his 1910 Broadway operetta, *Naughty Marietta*) is an outstanding example. For most other sentimental ballads the usual rhythms were the Viennese waltz (e.g., Herbert's "Kiss Me Again" from his 1905 show, *Mlle. Modiste*) or the metric patterns of European lieder. The release of Ernest R. Ball's 1906 "Love Me and the World is Mine," for example, is written in the 12/8 common to many lieder by Schubert ("Die junge Nonne," for instance) and Schumann, and many songs from the Broadway productions of Reginald De Koven are similarly rhythmicized.

Despite the widespread use of march and waltz rhythms in vaudeville and theater tunes before 1910, they were fundamentally neither danceable nor beat-driven. American popular music historians have long agreed on this: Nicholas

Tawa wrote of turn-of-the-twentieth-century songs that "there is no hint of dance rhythms in compositions in common time, and only weak references to waltz rhythms in those in triple time,"[4] echoing Sigmund Spaeth's 1948 comments that "there was little effort to give popular music a definite beat for dancing. Songs of the Foster type seldom suggested the possibility of a dance. They had to be arranged and adapted even for the old-fashioned soft-shoe and clog effects . . . in general, even if played in strict time, at the proper speed, the tunes would not be considered terpsichorean stimuli."[5] "Reuben, Reuben, I've Been Thinking" from the 1891 Broadway hit *A Trip to Chinatown* (a revised lyric of an 1871 tune) did not engender in the audience either toe-tapping or the urge to see energetic choreographed movement onstage. "After the Ball" from the same show, though a lovely waltz, was too leisurely to rouse the palpable momentum of Strauss's "The Blue Danube." Perhaps only the march tunes of Sousa's operettas (e.g., "El Capitan" from his operetta of the same name) had the ability to make a seated theatergoer tap his feet.

John Philip Sousa: The Rhythm King Who Soft-Pedaled the Beat

That Sousa's marches are as primally rhythmic as a heartbeat is known the world over. He himself said he wanted his marches to be so rhythmic that they would "make a man with a wooden leg step out."[6] That Sousa (1854–1932) also composed fifteen operettas, most of them produced on Broadway in the 1880–1913 period, conducted musicals composed both by himself and by others, played the violin in a theater orchestra conducted by Jacques Offenbach, and orchestrated the American premiere of Gilbert and Sullivan's *HMS Pinafore* is not part of the popular mythology of Sousa the "March King." (Nor is the fact that he published three novels and wrote lyrics and poetry.) Indeed, in composing his marches Sousa often borrowed tunes he had written earlier for his own operettas, such as the march "The Free Lance" (1906), which had been part of his 1905 operetta of the same name (he also cannibalized his earlier unsuccessful operettas for tunes for his later operettas). Yet Sousa's treatment of rhythm in the musical theater surprises our rock-assaulted tympanic membranes: he didn't think the beat was the main message.

In the theater Sousa modeled his orchestra on the ensembles of Mozart operas and Offenbach and Sullivan operettas, and like them he treated rhythm in the same understated way classical music generally treats rhythm: subtly distributing the pulsation among the various instrumental choirs rather than banging on the drum. Although Sousa certainly used his instruments to mark backbeats, he did not do so with strummed instruments or drums. Instead, he used the harp and the string bass. Like Verdi, he used the cymbals, triangle, and tambourine to color his strong beats, but, like Rossini, he would introduce them and the drums gradually, in a terraced, stepwise manner to build excitement as the tune went through reprises. Contemporary pop music uses the drum machine nonstop; Sousa did not use drums nonstop except during the final reprise of tunes. The many 1890–1910 recordings (both flat discs and hill-and-dale cylinders) of Broadway songs that survive suggest that the prevailing treatment of beat and rhythm in turn-of-the-century show music bore out Sousa's own practices; he may indeed have been the model for them. Sousa's typical theater orchestra consisted of one or two flutes (one doubling piccolo), two oboes, two clarinets, two bassoons, two horns, two cornets, one trombone, a first violin, a second violin, viola, cello, bass, percussion, and a piano part usually unused unless other instruments were missing—a setup similar to what Robert Russell Bennett described as "fifteen and piano."[7]

In the lyrical numbers of his operettas, Sousa did not force the rhythm to drive with a marcato downbeat; he did so only in the context of military numbers such as the title tune from *El Capitan* (1896), which later became a famous march. His waltz tunes tended to be gentle, light-footed, and somewhat Viennese. Only rarely and sparingly did he lay down the equivalent of a modern ostinato or rhythmic groove in his orchestration; one example was the "Rhine Wine" march, which became part of the 1923 revival of *The Bride Elect*. Even in his marches scored for band, he toned down and softened the genre he inherited; he revoiced the prevailing sound of the military band by increasing the number of woodwinds and reducing the number of brass and percussion. Thus Sousa's theater scores, while characteristically rhythmic, contained much music that was no more danceable than similar passages from his models Mozart, Offenbach, and Sullivan and would not necessarily be recognized as composed by Sousa by modern listeners familiar only with "Stars and Stripes Forever." Important as rhythm was to Sousa, he did not ram it into the ear of the listener, particularly not in the theater.

The March as Early Broadway Show Tune

Thus, although the most common rhythmic pattern of both the popular song and the theatrical song of the pre–Tin Pan Alley era was the march, it was not an out-front military or up-tempo danceable march. The waltz, then the second most common American song beat, was, with the exception of a few bowery waltzes, also characteristically soft-pedaled—less physical, less kinetic than the Viennese model. Victor Herbert, whose career in Broadway musical

126

theater started about a decade later than Sousa's and continued about a decade beyond Sousa's, had also been a professional bandmaster and wrote many songs built on march rhythms, whether implied ("Every Day Is Ladies' Day with Me" from the 1906 *The Red Mill*) or overt ("March of the Toys" from the 1903 *Babes in Toyland*). Herbert's theater orchestrations, like Sousa's, adopted the symphonic ideal of tonal balance and did not use drums, guitars, or pianos to propagate a dance beat in dance numbers.

The nineteenth-century American songwriter's march was an all-purpose template onto which most song lyrics were grafted, and despite songwriters' increasing resort to the 6/8 horse-trot rhythm as a way of bending the trochaic DAH-dit pattern, the march's ultimate lack of elasticity became a straitjacket that prevented further artistic development of lyrics and librettos. The tunes of the pre-1900 era seem to dominate their lyrics, not only as if they were composed first (they probably were), but as if the lyrics were crowbarred in to fit the melodies, however awkwardly. Frequently the lyrics of pre-1910 Broadway songs are either generic doggerel, stultifying pseudopoetry, or just plain inept (a typical Ned Harrigan couplet for the David Braham march-based tune "The Girl That's Up to Date": "She's really feminine / and she's never masculine"). The march tune did not admit the lyric as an equal and interactive creative partner, and the lyrics fitted to it lacked the ability to delineate individual characters or advance plot lines. Sousa himself composed ornate poetic lyrics to many of his tunes ("El Capitan" was a song with Sousa's lyrics before it ever became a band march), but they are not artfully integrated with their music and thus do not survive in the public consciousness the way his own best melodies, or the lyrics of Hammerstein, Hart, Porter, Berlin, or Ira Gershwin, do.

Sousa's march songs for the Broadway theater were organized as a series of "strains" yoked together like blocks; usually there are three (sometimes four) such strains. Scott Joplin's rags are built on the Sousa model: AABBCC (Joplin deviates by sometimes writing ABA or adding a D). But when theater songs are written this way, the verse can't be made psychologically or dramatically introductory to the words of the chorus. There is neither buildup between the verse and the chorus nor a contrast between them, just an aggregating of blocks. Thus, there was no musical scaffolding to support intricate, meaningful lyrics that would illustrate character and situation with more than generic, stock patterns.

Also, with both verse and chorus in a latent march rhythm, there was little ability to musically differentiate and contrast the lyrics of the two sections. Without a rhythm and sound that could foster the storytelling and character exposition of more complex situations and narratives, the musical theater could not progress beyond the ethnic caricatures of the Harrigan/Hart/ Braham musical comedies, the pseudoexotic operettic clichés of Sousa, Herbert, and De Koven, or the flag-waving folk parables of the Cohan shows.

By 1910 the American musical theater needed a new rhythmic template that would support the theatrical equivalent of sonata form in classical music—a sequentially developmental musical structure that could sustain longer narratives, stimulate more sophisticated lyrics, and achieve deeper dramatic expression. The horse-trotting march template had been unable to do this, and its companion, the waltz, had similarly failed. The horse needed to be replaced by a slyer animal. Perhaps a fox?

Scene Two. *The Foxtrot and Rhythm Section Revolution*

The Foxtrot Revolution

The "Broadway rhythm" of Nacio Herb Brown was a DNA mixture of centuries-old courtly dances with folk dances of European and African ancestry. From the fifteenth to the eighteenth centuries European composers had often written music to various courtly dance rhythms. Pavans, galliards, sarabands, saltarellos, allemandes, courantes, gavottes, and other such dance movements, written in various meters (4/4 for the allemande and gavotte, 3/4 for the sarabande, 12/8 for the gigue, and so on), were created in profusion by Bach and many other composers of the Baroque era.

By the late eighteenth century, European folk dance rhythms—minuets, ländlers, English country dances, Turkish marches—were also finding their way into art music. By the early 1800s, private dance salons and ballrooms in Europe were taking up then-daring new forms such as the waltz, and many of these newer society dances found their way into classical ballet scores and operas; others, like the can-can and polka, made their way into operettas. Ballroom dancing and dance instruction academies came to the United States as early as the 1840s, introducing to the American genteel class the waltz, the quadrille, the schottische, the polka, and other European social dances at about the same time, as we discussed above, that rhythmic folk dances imported from Europe and Africa (Irish jigs and African shuffles) were popular in the lower social echelons and on the street.

With the exception of the waltz, all the dances popular in America at the turn of the twentieth century—European and African alike—were written in the two-beat patterns characteristic of the march. Even the quadrille, a dance for four people (two couples) was written in 2/4 or 6/8, both duple rhythms. Ragtime was always written in two. The Baroque tradition of dance music in four-beat rhythms had virtually evaporated; no one danced the four-beat gavotte in 1900 or wrote popular songs based on its rhythm, as Gilbert and Sullivan had in *The Gondoliers* or Bernstein would later for *Candide* in the mid-1950s. A new four-beat dance rhythm was needed.

The separate Euro-American and African-American vernacular dance patterns had already reached a kind of street mix by the mid-nineteenth century. By the early twentieth century, the elegant/genteel ballroom forms and the scrappy street dance forms were also moving closer together, and by 1910 they began to syncretize. As African-Americans themselves had begun to appear in minstrel shows (often in blackface) in the post–Civil War period, they had refined and evolved tap dancing into a whole repertoire of steps: the stop-time, the soft shoe, the cakewalk, the buck and wing, and more. When white entertainers and composers began to bring ragtime into the song and dance of the first decade of the 1900s, they began to import these ragtime-based, African-Americanized dance steps to the ballroom. Usually these new dances had animal names—the turkey trot, the bunny hug, the camel walk, the grizzly bear—and required men and women to dance scandalously closer than in previous ballroom dances: cheek to cheek, or clasping each other's necks, or even, in the case of the grizzly bear, in full-bodied embrace. This menagerie of racy dances formed the first wave of a national dance craze that took place in cafés, on dance floors, and in restaurants from about 1910 to 1913.

Then the emergence of two dancing superstars paved the way beyond ragtime for a revolutionary change in American popular music. British-born Vernon Blyth (1887–1918) first appeared on Broadway around 1904, took the stage name of Castle, and in small roles for the producer Lew Fields made a modest reputation as an "eccentric dancer," that is, a lithe, athletic dancer physically adept at comedic dancing like the later Ray Bolger (who resembled the beanpole-thin Castle). Castle met a slim aspiring teenage actress named Irene Foote (1893–1969) at a party in 1910 and managed to get her cast in the show he was currently appearing in, *The Summer Widowers*. In 1911 they married and soon thereafter went to Paris to try their luck. There the young couple experienced bad breaks and poverty for some time until they began attracting attention as a dance team demonstrating the tango, the waltz, and American ragtime dances at the nightclub Café de Paris. They brought to the funkier dance steps a hitherto unseen elegance and swiftly became the sensation of Paris, hired by royalty to appear at private parties.

In 1912 Irene and Vernon Castle returned to the United States as dance stars and raised the already pitched dance craze several notches. They danced the Castle Tango, the Castle Gavotte, the Castle Hesitation Waltz, the Castle House Rag, the Castle Classic Waltz, and the Castle Walk at hotels, cabarets, and ballrooms, at private parties of the wealthy, and at posh restaurants like Louis Martin and Sans Souci. They returned triumphantly to Broadway in February 1913 in the musical *The Sunshine Girl.* They helped inaugurate thés dansants—afternoon teas at fine restaurants during which they demonstrated their dances. Imitation thés dansants sans Castles quickly sprang up at department stores and cheap dance halls, where bored housewives trying to emulate the hair-bobbed Irene were guided by male taxi dancers like Moses Teichman and Rodolfo Guglielmi (later to be better known under their noms de guerre Arthur Murray and Rudolph Valentino).

The Castles became an industry, starting several dance academies (including one on the roof of a theater called Castles-in-the-Air) and appearing in a series of illustrated articles in the *Ladies Home Journal.* Other dance teams formed in emulation of them, among them Clifton Webb and Mae Murray and the teenage brother-and-sister act of Fred and Adele Astaire. Ziegfeld quickly cashed in on the Castle craze by opening two dance nightclubs, the short-lived Danse de Follies Cabaret in 1914 and the more enduring Midnight Frolics in early 1915. The Castles' meteoric career came to an abrupt and tragic end with the February 1918 death of Vernon—who won the Croix de Guerre for bravery as a Royal Air Force aviator in World War I—in a flight training accident in Texas.

Although the Castles did not incorporate tap dancing into their demonstration dances, they fatefully ushered the African-American dance tradition into the mainstream of popular music. When they traveled to Paris in 1911, they brought along the Foote family servant, Walter Ash, a son of slaves. The Castles were relatively free of racial prejudice for their time, and once in Europe, where segregation didn't exist, Ash traveled, sightsaw, and boarded with them. In 1913 they engaged the African-American composer/conductor James ("Jim") Reese Europe (1880–1919) and his Syncopated Society Orchestra to be their band both in New York gigs and on the road. Though wealthy whites often hired

Europe and his musicians to play in their private railroad cars or yachts, the Castles went so far as to perform in front of black audiences and to refuse to perform with other orchestras; when the local musicians' union barred Europe from playing the Castles' engagement at the Palace Theatre, the Castles had Europe's musicians seated onstage, bypassing the rules.

Jim Europe, Alabama-born and Washington, D.C., bred, was an all-around musician who, like Sousa, had learned the violin first. Coming to New York about 1903, he quickly got involved in the city's burgeoning African-American musical theater, writing songs and conducting and arranging the all-black Broadway shows *The Shoo Fly Regiment* and *The Red Moon*. By 1910 he had formed the Clef Club, the premier contracting organization for the city's black musicians, and by 1912 his prestige was so great that he conducted the first of a series of all-black orchestra concerts of mostly ragtime music at Carnegie Hall. During World War I he achieved national celebrity as the army lieutenant leader of the all-black Hellfighters band touring the European front. At a rehearsal in Boston in 1919, he was stabbed to death by a disgruntled player. New York City accorded him a public funeral, the first ever for an African-American.

The Castles undertook a cross-country tour in the spring of 1914 with Europe and his Society Orchestra. For his 1913–15 work with the Castles, Europe gradually reduced his instrumentation to a seven-to-fourteen-piece combo that had an even distribution of strings, drums, piano, woodwinds, and brass—something very close to what would become the standard post-1920 small theater pit band. Between dances, the orchestra's drummer, Buddy Gilmore, performed energetic solo sets on the drum traps, anticipating the solo breaks of Gene Krupa and other jazz drummers by many years. So did Vernon himself; as Irene wrote in her memoirs, "Vernon was able to indulge in his favorite hobby, playing the drums. He played like a man possessed and from the audience all you could see was a blur of thin arms and drumsticks and feet. I think he felt he would have made as good a drummer as he was a dancer and any time he had the opportunity to play he took it."[8] In 1914 both Castles appeared in a Broadway musical with songs by Irving Berlin called *Watch Your Step!* In one number Vernon played the drums onstage.

Who Invented the Foxtrot?

In the same show Irene Castle sang a Berlin song entitled "Show Us How to Do the Fox Trot." But the question of precisely who did introduce the foxtrot remains unsettled. There are two leading theories of the dance's origin. The first credits the Castles and Jim Europe and has been supported by Europe, W. C.

Handy, Noble Sissle, and a 1920 letter written by Irene Castle to Sissle. In this account Europe, during the Castles' spring 1914 tour, was conducting W. C. Handy's "Memphis Blues" and asked Vernon Castle if he thought it would be suitable for dancing. Castle initially demurred, feeling the rhythm was too slow, but through trial and error and advice from Europe himself, evolved steps that seemed to work; he told one newspaper reporter at the time that the new dance had already been danced by blacks for fifteen years (that same year, the black composer-arranger Will Vodery published a piano piece under the title "Carolina Fox Trot").[9] In the December 1914 *Ladies Home Journal* article showing Vernon and Irene demonstrating the "Castle Fox Trot," Vernon writes that they had been demonstrating it at parties for three months. Describing the foxtrot, he said, "If you will play an ordinary rag half as fast as you would play it for the one-step, you will have a pretty good idea of the music and tempo."

But Irene claimed that she and Vernon at first referred to the new dance as the "fish walk" and cabled the *Ladies Home Journal* to change it to the foxtrot only when she and Vernon, abroad during the summer of 1914, heard that the new slower, four-beat dance was being called the foxtrot in the States. Indeed, surviving recordings of Europe's orchestra from the 1913–14 period reveal that he conducted in a fast two-beat ragtime tempo, although his October 1914 recording of a foxtrot does not survive.

Enter Harry Fox and "origin of the foxtrot" story number two. Fox (1882–1959), born Arthur Carringford Jr. (according to his press interviews), was a popular vaudeville and musical comedy singer-comedian of the interwar years who also appeared in silent films and a few early sound films. He claimed to be heir to a family of entertainers: in several interviews he asserted he was the great-grandson of the renowned nineteenth-century American clown-mime George L. Fox, whose life dates of 1825–77 cast considerable doubt on Harry's claim. (George L. Fox had been one of the first great stars of the American musical stage, producing, writing, and starring in *Humpty Dumpty*, an 1868 musical extravaganza. George L. Fox played the title character more than one thousand times, was the highest paid entertainer in the country for a time, and eventually went insane.) Harry began his own show-business career as a circus clown and medicine-show performer, moving into vaudeville and burlesque. In later years he also told newspaper interviewers that when the San Francisco earthquake destroyed the Belvedere Music Hall, it destroyed the only venue of his performing livelihood, forcing him to take his career to New York.[10] His real name may have been neither Fox nor Carringford; when his first wife, Lydia, sued him for divorce in 1914, the court case was listed as "*Messman v. Messman.*"

Fox was vaudeville incarnate: a fresh-faced, boyish-looking, fast-talking, straw-hat-twirling, comedic singer and piano player. In the show *Oh, Look!* (1918), he gave his most famous performance: he introduced the song standard "I'm Always Chasing Rainbows." He was married four times, notably to Jenny Dolly of the Hungarian-born dancing twins the Dolly Sisters (originally Roszika and Janszieka Deutsch—the Gabor sisters of their day). In the 1945 movie musical *The Dolly Sisters,* Fox (John Payne) is depicted as someone Jenny Dolly (Betty Grable) eclipsed in fame, but the film also credits him as the composer of "I'm Always Chasing Rainbows," whereas the song's tune was actually lifted whole from Chopin's Fantaisie-Impromptu in C-sharp Minor by the songwriter Harry Carroll. After a few bit-player stints in movies, Fox retired from show business and served out his later years as a photo lab technician for the Douglas Aircraft company in California. (The Harry Fox Agency in New York, the licensing rights organization for the performance of popular music, is named for a sheet music publisher of the same name, not the entertainer.)

Yet Harry Fox is credited by most authorities as the fount of the foxtrot. While some may feel advocates of this theory are always chasing rainbows, its source is impeccable: Oscar Duryea (1871?–1952), America's elder statesman of ballroom dance, who opened his New York City school of dance in 1889 and continued operating more than sixty years. Duryea was expert in both ballroom and ballet, and was a film studio choreographer in silent-film days, coaching Mary Pickford in the polka. In later years he taught dancing at the ballroom of the Ansonia Hotel on New York's Upper West Side. In the June 1951 issue of *Dance* magazine, he wrote:

In 1913—give or take a year—Harry Fox, a comedian, was doing "hot" trotting dance steps to a popular Ragtime song in a Ziegfeld Follies at the New Amsterdam Theatre in New York.

The theatre management, wishing to capitalize on Fox's trot hit, engaged the author of this story to introduce the dance at the Midnight Frolic, at the night club on the roof garden, atop the theatre. . . .

Arriving at the theatre roof garden at about 11:30 P.M. that night, after the show downstairs had ended, I was asked to dance with the pony ballet girls from the theatre, who were scattered among the patrons sitting at the tables.

We were told, the girls and myself, to run around, in dance position, with little trotting steps, to lively four-four time music.

This went on, at intervals, from twelve midnight, until two A.M.—every time the orchestra played Fox's trot music. . . . That's the way the Fox Trot was born.

For fifty years dance encyclopedias, ballroom dance instruction manuals, scholarly articles, and now Web pages have promulgated Duryea's story, notwithstanding that some of his facts are incorrect: Fox never appeared in a *Ziegfeld Follies* (the Dolly Sisters did), and the New Amsterdam roof garden was not the site of a show called the *Midnight Frolics* until 1915. But it seems unlikely that Duryea, given his stature in the profession, could have made the story up. According to Duryea, by late 1914 a "group of prominent teachers of dancing in New York City" had already codified the foxtrot into standard ballroom dance notation. In an undated memorandum in the New York Public Library, Duryea's daughter, Dorothy Duryea Ohl, amends her father's account:

> Harry Fox had nothing to do with its creation and no idea that the onlookers would tag it with his name. . . . [he] had a habit of trotting back and forth across the stage as he sang a number (his professional trademark). . . . Mr. Ziegfeld phoned my father: "Mr. Duryea, will you come to the Roof for after-the-theatre supper? . . . Then, when the orchestra starts to play, will you dance with each young lady in turn—to show the other patrons that this is the thing to do." The orchestra played a one-step, a lively fast-moving dance very popular at the time, with a step to every beat of the music (one step/one beat: One-Step). . . . It was nearing midnight when father bowed to young lady #9 or #10, and he was beginning to feel the pace a bit—and there were 16 young ladies in all. So he whispered to his current partner, "Let's do some of the steps in half-time," and proceeded to develop a pattern of two slow steps followed by three quick ones and hold (technical run-down: 8 beats in all—4 for the two slows and 4 for the three quicks-plus-rest).

A clip from a gossip column entitled "Town Topics" in an unidentified newspaper dated July 1, 1914, also in the New York Public Library, may have the final word: "Funny Harry Fox, languid comedian and inventor of the Long Beach Fox trot, is perhaps the most popular individual at that resort." Harry "Foxtrot" Fox, Q.E.D.

There is yet another theory that the new dance took its name from the equestrian trotting gait known as the foxtrot, in which the horse, instead of picking up a fore leg and the diagonally opposite hind leg simultaneously, raises the fore leg an instant before the opposite hind leg. In horses such as the Missouri Fox Trotter, this gait is said to be smoother and less jarring—something like a human being's slow foxtrot.

The Europe/Castle and Fox/Duryea stories are probably both true; the foxtrot may have coevolved out of a universally felt need to find an all-purpose popular rhythm to replace the duple gait of the march. (In his 1951 article

Duryea wrote that, before the invention of the foxtrot, "the Two-Step at the time was the universal favorite and was danced to all types of music, Sousa's Marches, Ragtime, Waltzes—any music that was danceable.")

The key phrase in Duryea's account of Harry Fox's trot is "lively four-four time music." The key fact about Jim Europe's claim that Handy's "Memphis Blues" became the foxtrot is that, like all blues, "Memphis Blues" is in a four-beat meter. Unlike the march, the two-step, or the turkey trot, the foxtrot is danced in four. There are many variations, but the basic pattern consists of a long gliding step equaling two beats followed by two quick, short steps taken one step per beat; an alternative version features two long, slow glides followed by two quick ones. Whatever the breakdown, stepping and gliding smoothly alternate in a four-beat box-step pattern. Thus the foxtrot combines slow and fast, rhythmic flexibility and downbeat regularity, in a unique way. It can be made to swing or syncopate, yet it gives off a subtle lilt even when the rhythm is foursquare and unswinging. It can be elegant and romantic or peppy and jazzy with a simple alteration of the basic tempo. It can equally be swank or earthy because it mixes courtly and folk dance elements in a way that no other dance ever has. Above all, a sung foxtrot rhythm always has a marked downbeat and feels danceable.

But tap dance, too, was an amalgam of tapping steps and shuffles. Why did it not form the basis for new song and dance? Because tap dance generated a foreground rhythm, a "top" rhythm, monopolizing the listener's perception. The foxtrot fostered a background rhythm, a "bottom" rhythm, present but not too present. Tap-dance rhythm is too florid and variable to guide melodies; it could only be center stage, in dance interludes, affording contrast with song choruses. However exciting and artistic a dance form, tap dancing did not provide a template for all-purpose songwriting—notwithstanding the Harry Warren–Al Dubin songs used in tap-dance numbers in Warner Brothers' Busby Berkeley musicals (most of which are fast foxtrots, anyway). Tap can't be sung, except possibly in a modern jazz vocalese style. Foxtrots can be.

The foxtrot is in four beats with the accents on the first and third beat. But the oom-pah of the march and the oom-pah-pah of the waltz are gone. The four beats of a foxtrot-based song typically correspond to the step-pause step-pause (slow, slow) rhythm of the feet. The foxtrot thus does not have heavy-footed beats; it has a cushioned, nonstomping downbeat and nontapping afterbeats. The nineteenth century's musical trochee of DAH-dit, DAH-dit gave way to the slow foxtrot's "DAH . . . dit . . . dah . . . dit" or the quick foxtrot's "DAH-dit-dah-dit, DAH-dit-dah-dit." In the 1910s the typical foxtrot was still fairly brisk in tempo; the slower foxtrot evolved in the 1920s as fast foxtrot–derived jazz dances like the Charleston took the public's fancy. A fast foxtrot usually is written alla breve, in "cut time" (2/2), but it is not beat or felt like a march: it is actually a crypto-4/8 time signature, with four beats implied, but conducted in two. The slow foxtrot is usually notated 4/4.

The foxtrot not only enchanted millions of ballroom dancers but also afforded lyricists and book writers an unprecedented expansion of verbal and dramatic possibilities. The backbeats of a foxtrot smoothly glide instead of boom-chucking, thus not distracting too much attention from the lyrics of a song. The four beats provide more space in which a lyricist could unfurl his thoughts, and more room for complex lyrics, than the 2/4 march template, yet obviate the need for the ungraceful martial 6/8 horse-trot of Victorian songwriters. Like the African-American blues and the European lied, its predecessors in 4/4 song forms, the foxtrot is built to accommodate and highlight narrative lyrics but, unlike them, does so while kicking up light, bouncy, danceably rhythmic downbeats. Its downbeat drives, but it drives gently, with a lilt and a sweetness that can endow a song with charm. It drives by soft selling, getting out of the way of lyrics so that complex wordplay and verbal character portrayal can come to the fore.

The foxtrot also gracefully allowed space for more florid melodies, previously the province of 3/4 time, giving them a new American feel. It gently supported less florid tunes as well, somehow wafting stepwise melodies like "Night and Day" to soaring. Its rhythmic signature was neutral and unobtrusive enough that a musical comedy number written in it could suddenly mutate into more aggressive dance rhythm for a choreographic interlude, even a different dance rhythm, and then return to the song lyric without breaking the dramatic line of the song. For example, the chorus of Cole Porter's "Were Thine Thy Special Face" from *Kiss Me, Kate* (1948) is marked "slow foxtrot tempo" in the published sheet music: onstage the dance break goes into a beguine rhythm and remains there through the song's climax. Other dance forms used in Broadway tunes would lack this chameleon-like elasticity to modulate into other rhythms. They were too distinctive to morph into dance episodes and variations; a Charleston was a Charleston, a rumba stayed a rumba.

The tango, despite a 1910s ballroom popularity rivaling that of the foxtrot, would never become a standard template for Broadway songwriters, notwithstanding occasional successful tango songs like "Hernando's Hideaway" (a hit from the 1954 *The Pajama Game*). Like tap dancing, the tango was merely genre painting in the American theater: decorative, but not narrative. Though in the

European theater Kurt Weill made the tango a narrative song rhythm, Weill's Broadway musicals did not sound fully American until he succeeded in writing, for *Lady in the Dark* (1941), American-sounding foxtrots: "This Is New," "My Ship Has Sailed," and so on.

Once the foxtrot was established as the default show-tune rhythm, even the march rhythm became viable only in generic march numbers, such as Jerry Herman's "Before the Parade Passes By" from *Hello, Dolly!* Only the waltz stayed on as a rhythm rivaling the foxtrot in versatility. But the foxtrot rhythm supports a far greater variety of song treatments, and emotional range, than the waltz.

The Sung Foxtrot as Show Tune

The Broadway composer of 1914 who could exploit the new rhythm in show music was in a unique position to expand the creative horizons of his medium. That composer turned out to be neither George M. Cohan nor Irving Berlin but Jerome Kern. Kern, usually cited as a melodist, was actually just as innovative a musical comedy rhythmist. Until the 1920s Berlin was still writing faux ragtime, and George Gershwin in 1914 was a kid yet to emerge. So Kern beat them both to the punch.

In the first decade of the 1900s Kern had composed tunes in the prevailing two-step march rhythm. One of his earliest hits, "How'd You Like to Spoon with Me?" interpolated in a 1905 show called *The Earl and the Girl*, was sung by women swinging on onstage swings and was advertised as the "the swinging song sensation," even though it didn't "swing." By the early 1910s Kern was writing ragtime-based rhythm songs; James Reese Europe recorded a driving version of Kern's "You're Here and I'm Here" in February 1914.

For the 1914 musical *The Girl from Utah*, Kern wrote several two-steppish danceable songs that were interpolated into a score composed mostly by Sidney Jones. But one song differed. It was a slow ballad written in cut time (2/2). Usually cut time indicated a brisk tempo. But despite the time signature on the printed page, the chorus of "They Didn't Believe Me" went at a new, different, walking gait—to quote Vernon Castle, "half as fast as you would play the one-step." "They Didn't Believe Me" was thus the first use of the most dominant song pattern of the next forty years: a slow or moderato foxtrot written in cut time, of which two measures constitute a single unit perceived by the ear as four beats. (Another song in the show, "Same Sort of Girl," was also a foxtrot, written in 2/4 but with the tempo indication "slow and well marked.") The song—the first hit song written in the foxtrot rhythm—shortly became a national sensation. George Gershwin heard "They Didn't Believe Me" played by a hired band at his aunt's wedding and was hooked; to get near his idol he would get himself hired as rehearsal pianist for the Kern show *Miss 1917*.[11]

In the spring following *The Girl from Utah*'s run, advertisements for Kern's new musical *Nobody Home* would describe the show as "a zippy, fox trotty musical treat." Kern shortly teamed with the librettist Guy Bolton (they were later joined by P. G. Wodehouse) to create a series of original book musicals for the 299-seat Princess Theatre at 104 West 39th Street: *Nobody Home* (1915), *Very Good Eddie* (1915), *Have a Heart, Oh, Boy!,* and *Leave It to Jane* (all 1917), and *Oh Lady! Lady!!* (1918). The young Richard Rodgers saw the Princess shows and later claimed to have found his lifelong ambition to be a theater composer in these productions, feeling that a new, breakaway American song style had been coined. The innovations Gershwin and Rodgers were responding to were not only in the melodies, as most theater historians have opined, but also in the rhythm. Kern's rhythmization of operettic melody with a smooth but danceable four-beat pattern in songs such as "They Didn't Believe Me" and "Some Sort of Somebody" was altogether new.

Irving Berlin's 4/4 songs invariably had been cakewalks: choppy, unsmooth four-beat ragtime marches with dotted rhythms and with the fourth eighth note syncopated, tied over the middle of the bar. Even Berlin's "Show Us How to Do the Foxtrot" had been a syncopated, double-dotted four-beat cakewalk, not a foxtrot. Kern's treatment of four-beat rhythm was truly unorthodox: Victor Herbert wrote in fours but did not write foxtrots, nor did Rudolf Friml, nor Sigmund Romberg, at least until years later. Berlin finally caught up with his own foxtrot tunes "A Pretty Girl Is Like a Melody" in 1919 and "Say It with Music" in 1921, but Friml's foxtrot "Chansonette" (later known as "The Donkey Serenade") debuted only in 1924, at the Paul Whiteman band concert at which Gershwin's *Rhapsody in Blue* premiered. That same year even Sousa tried his hand, composing a foxtrot he called "Peaches and Cream" that sounds more like a march or heavy-footed waltz.

Kern took a few years to break in his new style; most of the Princess Theatre songs were still two-steps or waltzes, as the public wasn't ready to accept the new rhythm in every song. The great Kern-Wodehouse ballad "Bill," which appears in *Show Boat,* was originally written in 1918 for *Oh Lady! Lady!!* but was dropped out of town because its slow tempo confused the audience. But the zippier "Till the Clouds Roll By" from *Oh, Boy!* made a hit at first hearing. A 1918 interview with the *Musical Courier* shows that Kern was well aware of what he was doing: "People won't take a man's work seriously if they have been dancing to one of his fox trots." Yet in show after show after his Princess Theatre period ended in 1918, he abandoned his earlier two-step style and wrote all his big hits in foxtrot rhythm: "Look for the Silver Lining," "Sally," "Whip-poor-Will," "Kalua," and others. It was the beat that marked his maturation as a songwriter. By the time Kern wrote *Show Boat* (1927), he had found ways to make the four-beat foxtrot support any dramatic situation. "Bill," rescued from the trunk, was now a foxtrot torch song. "Make Believe" and "Why Do I Love You?" are operetta love duets rendered as foxtrots. The verse to "Can't Help Lovin' Dat Man" is a blues, but the chorus is a foxtrotted blues. "Ol' Man River," though in four, is a hymn in the show and thus undanceable (though when bandleaders turned it into a hot swing number, it became danceable). Other Broadway composers would expand the rhythm's ambit, writing foxtrot comedy songs, foxtrot hymns, foxtrot ethnic numbers, and so on. In the 1930s and 1940s, most of Kern's songs continued to be foxtrots, from "The Song Is You" to "All the Things You Are."

By the late 1910s the word "foxtrot" was appearing on records as a generic term for any jazz or dance band treatment (usually hectic and wild) of almost any song. In show music, once Gershwin, Berlin, Porter, Rodgers, and everyone else got on the foxtrot bandwagon, it would eventually assume a similarly imprecise definition: a generic four-beat song tempo was a foxtrot and vice versa. For example, the published sheet music prepared by Albert Sirmay for Porter's 1948 song "Always True to You in My Fashion" gives the tempo indication of the chorus as "graceful foxtrot," which stretches the term liberally (in the *Kiss Me, Kate* vocal score the tempo for that song merely reads "medium bounce"). Throughout the belle époque, two-beat and three-beat show-tune rhythms persisted, but the majority of songs would be written as either fast, medium, or slow four-beat foxtrots.

Pace would determine whether the foxtrot was notated in two or four or conducted in two or four, but the feel was always four. Kern's "Bill" was notated in four and conducted in four. Gershwin's "Do Do Do" was notated both ways in different publications (in his own arrangement in the *Gershwin Songbook*, Gershwin notated it in cut time). Kern's "Why Do I Love You?" and Gershwin's "Embraceable You" are notated in two and conducted in two, but are quintessential foxtrots with a four-beat feeling. Jazz versions of many of these songs, of course, sometimes change the meter from four to three. But a substantial percentage of pop standards from the 1920–60 period are also foxtrots in their original rhythms, from "Sophisticated Lady" to "April in Paris" to "Moonlight Serenade" to "Stardust."

The foxtrot was to the Broadway musical what blank verse was to Elizabethan drama: a way of writing rhythm that liberated the artistic genius of an era. Before Kern invented the sung foxtrot, theater songs were catchy tunes by which lyricists illustrated prefabricated rhythms, making lyrics sound shoehorned in. Only tuneless, underscored patter songs like Cohan's "Life's a Funny Proposition After All" could spin out sophisticated language and thought. The Kern 4/4 allowed a character to talk through song and thereby liberated musical dramaturgy and textual sophistication while maintaining the catchy tune. The four-beat Broadway foxtrot is the song rhythm par excellence for dramatic exposition and narration. Even in the Rodgers and Hart book shows, when Rodger's rhythms were jazzier than in his Hammerstein period, Rodgers tended to use Kern's foxtrot rhythm for songs that required complex characterization: "Bewitched, Bothered, and Bewildered," "I Could Write a Book," and "Take Him," for example, delineate the inner drama of Vera Simpson, the society woman who keeps Joey in *Pal Joey*, and are foxtrots. But "Johnny One Note" and "The Lady Is a Tramp" from *Babes in Arms*—novelty numbers not rooted in the dramatic situation of the book—are not foxtrots. Porter did the same thing in *Kiss Me, Kate:* most of the songs that illustrate the essential sentiments of the characters are foxtrots (even "Why Can't You Behave?," a blues, is a foxtrot); those that stand outside the spine of the action are in other rhythms (the bowery waltz of "Brush Up Your Shakespeare").

The foxtrot concept of dancifying vocal music dominated not just Broadway but the entire popular music business for decades. The foxtrot rhythm was *the* sound of the dance band in the period before the 1950s. Practically any tune recorded by a name vocalist with a name dance band between 1925 and 1950 was some form of slow or fast foxtrot. Waltzes, Latin numbers, Charlestons, and other song rhythms were exceptions to the rule (and many were metric modulations of the foxtrot, as noted above of the beguine). Nor did the lindy hop and the jitterbug, the frenetic dance crazes of the swing era, persuade songwriters to retool their rhythmic lexicons. The belle époque songbook was a foxtrot songbook.

Still, the foxtrot was only one-half of the revolution in Broadway show music that began circa 1920.

The Rhythm Section Revolution: The Dancification of Song

The foxtrot beat was the catalyst in a chemical reaction that turned vocal music into dance music. But one more element was needed to complete the equation: that proved to be the rhythm section, which, once universally adopted, transformed theater music as well as all popular music.

The Castle ballroom craze of the 1910s moved social dancing from the salons of the rich to the dance floors of the masses and thereby ignited a huge demand for commercial dance bands. In the nineteenth century there had been no such thing as commercial dance bands. And only the minstrel show, which was dying out by the late nineteenth century, sported, with its ostinato drumming, a precursor of a rhythm section. Eventually the insistent rhythms of the brass marching band (as had the rhythms of Irish jigs before them) began to enter African-American music practices and to be cross-pollinated by them. By the 1890s the earliest black practitioners of ragtime piano were improvising syncopation to marches by Sousa; in the late 1940s Eubie Blake told the oral historian Rudi Blesh of one such late-nineteenth-century black pianist who Blesh said would "bring the house down with *The Stars and Stripes Forever* in march time, ragtime, and 'sixteen,' the latter meaning a fast boogie-woogie bass."[12] Conversely, the black ragtime piano style, when first borrowed by players such as the Kentucky vaudevillian Benjamin Harney, performing at Tony Pastor's Union Square Theatre in New York on February 17, 1896, was known as "jig piano," that is, Irish jig. (Some authorities believe Harney was a light-skinned black, but if this is so it appears he passed for white.)

In the pre-1910 period, when pickup groups for dancing played only in private salons, they were known as salon orchestras, a term that later came to refer to the style of music played and its typical instrumentation. The music's style was European light classical, sometimes "gypsy violin"–oriented, and the combo typically had no wind instruments. A salon-style combo was the band that played on the *Titanic*. Beginning about 1912, hotels began hiring standing salon bands to play for ballroom dancing. But with the thundering influence of ragtime and the new ballroom dances, and with Jim Europe's musicians being hired by rich whites to provide the dance music for their private affairs, the salon orchestra was under siege to change with the times. Joseph C. Smith, a classically trained violinist who led one of the early commercial salon dance orchestras at New York's Plaza Hotel in 1916, played ragtime syncopation in a Hungarian gypsy manner. Smith's orchestra later played in the pits of such Broadway shows as *Girl Crazy* (1930).

The salon-style dance band was not sufficient either in rhythm or in instrumentation to drive the new musical beat of the 1910s the way sheet music publishers and patrons of dance halls wanted, and wind instruments began to enter the band. (Later, in the period between the world wars, European salon bands, now sometimes joined by saxophones, were redubbed palm-court orchestras after the horticulture of the indoor hotel rooms where they typically would play music of Eric Coates, Ivor Novello, Albert Ketèlbey, and Noël Coward.) But more than new instruments, what was needed was a new musical way to jump-start dance rhythm, to propel its sense of downbeat.

Some of these changes actually began not on the ballroom floor but in the theater. Drumming was beginning to assume more prominence in show music. During the run of the 1908 musical *Miss Innocence,* the show's drummer achieved an unusual notoriety. According to *Variety,* "During a stage wait he announced the curtain with a roll of drums—but the curtain refused to go up. After several unsuccessful cues, he finally broke out into a rash of drumming. This solo made such an immediate hit that it stayed as part of the show."[13] The drum traps setups in theater pits followed vaudeville practice, and after 1910 added high-hat cymbals and the like. One of the two judges of a 1915 drumming contest held as a publicity stunt on the roof of the Strand Theatre was Jerome Kern.

Just as drummers were emerging as soloists in their own right, the strictly rhythmic side of the piano was beginning to play a role that keyboard instruments had not assumed since the late Baroque era of the 1700s, when harpsichords and organs (doubled by cellos) were used in orchestras as basso continuos—instruments that supplied the bass line of the entire orchestral texture and thereby also outlined the beat. By 1910 sheet music publishers were hiring song-plugging pianists to demonstrate new songs by playing them in a heightened rhythmic style that people could dance to, with a foot-stomping downbeat borrowed from ragtime and with a heightened emphasis on the bass line. These song pluggers were immortalized in the 1930s by several Warner Brothers movie musicals, which re-create scenes from Tin Pan Alley with shots panning room after room of song-plugging pianists banging out tunes for customers. Once dance music had entered the popular realm, the song-plugger style of unremitting pulsation in the rhythm of the accompaniment became de rigueur for the feel of a song. The young George Gershwin was a song plugger, and 1920s recordings of him playing his own songs abundantly demonstrate the song-plugging style, as he hits each downbeat with unvarying, relentless, almost monotonous rhythm, making each and every song a kind of fast foxtrot wind-up toy.

Eventually this hyperrhythmic style of solo playing also became a standardized aspect of the ensemble use of the piano within the dance band's rhythm section. The song-plugging pianist frequently graduated to rehearsal accompanist for show music (Gershwin himself did so), which often required him to read sheet music with fluency at sight. Rehearsal pianists of show music have to play with a rhythm-section feel; rehearsal pianists of opera do not. Baroque-era keyboard musicians who had performed basso continuo parts in 1700 had to read at sight a musical shorthand called figured bass and fill out the corresponding chords from it; the new rhythm pianist/accompanist would similarly be called upon to read harmonic notations in sheet music at sight and fill out the chords instantaneously.

The revolutionary popularity of the foxtrot forced what became a fundamental and enduring change in the makeup not only of the dance band but also of the theater orchestra. Before 1910 the salon orchestra and the theater orchestra were very similar: in 1931 Theodore Dreiser recalled a typical Warsaw, Indiana, opera house orchestra of the 1870s as having seven or eight players, including two violins, a cornet, a string bass, a cello, a flute, and a percussionist, much the same as the salon dance combo.[14] (Dreiser, the author of *An American Tragedy,* was the kid brother of the early Tin Pan Alley songwriter Paul Dresser [1858–1906] who wrote "On the Banks of the Wabash" and "My Gal Sal"). Sometime between 1910 and 1925 the dance band of salon orchestra instrumentation was replaced by a dance band built on the Dixieland jazz model—brass (trumpets and trombones), reeds (saxophones doubling on clarinets), and rhythm section, with occasional added strings for a "sweet" rather than a "hot" sound. No longer was the violin the lead instrument; now the trumpet was the leader. No longer was the marching band tuba the bass instrument; now it was up to the string bass. The rhythmic strumming function earlier taken by the harp and then assumed by the mandolin or banjo was now ceded to the guitar. For the first time the rhythm section was a separately constituted choir consisting of piano, drums, string bass, and guitar. In this grouping the piano, guitar, and string bass become a kind of vernacular basso continuo. Instead of playing coloristic punctuation only now and again, as did the percussion section of Sousa's theater orchestra, the dance band rhythm section played an unremitting four-beat pulse underneath whatever melody and harmony were being played by the other instruments, whether the piece was a fast trot or a slow ballad.

By the early 1920s and the heyday of Paul Whiteman's orchestra, all these innovations were in full swing in dance bands playing hotels and ballrooms. By sometime in the mid-1920s, the Broadway theater orchestra was adopting them, too. Until the mid-1910s Sousa's "piano and fifteen" had been the default plan of the theater pit, whereupon the orchestrator Frank Saddler began increasing the size of the pit band to twenty (for Berlin's 1914 *Watch Your Step!*)[15] or even twenty-six (for Kern's *Have a Heart* in 1917).[16] But Saddler's orchestrations still observed the classical music model rhythmically, assigning beat-outlining functions to the violas and harps. According to Russell Bennett, who succeeded Saddler as Kern's orchestrator in the early 1920s, neither Saddler nor Victor Herbert ever resorted to a dance band rhythm section.[17]

The rhythm section of the dance, jazz, or theater pit band fufilled a function that didn't exist in classical music orchestration: the propagation of a steady beat. Gone forever was the rhythmic backbeat function once performed by the violas. Instead the drummer would tap the snare drum with a stick four times a bar, while the guitar player would usually strum the chord four times per bar. The pianist customarily would play chords either on the downbeat and third beat or on the two backbeat chords (occasionally this was also done by the guitarist; usually one instrument would be assigned the first and third beats, the other the second and fourth). The bass player was the continuo part, playing the root position of the chords. (This is an oversimplified account of the rhythm section scheme; in performance there is often embellishment and syncopation of the four beats.) Jazz bands differed from dance and theater pit bands by taking these basic patterns and floridly elaborating on them: the rhythmic extrapolations on the basic pattern by the drummer became more complicated, the bass could play a melodically independent walking bass part, and so on. While it usually fell to the string and wind instruments of the dance band or theater orchestra to double the melody line, play countermelodies, or emit decorative licks, they could at times also double the accentuated foxtrot beats.

By the time the new guard of theater orchestrators had taken over in the late 1920s—Russell Bennett, Hans Spialek, Will Vodery, William Grant Still, Alfred Newman, and Max Steiner (the latter two soon departed for Hollywood)—the rhythm section had become a standard constituent of the Broadway pit, universally used as the infrastructure of both up-tempo songs and slow ballads. It was probably first used in African-American musicals such as Sissle and Blake's *Shuffle Along* (1921), James P. Johnson's *Runnin' Wild* (1923), which introduced the Charleston, and Lew Leslie's revue *Dixie to Broadway* (1924). It was certainly a part of the orchestra for such DeSylva, Brown, and Henderson shows as *Good News* (1927). By the late 1920s superb dance band players like Benny Goodman, Red Nichols, Glenn Miller, Artie Shaw, and Gene Krupa were all working in the orchestra pits of Broadway musicals.

The nineteenth-century minstrel-show band had been almost pure rhythm section, but it had little effect on popular songwriting. But after about 1920 all popular music and all show tunes were conceived and arranged for a dance band with a rhythm section. And with the addition of the rhythm section, theater music had taken a fundamental new turn: the Broadway pit band was now an orchestral version of the piano song plugger, and the sound and feel of the four-four beat and its characteristic downbeat would be inexorably placed in the ear as "Broadway rhythm": the suave tapping of a top-hatted Fred Astaire, the smooth refrain of "People Will Say We're in Love," the brassy belting of Ethel Merman in "There's No Business Like Show Business," or the lithe bounce of Ray Bolger singing "Once in Love with Amy." All of them were the end products of a vocalized foxtrot combined with a rhythm section.

The Foxtrot Rhythm and the Expository "I"

By the early 1930s the foxtrot template had transformed the language of every Broadway songwriter. Virtually every song in Porter's *Anything Goes* (1934) is a foxtrot. By the late 1940s and early 1950s, at the height of the belle époque, most show tunes still moved to the foxtrot rhythm of thirty years earlier, although jazz had already moved on to the irregular rhythms of bebop, and rhythm and blues was shortly to morph into rock and roll. In musicals, foxtrot song patterns outnumbered waltz patterns by a ratio of more than three to one.

The persistence of the foxtrot pattern in musicals attests not to the conservatism of the Broadway scene but rather to qualities inherent in the rhythm that are uniquely adapted to the theater medium. First, the foxtrot song is singularly suited to exposition of specific rather than generic narratives. The 1918 Kern-Wodehouse foxtrot "Bill" (later used in *Show Boat*) is a case in point. The singer tells the story of her specific relationship with a specific man; the lyric is not a generic blues about "my man," a somebody we don't know. The easy gait of the tune lets her fill in the details. The choruses of waltz songs or march songs had never been used as frames for specific exposition of character details; their verses were. The foxtrot song shifted the narrative exposition from the verse to the chorus, making the exposition more memorable and catchy. And once the foxtrot expositional song was established, the way was opened up for using rhythms in twos and threes for similarly specific character narratives (such as Og the leprechaun's 3/4 "When I'm Not Near the Girl I Love" in *Finian's Rainbow*).

Second, the foxtrot is singularly adaptable to spoken interior monologue. The literary critic Harold Bloom has observed that Shakespeare was the first writer in literature to portray human beings' consciousness through spoken asides and interior monologues. The lyrics of Frank Butler's song "My Defenses Are Down" from *Annie Get Your Gun* are remarkable in showing Berlin, master of simplicity, writing a Shakespearean interior monologue. The resemblance becomes especially clear when the lyric is run together as prose:

> My defenses are down; She's broken my resistance, And I don't know where I am. I went into the fight like a lion, but I came out like a lamb. My defenses are down; she's got me where she wants me, And I can't escape nohow. I could speak to my heart when it weakened, But my heart won't listen now. Like a toothless, clawless tiger, like an organ grinder's bear, like a knight without his armor, like Samson without his hair, My defenses are down; I might as well surrender, For the battle can't be won. But I must confess that I like it, So there's nothing to be done; Yes, I must confess that I like it—being mis'rable is gonna be fun.

What rhythm did Berlin set this Shakespearean monologue to? A 4/4 foxtrot. The same character, Frank Butler, also sings "The Girl That I Marry" in waltz time, but that song expresses a straightforward, unequivocal emotion. "My Defenses Are Down" shows the character in conflict, talking to himself, entertaining ambiguity out loud. If it had been set as either a bouncy two-step march or a waltz, the song would not have transmitted the same message, and the rhythm would have distracted the audience from the content of the lyric. Berlin knew this by instinct.

The psychological interiority of the foxtrot song can be further demonstrated by a comparison with Gilbert and Sullivan. Most of the lyrics in Gilbert and Sullivan are written as though they were the expression of a Greek chorus commenting on the dramatic action. Even when Gilbert's characters speak of themselves in the first person, the lyrics retain a certain third-person remove; in *HMS Pinafore* Sir Joseph, Captain Corcoran, and Buttercup characterize themselves in "When I Was a Lad," "I Am the Captain of the Pinafore," and "I'm Called Little Buttercup" as if someone else were referring to them, with no hint of interior monologue. Gilbert's lyrics are always in metrical verse, and that format, too, represents the speech of a Greek-chorus point of view: his characters speak a Greek-chorus mirror image of themselves rather than giving private utterance. By contrast, the foxtrot equally accommodates free verse, metrical verse, and prose but typically allows the characters to talk freely and unmetrically as themselves in their private interior voices, while still singing in tuneful regular rhythm. In *My Fair Lady* and *The King and I*, when Henry Higgins and the King of Siam deliver their interior monologues ("Why Can't the English," "Song of the King") they sing in foxtrot rhythm (with Gilbertian patterlike recitatives occasionally interspersed), not in march or waltz rhythm.

Third, the foxtrot rhythm rendered the singsong or patter treatment of complicated lyrics obsolete by improving upon it with danceable melody. Musicalized patter had been not only a part of Gilbert and Sullivan and George M. Cohan but a staple of vaudeville and burlesque, in which entertainers like Mae West and Gypsy Rose Lee performed a form of prose patter above musical underscoring. The striptease parody number "Zip" in *Pal Joey* (1940) not only wickedly satirizes the original burlesque genre, but goes the patter song one better by being wholly sung as a foxtrot.

Last, the foxtrot liberated the American musical theater lyric from the procrustean fetters of the march rhythm. For the chorus of the song "I Wish I Were in Love Again" from *Babes in Arms* (1937), Lorenz Hart wrote five-line stanzas that on paper scan as two lines of iambic dimeter followed by two lines of iambic pentameter followed by a single line of iambic tetrameter:

> *The sleepless nights*
> *The daily fights*
> *The quick toboggan when you reach the heights*
> *I miss the kisses and I miss the bites*
> *I wish I were in love again!*

For this lyric Richard Rodgers composed a clever repeating-riff tune in a bouncy foxtrot rhythm with a slight swing or lilt in the beat that is unnotated but felt in any performance of the song with a rhythm section. Hear the lyrics in your head set with Rodgers's tune, and then try fitting them to the tune of "Jingle Bells" or any two-step trochaic, DAH-dit march tune you can think of, starting the DAH accent on the syllable "sleep." The sense of the words is lost, and all you can think of is the beat of the rhythm. However, if you substitute the tune of "Tea for Two"—a foxtrot—the lyric works fairly well, the sense of the words again coming to the fore. Rodgers's tune and rhythm make you think of the words *and* the beat. As Alexander Pope wrote, "The sound must seem an echo to the sense."

As musicals from the 1920s on became more book-driven, theater songwriters instinctively gravitated to the foxtrot song. The more book-driven the concept, the higher percentage of foxtrot songs. Before 1920 Berlin wrote hardly any theater songs in foxtrot rhythm; in the 1920 to 1940 period he began to write them, but as late as Berlin's *Louisiana Purchase* (1940) most of the songs still have the vestigial syncopation of his 1910s ragtime songs. But in *Annie Get Your Gun* (1946), a show built on its book and its characters to a degree unprecedented for Berlin, half the songs are unsyncopated foxtrots, and only one other ("I Got the Sun in the Morning and the Moon at Night") is rhythmically cut to the prevailing popular idiom of the 1940s, swing.

The scores of the canonical musicals of the 1940s and 1950s consistently demonstrate how the foxtrot template adapted other rhythms and colors to it, not vice versa. They also demonstrate that songs carrying the principal plot, characters, or through-line of the show tended to be written in foxtrot rhythm, while subplots, Greek-chorus–style commentaries, or ethnic-color embellishments tended to be set in other rhythms. *Finian's Rainbow* (1947) has eleven songs; analyzed purely in dance beat, five of this "Irish" show's numbers are foxtrots: a folk foxtrot, "How Are Things in Glocca Morra?"; a slow swing foxtrot, "Old Devil Moon"; a fast swing foxtrot, "If This Isn't Love"; a blues foxtrot, "Necessity"; and a revivalist hymn foxtrot, "That Great Come-and-Get-It Day." Two other songs are also written in four, but, because they are not through-line material, they are not foxtrots but Celtic gavottes ("Something Sort of Grandish" and "When the Idle Poor Become the Idle Rich"). Lerner and Loewe's Scottish fantasy *Brigadoon* (1947) has five foxtrots, including a "Scotch snap foxtrot" ("The Heather on the Hill"); the show's musical numbers depicting the Scottish villagers tend to be in Celtic duple rhythms. The foxtrot rhythm psychologically says "I" to the theatergoer. When Rodgers and Hammerstein in *Allegro* (1947) stood the rule on its head and gave a Greek chorus foxtrot songs, the audience was confused because a Greek chorus, not a private character, was singing in the rhythm of "I."

Scene Three. *The Rock Groove Cataclysm*

Enter the Rock Groove, Exit the Melody

Ostinato rhythms have been a feature of folk music of different cultures for centuries, and an occasional feature of classical music occurring with more frequency in the twentieth century (Ravel's *Boléro,* as mentioned earlier, as well as the "Jeu des cités rivales" section of Stravinsky's *Rite of Spring* [1911] and the repeating left-hand pattern of the third movement of Prokofiev's Seventh Piano Sonata [1945]). However, before the second half of the twentieth century, ostinatos in Western music had never assumed a role equal in importance to other fundamental structural elements of music: melody, harmony, form. Even rhythm itself was judged a general structural function of which ostinato was a mere subset. But the popular music beat that succeeded the foxtrot beat in the 1950s did just that—it made the ostinato a fundamental parameter of music and had an inevitable, though not immediate, effect on Broadway theater music.

The earliest precursor of the rock groove is the boogie-woogie bass; some analysts call the fifteenth variation of Beethoven's Diabelli Variations for piano "Beethoven's boogie" because it anticipates the characteristic left-hand rhythmic piano pattern of boogie-woogie that became a popular piano styling in the 1930s and 1940s. Boogie-woogie was a variant of the classic twelve-bar blues. The 1919 Tin Pin Alley hit song "Dardanella" was perhaps the first pop tune to be built (in its verse) on a boogie-woogie–like ostinato. From the late 1940s to the middle 1950s, the blues-derived ostinato rhythmic patterns of African-American music started to migrate to music marketed to the white audience. In June 1951 a Cleveland disc jockey, Alan Freed, played rhythm and blues on his radio program and called it "rock and roll." Soon elements of white country and western were mixed in. The songs of early rock and roll that emerged from these influences—"Rock around the Clock," "Shake, Rattle, and Roll," "Hound Dog"—differed from traditional Tin Pan Alley songs in that their "top" or melodic rhythm did not develop independently of the underlying beat pattern; instead, the melodic rhythm and the beat pattern became one and the same. Standards sung by jazz vocalists from Ella Fitzgerald to Billie Holiday had always been melody-driven songs requiring an artistic interpreter. But the tune of Carl Perkins's "Blue Suede Shoes" is not really a melody at all: it merely repeats the notes of an up-tempo blues ostinato. It is a vocalized boogie-woogie. This new style required the vocalist only to hit the pitches of a melodized rhythmic groove, rather than interpret a song (although Elvis Presley still crooned a fair number of Tin Pan Alley–style ballads).

The new groove style of rhythm was born not only out of rhythm and blues but out of the rhythm section itself. Once dance orchestration had by the 1920s been changed to incorporate a rhythm choir, people began to hear music fundamentally differently. They now expected to hear rhythm as an independent voice, and their expectations were met with an increase in extended drumming solos and more complex fills in rhythm section parts. Ultimately these listening and performance habits gathered critical mass until in about thirty years' time a complete reversal of the conventional hierarchy of song occurred: the rhythm was made the melody, and the rhythmic groove became the new building block of a song. It was also at this juncture that a new instrumentation paradigm for the rhythm section developed: instead of the jazz/dance band model of acoustic piano, acoustic string bass, acoustic guitar, and drums, the rock band consisted of electric guitar, electric bass, electric keyboard, and drums. The dance band had been a melody/harmony orchestra with a rhythm section; the rock band *was* a rhythm section, with an adjunctive melody/harmony component.

A groove is fundamentally different from a beat. A groove is a motor-driven rhythmic impulse. With a groove the sense of the downbeat's inevitability is less important than the feeling of a persistently repeated pulse and an irregularly subdivided rhythmic pattern. A dance beat like the foxtrot or waltz is downbeat-based and drives a tune, makes a song danceable, animates a melody, but it doesn't mistake itself for the melody. The driving beat of Sousa and Gershwin marks the rhythm, even drives it, but does not upstage the tune. "Tea for Two," if driven insistently by a rhythmic groove, loses its melodic profile just as thoroughly as if its note values were rearranged in the manner I presented earlier. Yet non-grooved, artful jazz improvisations on "Tea for Two" do not destroy its essential melodic profile.

The rock groove was an atavistic throwback to the melody-denying rhythm band of the nineteenth-century minstrel show. The ragtime historian Rudi Blesh characterizes the origins of African-American ostinato music making:

> In Black America, from the first work songs of slavery on, duple or triple polyrhythms persisted as a basic practice. Without drums (which were eventually forbidden) they issued from the appositions of hand-clapping, foot-stamping, or the sounds of tools, and the sung melodic line. The first factor, regularly accented, formed a basic ostinato. The chant or melody (like the improvising drum in an African battery) was free to wander from the strong beats to the weak, to delay or to anticipate, to drop unpredictably between beats, and even to pose an odd meter to the even (e.g., 3/4 phrasing over 4/4). It was a drama of tensions: a rhythmic base of metric affirmation, and a melody of metric denial.[18]

Jazz can be built on a melody of metric denial. But the lyric theater, where melodic song is the fundamental vehicle of narrative communication, cannot be built on "melody of metric denial." It *must* be built on melody of metric affirmation. Scott Joplin himself, in his ragtime opera *Treemonisha*, realized this; he wrote tuneful melodies that, while not evading the rhythm, were also not predetermined by the rhythm. Race is not the issue—Duke Ellington and Fats Waller wrote songs that are rhythmic *and* melodic, while innumerable white rock songwriters have written unmelodious groove-driven songs.

With the sensational popularity of Presley, Jerry Lee Lewis, Chuck Berry, Carl Perkins, Buddy Holly, Little Richard, and other early rockers, composerlyricists like Jerry Leiber and Mike Stoller rewrote the rules for songwriting. Most of the familiar Leiber and Stoller songs of the 1950s—"Jailhouse Rock," "Trouble," even the more balladic "Stand by Me"—are constructed entirely of melodized rhythmic grooves rather than melodies. But while there were only two or three variations of the basic foxtrot DAH-dit-dah-dit, there are many varieties of rock groove, and for the last quarter century they have abounded in the songs of Broadway musicals. One common rock groove weights each of the four beats in 4/4 with a heavy downbeatlike accent (prosodically, a spondaic tetrameter). This groove drives the song "At the End of the Day" from the musical *Les Misérables* (1980). Another equally common groove, reproduced today ad nauseam by drum machine tracks laid onto just any song, places the heaviest beat in any group of four on the third of the four. This groove can be found in the chorus of prisoners' prologue to *Les Miz,* "Look Down, Look Down." See the accompanying examples of some other typical grooves from early rock-and-roll songs (they are not unique to each song):

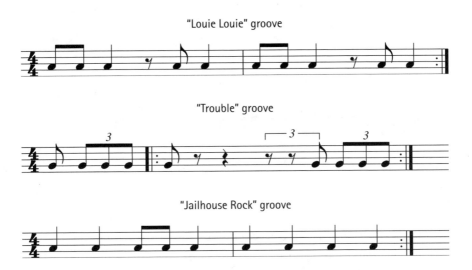

The grooves of rock songs are what first grabs the ear of the listener—quite the opposite of the Tin Pan Alley song, where the melody gets first dibs. The classic songs of the Beatles from their mid-1960s period (the albums *Revolver, Rubber Soul,* and *Sgt. Pepper*) differ from most rock-and-roll songs in that they more nearly follow the Tin Pan Alley model: although their songs certainly contain grooves, they subordinate the groove to the melody and integrate it into the whole. Much more frequently, the rock songwriter, instead of artfully manipulating melody and harmony to avoid monotony, tries to create variety and contrast by simply altering the groove. The groove shifts gears from one subostinato to another within the same fundamental pattern.

Early rock-and-roll songs were usually written down after they were first sung or jammed in the studio. Rock songwriting, unlike Tin Pan Alley and classic Broadway songwriting, has generally not been a notated medium or craft. As with jazz and swing, the actual feel of the rock groove is hard to capture on paper precisely because it is created in performance by tiny increments of prolonging or shortening notes' durations, a phenomenon music theorists call agogic accents and pop singers call backphrasing. Some sheet music tries to reproduce the exact groove feeling by asking the player to play "swing eighths"—

a convention in which ♪♩ is rendered with the triplet feel of ♩ ♪. Telling the performer to play swing eighths is an attempt to notate agogic accents. The difference between rock rhythmic feeling and Broadway rhythmic feeling can be illustrated by applying swing eighths to the song "They Call the Wind Maria" from Lerner and Loewe's *Paint Your Wagon* (1951). For this quasi-folk ballad meant to be evocative of a train rhythm, the composer Frederick Loewe wrote an ostinato accompaniment that on paper looks indistinguishable from a rock groove.

Ostinato for "They Call the Wind Maria"

If one plays these same notes in rock-accented swing eighths, it becomes a rock shuffle rhythm and the entire mood of the song is lost. It is drained of its specific theatrical color and becomes merely nonspecifically "groovy." If played with a rock beat but without swing eighths, this same Loewe rhythmic pattern becomes the beat of television's *Batman* theme of the 1960s or the groove of the early Bob Dylan song "I'd Hate to Be You on That Dreadful Day." Conversely, "Hit the Road, Jack," the 1961 Ray Charles hit composed by Percy Mayfield, is written on paper in a 4/4 that resembles a foxtrot, but which is certainly not a foxtrot in Charles's agogic-accented performance. Without the rhythm-and-blues feel, the notes and rhythms of "Hit the Road, Jack" become as pallid and meaningless as "They Call the Wind Maria" *with* the rock groove.

The first successful Broadway composer to adopt the new rhythmic sensibility was Charles Strouse, whose best-known shows over a forty-year career are *Bye Bye Birdie* (1960) and *Annie* (1977). Strouse made *Billboard*'s top-ten chart in 1958 with the song "Born Too Late," which was based on the groove ♫♩ ♫♩. Working primarily within the established Broadway bounce rhythm, Strouse introduced a light rock groove into his songs—not just in *Bye Bye Birdie* but in scores such as *It's a Bird . . . It's a Plane . . . It's Superman* (1966)—but did it so subtly that the public barely noticed. Strouse's score for *Annie* was probably the last Broadway use of the musical idioms of late 1950s–early 1960s rock, other than the nostalgia shows that directly quote from that era, like *Grease* and *Smoky Joe's Cafe*.

As rock and roll segued into rock through the 1960s, and electronic instruments and multitrack overdubbing became more prevalent, there was an evolution in the fundamental unit of the rock beat. Whereas the groove heretofore had been primarily quarter-note–based, now the pulsation of eight eighth notes replaced four quarter notes as the most common ostinato. Examples of this groove include Bruce Springsteen's 1975 song "Born to Run" and the title song to Andrew Lloyd Webber's 1987 *The Phantom of the Opera.* Whether the similar eighth-note pulsations of the minimalists Steve Reich and Philip Glass were a cause or an effect of the new rock groove is a matter of argument—but what is certain is that minimalism, like rock, uses ostinato rhythms as an organizing structural principle of form. Even Sondheim has adopted a minimalist groove for some of his later work, for example, the songs "Unworthy of Your Love" from *Passion* (1994) and "Happiness" from *Assassins* (1991).

Through the later 1960s, as rock became increasingly electrified, multitrack-layered, and manipulated by studio engineers, keyboard textures and drum tracks began to reflect a sense of perpetual motion, of motored ostinato arpeggiation and pulsating eighth-note beats, all of which were far removed from the original African-American rhythm-and-blues grooves. The first Broadway composer to write consistently in this new style was not Galt MacDermot, the composer of *Hair* (1968)—MacDermot wrote in a tuneful rock-cum–Tin Pan Alley style more akin to the Beatles—but Stephen Schwartz, the composer of *Godspell* (1971) and *Pippin* (1972). Across the Atlantic, Andrew Lloyd Webber also made use of it at about the same time in *Joseph and the Amazing Technicolor Dreamcoat* (1968) and *Jesus Christ Superstar* (1970). Schwartz went Lloyd Webber one better: he was the first composer to bring into the Broadway musical the notated backphrasing of melodic rhythm that was characteristic of recorded Motown music, but he superimposed it on the non-Motown eight eighth-notes groove. Compare the melodic rhythm of Schwartz's song "Corner of the Sky" from *Pippin* with the similarly backphrased melodic rhythm of the popular 1985 Stevie Wonder song "Overjoyed" (see accompanying music examples).

"Corner of the Sky" melodic rhythm

"Overjoyed" melodic rhythm

The rhythmic pattern of a melody notated in backphrasing, with its jagged syncopation and complex subdivision, is more characteristic of a rhythm-section line than a melody line. To write songs in this manner is to stabilize in the permanent notation of published sheet music the vocalese style of jazz singing, normally an improvised style. Bringing this kind of singing into the Broadway arena was as great a revolution as the advent of the foxtrot or of the 1950s-style rock groove. Schwartz is an unheralded Broadway revolutionary; his unconscious influence on young musical writers of the 1990s like Jonathan Larson is just as evident as that of Sondheim. With the increasing use in the 1970s of the new grooves as a basis for writing songs for Broadway musicals, the foxtrot beat, which already in the early 1960s was in retreat, went into exile, summoned back only for nostalgic period writing by older songwriters.

So fundamental is the groove to the construction of a rock song that on Broadway it has now upstaged the long-entrenched tradition of prefacing song choruses with verses. The song "Seasons of Love" from Larson's *Rent* (1996) begins with a repeating instrumental groove that continues under the vocals for the duration of the song; there's no verse. The *Rent* song "Out Tonight" is similarly written, and the show's title song is little more than a repeated-note patter melody with occasional skipwise movement over a constant eight eighth-notes pulsating bass. Likewise, almost every song in Paul Simon's *Capeman* (1997) begins in medias res, with an instrumental groove that repeats throughout the vocal line. It's as if the songwriter, lacking the patience to write a verse, reiterates a few rhythmic riffs as though one were cranking up a motor, and then when the motor catches, the riff becomes the groove and the song is expected to take off on its own steam. In songwriting technique there's little that differentiates this method from "Blue Suede Shoes" or "Jailhouse Rock."

The reader might well question what is so different about using rhythmic grooves as a basis for deriving melodies, when songs based on repeated-note riffs were typical of so much golden-age writing, from Youmans's "Tea for Two" and "I Want to Be Happy" to Gershwin's "Fascinatin' Rhythm" to Porter's "All Through the Night." To demonstrate the difference, let us compare a classic riff-melody show tune of the golden age—the Harry Warren–Al Dubin "Lullaby of Broadway," which appeared in the 1980 musical *42nd Street* almost fifty years after it was written—with a typical groove-melody show tune of the postrock era, "Your Daddy's Son" from the Stephen Flaherty–Lynn Ahrens musical *Ragtime* (1998). In "Lullaby of Broadway" the melody of the first twenty-four bars is entirely constructed out of a single repeating riff (see example).

Opening riff of "Lullaby of Broadway"

For the first eight bars it appears in the tonic; for the second eight bars, in the subdominant; for the third eight bars, back to the tonic. Simplicity itself. From bars 25 to 40 the melody shifts to a string of whole notes over an ostinato accompaniment (see example).

Bridge riff of "Lullaby of Broadway"

"Your Daddy's Son," rather than employing a verse like "Lullaby of Broadway," starts right in with a ten-bar vocalise vamp and thereafter consists of four consecutive twelve- or thirteen-bar blues choruses. The tune is a repeating pattern of the notes of a gapped blues scale going up and down, up and down, up and down. It is less a melody than a slowed-down boogie, a bass line rendered as a melody. Because this line doesn't generate tension through melodic interest, the songwriter unconsciously resorts to revving up the engine of the accompaniment to simulate excitement: at the end of the second thirteen bars, he injects a hint of a rock beat; to endow the end of the third thirteen bars with a feeling of operatic climax, the accompaniment, with the melody still treading water, reverts to a fortissimo spondaic rock groove: four equally heavy downbeatlike beats with a hint of eighth-note arpeggiation thrown in.

In "Your Daddy's Son" each successively louder repetition suggests a sameness, a lack of development that doesn't serve the song's lyric; the listener hears the lyric's emotion electronically amplified instead of musically developed. In "Lullaby of Broadway" each successive repetition of its ultrasimple riff somehow suggests a continuing momentum, whether of dance steps onstage or in the listener's aural imagination. "Your Daddy's Son" generates stasis from apparent movement. "Lullaby of Broadway" generates movement from apparent stasis. Harry Warren's repetitions ingeniously suggest an endlessness, a whole that is more than the sum of its parts. The listener fills in the blank without the need for a crescendoing groove.

The Rock Groove and the Fourth Wall

Since the mid-nineteenth century, the American musical theater of every epoch has mirrored the dominant popular dance music of each successive era: minstrel-show music in the 1850s and 1860s; marches in the 1880s; ragtime in the early 1910s; foxtrots in the 1920s–1960s golden age. The post-1960 influx of rock music—a culturally dominant popular music if there ever was one—into the musical theater is completely in keeping with this historical tradition. Yet for a hundred years the step-by-step migration of each era's popular music into the Broadway musical paralleled a steady artistic growth of the musical: an ever-increasing sophistication of songwriting, seamless integration of book, music, and lyrics, and structured use of dance and scenic design to enhance this integration. With the incursion of rock music into the theater, more than just the beat changed. The seemingly organic aesthetic growth of the musical as an art form abruptly stopped.

If evolving popular music has always promoted artistic progress in the musical, why would it not continue always to do so? Maybe the cause of this stoppage is some ontological change in the nature of popular music or how it is experienced. In its "millennium time capsule" issue of December 5, 1999, the *New York Times Magazine* explored this question. Gerald Marzorati noted:

> Take a half-hour or so and listen to Elvis Presley's "Mystery Train," the Beatles' "Ticket to Ride," the Four Tops' "Reach Out I'll Be There," Bob Dylan's "Like a Rolling Stone," Run-D.M.C.'s "Walk This Way" and Nirvana's "Smells Like Teen Spirit.". . .
>
> Pop music today is not what Americans called popular music as recently as 50 years ago. I do not mean merely that the *styles* of music have changed, though that is true enough. I am talking about music's sudden and astounding pervasiveness. . . . Pop music, circa 2000, might best be thought of not as one of the many cultural activities society avails itself of but as a new form of shared and evolving vocabulary—one committed to memory in youth; one *encountered or summoned, consciously and not, each day or even hour.* [emphasis added]

In the same article, Rick Gillette, a vice president for music programming at DMX, a company that provides customized, digitally delivered music to businesses, added: "Most any place you go now—offices, malls, lobbies, restaurants, gyms—there's music playing. I don't think we want quiet. I think what people have decided they want today is a soundtrack to their lives, and technology is going to allow them to have it."

This is a recipe for Muzak, not music. In the 1950s the term Muzak was originally a proprietary name for prepackaged recordings of easy-listening pop or semiclassical orchestral music that were sold on a subscription basis to corporations and piped into their elevators or offices. What Marzorati and Gillette are saying is that the rock groove has been "Muzak-ized" in America to a pervasive degree undreamt of by Mantovani or Guy Lombardo. The rock groove is the primal sound of postmodern Western civilization. It is heard 24/7 on every form of electronic broadcast media—television, radio, the Web—on jingles, station breaks, commercials, downloads, and on one's headphones while jogging or commuting to the office. It is heard in airports, on airplanes, in movie theaters, in sports stadiums. This was never true of the foxtrot, the waltz, the two-step, the march, the tango, or any other rhythm or dance pattern known to history. Our culture speaks the common tongue of the rock groove and exports it to Iceland, India, Italy, and everywhere else around the globe. The electronically generated and piped-in sound of the rock groove is the ostinato of life in the 2000s.

The popular musics that penetrated the legitimate theater in previous epochs were not experienced by the public as Muzak outside the theater, and were not transformed into Muzak inside the theater. The theater then was a kind of secular temple in which its own musical laws would be observed, and alien musics imported into it were adapted and subsumed. No more. The through-sung (and through-grooved) musicals so characteristic of the late twentieth century (*Les Misérables, Miss Saigon, Rent, Chess,* the Frank Wildhorn shows) don't reflect an artistic upscaling of the musical into opera—they reflect the pervasive habits of millions who are so accustomed to hearing the rock groove as an obbligato to daily life that they must have it inside the theater. Previously, dance beats and rhythm sections drove the rhythm but weren't conditions regarded as essential to music itself. But now, to *exist* as music, music has to be couched in the rock groove. Certainly, a new show cannot be commercially produced as a musical today on Broadway unless it is rock groove–based.

Until recently theater mandarins believed that the Broadway musical was impervious to a one-size-fits-all rhythmic treatment, that, as Lehman Engel wrote in the early 1970s, using one idiom "as the firm exclusive basis of a theatre-music score is impossible first because of a fundamental non-theatrical woodenness that each of them—rag, jazz, swing, rock—possesses as its very own hallmark. Furthermore, none of them in its authentic style allows for appreciable variety, a quality that is essential to the musical score of any show."[19] What has changed since then is the supposed immutability of the "fourth wall": the notion that the audience constitutes the fourth wall of an invisible room encompassing the stage and that this wall traps them within a suspension of disbelief. The rock groove—a form of music that is psychologically experienced in a way elementally different from any previous popular musics—apparently breaks down the fourth wall, dismissing Engel's notion of theatrical music and subverting the very experience of traditional musical theatergoing. How?

Remember how a slight alteration of agogic accent transformed the notes of "They Call the Wind Maria" into a beat that, instead of illustrating the mood and context of the song, dramatized only a preset feel-good emotion of the audience. A rock groove, unlike a pre-1950 dance beat, elicits a call-and-response emotional reaction from the theatergoer similar to the call-and-response of African-American gospel music and spirituals. But call-and-response, although visceral and valid, is a communal gesture of religious revivalism, not a mode of theater. It may well work in certain numbers (canonic musicals have many of them: "Sit Down, You're Rocking the Boat" from *Guys and Dolls,* for example), but if call-and-response became the rules of the game in the legitimate theater, audience members would constantly suspend belief and interrupt the performance of the actors onstage. At a performance I recently attended of the off-Broadway musical revue *Blue Man Group: Tubes,* during many of the musical numbers several young women from Germany stood up in the audience and rhythmically clapped, stomped their feet, and danced as though they were at a disco club or rock concert. At those moments the fourth wall in that theater disappeared.

Was this mere showstopping, or were the women engaged in a call-and-response reaction? If the latter, their response was arguably more self-centered, self-celebratory, and self-congratulatory than any matinee audience of blue-haired ladies from Scarsdale getting their liberal-bourgeois values massaged at a Rodgers and Hammerstein musical. The ladies from Scarsdale may applaud, but they don't interrupt the performance and tear down the fourth wall. As Elizabeth Swados put it, "Rock's confessional nature, though fine in itself, is a real stumbling block toward writing workable dramatic songs. . . . A dramatic song is organically connected to the individuality of the character who sings it. The urgent 'I' and 'he' or 'she' in rock are usually a standardized self and other in a situation of pleasure and/or pain, and whatever narrative there is gets dropped for the duration of a chorus in which everyone joins. . . . Because such songs are written to be complete in themselves, they leave nothing to be developed and usually pull out all the stops for an emotional build. . . . The very elements that make good rock make bad theatre. You should not want to get up and dance with a character who is not even supposed to know you're there."[20]

With the rock groove, gone is the onstage expositional "I" of the foxtrot beat. The rock groove tells the audience the "I" is them, not the character onstage. But theater loses richness and power as a narrative and literary medium when it panders to the audience before it serves the play. Such a theater may well generate a carnal excitement, but it cannot function as an evoker of Aristotelian pity and terror. Paradoxically, heightened engagement of sensation and rhythm alienates the theatergoer from a true emotional engagement with the drama. It is as Brechtian as Brecht's own alienation effect, *Verfremdung,* which may be one reason why Brecht-Weill songs are so popular with rockers. Another likely reason is that Weill's Berlin theater music used an agogic backbeat that is closer to a modern rock groove than any other American or European show music of the first half of the twentieth century. Typical Weill-Brecht songs have strong beats on two and four, much like rock, instead of on one and three, like most Broadway foxtrot songs of the 1920s, 1930s, 1940s, and later.

When four equally accented quarter-note beats or eight eighth-note beats accompany a lyric, the emotion of the lyric is attenuated by the beat's very sameness. A novelist (except perhaps a Gertrude Stein) doesn't describe a character's weatherbeaten face by writing "ruddy! ruddy! ruddy! ruddy!" because it would draw the reader's attention away from the character and toward the odd repetition of one word. The use of such language would be in cognitive dissonance with the object of its description. The same thing happens when the monotony of grooved rhythms is used to deliver complex, nuanced lyrics; it can't work, because the ear is hearing one signal from the music and the brain is getting another from the words, and the brain can't make sense of the combination.

Musical shows that subordinate the rock groove to the drama, that put the "I" onstage rather than in the audience—shows like *Dreamgirls* (1981)—can work just as well as the classic belle époque shows. Through-sung shows written in American pop music idioms *can* be both melodious and dramatically mature—witness Galt MacDermot's 1984 *The Human Comedy.* But more often than not, the rock groove atavistically returns the theater to the inflexibility of the nineteenth-century march beat. It dismantles, if not destroys, the evolutionary accretions that created the finely crafted foxtrot song, as if fifty, seventy, or a hundred years of theater history had never happened. Lyrics are once again shoehorned in or of patently diminished importance. What's more, the notated backphrasing of rock tends to break up melody lines into cells strung together in the manner of rhythm grooves, which defeats a tune's becoming catchy. Since memorable tunes are essential to binding the narrative structure of book musicals in the audience's ears, backphrased tune writing tends to subvert the entire genre; the audience can't whistle a rock groove. As Nicholas Tawa wrote of the similar limitations of musical theater in 1900, "Melody was at the center of every song, even the rag song—whatever its rhythmic attractions. . . . Audiences had to go away humming a tune; they could not hum rhythms, however catchy."[21]

Songs of Tin Pan Alley and the theater's belle époque have a structure of periodic phrases. The classic periodic form is four groups of eight-bar phrases—AABA—with B as the bridge or release (of course, some Tin Pan Alley songs deviate into Cs and Ds and other patterns, but AABA is preponderant). The syllogistic form of the basic $A^1A^2BA^3$ pattern is like a miniature version of classical music's sonata form: exposition (AA), development (B), and recapitulation (A). The bridge section also bears a structural resemblance to the Aristotelian concept of peripeteia, a reversal in the course of the drama before the final outcome. Thus the AABA structure not only spotlights catchy tunes but gives listeners a subliminal miniaturization of the architectural trajectory of great music, drama, and literature. But the latter effect depends on the extent to which the release contrasts with the "A" phrase. The song has to make listeners feel they've been on a journey from A^1 to A^3. With rock groove songs—even those nominally written in eight-bar phrases and thirty-two-bar choruses—the insistent, foreground nature of the groove attenuates listeners' awareness of the bridge's distinct borders from the rest of the song. The very motor continuity of the groove tends to take away the bridge's peripeteian effect and makes the return of the A phrase a less satisfying payoff to the listener. Thus, the rock groove dilutes some of the satisfying aesthetic symmetry of the AABA song form, flattening the three-dimensional feeling of story-reversal-denouement into one plane. To populate musical plays with songs that in their very structure work against the narrative function of song is another way of weakening the fourth wall.

The rock groove's motor continuity can paradoxically disrupt continuity in a theater song. Rock grooves tend to morph kaleidoscopically into different grooves throughout a song. (Burt Bacharach's songs are rhythmically vibrant because they frequently change their meters, not their grooves.) By fixing on a steady, undergirding dance beat, the golden-age songwriter anchored the listener both to the tune of the song and to the story of the lyric. Kaleidoscopically shifting grooves impose an attention overload on the theatergoer's ear, distracting from the message of melody and story and thus disrupting the fourth wall.

However, the opposite can occur, too. When rock grooves are used song after song to illustrate every variety of dramatic moment, or when a single groove is sustained for an entire song, the result is an aural monotony that works against drama and suspense. Theater scores with musical rhythms that shift with the mood, both within songs and from song to song, avert this monotony and heighten drama. In *110 in the Shade* (1963), with lyrics by Tom Jones and music by Harvey Schmidt, the underlying rhythms change within the same song as the drama, mood, or character changes. In "The Rain Song," there's a bluesy four, a fast four, a beat in one, a couple of cowboy country-and-western grooves, and so on; they all occur in the same song as Starbuck's mood changes. The same thing happens in Starbuck's song "Melisande." Lizzie's song "Raunchy" starts as a funky blues but Schmidt cleverly reinserts the galloping cowboy rhythm of the earlier song "Lizzie Is Comin' Home" to keep her in character. Thirty-five years later, Jason Robert Brown, one of the better young rock-idiom composer-lyricists, used rock grooves for most of the songs in *Parade* (1998), typically sticking to the initial pattern throughout the lyrics' shifts in mood and emphasis. Set in 1913–15, *Parade* earnestly interpolates a few actual march and hymn tunes of the 1800s, but, far more frequently than *110 in the Shade*, it relies on the clichés of contemporary rock/pop to evoke the colors of the time period of the show.

Parade also uses idioms like hot Dixieland rhythms that are neither from the 1910s nor from 1998, but then Meredith Willson inserted the anachronistic 1940s crooning ballad "Till There Was You" into his 1910-set *The Music Man*. The problem comes when a theater audience is made more aware of the contemporaneity of a show's pop idiom than of the dramatic demands and musical context of its book. Rock-era shows tend to do the former. As theater music, contemporary pop is self-reflective; it tends to see itself in the mirror no matter what style it's trying to depict dramatically. When Kurt Weill composed *Lost in the Stars* (1949), based on Alan Paton's novel of South African apartheid, *Cry the Beloved Country*, he made up his own South African musical idiom. He inserted only a hint of African-American rhythm and blues and jazz elements, and he used neither Zulu music nor Afrikaaner music nor the popular song clichés of his time. In spite of that, *Lost in the Stars*' music is abundantly rhythmic, melodious, and *specific.*

The Audience Doesn't Go Out Humming the Rhythm

There were two authentic musical revolutions in Broadway history, both originating in popular dance music. The circa 1913 foxtrot erupted on Tin Pan Alley, revolutionized songwriting, and created a template upon which the great songwriters of the Broadway canon forged compelling *Gesamtkunstwerke* that even Wagner might have approved. The circa 1954 rock groove revolutionized songwriting more globally than any other dance rhythm in previous history. Both the foxtrot and the rock groove were eventually incorporated by the Broadway musical. The former led to a golden age of inspiration. The foxtrot's strength as a theater song template was its separation of "top" and "bottom" rhythm, allowing the melody and lyric space to breathe, to dance, to dramatize. The rock groove fused the "top" and "bottom" into a single rhythm, fettering the melody, the lyric, and the drama to its rhythmic ball and chain. This is antitheatrical.

Today the rock groove is leading to the complete displacement of melody in musical theater. *Bring in 'Da Noise, Bring in 'Da Funk* (1996) was a show completely constructed on rhythm grooves. Its melodies, lyrics, and dialogue were secondary to the sounds and sights of its dance steps. The inevitable next step was the introduction of rap and hip-hop into musical theater. Rap music is a retreat to musicalized patter, a form once popular in vaudeville. But the language used in rap, while rhythmic, is altogether lacking in the poetic qualities of verbal density and metaphor that made the lyrics of W. S. Gilbert, Ira Gershwin, Cole Porter, Lorenz Hart, and the rest . . . *lyrics.* The rhyme of rap is not the rhyme of versification. Rather it is the verbal equivalent of the rock groove: an unflagging, unchanging ostinato. And where is the melody? Notes linguistics expert John McWhorter:

> A good two generations have grown up with a musical sensibility based on
> beat. . . . Whatever residual response one has to the melody and harmony, take
> away the beat and the cool voice and we lose interest. . . . The youngest generation
> of theater composers, having known nothing but an America where music talks,
> often write vamps (repetition) and burbling ostinatos (more repetition) in the left
> hand and place a melody on top . . . [not] mated to those particular harmonies. . . .
> Some . . . sense self-standing melodies as corny.[22]

164

It is entirely possible that new twenty-first-century oral forms like poetry slams could form the basis of viable musicals. The poetry at slams tends to be narrative and dramatic. If a way could be found to mate real melody with the rhythms of slam poetry—as the foxtrot mated melody with rhythm and story—it could be a path back from the wilderness.

But only if the rhythm does not continue to drive all else out of the picture. On June 8, 2003, a *New York Times* reporter, previewing the New York City Hip-Hop Theatre Festival, wrote, "Hip-hop theatre's fusion of verse and song makes it a kind of natural successor to the traditional musical."

Or is it the Broadway theater's version of what Don McLean wrote about in his 1972 song "American Pie": the day the music died?

ACT FOUR

The Loudspeakers Are Alive with The Sound of Music:
How Electronics Trumped the Artful Acoustics of Broadway

> In the early part of the century there were no
> "little" theatres; all of them, indeed, seemed very
> "big," yet the lightest whisper of a good actor
> (long before amplification!) was as audible in the
> remotest gallery, as his loudest tones. Perhaps it
> was that he knew how to act.
> — John Murray Anderson, 1954[1]

> We are in danger of producing a generation of
> composers, directors, sound designers and audi-
> ences who have never heard a live performance by
> real musicians.
> —John A. Leonard, British sound designer, 2001

The creative team of a musical is usually understood to consist of the composer, lyricist, book writer, director, and choreographer. Those are the principals who participate in any royalties the show generates. Yet theater posters
and display advertising clearly cite important additional collaborating artists:
the set designer, the lighting designer, the costume designer. Although the best
of these become familiar names to serious theatergoers, they are never viewed
as members of the primary creative team by the public, nor do they participate
in royalty income. Still, as underappreciated as a musical's scenic artists are,
they receive more respect and attention than two other players in the supporting hierarchy who arguably have been the most significant secret sharers of the
course of the Broadway musical: the arranger-orchestrator and the sound designer. (A third unheralded artist, the show's orchestra conductor, greatly
abetted the first of these two.)

In Broadway's first century (pre-1966), the score of a musical was created by the arranger and orchestrator as much as the book was created by a collaborating librettist. In Broadway's second era (post-1966), technology in the theater grew from a modest enhancement of the arrangements to the point where electronics took over not only the instrumentation but the entire sound environment of the show. In the golden age, the heard-but-unseen efforts of arrangers contributed as much as the tunes themselves to the elevation of Broadway musicals from a vaudevillian hodgepodge to an enlightened art. That's because arrangers were the real, secret composers, the ghostwriters of the Broadway musical; it was they who stitched one-fingered pianists' ditties into coherent theatrical form. In postlapsarian Broadway, sound design entered the arena as a benign reinforcement of natural acoustics only to become the sorcerer's apprentice, abused to the point where the natural balance of song, dialogue, staging, and underscoring was undone, and thus was lost much of the art of the musical itself.

The histories of arranging and sound design have also intertwined in the recording of Broadway shows. In the golden age, original-cast albums promoted the appreciation and practice of live theater values. They were recorded after the show opened, reflected onstage performance, and served as mementos with which the audience could reconstruct that onstage performance. In recent decades cast albums have frequently been recorded before theater production, forcing an alien pop music model on the sound of the musical, causing the audience to expect to hear a sound-designed re-creation of the album when they entered the theater, and thereby destroying the traditional live theater values that had distinguished golden-age Broadway musical productions.

Long before musicals ever required the services of a sound design team to balance the acoustics in the theater, the live sound of musicals was self-balancing thanks to the art and craft of the orchestrator, musical director, and actor-singers well trained in vocal projection. To understand how this evolution came about, let's retrace how the original, pre-electronic Broadway sound came to be, and explore the hidden history of how that untouted mastermind, the arranger, was often the primary composer of what the audience heard in the theater.

Scene One. *Orchestrators*

How One-Fingered Tune Pickers Were Turned into Composers of Musicals

> If I did not work out my own orchestrations, it
> would be as if a painter conceived the idea of a
> picture and then had someone else paint it.
> —Victor Herbert[2]

Nobody would call an artful doodler who hired a team of easel painters to re-produce his doodles in oil a painter. Yet that's exactly how most Broadway mu-sicals since the dawn of the golden age (circa 1927) have been "composed." This glaring anomaly about how a musical's score is manufactured goes virtually un-remarked by every historian of the musical, perhaps because it is considered po-litically incorrect to question our popular music gods. In no other art form is the creator of such a small percentage of the final material adjudged the presid-ing genius of it. Old master paintings are authenticated and attributed either to "the school of" when the principal artist had assistance, or to the artist himself. Not long after the novelist Jerzy Kosinski was found to have employed ghost-writers for the creation of *The Painted Bird* and his other fiction, he committed suicide. When Richard Rodgers was asked by the critic Winthrop Sargeant whether he wished he could arrange his own music instead of leaving the job to Russell Bennett, Rodgers proudly demurred. And Sargeant concurred in the wisdom, elegantly stating the case for the art of the popular song melodist:

> The ability to create successful tunes is a special talent, often lacking among the most learned and technically accomplished musicians and sometimes found, par-adoxically, among men of the most rudimentary musical knowledge. . . . "Some Enchanted Evening" is [no] less a work of art than a comparable "classical" tune. . . . Its very simplicity is a virtue at a time when melodic simplicity is shunned by nearly all highbrow composers. It contains the attributes of charm and mood that are the minimal requirements of all important music. It is, indeed, a work of art.[3]

One can heartily endorse Sargeant's view yet at the same time not be blind to this fact: *Victory at Sea,* a 1952 NBC television documentary broadcast in twenty-six half-hour episodes with virtually continuous orchestral underscor-ing, was billed as "music by Richard Rodgers" even though Rodgers wrote only about thirty minutes of music, mostly thirty-two-bar tunes; the rest of the ap-proximately eleven hours of music was composed by Russell Bennett, building on Rodgers's tunes. (Rodgers later recycled one of the tunes as "No Other Love Have I," the only song in his 1953 musical *Me and Juliet* to become a hit.)

The typical golden-era Broadway musical had a less drastic but still lopsided ratio between tunes actually composed by the "composer" and all the under-scoring, vocal reprises, and dance music that form the show's musical connec-tive tissue. "Few Broadway composers are responsible for any of their own or-chestrations. Most of them furnish only the song melodies, while the overtures, the incidental action accompaniments, the transition pieces, the ballet and vo-cal variations, the musical reinforcement and 'glue' of the show will be arranged by someone else," wrote Agnes de Mille, who was there in the trenches.[4] Most Broadway composers could be described with the adjective "primitive" as it is applied to painters. Even today, Henry Krieger (*Dreamgirls, Side Show*) cannot read or write music, William Finn (*Falsettos*) is challenged when writing ac-companiments, and so on.

This was not always true. Before about 1915, the operettas and musicals of other countries that were brought to Broadway, and many by Americans as well, were fully composed and orchestrated by trained composers. In England, not only was Sir Arthur Sullivan a full-fledged symphonic composer, but most of his less well remembered light opera colleagues (Julian Edwards, Lionel Monckton, Edward German, and Sidney Jones), several of whom came to the

United States to write musicals produced on Broadway from the 1890s to the 1910s, were also symphonically trained. Similarly, the French operetta tradition of Offenbach was carried on by his successors, such as the Belgian Ivan Caryll, who came to the United States to write Broadway musicals. The Viennese operetta composers Suppé, Johann Strauss Jr., Lehár, Oscar Straus, Imre Kálmán, Ludwig Engländer, and others, many of whose works played in Broadway theaters with great success before 1920, were all legitimately trained, as were the German-born Gustave Kerker and Gustav Luders, who also wrote musicals produced in the States before World War I. Almost all these "Broadway" composers (i.e., they were produced on Broadway) orchestrated and sometimes conducted their own scores.

Several American composers who wrote for Broadway before 1915 also were legitimately trained, and they composed and orchestrated every note of their own Broadway works. These included John Philip Sousa, Victor Herbert, and the American-born, European-trained Reginald De Koven. Herbert continued his forays into classical composition even while writing for Broadway and saw no contradiction: he famously asked of his Broadway scores, "Is it a crime to be popular?" De Koven, a musical snob, decried what he called the "one-fingered composers" of "ragtime, coon songs, and Tenderloin ditties." He was referring to musically unlettered upstarts such as George M. Cohan and Irving Berlin, who in the 1910s were beginning to poach on his territory even though each could play in only one key on the piano (F-sharp—whereas Noël Coward could play only in E-flat). "I could play four chords on the piano in F sharp," Cohan wrote in his 1924 autobiography. "I'd vamp these four chords and hum tunes to myself for hours at a time. I never got any further than the four F sharp chords, by the way. I've used them ever since."

Even as long ago as 1874, the year of the first American musical considered wholly composed by one man—*Evangeline*—the show's composer, Edward Rice, "dictated it to a secretary with suggestions about its instrumental effects."[5] Charles K. Harris (1867–1930), the "composer" of the biggest song hit from a nineteenth-century musical—"After the Ball" from *A Trip to Chinatown* (1891), a song quoted by Kern in *Show Boat*—spoke for the typical Broadway songwriter when he wrote in his 1926 memoirs: "The reader will naturally wonder how it was possible for me to write music to a song when even to this day I cannot distinguish one note from another. The answer is simple. As soon as a melody occurred to me, I hummed it. Then I would procure the services of a trained musician for the purpose, hum or whistle the melody for him and have him take it down on paper with notes. He would then arrange it for the piano."[6] Sigmund Spaeth (known on 1930s radio as the "tune detective") later wrote that the songwriters of early Tin Pan Alley were

> often unable to play on any instrument and entirely lacking in the ordinary technique of composition. Stephen Foster was an authentic genius, but worked mostly by ear, barely able to write out the most conventional arrangements for his inspired melodies. . . . Paul Dresser . . . picked out his tunes at a portable organ. . . . Charles K. Harris could strum a banjo and play the piano on the black keys. (He was the first to use a movable keyboard to transpose his tunes into the right keys for singing, as was done later by Irving Berlin.) Harry von Tilzer was probably the best-grounded of such natural composers, with definite skills at the piano and a good singing voice; but he knew nothing about orchestration or the larger forms of music.[7]

The Boston-born Henry Woolson Morse, who composed DeWolf Hopper's Broadway musicals in the 1890s, was deemed solid enough a composer by W. S. Gilbert that Gilbert invited Morse to collaborate with him and replace Sullivan, even though Morse composed only at the harmonium. David Braham, the composer of the Harrigan and Hart shows of the 1880s, worked out his tunes on the violin but had someone else arrange them.

Most of the arrangers and orchestrators of the pre-1910 period are lost to history. But Sousa was one such early Broadway arranger-orchestrator, and another was the Wisconsin-born classical composer Edgar Stillman Kelley (1857–1944). Kelley orchestrated Edward Rice's post-*Evangeline* work, commenting, in a pre-echo of Winthrop Sargeant, "Mr. Rice is really a very musical man—although he does not read music, but his melodic and harmonic instinct is naturally far superior to those of many trained professionals."[8] For the New York stage Kelley himself composed incidental music for productions of *Macbeth* (1887) and *Ben-Hur* (1899) as well as an early version of a "poperetta," *Puritania* (1893). But apart from Sousa, De Koven, Herbert, and Kelley, until the early 1900s songs were so freely and cavalierly interpolated from show to show that it is hard to refer to the musicals (as opposed to the operettas) of that era as "composed" at all. The performed score of a given musical could change substantially within its run, sometimes even nightly.

It is important to remember that Offenbach, Franz Lehár, Arthur Sullivan, and Victor Herbert *wrote all the tunes,* not just the dance music, overtures, and orchestrations. What happened between Victor Herbert and Irving Berlin to cause the almost complete blackout of the one-man–composer/orchestrator musical? After about 1910, when American musical comedy started to introduce singers who had vaudeville-style rather than operettic voices, and the growing dramatic integration of book musicals made acting and dancing a factor equal to singing in casting decisions, keys could no longer be set in advance as they had been for operettas. A given song had to be transposed to accommodate the range of whatever actor was cast, and songs sometimes changed well into rehearsals, meaning that entire orchestrations had to be rewritten in a new key overnight.* In operetta the librettist writes the libretto and the composer musicalizes it, complete with all vocal arrangements and orchestrations but with the expectation that directors and choreographers will adapt to the already scored music, not the other way around. As book musicals evolved in the decades after 1910, scenery changes and dances were allowed to develop freely during rehearsals and only then could it be determined what amount and kind of music would be needed where. The medium's growing tendency to favor authorial contributions by all the creative collaborators forced constant revisions of the music, whether revised vocal arrangements, dance arrangements, new songs, or other producer- or director-ordered alterations. The only Broadway composer after Victor Herbert who stubbornly rewrote his own orchestrations single-handedly during rehearsal changes was Kurt Weill, a human computer who reorchestrated in ink "on the back of a Steinway, standing up" in the theater or in his hotel room.[9] Undoubtedly Herbert had been called upon to rewrite and reorchestrate music much less than Weill was by the 1940s. Weill's librettist on *Street Scene* (1947), Elmer Rice, noted that "every time a change was made, he had to alter the score substantially. I was afraid he would crack up."[10] Six weeks after the opening of *Street Scene,* Weill wrote to a former colleague in Europe, "I was so totally exhausted after the premiere of *Street Scene* that for weeks I couldn't gather enough strength even to write a letter."[11] A smoker with high blood pressure, Weill succumbed to a heart attack at age fifty.

So the evolving modern Broadway musical of constant rehearsal revision, collaborative changes, and time limitations mandated a division of musical labor: composing by team. Rehearsal time limitations are also the main reason those Broadway composers able to arrange and orchestrate their own scores—Leonard Bernstein, Vernon Duke, Marc Blitzstein, Duke Ellington, Meredith

---

*When musicals are in production, sometimes just the two or three measures of the rideout of a single song need to be transposed because of a singer-dancer's inability to hit the original notes as written. Such mini-transpositions required on-site during rehearsal can multiply exponentially, forcing the use of a team of arrangers and copyists.

Willson—have usually farmed at least some of it out to others. Gershwin did not undertake the complete orchestrations of his Broadway shows until *Porgy and Bess* (1935), the orchestration for which took him seven months (the average book musical, which is shorter than *Porgy and Bess,* usually has to be orchestrated within six weeks or less). After 1940 only Weill, Morton Gould (*Billion Dollar Baby,* 1945; *Arms and the Girl,* 1950), and the bandleader Raymond Scott (*Lute Song,* 1946) did most or all of the incidental arranging and orchestration themselves.

Before the well-integrated musical took hold, theater arrangements and orchestrations were strictly boilerplate. The orchestrator often wasn't in the theater or even in the same town; it was a mail-order business. "In the old days orchestrators didn't have to know what the show was all about," recalled Russell Bennett in 1951. "They simply translated the melody notes on the composer's lead sheet into straight instrumentation for the pit orchestra. A producer could send a bundle of lead sheets to a fellow in Chicago or St. Louis and get the arrangements back by mail the same week."[12] Thus, the orchestrations for team-composed musicals in the pre-1920 decades of Broadway had no dramatic or stylistic variety and almost no connection with what was going on onstage.

Perhaps the first Broadway orchestrator to connect the orchestration with the show's plot and its performers, and to do so with a sense of humor and style, was Frank Saddler (1864–1921), an American who trained musically in Europe. Saddler started as an arranger for the huge orchestra at the Hippodrome in the 1900s, but in the 1910s he became orchestrator of choice for Jerome Kern's shows at the Princess Theatre. At the Princess, Saddler had to write for a small ensemble, for which the broad brushstrokes of Hippodrome orchestration wouldn't work: every detail had to tell. Said Russell Bennett of Saddler's Princess Theatre charts, "He'd come up with a low woodwind that was just right for some little looker with a little voice."[13] Saddler was an unsung contributor to the much heralded integrated quality of the Kern-Wodehouse-Bolton Princess Theatre musicals. In 1929 the *New York Times* published a letter by a young orchestrator who had trained with Saddler, Maurice De Packh (1896–1960). De Packh "felt that the intrusion of jazz-band instrumentation and scoring into the theater pit had caused his mentor's 'life work [to] crumble to ruin'" and that the Saddlerian theater orchestra had become a "friendless orphan."[14] (Ironically, with the arrival of talking pictures, De Packh went on to become one of Hollywood's busiest orchestrators.)

When Saddler died suddenly in 1921, another young man named Russell Bennett took over as Kern's arranger. Some people feel that there wouldn't have been a Beatles without their producer and arranger, George Martin, a trained composer. Others feel that way about Russell Bennett and Broadway musicals.

Robert Russell Bennett: Transforming Musical Hamburgers into Haute Cuisine

> If you have some tune jingling in your head, you have only to go to Harms and . . . hum it or play it with one finger to Russell Bennett and it will presently emerge fully arranged or scored, suavely and colorfully, for a modern orchestra. It is as if an aspiring writer who could neither read nor write were to go into Scribner's, whisper an idea to the editor, and get it written for him in novel form by John Galsworthy.
>
> —S. N. Behrman, 1932

> A program credit, instead of stating "Orchestrations by Russell Bennett," should read: "You can thank Mr. Bennett for the music sounding nice. All he had to start with was a one-finger piano outline of eight song choruses."
>
> —John Chapman, 1937

Robert Russell Bennett* (1894–1981) was not famous, but he was arguably one of the most gifted musicians in American history. The dean of Broadway orchestration, the man who orchestrated some 300 shows from the 1920s to the 1970s, he was also a serious composer of more than 175 legitimate works: symphonies, orchestral suites and tone poems, operas, band pieces, incidental music, and choral works. They were widely performed during his lifetime and are beginning to enjoy a renaissance today. The Bennett scholar George J. Ferencz believes that Bennett as composer and arranger may have produced more pages of musical manuscript in his lifetime than *any* other composer past or present, including Bach, Mozart, Wagner, et al. His composing and orchestrating the overture to *The King and I* in the twenty-five hours before the opening night curtain in New Haven previews—in ink, no less—as a feat of speed certainly bears comparison with Mozart's composing and orchestrating the overture to

---

*His name was Russell Bennett but a numerologist suggested he would have better professional success with his full birth name, Robert Russell Bennett. Bennett openly admitted to consulting astrologers, numerologists, and other occultists.

Don Giovanni in about the same amount of time. Enhancing the sometimes one-fingered, sometimes two-handed ditties of the great songwriters—Berlin, Gershwin, Kern, Porter, Rodgers, Youmans, et al.—was not just a day job but a strenuous, round-the-clock challenge requiring Olympic *sitzfleisch.*

Bennett grew up in Kansas City in a musical family—his father was a professional trumpeter and violinist, his mother a pianist—and by his teenage years he was already able to play violin, piano, organ, and most of the brass and woodwind instruments, and was making arrangements for community groups. He survived a childhood bout of polio and grew quite tall; as an adult he had indefatigable stamina and was able not only to work back-to-back sixteen-hour days bent over his desk orchestrating but also to play vigorous tennis and handball. Bennett must have had an inborn genius for musical instruments and their sounds, although as a teenager he diligently studied harmony and counterpoint with Carl Busch, a Danish composer who had become conductor of the Kansas City Philharmonic in the 1910s. Coming to New York in 1916, Bennett began as a music copyist for G. Schirmer music publishers and soon had a private practice "taking down" the melodies of untutored songwriters and writing out accompaniments for lead sheets. In 1917 he played piano in a small incidental music orchestra for *Peter Ibbetson,* a Broadway play mounted for the Barrymore brothers. At one point in the script Lionel Barrymore, a decent amateur pianist, had to play the piano in his role as Ibbetson. Barrymore artfully faked Liszt's Hungarian Rhapsody No. 14 while the twenty-three-year-old Bennett played the real thing behind a curtain.

In 1919 Bennett made a stock arrangement for the Harms Company of his first Broadway song, the then-unknown Cole Porter's "An Old-Fashioned Garden" from the Raymond Hitchcock revue *Hitchy-Koo* of that year. Bennett also composed incidental music for plays in the late 1910s and early 1920s, including the legendary John Barrymore *Hamlet* of 1922. His first orchestration assignment for a complete show was the 1922 *Daffy Dill,* with music by Herbert Stothart and lyrics by the young Oscar Hammerstein II.

By the mid-1920s Bennett had become the favorite orchestrator of the Broadway crowd and was flush enough to take his wife and daughter with him to Paris in 1926 on a sabbatical to pursue his own serious composing. He studied there informally with Nadia Boulanger, the guru of choice for expatriate American composers. But Bennett from the beginning had been a natural musician, endowed with a brilliant ear, so fully formed that Boulanger wrote the Guggenheim Foundation that she had little to teach him: "Robert Russell Bennett is a born and an accomplished musician. . . . His form, his writing, his orchestration are absolutely achieved—and I have always wondered why he asked me advices [*sic*]—He is completely able to realize what ever he has planned."[15] (Even so accomplished a composer as Sergei Rachmaninov later sought Bennett's advice on how to write for the saxophone for his 1940 Symphonic Dances.) Bennett was awarded two Guggenheim fellowships but soon enough returned to America and the Great White Way.

On Broadway Bennett was both an arranger and an orchestrator, and it is important to clarify the difference. An orchestrator takes a completed arrangement—fully notated melodies, countermelodies, accompanimental pattern, rhythm, harmony, and so on—and sets it for a designated instrumentation. An arranger begins earlier in the process, introducing his own tunes, riffs, licks, connective material, and harmonies to color and fill out the so-called lead sheet—the melody of the song with a few skeletal harmonies. An arranger is really a ghost composer, a kind of musical ventriloquist for the songwriter who can only whistle his or her tunes. A skilled arranger can be like a makeover artist, extracting musical silk purses from sow's ears. Bennett's autobiography reads like a polite exposé of the musical illiteracy of Broadway's post-1920 composers. While it is unsurprising that songwriting actors such as Nöel Coward and George M. Cohan would have required a musical amanuensis to transcribe their tunes, it is a little startling to read, "I took down some of Jerry's [Kern's] songs from his performance at the piano" and "I sat with Kern and took down the tunes before making the *Show Boat* rehearsal copies for voice and piano."

It appears that Bennett may well have been *the* ghost composer of Broadway's golden age, having been largely responsible for the harmonies, accompaniments, and God-knows-what-else of many of the scores of the canonical tunesmiths. It is not overreaching to speculate that the very tunes as the public knows them were in part composed by Bennett or other arrangers: for instance, the responsorial orchestral "boom boom boom" that occurs after the initial sung phrase of "Shall We Dance?" in *The King and I* is Bennett, not Rodgers. Broadway arranging, Bennett wrote, meant being "a writer of whatever wasn't already written in their music." The only composer he singled out for consistently writing his own fully voiced chords was George Gershwin. (According to both Bennett and Hans Spialek, Vincent Youmans, composer of "Tea for Two," had the keenest natural ear after Gershwin.) The typical tunesmith "couldn't write two bars to save his soul," wrote Bennett. "He called in a music arranger and sang, whistled, or one-fingered it on the piano and the arranger took it from there. The typical story is that it caught on and made a hit. The arranger got paid by the page—say, a total of fifty dollars, and the composer made a pile—something in five figures." Then, once the arrangement was made, "the vast majority of Broadway's tune-writers didn't know their ankles from their uncles when it came to the orchestrations and that's how we all got to assume a certain importance."[16] The importance Bennett assumed amounted to a fee of about $5,000 per show by 1951, equivalent to about $35,000 in 2004 dollars.

Perhaps mindful of not biting the hand that fed him, Bennett late in life was respectful enough to credit the great tunesmiths with brilliant instincts for harmony:

> Irving Berlin, working with the arranger, would sometimes stop at a chord and say, "is that the right harmony?" We would say, "It's probably not the one you want, how about this?" We would strike a chord and he would say, "That's it!" Which means that his inner ear was way ahead of his fingers on the black keys of the piano. The right harmony, as he called it, was a part of the original inspiration, whether he could play it for you or not.[17]

At other times, he calls a spade a spade. Here's Bennett on the origins of one of the greatest of all theater songs, Jerome Kern's "Ol' Man River":

> . . . when he handed me his sketch it had no name and no lyric. It was thirty-two not wholly convincing measures that sounded to me like they wanted to be wanted. In the first place it starts with two harmonically powerful and self-reliant bars and then comes to a mud puddle and doesn't know where to put its feet for the next two. Perhaps that isn't important, but to a musical snob it is. . . . Anyhow the Muse of Music never spat at either Jerry or me for not finding the chords that should have been there. I found some rather nice fills for the ends of phrases and didn't worry about it until a few days later when I looked at it with Oscar Hammerstein's words written in. I didn't worry about it then either—just said to Jerry, "Gee, that's a great song!" Kern said, "You didn't say that when I gave it to you." He knew as well as I did that it wasn't a song at all until Oscar came in with the words.[18]

In 1974 Bennett told a reporter for the *Pittsburgh Post-Gazette,* "When I was working on Jerome Kern's *Show Boat* his publisher said to him one day, 'Jerry, this is the finest thing you ever wrote,' and he replied, 'Well, I just wish Russell Bennett thought so.'" Yip Harburg once told Jonathan Schwartz in a radio interview, "Jerome Kern was not a very good player. In fact, I had to listen to the tune many times before I could get it. He was always mechanically figuring out the tune." Bennett, though outwardly courtly and tactful, privately was unimpressed by the musical attainments of those whose lead sheets and whistled tunes he turned by some alchemy into logically harmonized and sequenced music for twenty-five-piece orchestras. He rebuffed writers' attempts to induce him to utter starry-eyed rhapsodies on Kern, Porter, or Rodgers, instead writing, with a certain ring of truth, "Tune-writers are fundamentally a bit awed by their music arrangers." In fifty years Bennett never did lose his preference for classical music, which he called his "musical snobbery":

> I remember saying to Nadia Boulanger . . . that "Tea for Two" would always sound a little cheap to me. . . . "Tea for Two," along with about all the two-hundred-and-fifty-odd theatre scores I've sat with, still sounds a little cheap to me. . . . the truth of the matter is, twenty-seven bars of Beethoven's opus 84 is worth the whole output of musical comedy since I *started* working on it.[19]

Bennett and Company: Ghostboosters of Broadway Tunes

Bennett wasn't the only midwife to the birth of Broadway songs. Albert Szirmai (1880–1967) first came to the United States in 1921 after a career as one of the most successful composers of operetta in Hungary, but he was unable to re-create his European eminence here. Only two Broadway musicals had music by Szirmai: a 1913 show entitled *The Girl on the Film,* and a 1930 flop, *Ripples,* which he cocomposed with Oscar Levant. His biggest hit, the 1925 *Princess Charming,* played London's West End but didn't make it to New York. Late in life Szirmai returned to composing, writing two operettas that were produced in his beloved native Budapest; one of his earlier Hungarian musicals was revived there as recently as 1990.

Although Szirmai's operettas had failed to travel to the New World, he himself became almost the incarnation of a comic opera character. He anglicized his name, added an honorific "Dr.," and as "Dr. Albert Sirmay" became, in the orchestrator Hans Spialek's words, Cole Porter's "errand boy deluxe." Szirmai "worked very closely with Cole and saw him every day in the course of editing his music," according to Bennett. Porter's biographer William McBrien writes that "Sirmay faithfully took down the melodies as Cole dictated them. . . . though the melodies came from Porter, it was Dr. Sirmay, some say, who supplied the harmonics [sic]. His chordal ideas were often superior to Porter's. Sirmay did the voicing of the chords, not changing a note of the composer."[20] Szirmai, first at Harms and then at its successor, Chappell, became the chief editor for publication not only of Porter's music but also of that of Kern, Rodgers, Gershwin, and other canonical Broadway songwriters, and it may well be that he enhanced some of their songs, too.

Bennett wrote that Porter "called on one or two or three other men to work with him at the piano to prepare his voice-and-piano copies as the songs first went on paper. . . . His not writing out every detail of the harmony himself surprised me. . . . Cole at an orchestra reading of a new show would sit in the back of the empty theater with his principal music editor, Dr. Albert Sirmay, and every time he wanted to make a little change Dr. Sirmay . . . would have to come running down the aisle to tell the conductor to tell the oboe player to accent the F sharp a little more. That went on all day."[21]

Some Broadway composers found other modes of assisted composing. According to Alan Jay Lerner, Sigmund Romberg

> had assembled over the years a library of all the great operas, operettas, lieders and orchestral works that had ever been written. He read them all carefully and made notes next to hundreds and hundreds of orchestral and vocal parts. Perhaps it would only be four bars, but next to it he would write "good baritone solo," or "soprano." When the time came to sit down to write a score, if he were about to write a baritone solo, he would check his files for "good baritone solo," etcetera. Perhaps he would not use it verbatim, but it would give him a start.[22]

From the beginning of his long career, Irving Berlin employed a series of musical dictation takers, principally including Clifford Hess, Arthur Johnston, and, from 1927 to Berlin's death in 1989, Helmy Kresa (1904–91), a German-born pilot, photographer, and songwriter who is also said to have been an arranger for Porter, Johnny Mercer, Harold Arlen, Burton Lane, Harry Warren, and Harry Ruby. When Will Irwin, an all-around musician and sometime lyricist who had worked for the Gershwins as a pianist, was brought into Berlin's studio during rehearsals for the revue *As Thousands Cheer* in 1933, he "had been accustomed to George Gershwin's able, pulsing style of pianism, but when Berlin sat down to play, the result defied description—eerie, disjointed meanderings across the keyboard." Irwin said, "Mr. Berlin, why don't we be content with this: you sing it for me, and I'll write it down."[23] (The multitalented Irwin later coauthored the libretto of *Lute Song* [1946] and conducted *The King and I*.)

Helmy Kresa sometimes took dictation from Berlin's singing voice over the telephone (until Kresa lost his hearing late in life).[24] Berlin's fabled trick piano was

> a Weser Brothers model that he had acquired, secondhand, for a hundred dollars. . . .
> On the right-hand side, at the treble end of the keyboard, was a small wheel, not

unlike a miniature version of that used to steer an automobile. By turning it, Berlin could shift the keyboard and, still using only the F-sharp black keys, play the melody in other keys. This type of piano was widely used by unskilled pianists, called "fakers," in Tin Pan Alley, vaudeville, and cabaret. Perhaps cued by the wheel, Berlin referred to this contraption as his Buick. A later Buick was equipped with a less obtrusive shift, a crank under the keyboard.[25]

George M. Cohan once sent Nöel Coward a transposing piano just like Berlin's.[26]

Dictation takers and orchestrators are only a few of the personnel in Broadway team composing. There are also vocal arrangers like Hugh Martin, who set "Sing for Your Supper" as a vocal trio in *The Boys from Syracuse* when Rodgers wanted to but didn't know how. Who is primarily responsible for the "Fugue for Tinhorns" (actually a circle canon, or round) in *Guys and Dolls* and the comic ensemble writing in "Abbondanza" in *The Most Happy Fella:* the shows' composer, Frank Loesser, or the shows' vocal arranger, Herbert Greene? Did Irving Berlin or did Helmy Kresa write the contrapuntal dual vocal lines for "You're Just in Love" from *Call Me Madam* (when the first person ever to hear them, cast member Russell Nype, came into Berlin's studio, he found Kresa standing there with Berlin)? While Stephen Flaherty (*Once on This Island, Ragtime*) is clearly a skilled vocal arranger, Stephen Sondheim's shows, whose music is often distinguished by its elaborate vocal part writing, have not credited a vocal arranger since he began working with the orchestrator Jonathan Tunick. By his own admission, Sondheim writes his own choral parts but has the conductor Paul Gemignani tweak them. Sondheim notates very complete piano scores, but his orchestrator (usually Tunick) takes it from there. Of course, a ghost composer can be a true alter ego, a secret sharer, as the arranger Billy Strayhorn was for Duke Ellington by Ellington's own admission. Nobody is at all suggesting that Tunick has written any Sondheim tunes, but much of the Sondheim sound could rightly be ascribed to him.

Another trade secret is that the person given the program credit for a show's orchestrations almost never is responsible for all of them. This has been true since before Robert Russell Bennett's time and it is still true today. Thus, although Bennett's name appeared as the lone orchestrator on the playbill and posters for *The King and I* (1951), Hans Spialek, the orchestrator of *On Your Toes* and *Babes in Arms* in the 1930s, actually orchestrated some of *The King and I. Carousel* (1945), nominally credited to the orchestrator Don Walker, was also partly orchestrated by Spialek ("When the Children Are Asleep"), Stephen Jones (1880–1967), and Bennett himself. A golden-age show credited to Bennett was often partly the work of Spialek (1894–1983), Don Walker (1907–89), Philip J. Lang (1911–86), Ted Royal (1904?–76), and others (sometimes Walker, Lang, or Royal had head billing and Bennett was uncredited). Even in today's era of computerized scores, time is so limited in rehearsal that the orchestrator named on the program will farm out some of the work to his colleagues.

As more artistic choreography became an integral dramatic part of the musical in the late 1930s and early 1940s, yet another musician was added to the team roster: the dance arranger (sometimes called a continuity composer when the dance arranger's task included underscoring dialogue). The dance arranger was no less a ghost composer of the show than the arranger/orchestrator, as demonstrated by an anecdote from *South Pacific* (1949). Joshua Logan, the show's director, felt that the song Rodgers had supplied for a climactic musical moment between Nellie Forbush (Mary Martin) and Emile LeBecque (Ezio Pinza) wasn't working in rehearsal. Finally, as Logan recalled, the show's dance arranger, Trude Rittmann, devised a solution:

> the two of them began singing Dick Rodgers' insistent, marvelous tune, "Twin Soliloquies" ["Wonder How It Feels"]—each using the same melody, but at a distance apart, with Oscar's words of tentative, doubting love. This was the moment when for me the show became great. But the song stopped too quickly; the music had to continue to strengthen the passionate, almost sexual, feeling. Trude provided the thrilling continuation later.[27]

Rittmann's solution, which can be heard on the original cast album and is in the published vocal score, was to create a surging orchestral reprise of Rodgers's tune in the manner of Wagner's "Liebestod" from *Tristan und Isolde,* with the two actors mutely yearning. It was an ingenious coup de théâtre. Two years later Rittmann composed sixteen minutes of ballet music for "The Small House of Uncle Thomas" for *The King and I,* not basing it on any Rodgers tune. It was many years before the Rodgers and Hammerstein organization allowed her to take public credit for that number. When Leonard Bernstein ran out of time finishing the score for the Jean Arthur–Boris Karloff version of *Peter Pan* in 1950, he personally called Rittman to ask her to take over not only the dance music but the composition of the songs. She has never received credit for this. But that's not untypical in the world of Broadway ghost composing. Writes Frank Loesser's daughter:

> My father would give the conductor a melodic line and perhaps some incomplete counterlines. The conductor would work out a piano arrangement, which my fa-

ther would edit verbally. Then it was orchestrated. . . . Every musical assistant who worked for Frank Loesser was required to sign an agreement specifying that—for a fee of one dollar—anything they wrote, fixed, or changed became Frank Loesser's (or his heirs' or assignees') property.[28]

Some enterprising scholar will someday measure the exact yardage of Trude Rittmann's (and Genevieve Pitot's, John Morris's, and other continuity music composers') contribution to the final performance versions of Broadway classics. Rittmann had studied composition for four years in Germany with Philipp Jarnach, a pupil of Busoni. Establishing herself in America as Agnes de Mille's piano accompanist of choice, she went on to become Broadway's leading dance arranger for thirty years, working with most of the significant Broadway composers. There were only three she found musically well educated: Kurt Weill, Marc Blitzstein, and Frederick "Fritz" Loewe (an unfathomably underappreciated Broadway composer). "Loewe studied at the Hochschule in Berlin, and he improvised brilliantly," Rittmann recalled. "He did the choral arrangements for *Brigadoon*. But with dancing he didn't know what to do. With Fritz in *Brigadoon*, he didn't like someone fooling around with his stuff. Weill definitely didn't want anyone fooling with his stuff, nor Blitzstein." When asked whether Rodgers, her frequent boss, wrote out the harmony for his songs, Rittmann replied, "Yes, but in a sort of primitive way. It was not very elaborate. He was not at all well educated in music. Rodgers was difficult. We finally hit it off, but he was a tough man and did lots of things I didn't agree to."[29] (Rodgers's rehearsal pianist Margot Hopkins [1904–67], a brilliant improviser on his tunes according to Rittman, also may have had a hand in shaping his material.) Rodgers once quipped, "It's supposed to be Rodgers and Hammerstein, not Rodgers and Rittman!" In 1970, during rehearsals of *Two by Two,* after twenty-five years of working together with Rittmann on his shows (longer than his partnership with Hammerstein), Rodgers told her that he was—sometimes—"afraid of her."[30]

Do orchestrations ever really make the difference? Yes. The notion that great tunes of great songwriters invariably sell themselves is simply not so. Case in point: Irving Berlin's greatest musical, *Annie Get Your Gun* (1946). The show's producers, Rodgers and Hammerstein, originally commissioned Philip J. Lang to prepare the orchestrations. But in the New Haven tryouts the orchestrations fizzled; the charm of the tunes did not come through. (It was only Lang's second Broadway assignment; he went on to become perhaps the leading post-Bennett orchestrator for Broadway in the ensuing thirty years.) The musical director Jay Blackton, colibrettist Dorothy Fields, and Berlin were despondent. Rodgers put out an SOS to Bennett, and "Bennett's new orchestration rescued Berlin's score from disaster."[31] Patricia Morison, the original Lilli Vanessi in *Kiss Me, Kate* (1948), told interviewers, "When we were rehearsing *Kate*, we rehearsed with piano, of course. . . . It was disjointed, and we didn't think we had a hit. . . . it wasn't until we heard Robert Russell Bennett's orchestrations [in Philadelphia tryouts] that all of a sudden we got really excited."[32]

Before Bennett, reprises of songs in musical comedy were uncommon, and transitional underscoring often consisted of musical material extraneous to the show's songs. Vocal scores from the 1900–1920 period show that musical numbers then were more like isolated set pieces; the music for scene changes used stock patterns rather than tune reprises, and frequently there were no overtures. (Overtures are usually the last piece to be written by the orchestrator. One notable exception: Sid Ramin and Robert Ginzler's overture of Jule Styne's music to *Gypsy* [1959], written first.) The first theater composer to understand that reprising songs not only would reinforce the tunes in the audience's ears but also could dramatically integrate the musical was Jerome Kern. The Kern-Bennett shows were the first to consistently weave the show's main melodies within the underscoring, laying the groundwork for the later, even more integrated musical. Alhough Bennett took dictation from Kern's piano improvisations, he did say that Kern "was rather better schooled than the majority and was very sensitive to harmony and orchestral color. . . . he was actually the composer of a great deal of the background music behind scenes, and some of the counter-melodies."[33]

Kern may have intended his reprises as Wagnerian leitmotifs, and *Show Boat*'s score incorporates both reprises that bind the sprawling story and underscoring that brings in extraneous source music. But in his 1930s shows Kern began to over-reprise the melodies, overtaxing their capacity to tell the story and allowing them to become tediously repetitive song plugs. Undoubtedly this is one of the reasons his 1930s musicals have not stood the test of time as well as *Show Boat.* Other composers Bennett later worked with had the judgment and taste not to push Bennett as Kern did into endless reprises of, for example, "All the Things You Are" in *Very Warm for May* (1939).

"Over the years," Bennett commented in 1951, "the musical numbers have been woven more and more tightly into the telling of the story. Today, the orchestrator has got to live in the theatre not only during rehearsals but while the show's in Philly or Boston or wherever it's trying out. Every change in production means a change in orchestration."[34] The result of this approach was that

Bennett and the other orchestrators who emulated him raised the tune to a level of dramatic power it would not have otherwise possessed. Albert Szirmai, who had helped Porter compose *Kiss Me, Kate*'s piano score, marveled at Bennett's transformation of the score to the orchestra in the theater, "You listen to 'Too Darn Hot.' Zingo! It gets so hot, so jazzy, so American that the audience is overcome by the fieriness of the orchestra. Next, maybe, 'Were Thine That Special Face.' Ah! You feel Russell building the melody, then setting it off with the perfect counter-melody. It has the charm of de Falla, Debussy. You smile. You lean back. All of a sudden—what is this?—you think you face a madrigal by Mozart: 'I Am Ashamed That Women Are So Simple.'"[35]

Just as the dancing in musicals became more integrated, more at one with the through-line, so did the orchestration. In "I'm Always True to You in My Fashion" in *Kiss Me, Kate,* Bennett comically echoes the coy sex-kittenish lyrics like "From Milwaukee, Mister Fritz / Often moves me to the Ritz" with sassy waawaa-mute trumpet rips. The orchestral intro to *Guys and Dolls'* opening number, "Fugue for Tinhorns," is a familiar trumpet racetrack call, immediately characterizing the tinhorns before they sing a note. The characters literally speak through the orchestra in both *Kate* and *Guys and Dolls* (orchestrated by Ted Royal). Hans Spialek, who worked on many of the Rodgers and Hart shows, inserted frequent musical puns in his orchestration of the shows' ballet music, including quotes from Debussy's *Prelude to the Afternoon of a Faun* in *The Boys from Syracuse* "Twins" ballet and from Rimsky-Korsakov's *Scheherezade* in the "Imagine" ballet from *Babes in Arms.* Humorous classical music quotation was not uncommon in big-band arrangements of that time; they run all through the Paul Whiteman band recordings. The songwriters did it, too; the middle section of Harry Warren's "Lullaby of Broadway" quotes the middle section of Brahms's Hungarian Dance No. 5. Today there is no common fund of musical vocabulary on which to make musical puns. What musical pun can orchestrators insert today that audiences would recognize? A television sitcom theme? A video game jingle?

Bennett's credo of being present in the theater also speaks to the orchestrator's then de facto function as acoustician; the orchestrations had to be scored so that the music and lyrics could be heard in the theater without artificial enhancement:

> While Bennett is sitting out front at rehearsals, he jots down, in a personal shorthand, a description of each routine, noting the timbre of a singer's voice during a certain passage of a song, the way a dancer moves his feet at a critical point in his

dance, and other idiosyncrasies that demand custom tailoring. . . . [For Hammer-stein's lyrics in *Carmen Jones* (1943)] Bennett subdued his orchestrations as he had never done before in order to make every phrase stand out boldly above the accompaniment. He felt confident that nothing could go wrong, as he was personally conducting the pit orchestra at the Philadelphia tryout. "Opening night was a catastrophe," Bennett recalls sheepishly. "You heard Oscar's lyrics, all right, but you couldn't hear the orchestra at all. Fill a theatre with people and you set up new vibrations that completely change the acoustics. It's a strange business. Human bodies seem to sop up an orchestra, but the voice on the stage gains much more projection. The crowd is part of the orchestration, and I shouldn't have forgotten it."[36]

The theater orchestrator's collaborator in regulating the balance of acoustics was the conductor of the pit orchestra, called the musical director. Lehman Engel, perhaps Broadway's busiest musical director from the 1930s to the 1960s and the only one to write extensively about it, said that he would set up

times when the arranger may come in to hear and notate certain completely rehearsed numbers so that the arranger can set their proper keys and layouts and note any special performance difficulties that may affect his orchestration. An example of this would be a singer's having to perform a song while running around a great deal and becoming short of breath. In such a case, the orchestrator has to lighten the supporting instrumentation. . . . Sometimes a phrase is played an octave lower or higher in order to minimize the amount of conflict with a singer. Often a melody doubled (for example, the bassoon may be doubled by the trombone) is thinned out so that only one of the instruments plays.[37]

Before sound design, the audience seated in the front rows of the orchestra and balcony sometimes complained that the orchestra was too loud. The reason for this often was that the song might have been orchestrated so that the singing was obscured, because "choreographers complained that the percussion, which generally defines the rhythm, [was] too quiet for dancers" and the orchestrator reorchestrated accordingly. In pre–sound design days, the orchestra pit was hard to hear from the rear of the orchestra seating section in some Broadway houses.

It was a given in the pre-1940 theater that it was the orchestrator's job to make sure the singers could be heard. Vivienne Segal played the leading role in both the 1940 and 1952 productions of *Pal Joey*. Spialek's orchestration of "Bewitched, Bothered, and Bewildered" in 1940 doubled the tune on the violins. In the later production Segal asked Spialek to remove the doubling so that she could phrase the song without interference from the strings.[38] In the song "Glad to Be Unhappy" from *On Your Toes* (1936), Spialek used a light accompaniment of string quartet, celesta, and glockenspiel, not just to permit the voice to come through but to etch a toy piano sound that cleverly complements Hart's lyrics about babies. For the same song in the 1954 Broadway revival of *On Your Toes,* the orchestrator Don Walker used more strings, muted trumpet, and woodwinds, making the background less like chamber music and more like a nightclub. Spialek closed the song with a pianissimo gong and celesta, which recalls the end of Strauss's *Der Rosenkavalier.* Walker ended the song with a big flourish, including a timpani roll and a harp sweep. Walker's orchestration no doubt reflects the fact that by 1954 concealed foot mikes were in use. It also reflects the fact that the number of nonstring instruments in pit orchestras had almost doubled from the 1910s to the 1950s. (Spialek's original orchestrations were revived for the 1983 Broadway revival of *On Your Toes,* but the production also used a sound man.)

Bennett considered Philip J. Lang, the fall guy in 1946, an excellent orchestrator and said that "What bothered the producers [of *Annie Get Your Gun*] was the use of modern technique in the accompaniments under vocal solos, wherein the actual tune was left to the singer or singers and the orchestra avoided competing with the soloist on the melody. That was called 'microphone technique' and was the best way to do any song for recordings of any kind. In the theatre (live sound) the music is under the singer, physically and sound-wise, and the orchestra can sing the tune along with the singer without tying him or her up in any way."[39] Bennett retired from Broadway after orchestrating *On a Clear Day You Can See Forever* in 1965, just in time to escape the new regime in sound. As Louis XIV said, "Après moi, le déluge."

Scene Two. *Sound Design*

I Sing the Body Electric: The Invasion of the Sound Designers

Before the development of the microphone and theater loudspeakers for talking films in the 1920s, the only artificial device that had been used to amplify the voice in the theater was the megaphone, and its use was confined to rehearsals of large ensembles when directors like Julian Mitchell, Ned Wayburn, or Rouben Mamoulian needed to be quickly heard. Only one popular singer ever used the megaphone to effect—Rudy Vallee, for a few years in the 1920s—but his megaphone style was made obsolete by Bing Crosby in the early 1930s. (Crosby himself briefly experimented with the megaphone in the 1920s.) For at least 350 years before, onstage performers in the Western world made their lines or songs heard unaided, despite noisy, indecorous audiences and cavernous spaces. How were the actors at the Globe Theatre heard performing Shakespeare without microphones? How were the songs of *The Beggar's Opera* (arguably the first English-language musical comedy) heard at the Theatre Royal in London in 1728 without loudspeakers? How were W. S. Gilbert's lyrics heard over a thirty-five-piece orchestra at the 1,292-seat Savoy Theatre in London so clearly that his enduring reputation as a lyricist was established without sound design?

Most authorities believe the answers are to be found in the architecture of early theaters and the training and practice of vocal projection among pre–microphone-era singers and actors. Says the theater historian Mary C. Henderson, "In Elizabethan theater they were shouting. Actors bellowed in the nineteenth century. There was no subtlety to it. With the advent of realistic acting styles in the twentieth century you didn't shout."[40] Before the movies and television, the art of live vocal projection was considered an essential part of learning the craft of acting. A substantial portion of Zeke Colvan's 1940 text for actors, *Face the Footlights!,* deals with vocal projection; Uta Hagen, in her 1973 book, *Respect for Acting,* omits the subject except briefly to advise the student to seek vocal teachers. Some observers also credit a habit of more active, involved listening on the part of audiences in the past, arguing that phonographs, radio, television, and movies taught new generations that sound was something that would reach them without being reached for. Recalled Harold Prince in 1974, "The advent of television and electronic instruments has pushed the audience back in its seats. I remember when I first went to theatre, having to adjust for perhaps five minutes to the sounds of the actors. I would sit forward in my seat and the connection that I made with the stage was an investment in the experience."[41] (Thirty years later, however, Prince has joined the devil's party and uses overproduced sound design like the rest of the Broadway theater.)

It is true that most singers who performed with orchestra in theaters before the early twentieth century had legitimate voices, but this fact does not account for how nonlegitimate-voiced vaudeville performers were heard above live fifteen-piece (or larger) orchestras in big-time vaudeville theaters like the Palace, Victoria, or Orpheum in the 1910s, or how similar singing voices were heard in comparable Broadway theaters before microphones came into wide use. While Lillian Russell sang in a legitimate soprano that carried, George M. Cohan talk-sang like Rex Harrison in *My Fair Lady* but was still heard above an orchestra of some fifteen pieces in large theater. "Coon shouters" like May Irwin and Stella Mayhew were Merman-like belters, but Eddie Cantor sang in a slender tenor and Eva Tanguay was also light-voiced, yet they too were heard in both vaudeville theaters and legitimate theaters of 1500–2000 seats. Vaudeville comedians like Weber and Fields walked to the apron of the stage and, joking confidentially with the audience, could be heard throughout the house. The actress Sarah Bernhardt played vaudeville, too, and she certainly was heard to the back of balconies. The Palace, built in 1913, seated 1,736. It was renovated in 1965 for Broadway musicals (at this writing it houses *Aida*) but now requires elaborate sound design. How could the same space earlier have worked with no amplification? The veteran Broadway sound designer Jack Shearing offers one explanation: "There were spots on stage at the Palace Theater that Al Jolson would go to. He knew where his voice would carry."[42]

Howard Whitfield (1914–2001), an actor and stage manager who was the production stage manager for Irving Berlin's last musical, *Mr. President* (1962), offered this reminiscence in 1998:

> When you went on the road, you'd go out on the stage and check your voice in the house to know just how much you needed to fill that house, allowing for an audience. Knowing that an audience would deaden the sound, you'd just say a few words of the play and listen to see how your voice would fit in that house. For instance, each time we changed houses on the road tour with *The Country Wife*, Julie Harris would ask me, "Howard, go up into the balcony and tell me if I'm all right."
>
> Most theaters then were built for you to be heard, and the actor was taught to be heard. No one wore a microphone. They just said their words and were heard. They sang their numbers and were heard. Probably *Mr. President* was the last musical show that was not amplified at all. We did not have mikes in the footlights. The performers did not wear body mikes. Everybody knew how to speak. Of course, I know how things have now changed. I've seen it and cringed. Although now I haven't been to the theater in almost twenty years, because we did not like what we saw.[43]

The actress Bethel Leslie, who appeared in many Broadway plays in the 1940s, recalled that the less mobile set construction of that era acted as a natural soundboard. "When you had a set, you had something behind you to bounce your voice off of. That isn't happening now in musicals. Now you have scrims coming in and out, you have a lot of things come popping up from the floor, so you don't even have a floor underneath to support your sound."[44] George Izenour, the emeritus theater design and technology professor at the Yale School of Drama, explains it this way:

> Proper placement of the voice for the stage actor is forward in the mouth on the hard palate. . . . This placement in turn energizes the bony structure of the head, notably the antrum (sinuses) which is the most efficient (physical) radiator of acoustical energy (both of the speaking and the singing voice). . . . With the microphone and the attendant audio amplification as first used in radio and its continuing use in sound motion pictures and now television where actors are instructed (on purpose) to speak as one does in conversation and sing as per "supper club" intimacy [there is] no particular placement and no projection whatever of the voice.[45]

Before sound design, extra-large theaters like the Hippodrome (5,000 seats) did present an audibility problem. The producer John Golden said that the Hippodrome was so large that audiences could never hear the lyrics.[46] To enhance the sound in the 3,000-seat Earl Carroll Theatre, "5,000 acoustic discs were placed throughout the auditorium to assure easy hearing," but ultimately the sound was judged too tenuous and the theater closed in 1939.[47] In a 1982 study of Broadway theater acoustics, the consultant Peter George concluded that natural sound in a well-designed theater of fewer than 2,000 seats should not need electronic enhancement. All contemporary Broadway "tuner" houses do have fewer than 2,000 seats—yet all now use electronic enhancement. *Show Boat* played in 1927 at the 1,632-seat Ziegfeld Theater without benefit of microphones or loudspeakers. The Ziegfeld was demolished years ago, but the St. James, the Majestic, and the Winter Garden still stand. The Majestic, with 1,629 seats, was built in 1927 and was home to many great unmiked musicals, including the original *Carousel* (1945). Today it houses Martin Levan's souped-up sound design for *The Phantom of the Opera.* The Winter Garden, built in 1911, was home to most of the big revues of the 1920s and 1930s, all performed sans loudspeakers. Today it is home to *Mamma Mia!,* a show amplified like a rock concert. The St. James, built in 1927, housed the original mikeless productions of *Pal Joey* and *Oklahoma!* At this writing it is home to *The Producers,* while the recent revival of *Oklahoma!* at the George Gershwin Theatre used artificial sound.

Newer theaters like the Gershwin (originally named the Uris and constructed in 1972) simply aren't the acoustic gems their predecessors were. The sound designer Tony Meola told an interviewer that with the older theaters, "the architects took a lot of care to make sure that an even frequency spectrum got to the back of the house. Older theaters also tend to have a lot of the ornate, decorative plasterwork, which spreads the high frequencies around evenly. In some newer theaters, the rear of the house becomes a bass trap, with the bass rolling around in the back behind the seating. If you come to New York and go to the Majestic, the Ambassador, the Shubert or the Imperial, you'll find that they are all wonderful."[48]

The debut of microphones and loudspeakers in the theater is hard to pinpoint. The veteran sound designer Abe Jacob says the Broadway revue producer Earl Carroll imported a Hollywood sound man in 1933.[49] Musical theater historians Lehman Engel, Miles Kreuger, and Gerald Bordman all favor 1939–40 as the beginning. The vocals in the Cole Porter show *DuBarry Was a Lady* (1939), though Ethel Merman was in the cast, secretly used amplification because of heavy brass orchestrations. The *Earl Carroll Vanities of 1940* used microphones publicly, and the critics Brooks Atkinson and Richard Watts took Carroll to task for it. Two spectacle shows in the 1930s used remote sound with loud-speakers. *The American Way*, a historical pageant by George S. Kaufman and Moss Hart with music composed and conducted by Oscar Levant, featuring a cast of 250 and 2,200 costume changes, opened in 1939 at the Center Theatre, a 4,000-seat space built in 1932 in Rockefeller Center. The stage had to be enlarged to accommodate the gigantic cast and sets, so the orchestra pit was covered, necessitating the placement of the orchestra in a different room. "When *The American Way* finally opened, on January 21, 1939, Levant was conducting a small band of musicians in a seventh-floor studio, his music piped into the theatre and cued by means of flashing lights."[50] A *New Yorker* writer reported:

> To keep Mr. Levant in touch with the action on stage six stories below, there are three signal lights: a blue one, a white one, and a red one. Blue means, "Get ready," white means "Go," and red means "Stop." In case these should fail, there is a supplementary mike, from which a tinny voice says, "Go ahead.". . . [Levant] . . . has never seen "The American Way" and probably never will unless he loses his job.[51]

Two years earlier, another mammoth production, *The Eternal Road*, a sung-through spectacle with two hundred performers, written by Franz Werfel, composed by Kurt Weill, and directed by Max Reinhardt, necessitated a similar restructuring of the interior of the Manhattan Opera House (a Broadway theater despite the name). The result was arguably the first case of sound design on Broadway and an eerie precursor to the live-versus-canned-music labor dispute between the musicians' local and the League of Broadway Producers in 2003. "The set appropriated the orchestra pit for the staging . . . requiring the score to be prerecorded using a new sound-on-film process developed by RCA."[52] Originally the plan was to prerecord the entire score. But "the American Federation of Musicians had intervened, and [the producer] had been forced to hire a live orchestra of sixteen instrumentalists, to be used in conjunction with the recorded core. This group . . . was stationed in a soundproof room high up on the left side of the auditorium, from where the occasional effects that it supplied were piped onto the stage, just as the recorded accompaniment was."[53] (The instrument-upon-instrument reinforcement of *The Eternal Road* is still practiced. Today it is not uncommon in Broadway pits for synthesized violin to double real violins.) The remote orchestra also played "the musical numbers added to the score after the recordings were made. The sound from the live ensemble was apparently played back electronically in the theatre so that it sounded to the audience just like the prerecorded parts."[54]

In her book *And Promenade Home,* Agnes de Mille says sound equipment was used in *One Touch of Venus* (1943); the person responsible, Saki Oura (1915–94), was probably the first to receive playbill credit as "consulting sound engineer" (and again in 1944 for *Follow the Girls*). By the 1950s if not earlier, "Electric amplification became a necessity even for such 'vocal' performers as Ethel Merman and Alfred Drake," according to Lehman Engel. "Six or seven microphones were spaced out evenly in the footlight troughs. Sometimes mikes were also hidden in scenery when singers had to perform at too great a distance from the forestage. For two decades this crude method of amplification sufficed."[55] *West Side Story* (1957) was staged with foot mikes.

Trude Rittmann, asked how the balance between Mary Martin's almost vibratoless voice and ex-Met basso Ezio Pinza was achieved in *South Pacific* (1949), said, "We never had amplification. Ever!"[56] Rodgers told the Columbia University Oral History project in the late 1960s that *Carousel* was his last show without microphones,[57] while in his study of Rodgers and Hammerstein, Ethan Mordden writes that ex–opera singer Helen Traubel in *Pipe Dream* (1955) was (ironically) the first R&H performer to be miked.[58]

The dean of veteran Broadway sound designers, Jack Mann, who started in the late 1940s, recalled that the stage manager was the sound designer in the old days. When the director asked for a sound effect, the stage manager would furnish it. Later, electricians took over sound from the stage manager. Before the 1960s "there was no such thing as a sound operator," said Mann. "The switchboard operator had the sound system as a side job."[59]

The first reported example of a sound-mixing console in the back of the theater's orchestra section—by the 1980s a fixture of all Broadway musicals—was for the 1957 musical *Jamaica* at the Imperial Theatre starring Lena Horne. While the show's nominal orchestrator was Philip J. Lang, the star wanted her own songs orchestrated by her husband, Lennie Hayton. The Hayton arrangements featured five saxophones, and Horne's voice required electronic boosting from the back of the house to be heard over the saxes. The conductor, the ubiquitous Engel, ruefully reported that the amplification would have been unnecessary if woodwinds had been substituted for the saxophones.[60] (The same reed players in Broadway orchestras normally double on woodwinds and saxophones.)

A quarter century after *The Eternal Road* and *The American Way,* Richard Rodgers designed his 1962 musical *No Strings* so that the orchestra sat behind the stage and its sound was piped into the theater by two sound operators; part of the time the musicians were actually onstage. (This was not the first time a small band of musicians was placed with the actors; in Kern's last show, *Very Warm for May* [1939], accordionist Milton DeLugg and a small combo appeared onstage.) The director Gower Champion was another early user of sound design: Carol Channing was miked by the sound designer Robert Maybaum in *Hello, Dolly!* (1964). But as late as *Fiddler on the Roof* (1964), there were only two sound cues, a dialogue cue and a music cue, and one automatically adjusting level (it toned down when people shouted onstage). The audio budget for *Fiddler* was less than $6,000. A quarter century later, the sound budgets for *The Phantom of the Opera* and *Aspects of Love* were closer to $600,000.

How did the steady advance of sound design affect orchestrators like Robert Russell Bennett? Bennett had customarily doubled the vocal line in his orchestrations, although usually in a pitch register above or below the singer (flute above, oboe unison, cello and bassoon below). He always maintained that the orchestrator had to take care to arrange, and the conductor to maintain, what he called "playing under" "voiceless voices," which he claimed "necessitated for years the presence of the melody strongly played in the orchestra. . . . Not until the use of microphones, which transform a 'croon' into a full vocal tone, was it thought possible to make the orchestration into pure accompaniment."[61] Bennett apparently remained an apostle of sound balance by natural means, although he admitted that "recorded music, which removes all dynamic distinction between a muted viola and the Battle of the Marne with a sweep of the engineer's touch, has conditioned the ears of our generation until a study of live-music values begins to sound a little quaint."[62] He stubbornly stuck to recommending doubling the vocal line in his 1975 text on theater arranging. Today, in an ironic reversal, many sound designers say the problem is with the orchestrations: "The charts are changing what happens to the voice," said Jack Shearing in 1990. "*The Sound of Music*'s arrangements underscored the voice. Today that's impossible because of the way charts interfere and compete with the voice. You get a record orchestration in the theater now."[63] Otts Munderloh agrees—"Orchestrators are now writing for the record charts and then they get into the theater and say why can't we hear?"—although he adds that the better orchestrators like Tunick are savvy enough to avoid this problem.[64]

Thus, miking crooning voices enabled louder orchestration, which in turn forced louder and heavier vocal amplification. Also, with the ascent of choreographer-directors, performers were being placed above stage level in newly complex scenery, such as Champion's "living comic strip" backdrop for the song "The Telephone Hour" in *Bye Bye Birdie* (1960) (later copied by Harold Prince in *It's a Bird! . . . It's a Plane! . . . It's Superman* and *Company*). Such cinematic stage movement, while visually dazzling, was not always optimal for vocal directionality (one source claims Carol Channing was on a wireless mike as Dolly even in 1964). After *West Side Story*, singing and dancing were more frequently consolidated in the same performer, and singing dancer/actors could find themselves singing while facing toward the wings or even upstage, instead of downstage in the style of early golden-age musicals. The obsolescence of choruses exclusively made up of trained singers (common in the 1940s and earlier) also reduced the sheer volume of group singing that had obviated amplification.

Then came along two watersheds: *Promises, Promises* (1968) and *Jesus Christ Superstar* (1971). For *Promises, Promises*, Burt Bacharach's only book Broadway musical, Bacharach engaged the record producer Phil Ramone to simulate a recording studio setup and design the sound. The musicians were miked in the orchestra pit, and cubicles were built around each player in the pit. As for Lloyd Webber's contribution,

> In the UK, the musical *Jesus Christ Superstar* started life as a recording, and only after the success of the record was it presented at the Palace Theatre in London in 1972. . . . What was unusual about the show was the fact that, as well as the traditional band in the orchestra pit of the theatre, a rock band was on stage next to the performers. The pit musicians were amplified to bring them up to a similar level to that of the on stage band, and so that the performers could be heard, handheld microphones were used. After each song, the microphones were either placed on the stage to be picked up by the next singer, or hauled into the wings by their cables. . . . the overall effect was more that of a rock concert than a traditional musical, but the show started a rise in the tide of amplification in musical theatre. . . . The use of cabled hand microphones was obviously not appropriate for all musicals, and sound engineers started to exploit the availability of miniature wireless transmitters coupled with small electret-condenser microphones.[65]

Wireless radio microphones were first produced in the early 1960s but didn't become widely used until the 1970s. *Cats* (1982) was probably the first show in which every single performer onstage wore a wireless mike. Even as late as 1981, *Dreamgirls* used only five wireless mikes; when the show's other performers "came down across the stage, the whole orchestra had to come down in volume, because the performers were coming off the foot mikes," recalls the show's sound designer, Otts Munderloh.[66] According to Munderloh, Michael Bennett, unlike Champion, moved performers downstage to be on foot mikes when their voices were weak, instead of fitting them with body mikes. Since performers need to hear the orchestra, yet with wireless mikes are frequently directed not to face the orchestra pit, they now listen to the orchestra through a loudspeaker concealed in the set. With both microphones and loudspeakers concealed onstage, the performers' own wireless mikes are constantly at risk of picking up not only their own voices but also the sound coming out of the onstage loudspeakers, further corrupting the sound signal and forcing the operator to raise volume levels, equalize, compress, or otherwise artificially alter the sound that the audience hears.

Video monitors are also a part of the loop that corrupts the sound that microphones pick up. In cases where orchestra players are not in the pit—and in some cases where they are—they view the conductor on a video monitor. Because orchestra pits are frequently covered today and the conductor may not be naturally visible to the actors, video monitors are also mounted close to the stage so that the cast can see the conductor. The conductor in turn may also need a video monitor of the stage, as will the sound operator in the rear of the theater and the stage manager in the wings. Another byproduct of this setup is that the conductor may hear his players more from the monitor than from the live sound; says the Broadway conductor David Chase, "I am mostly hearing from the monitor when I'm low in the pit."[67] Among shows running in 2003, the actors had an unobstructed view of the conductor in *Man of La Mancha, Aida,* and *The Lion King.* For the revival of *Flower Drum Song,* however, the orchestra was onstage, yet the actors watched the conductor on a video monitor. The audio from a monitor, just like the audio from loudspeakers, can enter the microphone chain, causing further corruption and distortion in what emerges from the theater's loudspeakers and is heard by the audience. If the monitors onstage are turned down low to prevent their sound from being picked up by microphones, sometimes the actors can't hear the music or even the other actors. In *Passion* (1994), the actor Jere Shea was stage right and Donna Murphy was stage left in a scene. Recalls Munderloh, "Jere Shea said, 'How will I hear her? Will there be monitors?' There were a lot of complaints from performers onstage not able to hear Donna Murphy singing; the conductor Paul Gemignani couldn't hear her."[68]

With the Lloyd Webber and Boublil-Schönberg shows of the 1980s, what had started as a benign reinforcement creep became a runaway SPL (sound pressure level) mushroom cloud. Writes John A. Leonard, "So that vocals could still be heard, sound designers were forced to use recording studio techniques such as compression to reduce the natural dynamic range of the human voice. . . . Musicals became, in some cases, almost unbearably loud. . . . It was often impossible to work out which character was singing, as all directional information from the stage was being swamped by the sound from the loud-speaker system." Loudspeakers have multiplied exponentially. *The Lion King* has more than eighty loudspeakers and thirty-five performers with body mikes. Jonathan Deans, the sound designer for *Fosse* and *Ragtime,* used forty loudspeakers in the theater for *Seussical* (2000). Forty, it should be noted, is a greater number than either the total number of actors or the total number of orchestra players in *Seussical.* For the rear of the Richard Rodgers Theatre in *Seussical,* Deans told an interviewer, "I was able to use a digital mixer board that only took up six seats instead of twenty, which would have saved $11,000 a week if the seats had sold."[69]

The ability to manipulate sound can be good or bad from the point of view of stagecraft. Certainly amplifying the sound of the entire onstage dance ensemble's tap shoes striking the floor in *42nd Street* (also done in the 1933 movie) was exciting and justifiable. But in the same show, the character Peggy Sawyer walks offstage at one point and one still heard her speaking on mike while one's eye was being drawn to other actors onstage. Such scenes are now common-place in musicals: many performers are onstage, a single actor's voice is ema-nating from a loudspeaker, and the audience searches in vain for the face to match the voice. Visual/auditory directionality dissonance also afflicts the sound design of the orchestra: in the 1999 *Annie Get Your Gun* revival, the pit to the main orchestra was almost entirely covered, while a smaller band sat on-stage. The loudspeaker distribution was such that it seemed as if the sounds of different instruments were emanating from physically impossible directions. In extreme cases, the director and sound designer may even ask singing dancers to lip-synch to their own prerecorded singing: this was done as long ago as *Follies* (1971) by codirector Michael Bennett. "It takes away from that 'live' feel," admits Tony Meola. "I will do it occasionally, usually on chorus numbers, maybe eight bars of a number where they have just come off danc-ing and can barely catch their breath enough to start singing. In that case, we will augment live singing with a little bit of click track."[70] *Side Show's* song "Tunnel of Love" had backup vocals on a click track, and the title song in *The Phantom of the Opera* is on a prerecorded click track because of the drum ma-chine in the arrangement.

Because every performer (principal and ensemble alike) now wears a wire-less onstage, and because only one mike is on at a time, the sound operator who sits in the rear has to memorize every line in the show. His sound plot literally operates the entire show. If he gets sick or has no trained sub, the show can't go on. "The sound has become indispensable," says Meola. "For example, if the lighting board goes down in a show and you have to turn up the house lights, the show can go on. But on many shows, if you lose the sound board, the show can't go on. The people can't sing loud enough."[71] The pantomime of the long-running off-Broadway show *Blue Man Group: Tubes* is supported almost gesture for gesture by sound cues. There'd be no show without the sound plot.

Who is the auteur or "muscle" behind sound design of a musical? In the vast majority of cases, either the producers or the director. Except for Andrew Lloyd Webber, who famously fired the Broadway sound man Abe Jacob (who had done *Evita*) and replaced him with the British sound man Martin Levan on *Cats* and subsequent Lloyd Webber shows, the composer, orchestrator, and even the sound designer have little to do with deciding how the sound is used (although the orchestrator Jonathan Tunick has it in his contract that he retains approval of the sound). Contrast this with the old days, when Rodgers, Porter, Gershwin, Kern, and Loewe had much to do with deciding whether the orchestrations—the sound design of their era—were acceptable. Many of the older sound designers are appalled by the uses to which they've been put. "We've gone from a human-sized theater to a theater much more than life-sized," lamented Jack Shearing, whose work as a sound man dates back to before the 1970s. "It's easier to be bludgeoned into a sense of spectacle than to critically think about what's going on onstage. Young people today are used to hearing music that eclipses all thinking about it. We can amplify voices so they can overcome electronic instruments. A great deal of theater has become destroyed by technology. You become overloaded and lose a certain amount of judgment. A lot louder is the imperative if the show doesn't have content."[72] Adds Munderloh, "We can only make it louder and still bad, not louder and better."[73] George Izenour agrees: "The tendency is to overdrive, overamplify the system. Personally I hate with a vengeance the whole business to the extent that I have not attended a Broadway musical or a play in over twenty years. Technology has its uses and its misuses. Take your pick."[74]

Whereas in traditional theatergoing prior to about 1965, it was expected that the sound would vary at different spots in the house—fifth-row center was always regarded as optimal—now the guiding philosophy among producers is that every seat in the house has to sound the same.* In 1985 Shubert Organization chairman Gerald Schoenfeld, a producer of *Harrigan 'n Hart,* complained

---

*If producers spend money to ensure that every seat in the house sounds the same, why are patrons being charged differential rates for seating? Especially since the added costs of sound design are inflating the cost of theater tickets?

that the sound in the fifth-row orchestra sounded as if it were coming from the orchestra pit. (In a later show he leaned over the orchestra pit and asked why any strings were needed.) Says Munderloh, who has been working as a sound designer since about 1970, "Directors never run to the orchestra pit anymore to solve problems. They're not like Jerome Robbins. When I did *Jerome Robbins' Broadway* (1989), Robbins ran down to the pit and said 'too loud, too loud, I can't hear Debbie Shapiro' to Paul Gemignani [the conductor]. Robbins would go through orchestrator after orchestrator to get the right sound balance." Today the conductor and the orchestrator are at the mercy of the producer, the director, and the sound design. "Producers don't listen to me," says Munderloh. "They think louder is better." Abe Jacob says, "The audience now expects to hear in the theater what they hear in their living room. Machines have become the standard of performance instead of performance in a public place. There's a decline of listening literacy."

Wireless mikes and sound design have also revolutionized the casting and marketing of Broadway musicals, permitting television and film actors with little or no traditional singing chops or theater technique to play leading roles in even old-time classic musicals. In fact, technically able singers are sometimes asked by the sound designer to sing softly so that the sound operator can tweak them to blend with less capable singers (one such occurrence was reported to me from the 1996 revival of *The King and I*).

To summarize, if you went to see any Broadway musical at the time of this writing in 2003,

(1) every performer onstage was wearing a wireless microphone;

(2) every musician in the pit (or elsewhere) was individually miked;

(3) there were probably more loudspeakers in the theater than there were musicians or performers;

(4) there were an uncounted number of hidden video screens actively being monitored during live performance by the actors, musicians, conductor, and other tech people;

(5) the sound operator who sat in the rear of the theater at the mixing console was arguably more important than either the stage manager or the conductor in running the show; and

(6) the overall decibel level as a result of all the above approached rock-concert levels, even for most nonrock musicals.

Another factor governing the experience of hearing a Broadway musical today is the frequent covering of orchestra pits. Orchestra pits in Broadway theaters have always been sunken to some extent: originally orchestras were put in pits to subdue them slightly. But the problem has gotten worse in the last twenty years with the trend toward covering the pits. Opera pits have always been open (except for Wagner's Festspielhaus at Bayreuth, a uniquely designed acoustic space that is the exception that proves the rule). "If you go to any good opera house or any well-designed theatre," said Jonathan Tunick back in the early 1970s, when covered pits first became an issue on Broadway, "you'll see an orchestra pit that's fairly shallow and extremely wide which is very desirable because it allows the sound to rise through a large opening and become diffused in the air."[75] Probably a substantial reason vaudeville singers could be heard above their orchestras was that the pits were uncovered (old photographs support this), and the performers knew how to project their voices from the foot of the stage to the back of the house. "Broadway producers decided with the advent of mikes that it was all about real estate, so they moved the orchestra underneath the stage and fit the musicians into the new pit," says Munderloh. "If the pit were extended further out into the theater, the sound would rise. But producers don't want to give away the ticket revenue." One casualty of this has been the traditional excitement of hearing the overture played from a semi-open pit. The overture, like everything else, now is piped in through loudspeakers. The opening of the 2000 revival of *The Music Man* arrived at a novel and effective solution to this problem, with musical director David Chase in bandmaster costume conducting a band onstage in the actual overture.

The musical director in the old days was the master link in the chain of the self-sound-balancing of musicals; *he* was the sound operator, to all intents and purposes (the stage manager merely operated special sound effects). Today the musical director is a cog in a larger machine. Eric Stern, an arranger and conductor who conducted *The Will Rogers Follies*, *Carousel*, and other shows of the 1980s and 1990s, describes how it was conducting *Parade* in 1998:

> Set designers and directors apportion the pit without even consulting a conductor. The two elevators on the aprons of the stage that brought set pieces up literally ate up a third of my pit for *Parade*. I had a drummer in the pit but a percussionist in an entirely different room all hooked up by video and audio. My bass clarinet/bassoonist was playing behind me on my right, positioned so that he has absolutely no shot of me at all. He played off the monitor. He was sitting next to a man who *could* see me, but *he* couldn't see me. During *The Will Rogers Follies* I had my entire string section on the eighth floor.
>
> You tell the sound people that the right side of the pit can't hear the left side.

What do you say when you have a flute player who says, "I can't hear the piano or the strings. I have no idea how my intonation is. I can't hear ANYTHING"? You go to sound and say, "Do we want a hot spot from the right side to the left side?" No, because then the mike will pick up that. My percussionist is wearing a head-piece. He's hearing the band in his ears. So it's not even live in the room.

You have to remember that sound designers are basically miking each instrument separately and then creating a blend out in the house. Same with the vocals, by the way. Every single singer in the ensemble is wearing a wireless. And as a result, what you're getting here is you work for eight weeks for choral blend, and then for the first two weeks of rehearsal in the theater you're hearing nothing but individual voices with absolutely no blend and absolutely no choral presence, no choral field. The same thing happens with the orchestral mix. It takes ages to get to the point where the saxes sound like a choir, where the strings sound like a choir. And you're on the podium, you can't hear the whole show from the back and say "No, this isn't mixed right."[76]

In pre–sound design days, it was the job of the assistant conductor, who was the musical director's understudy, to check the sound balance live by walking around the house. Stern continues,

Sometimes you have to go back and say to the sound designer, "You know, I rehearsed a diminuendo there. Don't dig them out," because the guy who's mixing the show is undoing everything you told him. There was a spot in *Parade* where the chorus on the courthouse steps sang "It is time now, it is time now" and I had rehearsed the chorus so that they went into one long diminuendo as the steps disappeared. But because sound effects had to be audible during the crowd moment, the sound designer had to turn the chorus up!

"A producer or director might step in and ask that the volume be pumped up to generate more excitement," says Tony Meola. "It's funny the euphemisms you hear for that—like 'presence' or 'excitement'—when it's really only volume. I always say sound is exciting when there's a difference, when you have dynamics. Going from pianissimo to fortissimo can be exciting. But if the quietest you ever get is mezzo forte, and you never get to pianissimo, then you have to go louder to get the dynamics. It can be too much." Adds David Budries, the chair of sound design at the Yale School of Drama, "If we don't have silence, a noise floor, we really can't perform properly."[77]

What today's producers and directors are really trying to replicate in the theater is the sound environment Americans experience at the movies, on boom boxes, on Walkman earphones, and even from overamplified background music in restaurants, airports, and other public spaces, piped in at a louder volume than 1950s Muzak ever was. Americans hear constant "live soundtracking" even in their cars, and producers believe that to sell tickets they must provide a similar sonic assault in the legitimate theater, including Sensurround, used in some Broadway musicals. Social norms of sound levels have changed with the universalization of loud pop music and the ever-increasing use of noise-making appliances. In the 1940s—the decade when the musicals of Rodgers and Hammerstein, Lerner and Loewe, Kurt Weill, and others made their splash—the noise of an airplane flying overhead in Manhattan was still such an event that pedestrians would stop in the streets to look up.

In the 2000s, far too many people expect to hear in the theater the sound levels and balances they are accustomed to hearing on recorded pop music, in which there is no noise floor. But indiscriminate loud sound assaults the very essence of live theater, which requires discriminating among different expressive levels of an actor's speech and singing. Leveling all sound onto one high plateau of excitement removes the capacity to build excitement by the traditional dramatic means of narrative suspense, which is sometimes achieved by a diminution of sound, not an increase. Even the overture, the traditional rabble-rouser of the old-style musical, is rendered feckless by the new sound levels, because the shows now often get even louder after the overture is over.

The final indignity is that no longer is any attempt made to conceal the performers' wireless mikes. The sound designer Jack Mann recalled that "in the old days, the sound system had to be invisible or the producer would get mad. Speakers then were invisible. The mikes were floor mikes housed in doghouses so as to be invisible on the floor of the stage." For the first decade or two of their use, transistor mikes were strapped to performers under their costumes. If they couldn't be concealed that way, other stratagems were used: as recently as *Crazy for You* (1992), wirelesses were put under the wigs of women costumed in strapless gowns. But now the wireless transmitter is often freely displayed on the performer's ear; even publicity shots show the performers with the earpieces visible, making them look like mutant aliens. Visible radio mikes destroy the fourth wall. They suspend the suspension of disbelief. They break the spell of the magic of live theater.

Sound design is not inherently an evil. It can be artful and necessary. But it's a slippery slope between discreet and necessary sound reinforcement and the creation of a too-dominant "sound environment." Sound designers and operators are not the ones at fault; they are merely executing what producers and directors demand. Visible mikes belong in the rock concert arena and the night-club, not in the theater. Controlled sound environments can work. Runaway sound environments in musical theater production, like the rock groove in theater music, batter the fourth wall and cheapen the experience of live theater.

Otts Munderloh thinks the solution might lie in going back to foot mikes only: "It would demand that the performers be louder and have more training." Yet there are practical limits to foot mikes: Julie Andrews claimed that playing Eliza Doolittle in the original *My Fair Lady* eight times a week without any sound assistance other than foot mikes overtaxed her highly trained voice.[78] Still, John A. Leonard, the sound designer for the Royal Shakespeare Company, believes that "tempting as it is to fill our . . . productions with continuous sound effects and music, very often less is more."[79] The most elegant demonstration of this dictum was by that ageless doyenne of musicals, Barbara Cook, in her recent one-woman show, *Mostly Sondheim*. At seventy-four, after singing for some eighty minutes, she sang the final number of the evening—"Anyone Can Whistle"—off microphone and was heard to the back of the rafters.

How the Recording Studio Transformed Musicals

Contrary to received wisdom, recordings of original casts of Broadway musicals did not begin with record producer Jack Kapp's *Oklahoma!* in 1943. Singles of songs with original cast members were commercially recorded as long ago as 1890. Such stars of the pre-1920 musical comedy stage as Nora Bayes, Blanche Ring, George M. Cohan, Chauncey Olcott, Raymond Hitchcock, and Joseph Cawthorn recorded songs from their shows with orchestra on flat 78-rpm acoustic discs, for which they had to perform in front of large acoustic horns (electrical recording microphones were introduced in 1925). Broadcast radio started only in 1920. The pre-1920 records are particularly powerful documents because the performers did not yet have microphone technique or radio experience and re-created their numbers before the acoustic horn pretty much as they performed them onstage. Because the technology for editing had not yet developed, these primitive recordings are truly live performances and have a surprising presence when played back today on modern equipment (although their orchestrations may not represent an exact replica of what was heard in the theater). In listening to them, one can almost see the acting—quite the opposite of today's multitracked, hyperlayered preproduction "studio cast albums" with their sometimes acting-deficient vocalism.

By the 1910s "original studio cast" recordings were already being made by the Victor Light Opera Company, Columbia Light Opera Company, and other such groups cobbled together by the recording labels. On each of the 78-rpm singles a song from the show would be sung by a chorus, not a soloist. Most of the songs from Jerome Kern Princess Theatre musicals were thus recorded by the Victor Light Opera Company, while Victor Herbert himself conducted the VLOC recording of songs from his *Eileen* (1917).

In the late 1920s original cast members Helen Morgan and Jules Bledsoe of *Show Boat* made recordings of their songs, and *Blackbirds of 1928* was recorded by its original cast almost completely in 1932 and 1933 by Jack Kapp, then with Brunswick Records. But singles made in this period by original cast members were usually designed as song plugs for the radio and home phonograph rather than documents of the shows, and as representations of the original orchestrations or even tempi they must be assessed cautiously. When the conductor John Mauceri played Ethel Merman's 1934 recording of "I Get a Kick Out of You" from *Anything Goes* to Hans Spialek (who co-orchestrated the show with Bennett) in the early 1980s, Spialek at first didn't even recognize her. Then Spialek noted that the recording was a dance band arrangement (by Johnny Green's orchestra), not the one played in the theater, and that its tempo was so different from what he remembered live in the theater that he didn't recognize Merman.[80]

There is a July 1935 rehearsal recording of excerpts from *Porgy and Bess* with Gershwin conducting (the show opened in October 1935), but it wasn't until 1942 that Decca recorded parts of the 1935 and 1942 revival cast of *Porgy and Bess* in a true cast album. Still, that was not the first original-cast album. Pride of place for that honor goes to the April 1938 recording of the 1937 Orson Welles production of Marc Blitzstein's *The Cradle Will Rock,* released on a seven-record set by Musicraft Records for $10.50. (Four years later, Blitzstein's short-lived *No for an Answer* was partially recorded.) Meanwhile, singles continued to be issued until the dawn of long-playing records. Gene Kelly recorded "I Could Write a Book" from *Pal Joey* in 1940; Gertrude Lawrence recorded several songs from *Lady in the Dark* in 1941. In the late 1930s and early 1940s the Liberty Music Shop in Manhattan issued singles with original Broadway casts, including several songs from Rodgers and Hart's *I Married an Angel* (1938) and Ethel Waters in *Cabin in the Sky* (1940).

But absent from the recorded history of musicals is what is abundantly present in the recorded archives of opera: recordings of live performance in the house. Without such live recordings, a reconstruction of actual sound balances in the theater remains guesswork and memory. Surviving live Broadway recordings from before World War II are extremely rare. The outstanding example is a recording of the *Ziegfeld Follies of 1934* on tour at the Shubert Theatre in New Haven, Connecticut: a complete, uncut live seventy-five-minute performance from March 16, 1935, with all the original cast, recorded on acetate discs in the theater. Three songs sung by Ethel Merman were recorded live from the wings by a wire recorder during a performance of *Panama Hattie* (1940). After about 1950 and the invention of the magnetic tape recorder, private tapes began to be made secretly in performance; copies of some of them now repose in the Institute for the American Musical in Los Angeles. The collection of the Theatre on Film and Tape Archive of New York's Performing Arts Library at Lincoln Center doesn't really begin until the 1960s. Since about 1970, most Broadway musicals have been archivally videotaped for this collection, although the audio quality of videotape is not equal even to a state-of-the-art magnetic tape recorder of the 1950s.

The major labels began recording original casts in the studio in the late 1940s and have done so ever since. At about that same time Goddard Lieberson, a composer who was executive vice-president of Columbia Records, engaged Lehman Engel to record the scores of musicals that predated original cast albums. Using the original orchestrations and hiring superb singers, Engel and Lieberson recorded the complete *Porgy and Bess,* many Rodgers and Hart scores, *Roberta, Brigadoon, The Student Prince,* and others. One such studio re-creation, the September 1950 recording of *Pal Joey* with Harold Lang replacing Gene Kelly and Vivienne Segal recreating her original 1940 role, was the first studio album in history to lead directly to a Broadway production: the successful 1952 revival of *Pal Joey* ran for 542 performances.

Yet the Engel-Lieberson studio recordings, well executed as they are, leave a mixed legacy. At that time (and now), the economic argument was compelling: it was much less expensive to hire a studio cast of excellent singers than the original stage cast, who were required to be paid Actors Equity scale. But such studio casts, for Lehman Engel as well as for much later conductors of studio cast albums such as John McGlinn and even Leonard Bernstein in his 1985 *West Side Story* and 1989 *Candide* recordings, inevitably deliver a cantata reading, not an inhabited, fully experienced dramatic reading. (Engel himself recognized this dilemma and wrote about it.) They tend to slower, reverential tempos that don't reflect the tempos used in the theater. To that extent they are a falsification of musicals in a way that studio recordings of opera are not, because opera drives on its music alone, while even the aural performance of musicals is a compendium of musical, dramatic, and literary values.

Of course, even original-cast recordings are audio falsifications, since they are recorded not onstage in performance (as operas frequently are) but in the studio, where the sound is mixed and controlled artificially so that the microphone boosts the singers over the orchestra like movie dialogue over a film soundtrack. They are also falsifications insofar as the string section on original-cast recordings has traditionally been enlarged well beyond what the orchestra pit contains live in the theater. *Titanic* (1997) was orchestrated for twenty-six players, but its original cast recording has thirty-eight players, including twelve violins, four violas, four cellos, and three basses.

But more important, an original-cast album in its every spoken and sung nuance reflects the end product of many weeks of a cast living in their roles and being molded by the stage director and other creative personnel. It represents a record of three-dimensionally achieved theater, rather than an ad hoc "staged reading," however expertly performed. Thus, the 1947 original-cast recording of Lerner and Loewe's *Brigadoon* (RCA Victor's first venture into the field), though less slickly sung or orchestrally played than Lehman Engel's 1957 studio re-creation, is in every important theatrical way superior to it: it exudes the set designs of Oliver Smith and makes the chase ballet palpably dramatic in a way that the Engel recording does not. Original-cast recordings are now up to sixty years old and have become historical artifacts of a bygone age, like the Mapleson opera cylinders of the early 1900s. Instead of being merely reminders of the songs, they are now reminders of the art form that no longer is, and of its finest performers. We can listen to the remarkable detail of the October 1944 recording of *Bloomer Girl* and somehow see with our ears the entire panoply of 1940s Broadway. We cannot hear James O'Neill play the Count of Monte Cristo or Sarah Bernhardt as Camille, but we can hear Alfred Drake whisper the last verse of "The Surrey with the Fringe on Top" and immediately understand why he was a great singing actor, as readily as we can hear Fyodor Chaliapin sing Boris Godunov or Claudia Muzio sing Mimì. We can hear the acting depth Shirley Booth brought to musicals on the albums of *A Tree Grows in Brooklyn, By the Beautiful Sea,* and *Juno,* the velvety warmth and heart of Mary Martin, or the inimitable Broadway spinto of Stubby Kaye's voice raising the roof with *Guys and Dolls'* eleven o'clock number, "Sit Down, You're Rocking the Boat." The voices of Edwin Forrest and David Garrick are lost to history; these voices are preserved.

The single most important new development for the original-cast album since Jack Kapp recorded *Oklahoma!* in 1943 was the 1967 release of the Beatles' "concept album," *Sgt. Pepper's Lonely Hearts Club Band.* This watershed event in pop music ultimately altered the course of history for the Broadway musical. Immediately there was a stream of similar rock "concept albums": the Moody Blues' *Days of Future Passed* in 1968, the Who's *Tommy* in 1969, and others inaugurating what would become known as classical or progressive rock. Two young Englishmen named Andrew Lloyd Webber and Tim Rice took note and released as concept albums what would in a few years become their first two musicals staged in London and then New York: *Joseph and the Amazing Technicolor Dreamcoat* (1968) and *Jesus Christ Superstar* (1970). Because both works were written and conceived as cantatas, they naturally adapted to studio cast recording with its inherent bias toward cantata values. The team later issued *Evita* as a concept album before the stage show, and soon it became standard operating procedure for rock musicals to be test-marketed by a concept album, a practice followed by Alain Boublil and Claude-Michel Schönberg for *Les Misérables* and by Frank Wildhorn, a recording company executive/composer, for his 1990s musicals *Jekyll and Hyde* and *The Scarlet Pimpernel*.

For musicals already presold to the public as hit albums, "the theatre had to replicate the recorded sound," as the producer Stuart Ostrow says.[81] But the Lloyd Webber–Rice works are cantatas, completely through-sung with no spoken dialogue, and as theater they are primitive, with no in-depth characterizations, literary cleverness, or narrative sophistication. The crucible of lived-in onstage performance and backstage preparation, of research and investigation into the characters and the play—essential elements of fine theater—is missing. The achieved depth of performers' playing and "living" in the roles in front of live audiences that earlier original-cast albums had documented was made otiose by concept album–driven theater. There are no acquired theatrical values in concept albums. So the concept album, from the Beatles to Lloyd Webber, rebuilt the Broadway musical on the pop music model, and of course sound design had to re-create the sound of concept albums.

Recording albums of shows before they're written is about marketing, not dramaturgy, and inevitably weakens traditions of strong writing for the musical theater. A cast album made prior to staging is a kind of backers' audition (some, like Maury Yeston's concept album *Goya* [1989], never make it to the stage).

If producers wanted to reconstruct live the sound of the pre–decibel-overload musical, they could either study original-cast recordings or listen to the private archival tapes recorded live. Or simply exercise taste and common sense and achieve the same result.

Virtual Orchestras Mean Virtual Theater

In March 2003, Local 802 of the American Federation of Musicians (AFM), the labor union for orchestra players in Broadway pits, went on strike against the

League of American Theatres and Producers (LATP). At issue was the minimum number of live musicians producers would be required to hire for musicals. The musicians wanted the minimum for large houses at twenty-four; the producers initially tried to bargain for a minimum of only seven, then went to fourteen, then fifteen. A statement supporting the Federation's position and signed by most of the leading composers, conductors, and arrangers of Broadway said, "The great classics of the past are now performed with synthesizers replacing full string sections; one show is even performed to taped music." Members of Actors' Equity and the stagehands' union refused to cross the picket line, effectively closing Broadway, and the strike was settled in four days. After mediation at Gracie Mansion under the eye of Mayor Bloomberg, the two sides agreed on minimums of eighteen and nineteen, depending upon the theater—a 25 percent reduction in employment for Broadway pit players, one of the most skilled labor pools of musicians anywhere.

For decades, New York theater producers had been required to employ a set minimum of musicians for each house even if the orchestrations didn't need that number. A 1993 labor agreement ended this featherbedding of paid nonperforming musicians, called "walkers." Local 802 at that time agreed to lower the minimums to three to nine musicians for small houses, fifteen to twenty in four medium houses, and twenty-four to twenty-six in about a dozen larger houses. In the past at these larger houses, there have been orchestras as large as forty-five (for Vincent Youmans's 1932 musical *Through the Years* at the Manhattan Theatre, now the studio for David Letterman's television show), forty-four (for *Porgy and Bess* in 1935 at the Alvin Theatre, now called the Neil Simon Theatre), thirty-five (for *Street Scene* in 1947 at the Adelphi Theatre), thirty-three (for *The King and I* in 1951 at the St. James), thirty (for *West Side Story* in 1957 at the Winter Garden), and twenty-eight (for *Follies*, as recently as 1971, at the Winter Garden). *A Chorus Line* in 1975 had only a sixteen-piece orchestra.

In the first few decades of the twentieth century, Broadway orchestras had more string players than nonstring players. Saxophones may have been used as early as *Oh, I Say!*, a 1913 musical, but didn't get established as part of the reed section until the late 1920s. Once rhythm sections entered the pit, the balance started shifting to jazzier instruments and players. Glenn Miller, Gene Krupa, and Benny Goodman all played in the pit of *Girl Crazy* (1930). The 1948 orchestration of *Kiss Me, Kate* by Russell Bennett and his colleagues relied on a strong string section to underline the schmaltz in songs like "So in Love" (which includes a solo violin cadenza). The producers of the 1999 *Kiss Me, Kate* revival at the Martin Beck Theatre took advantage of that theater's AFM/LATP minimum of fifteen and commissioned Don Sebesky to reorchestrate the entire show for fifteen players (including only four live string players). Only a few Broadway musicals of the last thirty years have had prominent string writing—*A Little Night Music, On the Twentieth Century, Titanic*—and some that sound as if they do are actually augmented by "string synth."

The use of keyboard synthesizers that can digitally sample the sounds of live acoustic instruments is to the Broadway orchestra what the "concept album" was to the original-cast album: an alien influence dumbing down the nuances of good theater. Digital synthesizers can produce credible imitations of many instruments and thus reduce the number of musicians needed for hire. They were introduced into pit orchestras in the 1980s and quickly became the medium of choice to replace string players. (Sometimes they are used to "thicken" the sound of live string players.) Synthesized electronic orchestration has been the sound millions of Americans have heard on television commercials and movie soundtracks for two decades. And in the last fifteen years, there has been an inexorable march toward replacing larger and larger parts of the theater orchestra with such synthesized sound. Synthesized orchestration can be convincing in small theater venues if handled artfully. Peter Jones's two-handed electronic arrangement for the 1998 off-off-Broadway revival of *Flahooley* was uncanny in its illusion of orchestral detail.

Broadway orchestras in the early 2000s employed about 275 regular musicians and 1,500 substitutes. Almost all these players freelance extensively and are adept in all styles of performance—classical, jazz, and rock. But, like Gary Kasparov versus Deep Blue, they now compete with computers in a shrinking job market. Recently two different versions of a digital one-man-band dubbed the "virtual orchestra" have been used on Broadway and on tours. Until the actors and stagehands refused to cross the picket line during the March 2003 strike, the producers were threatening to run their shows with virtual orchestra accompaniment (at no reduction in ticket prices, it must be added). Virtual orchestras are of course cheaper to hire than live orchestras. One such "VO," called "the Most," "consists of a laptop computer and a keyboard that hooks into the house sound system. The show's score is programmed into the computer. Playing a minimal part on the keyboard triggers the synthesizer's programmed sounds. As the score scrolls across the computer screen, the operator/conductor can presumably speed up or slow down the machine to accompany the onstage performers."[82] The Most was used on Broadway together with live musicians for *Swan Lake* (1998). To hire it at the time of this writing costs an initial fee of up to $50,000 and then only $1,000 a week plus the salary of one keyboard player/conductor. The payroll for a large theater orchestra of up to twenty-six musicians costs up to $40,000 weekly. For comparison's sake, note that out of one $100 ticket to *Mamma Mia!* in 2003, 2 percent went to musicians' salaries, 5.3 percent to cast salaries (cast of 35), 6.9 percent to crew salaries, and 15.7 percent to creative team royalties.

It has been bruited that the Most and the other VO, the Sinfonia, have had some problems handling the subtle shifts of tempo that inevitably occur in live performances supporting live singers (until they, too, are replaced . . .). As the sound designer John A. Leonard has written, "No amount of technology can make up for the instant reactions and subtlety of shading that a skilled pit or session musician can bring to a performance."[83] The operator of the Sinfonia "controls the tempo of the digitized musical lines by tapping on a single key, following the conductor on a video screen in front of him and listening through headphones to the sound of the orchestra as a whole."

We're back to Irving Berlin's Buick, digitized. People in the trade have taken to calling VO operators "tappers."

Fred Astaire would weep.

ACT FIVE

*Wagging the Musical: How Director-Choreographers
Co-opted a Writer's Medium*

> The bankable part of the theatrical team now is
> the director, with Michael Bennett, Trevor Nunn,
> Bob Fosse, Mike Nichols and Tommy Tune heading
> the list. This in itself is an unhealthy symptom. The
> theatre flourishes when it is a writer's theatre.
>
> —Alan Jay Lerner, 1986[1]

> The director is a conductor, not a composer.... The
> interpretation the creative director contributes
> has its seeds in and grows out of the composer-
> playwright's text and is not some smart-assed ego
> trip of a fancy director pasted on to the text and
> destroying it.
>
> —Bobby Lewis, 1984[2]

Does history judge the literature of the drama by recalling the names of the directors who staged the greatest plays? The literary critic Alfred Kazin once wrote, "Literature is news that stays news." A century after most great plays were written, the names of their original directors were no longer news; yet the plays still were. The great dramatic literature of the Western world is indivisible in our minds from its playwrights—Shakespeare, Molière, Ibsen, Chekhov, Strindberg, Shaw, Calderón, Lope de Vega, et al. When we think of Hamlet, Falstaff, or Lear, we think of Shakespeare; our minds don't conjure up stage directors at the Globe Theatre (who didn't exist). When we think of Tartuffe, Hedda Gabler, Uncle Vanya, or Major Barbara, we don't tend to think of the personnel who devised blocking or painted backdrops. Even with recent classics such as *Strange Interlude*, *The Glass Menagerie*, or *Death of a Salesman*, the names of their directors Philip Moeller and Elia Kazan, whose interventions contributed meaningfully to their final form as plays (Moeller, not O'Neill, created the freeze-frame action of the spoken asides in *Strange Interlude*), don't come to mind before we first think of Eugene O'Neill, Tennessee Williams, and Arthur Miller.

Likewise, the titles of the greatest operas of the repertoire are undetachable from the names of their composers: Mozart, Verdi, Wagner, Puccini, Bizet, Richard Strauss. When we think of *Don Giovanni*, or *Carmen*, or *Tosca*, we don't immediately think of the stagers or designers of opera house productions; we think of the composers. Many connoisseurs know the names of the most illustrious opera librettists—Da Ponte, Boito, Hofmannsthal, Maeterlinck, and so on—but even these connoisseurs do not refer to the "Boito-Verdi *Otello*," or the "Debussy-Maeterlinck *Pelléas et Mélisande*." With ballet and modern dance there is more cocrediting: the names of the great choreographers are as well remembered as the ballet composers. Petipa, Fokine, Massine, Balanchine, and Graham are sometimes even better remembered than the composers of the music they set (Adam, Delibes, Rieti, Horst). However, as with opera, in ballet and modern dance the scenic designer, no matter how illustrious, is not the primary artist for whom the work is remembered. One doesn't speak of a Léon Bakst ballet, one speaks of a Michel Fokine ballet.

But the Broadway musical, a popular art with occasional aspirations to high art, is a special case. Not only is it both commercial enterprise and vernacular *Gesamtkunstwerk*, but also, with the substantial role played by dance and movement, it is a hybrid of writing and staging. Is it primarily a writer's theater or a stager's theater? It would seem that the answer is suggested by the winnowing process of history: today we don't remember or care who first directed or designed *Oklahoma!* or who first choreographed *Show Boat* or *My Fair Lady*; what we do remember and care about are these shows' composers, lyricists, and librettists and their creative inventions: the songs, plots, and characters. Yet perhaps this isn't entirely fair to the visual element of musical productions, less easily preserved than the music, lyrics, acting, and general "sound" so often immortalized on original-cast albums. The design, the dances, the pace, and the staging are ephemera of live performance that inevitably vanish, except in the memories of theatergoers and on the pages of theater history books. You can't hang the look and movement of a musical show on a wall permanently like a painting.

With motion pictures, a more permanent medium, the preeminence of the director has never been in doubt. In Hollywood the screenplay has always played second fiddle to the film director's conception: the screenwriter is a well-paid if expendable journeyman whose words and concepts are unprotected by contract and whose name is unglorified by history or tradition. By contrast, the Broadway playwright or musical book writer is protected by the contract of the Dramatists Guild, which stipulates that nary a word of the script can be changed without permission. In actual practice, the Guild contract is rarely invoked to the point of a legal facedown among the principals. Nevertheless, the legitimate stage is proverbially an author's medium, the sound stage, a director's medium. During Broadway's 1920–60 belle époque the public never recalled the names of the directors of musicals as they would recall the names of Cecil B. De Mille, Alfred Hitchcock, John Ford, or Orson Welles.

During Broadway's golden age the auteurs of the show were its actual authors. "Concepts" were devised by one or a combination of the composer, lyricist, and book writer. At most, the director was another collaborative voice, not a generalissimo. But beginning with the Broadway ballets of Agnes de Mille and Jerome Robbins in the 1940s, choreographers began to ascend the chain of command. Starting in 1957 with Robbins in *West Side Story,* there appeared on theatrical posters and playbills for Broadway musicals a special encircled box enclosing the name of one primary person: the director-choreographer, or the person credited with "entire production supervised by," or "conceived by." Though such "entirety" credits occasionally appeared in earlier decades, the bordered box around the name was new, symbolizing a sea change in the art form. By the early 1960s the names encircled in this playbill box—Robbins, Gower Champion, Bob Fosse, and, later, Michael Bennett and others—were the dramatis personae of a new breed of superdirector who was usurping the places not only of the old-style director and choreographer but also of the lyricist, book writer, and composer.

Still later, from the 1970s to today's *The Lion King,* the production design of a show—hitherto subordinate to the primary arts of music, words, and acting—began itself to assume an independent (if superimposed) expressive role in the overall character of a musical. For a generation it was dogma that the guiding star of the Broadway show was not the writing team but the director. And although the major choreographer-directors who inaugurated this trend have died, they have left to their successors a permanent legacy: the notion that the previous belle époque paradigm of composer-lyricist auteurship has been supplanted by a movement-based, visual storytelling, design-heavy premise of equal artistic merit.

But *is* it of equal artistic merit? Will history accord the names of Michael Bennett and Bob Fosse an equal pantheonic footing with those of Irving Berlin and Jerome Kern? Was the cultural ascendancy of the design-driven director-choreographer a superior artistic evolution, or a false dawn, a cul-de-sac? To answer these questions requires a complete reexamination of the first hundred years (we'll call it 1866–1966) of choreography, stage direction, and scenic design in our musical theater—underexplored historical pathways, far less often revisited than the much-rehashed biographies of the great songwriters. One learns that today's musical has experienced a retrograde evolution, perversely reverting to its nineteenth-century beginnings in spectacle and rejecting the power of words and music.

Scene One. *From* The Black Crook *to Balanchine*

Terping on Paleozoic Broadway: French Ballet, Pink Tights, and Tiller's Girls

Forms of show dance distinct from both folk dance and ballet have existed on the professional American stage since before 1800. *The Archers* (1796), an adaptation of the William Tell story considered by some scholars to be the earliest example of American musical comedy, featured not only songs but dance numbers described in contemporaneous accounts as hornpipe, an Anglo-Irish step-dance ancestor of tap dancing. Rope dancing (both tight and slack) was regularly performed in musical shows before 1800 and after. Surviving accounts of French ballet troupe tours of the American colonial era often report song performances interpolated in the dancing, as though song-and-dance was even then rooted in the American psyche.

Ballet's connection with opera, however, is centuries older than choreography's connection with musical comedy. Long before either ballet or step dancing was transplanted into any musical comedies, ballet sequences were featured in such still-performed early operas as Monteverdi's *Orfeo* (1607) and Purcell's *Dido and Aeneas* (1689). The Paris Opéra Ballet goes back two centuries. Other leading opera houses have also had resident corps de ballet for as long, and both Verdi and Wagner used ballets integrally in their works.

In 1866 a fire in a theater fortuitously led to the injection of ballet into the

215

veins of the American popular musical. Henry Jarrett and Henry Palmer, two American producers, had imported a French ballet, a London pantomime troupe, and special scenic effects for New York's Academy of Music. But the Academy of Music burned down before the show could open, leaving the producers without a venue for their performers and sets. Jarrett and Palmer persuaded another producer, William Wheatley, to shoehorn their stranded show into a potboiler melodrama Wheatley was about to open at his own theater, Niblo's Garden. Unrelated songs and incidental ballet music, some written expressly for the occasion, some purloined from sheet music shops, were interpolated to fudge the incongruous presence of the dancers. The resulting mélange, *The Black Crook* (1866), introduced a stageful of some one hundred shapely chorines in pink tights to a New York audience desperate for escapist entertainment since the devastation of the Civil War and the theater-tainting trauma of John Wilkes Booth's assassination of Lincoln. (In 1866 Booth's brother and fellow actor Edwin was still in a temporary retirement from the stage out of respect for the tragedy.)

The scenic effects created by Jarrett, Palmer, and Wheatley for *The Black Crook* were unprecedented for their time and launched the American musical not merely as a song-and-dance show but as a circuslike spectacle much in the style of some of the Lloyd Webber musicals of the 1980s and 1990s. *The Black Crook* was the first smash-hit musical: it made its producers and writers rich, and it played off and on for the rest of the nineteenth century. Its elaborate ballet numbers with fairyland motifs crossed with risqué suggestion were devised by the French troupe's Italian ballet master, Davide Costa (1835?–73), who could fairly be called America's first notable stage-musical choreographer. Costa choreographed a sequel to *The Black Crook*, *The White Fawn*, in 1867; he was signed by the impresario-mime-clown George L. Fox (Harry Fox's supposed ancestor) to arrange the dances for Fox's hit musical production *Humpty Dumpty* in 1868 and for a musical extravaganza entitled *The Twelve Temptations* in 1870.

Costa's choreography for *The Black Crook* and *The White Fawn* seems to have inaugurated the chorus line in American musical theater, although some commentators also credit the New York appearances from the late 1860s of "Lydia Thompson and her British Bleached Blondes" for popularizing the high-kicking chorus line, a borrowing from Offenbach and the Folies Bergère. The development of the Broadway chorus line received a further high kick in the pants in 1899 when George W. Lederer (1861–1938), who had in 1894 produced the first Broadway revue, *The Passing Show*, imported the Tiller Girls from England to perform in his musical extravaganzas *The Man in the Moon* and *The Casino Girl.*

John Tiller (1851?–1925) was a British businessman who had staged church pageants using march steps in military drill formation. His church work became so popular that he had to open a dance school in London; soon he added can-can kicks and other vaudeville-derived steps to the march step routines. The Tiller Girls were the original model for the Rockette-type chorus line in which each girl's movement is exactly matched with each other's in geometrical precision; Tiller is thus also the artistic godfather of Busby Berkeley's film choreography. Over the ensuing quarter century the Tiller Girls frequently appeared for such other Broadway producers as Hammerstein, Frohman, and Dillingham, but they achieved their greatest fame dancing in several *Ziegfeld Follies* in the early 1920s. Tiller's invention of the precision chorus line has had an extraordinarily durable cultural influence, extending all the way to the Moiseyev dancers of the Soviet Union, the 1975 musical *A Chorus Line,* disco dancing, and the precision-coordinated dance movements of Janet Jackson, Britney Spears, and others.

There were probably other ballet masters besides Davide Costa who choreographed Broadway musical shows in the 1866–1910 period, but they were given billing in theater programs very seldom, less frequently than the lighting and costume designers. By 1910 the anonymity was giving way: Pauline Verhoeven, the ballet mistress of the Manhattan Opera Company, choreographed the dancing (presumably all ballet) in Victor Herbert's popular show of that year, *Naughty Marietta,* while the dance director for the circuslike Hippodrome shows of 1905–20 was a ballet master, Vincenzo Romeo.

Later nineteenth-century revivals of *The Black Crook* tended to substitute vaudeville dancing for the original ballet. It appears that just as the vocal side of musical comedy sprang from a genetic mutation of operetta and vaudeville, the choreography of musicals eventually evolved as a blending of ballet steps and vaudeville hoofing—with a soupçon of modern dance thrown into the mix. The great modern dancer Ruth St. Denis (1877–1968) not only hoofed in the chorus line of George Lederer's 1899 *The Man in the Moon* but also did so in several Broadway straight plays of 1900 and 1901. Martha Graham (1894–1991) danced in the "ballet ballad" *The Garden of Kama* in the popular Broadway revue *The Greenwich Follies of 1923.* Ballet, hoofing, and modern coexisted on the musical stage, but did not meld for a long time. Vaudeville programs from 1880 to about 1920 commonly featured "toe dancing"—ballet acts presented as acrobatic novelties—cheek-by-jowl with tap acts and, occasionally, modern. When ballet and modern dance did appear in book musicals before about 1920, they tended to be presented as "numbers" disconnected from the plot, just as the songs of that era were nonchalantly unrelated to the story line. The 1912 Victor Herbert musical, *The Lady of the Slipper*, a treatment of the Cinderella story, featured dance numbers alternating between the eccentric dancer Fred Stone and the Russian ballerina Lydia Lopokova. Integration of dance with plot and subtext lay well ahead in the future.

The Theater of Spectacle-as-Content, Starring Arthur Voegtlin, Auteur of Musical Extravaganza

> [*The Black Crook*]'s priorities were visible from its
> advertising: the splendid "Tableaux, Costumes,
> Marches, Scenery" ("operated by 71 stage-hands")
> and the "premium transformation" ("purchased
> entire from Astley's Theatre, London") were
> splashed large across announcements which did
> not even mention the text or the music.[3]

Special effects were as much a part of the sensation of *The Black Crook* as dance and womens' legs. Scene changes effected before the audience's eyes were made possible by trapdoors, sets that could sink in full audience view below the level of the stage, and other machinery. The *New York Tribune* critic wrote of the finale, "One by one, curtains of mist ascend and drift away. Silver couches, on which the fairies loll in negligent grace, ascend and descend amid a silver rain. From the clouds drop gilded chariots and the white forms of angels."[4]

From *The Black Crook* to *Show Boat*, a significant component of American musical staging would continue to be spectacle or, in the parlance of the time, extravaganza: the design of physical properties and onstage movement to achieve circuslike effects that emphasized visual excitement untethered to plot, character, or organically developed drama. Much of this scenic legerdemain was achieved with primitive machines, and in the nineteenth century the very word "machinist" was a generic term for a theatrical technical designer or carpenter. Other producers of musical theater quickly tried to outmachine each other. *Humpty Dumpty*, the 1868 George L. Fox show which ran even longer than *The Black Crook*, sported live roller skaters (more than a hundred years before Lloyd Webber's *Starlight Express*) and a trick steamboat that exploded onstage. "Great prominence was given in the program to the names of the two scene designers, Minard Lewis and J. A. Johnson," noted Cecil Smith of *Humpty Dumpty.* "Their names appeared after the titles of each scene, much as composers' names are printed opposite the titles of their works in contemporary musical programs."[5]

The leading exponents of the nineteenth-century machine spectacle, and arguably the forerunners of the modern design-heavy concept musical, were the Kiralfy brothers. The Kiralfys were three Hungarian dancers who immigrated to the United States in 1868 and quickly found work dancing in revivals of *The Black Crook* and *Humpty Dumpty.* After several years of dancing in other producers' extravaganzas, they turned impresario in 1874 and set about producing musical spectacles such as *Around the World in Eighty Days* (1875), with its eighteen different exotic locales represented onstage. The Kiralfys' productions were among the first to use electric lighting, to introduce verisimilitude in stage properties, and to use imaginatively painted cycloramas to create the illusion of expanded space. As dancers themselves, they greatly enlarged the role of dancing in musicals, importing three European ballet troupes to appear in their biggest production, *Excelsior* (1883). The songs in the Kiralfys' productions were not, and didn't need to be, memorable, and frequently the only conceptual thread binding the pageantry was vague: in *Excelsior* the concept was nothing less than the rise of modern civilization, with the final stage tableau entitled "The Triumph of Light Over Darkness and the Peaceful Union of Nations." *Cats* (1982) is essentially a Kiralfy show gussied up with computerized stagecraft.

Machinery wasn't the only component of nineteenth-century stage design. The prevailing method of designing scenery was still the painting of flat backdrops, and much of *The Black Crook's* and *Around the World's* extravagance came from their eye-popping profusion of these. Scene painters for the theater were then trained easel painters; sometimes their backdrops deliberately simulated well-known paintings just as movie music of the 1930s and 1940s copied or simulated famous classical orchestral works. One of the first American stage designers to become prominent was William T. Voegtlin, a Swiss-born painter who worked in New Orleans and San Francisco before designing the 1870 New York revival of *The Black Crook* and a number of other subsequent musical extravaganzas.

It was as typical of hit musicals a century ago as it is now to emphasize visuals at the expense of all else. Lew Fields of the "Dutch" comedy team of Weber and Fields took note of this as soon as he started producing:

Fields's 1907 offering, *The Girl Behind the Counter* . . . allowed Fields to do almost anything, and one thing he wanted was a spectacular scene or two. From the start, his soda fountain scene was a show-stopper. In it, [he] attempted to match the color of his customers' dress or tie. One particularly difficult young man demanded his striped tie be duplicated. [Fields] succeeded, to prolonged applause. Another scene for which Fields held high hopes was a romantic one, a summer arbor at night, bathed in soft lights with additional trick lighting to simulate fireflies. The scene made an excellent first impression, but then fell apart when nothing of interest followed. . . .

Fields learned . . . the value of spectacle. . . . to bolster a limp score, [he inserted] an airship sailing across the stage. . . . [In] *The Midnight Sons* . . . Fields began the show with a stunning effect that helped set the mood. The real audience found itself gazing at an imaginary audience in an imaginary theatre, "with orchestra, balcony, and boxes filled." Indeed, the actual audience found itself on an imaginary stage, with footlights shining out at them and performers giving them not so much their all as their backs.[6]

The Summer Widowers had other stage effects, including "an entire apartment house, with its several floors all bustling with activity. Later in the show, Fields sent miniature airplanes flying through the theatre." Another Fields show had live farm animals scurrying around onstage. Such special effects were sensational but vacuous, "sight gags" divorced from dramaturgic necessity.

The onstage special effects known as "transformations" were as definitive of American musicals circa 1900 as show tunes became a few decades later. *The Wizard of Oz* was the biggest hit of 1903; newspaper advertisements for the show warned patrons that if they were late they would miss the opening cyclone scene in which a stereopticon (a slide projector that simulated cinematic dissolves) kaleidoscopically transformed the stage from Dorothy's Kansas house to a house uprooted by cyclonic gales and then dropped into the land of Oz. Reviewers had no good words for either the book or the songs; the show ran on the basis of its spectacle, devised by the director-choreographer Julian Mitchell and his scenic designers, John Young, Walter Burridge, and Fred Gibson.

Perhaps the outstanding exponent of the notion that spectacle *is* the content in musical theater was William Voegtlin's son Arthur (1857?–1948), who eventually eclipsed his father in influence and notoriety and is a missing link between the Kiralfys and Ziegfeld, a unique Barnum of the Rialto. (Arthur's son Jack Voglin [1904–82] was a second unit director and production manager for films and television programs from the 1940s to the early 1970s.) If the Kiralfys were the first director-choreographers, Arthur Voegtlin was the first director-designer. He has rather astonishingly been left out of most histories of American musical theater, even though he is arguably the truest precursor of the conceptual stage directors and the packaged musical of the late twentieth century. His unique conceptual authorship of musical extravaganzas has often been conflated with and misattributed to R. H. Burnside, who replaced him as the supervisor of Hippodrome extravaganzas and earlier had directed some of the Hippodrome shows Voegtlin conceived and designed. But Burnside's modus operandi was to write scripts and stage them; Voegtlin's m.o. was to conceive a staging and then get others (including Burnside) to write the script to support it. It was Arthur Voegtlin, not Burnside, Orson Welles, or Jerome Robbins, who invented "concept" as the ur-factor governing design, dialogue, plot, music, and lyrics—a notion that returned in the late twentieth century to unharness the glory of the book-driven integrated musical.

Born in Chicago, Voegtlin initially trained as a serious painter but shortly followed his father into the commercial theater, working for Charles Hoyt and painting some of the flats for the great 1891 musical hit *A Trip to Chinatown.* In the early years of his career he designed mostly for straight plays. His career took a fateful turn in 1905 with the construction of the colossal Hippodrome, the largest legitimate theater in the world, occupying the entire city block of Sixth Avenue between 43rd and 44th Streets, with over five thousand seats and a stage the size of half a football field. Built by the architects of Coney Island's Luna Park, the Hippodrome housed musical extravaganzas that dwarfed *The Black Crook:* for the opening-night show, *A Yankee Circus on Mars,* Voegtlin designed a battleship-sized space travel vessel that vividly depicted the title. He later designed onstage Hippodrome earthquakes and auto races, as well as his own versions of *Around the World in Eighty Days* and *HMS Pinafore* (with a complete life-sized replica of the boat, of course).

Voegtlin was the de facto commander-in-chief and auteur of all Hippodrome productions. Although Edward Temple, William Wilson, or Burnside was nominally credited in Hippodrome programs as stage director, Voegtlin, fifty years before Robbins's *West Side Story,* was apparently the first person in American musical theater ever given the handbill credit "conceived by." He told a reporter that his scene plots were "generally mapped out before the book, lyrics, and music are written" (though he hastily added that the "author, composer, costumer, stage manager, and artist were in conference every day for six months" before the Hippodrome show opened). Literary quality was not a criterion for Voegtlin; he once told an interviewer that he "never reads books."[7]

> Voegtlin originated basic story ideas, which took shape through mentally map-
> ping out individual scenes. . . . This was the starting point for a Hippodrome
> show—a scene conjured up and planned. Playwrights like R. H. Burnside, John P.
> Wilson, and Carrol Fleming supplied a story to accommodate it: a story whose
> plot would be dictated by related scenic ideas. . . . The Hipp's writers were
> bounded by scene requirements, and under only slight obligation to make the plot
> matter much.[8]

Needless to say, music and lyrics were also secondary to spectacle (Voegtlin
himself designed an onstage pool into which horses jumped) and dance (the
Hippodrome had a standing corps de ballet of two hundred). Once his run at
the Hippodrome ended, Voegtlin produced site-specific spectacles, such as an
installation in New York's Grand Central Terminal that simulated the battle-
fields of World War I, including trenches. (In the 1920s the Hippodrome was
used as a venue for vaudeville; in 1935 the last stage show, Rodgers and Hart's circus musical, *Jumbo*, was produced there. The theater was torn down in 1939.)

Not a modest man, Voegtlin once argued so undeferentially with the Hippodrome's owners, the Shubert brothers, that they had him physically ejected
from the theater. The avant-garde novelist Djuna Barnes (1892–1982), in her
early days a journalist who frequently interviewed theater personalities, entitled
her *Brooklyn Eagle* piece about Voegtlin "Interviewing Arthur Voegtlin Is
Something Like Having a Nightmare." In a newspaper interview in the January 3, 1915, *Hartford Courant*, Voegtlin said of his Hippodrome production of
Pinafore, "Realism—that's the keynote of my work. I suppose if Max Reinhardt
were to produce 'Pinafore' he would give us a violet ship with red trimmings
on a purple sea. That sort of impressionistic art is a joke, in my opinion."

During the first two decades of the twentieth century the Hippodrome
was perhaps New York City's number-one tourist attraction, and before 1915
Voegtlin, not R. H. Burnside, was repeatedly credited by drama critics and newspaper editorialists as the brain behind the shows. His photograph was the first,
and largest, in the Hippodrome's souvenir program, larger than the stage director's. In 1913 life almost imitated art for Voegtlin: while he was at home sitting in his dining room the ceiling suddenly collapsed, nearly killing him. The
narrow escape made the newspapers, which referred to the event as an "ava-
lanche" and to his miraculous survival as if it were a special effect from one of
his shows.

Voegtlin's Rialto nickname was "the Silver King"; the nickname of the other
great influence on New York's cult of spectacle was David Belasco's—"the

Bishop of Broadway"—because Belasco, though of Jewish origin, always wore a clerical collar in public. Belasco (1853–1931) was a producer-director-playwright whose plays *Madame Butterfly* and *The Girl of the Golden West* were immortalized when Puccini turned them into operas. Belasco became famous for his pioneering use of detailed, three-dimensional stage properties—actual, not painted, windows, doors that opened and shut, worn-out period furniture—as well as for his realistic lighting. The *New York Times* critic Brooks Atkinson wrote he was "the first manager to conceal footlights in the interest of reality."[9] But Belasco's career, like Voegtlin's, epitomizes the flip side of making a cult of extravagance. None of the many plays he wrote and gave super-productions to are revived today. Wrote Atkinson:

> He seldom presented . . . dramas of genuine distinction. He was a showman masquerading as an artist. To him, the theatre was on a higher plane than the tent-show or the carnival but essentially the same thing. . . . Everything was spectacular; everything was elementary; everything was in falseface. . . . He could buy the materials of reality. It was paradoxical, nevertheless, that the truth of reality escaped him. He did not believe in reality. He believed in stage buncombe . . .[10]

The Invisible Prehistory of Broadway Musical Stage Direction

> In the forgotten days of the actor-managers no
> director was in evidence; the stage manager
> moved the supporting players around the stage
> out of the path of the star's travels.
> —Howard Bay, scenic designer[11]

> In my early days as a playgoer—in the "teens"—
> hardly any director except David Belasco enjoyed
> program credit.
> —Harold Clurman, director[12]

Stage direction as an independent function, separate from but equal with acting, playwrighting, and technical management, is a relatively recent phenomenon in the history of the theater. Until the mid-nineteenth century, rehearsing and blocking the actors in Britain and America was handled by the actor-manager of the company, by the promptbook keeper (equivalent to the modern stage manager), or by the playwright (who not so infrequently was also the actor-manager). This was no less true in musicals. In the nineteenth century, more often than not the name (if any) to enter the historical record as the book director of a musical was the actor-manager or writer-manager, such as George L. Fox, Ned Harrigan, or Charles H. Hoyt. Even into the early 1900s, a musical's staging could be the work of so many hands that Oscar Hammerstein II, as a young stage manager in the 1910s, sometimes had the job of teaching dance steps to chorus line replacements, although he was completely untrained as a dancer.

Before 1920 it was considered respectable, maybe even the test of professionalism, for an actor to be able to play any part or for a director to be able to stage any kind of show. Recalled the actor DeWolf Hopper (1858–1935), "The type system, whereby an actor or actress is condemned for life to play only the sort of characters which he or she had first done conspicuously well, was not yet in vogue. Versatility was the first demand of the theatre—without it one was not an actor. . . . every player in his or her time ran the gamut from blank verse to low comedy."[13] The role of stage director was likewise that of a generalist: any director had to be equally prepared to direct comedies, tragedies, melodramas, or song-and-dance shows. One such director was Augustin Daly (1838–99), the leading author of American melodrama in the late nineteenth century, best known for his 1871 play *Horizon,* the first widely popular stage treatment of cowboys and Indians in the Wild West, and his 1867 melodrama *Under the Gaslight,* which introduced the now iconic device of tying an actor to a railroad track. Daly also directed musicals. The young Isadora Duncan played bit parts in touring Daly shows for two years, even singing in his 1896 musical *The Geisha.* Daly's staging style was kinetic, with lots of crossovers, and may well have influenced the young George M. Cohan's directing style.

In the less specialized theater of the early 1900s, the craft of stage managing was far closer to acting and stage direction than to technical production. It was standard operating procedure then for the stage manager to direct the rehearsals—which prompts the question, what did the "director" contribute? The answer appears to be the finishing touches. According to George Abbott, Belasco directed only the stars in his productions.[14] Jack McGowan (1894–1977), an actor (also director and librettist) whom Cohan directed in the musicals *Mary* (1920) and *The Song and Dance Man* (1923), said Cohan "would never fully direct his shows. Sam Forrest or Julian Mitchell or Johnny Meehan would block them out and then George would take over, sometimes as late as two days before the opening, to give it his special touch."[15]

This confusing near-interchangeability of directors and stage managers in early-twentieth-century musical theater is poignantly illustrated by the forgotten career of Ezekiel Bredin "Zeke" Colvan (1880–1945). Originally an actor,

Colvan stage-managed many *Ziegfeld Follies,* Ziegfeld-produced book shows, and shows produced by the Shubert Brothers, the Theatre Guild, and others. He was at times credited with the stage direction of shows he stage-managed, and at other times, vice versa. When the Depression hit Broadway, Colvan found steadier employment as a general stage manager of several municipal opera companies: St. Louis, Detroit, and finally Los Angeles. Colvan and his wife, Doris, cowrote the play on which the screenplay for the 1944 movie musical *Hey, Rookie* was based. He died in Hollywood.

For years Colvan's claim to immortality appeared to be his direction of the original production of *Show Boat.* The 1927 Ziegfeld Theatre playbill reads, "Dialogue staged by Zeke Colvan." But *Show Boat*'s librettist-lyricist Oscar Hammerstein told the theater scholar Miles Kreuger in 1960 that he himself had directed the show, ceding the billing credit to Colvan, who was the production stage manager, as a reward for his assistance in shepherding such a massive staging. Hammerstein's remark has given rise to an understandable misconception that Colvan was a mere traffic manager, a Ziegfeld hack. But Colvan wrote a remarkable book entitled *Face the Footlights! A New and Practical Approach to Acting* that corrects this misconception. The inside covers of the book reproduce a painting with a caption that reads, "The author (E. B. Colvan) directing the final dress rehearsal of the American classic *Show Boat.*" Throughout the book Colvan refers to his "25 years" of professional experience as a "director," "actor," and "producer." He never uses the term stage manager. Was he flattering and aggrandizing himself, or was the theater different then? He regales the reader with anecdotes from his directing experience, such as his being called in to direct the young Fred and Adele Astaire in vaudeville "fifteen years before" Ziegfeld's production of *Smiles* (1930). His obituary in the *New York Times* also refers to him only as a director, not as a stage manager.

Before the advent of the Actors Studio and before postwar books like Uta Hagen's *Respect for Acting* supplanted it, Colvan's *Face the Footlights!* was the leading textbook for aspiring actors in colleges and universities throughout the United States. It is a stunningly encyclopedic method for the apprentice stage actor, still valid today. Every tool—voice projection, gait, carriage, makeup, "beats," the eyes, the hands—is treated as constituent "stage mechanics" with which the actor can systematically build convincing character and motivation. Colvan meticulously describes the direction of the original 1927 *Show Boat,* breaking it down into discrete moments: Helen Morgan's use of her hands to pantomime a reaction in a scene with Magnolia; Charles Winninger's delivering a line with his eyes gimleted at another actor; Edna May Oliver's "explosive attack and quick cue pickup." Part of the stage manager's job has always been to train touring companies in the stage direction of the original. But Colvan's book goes beyond that. He also re-creates moments of performances by the Lunts, Helen Hayes, and other leading actors in plays of the time with exquisite nuance, recalling line readings and facial gestures most nonprofessionals would never notice. Colvan's book is an incunabulum of lost theater history; after reading it, it is impossible to think of him as merely running the call board, calling out prompts, and blocking crossovers for *Show Boat,* even if Hammerstein was the primary director. (The playbill for the 1932 Ziegfeld revival of *Show Boat* does not credit a stage director.)

Directing a musical demands a peculiar array of technical skills before it can progress to any kind of visionary statement. Some of the great directors of the twentieth century never directed a Broadway musical: Jed Harris, Gilbert Miller, Philip Moeller, Guthrie McClintic, Alfred Lunt, Eva Le Gallienne, Margaret Webster. Others equally distinguished directed only one or two with results ranging from indifferent to disastrous: José Quintero, Peter Brook, Lee Strasberg, Elia Kazan, Tyrone Guthrie, John Houseman, Alan Schneider, John Gielgud, José Ferrer. Harold Clurman, the cofounder of the Group Theatre and perhaps America's greatest authority on stage directing, directed only one Broadway musical in his long career, Rodgers and Hammerstein's 1955 flop, *Pipe Dream,* and his direction was doctored by Hammerstein and Joshua Logan. Of directors of musicals, Agnes de Mille wrote in 1956 that

> their work is considered sufficiently useful to be recorded exactly in complete detail and forwarded to the producer of each subsidiary or stock company, domestic or foreign . . . [in] extensive and detailed blueprints ("on the word 'cut' Donald sits on the left stool, crosses his legs and takes cup in right hand, looking over his shoulder"). . . . Mamoulian's direction in *Oklahoma!* and *Carousel,* for instance, is always reproduced.[16]

The "blueprints" de Mille refers to are the published librettos, as distinguished from the published play scripts, which condense the stage directions and eliminate the technical cues. Stage managers work from the former. In 1989 Harold Prince further commented:

> It makes me crazy that critics and theatre aficionados never acknowledge the fact that a show is originally directed the first time. The original director cut it, inspired rewrites, altered the cadence of sentences, chopped up a scene so that instead of it being one scene it's three scenes interpolated by a musical fragment,

put a blackout right in the middle of a scene that never expected one and then brought the lights up again to shock the audience. That, in fact, becomes part of the finished script of a show. So directing a show for the first time and directing a revival of the show are two very different things.[17]

Yet it is not clear that de Mille's and Prince's descriptions of what eventually crystallized as the craft of directing musicals had taken hold during the 1866–1927 period, because there are so few backstage accounts of musicals' directors during that time, and because the art form had yet to reach its highest maturity.

The evolution of the role of director from stage manager to conceptual and interpretive visionary happened in the European legitimate theater almost a century before it became the vogue on the American commercial musical stage. In Europe the two earliest exponents of the notion that a single controlling intelligence must unite all aspects of a play's production were, interestingly, both scenic designers. The first was Duke George II of Saxe-Meiningen, a scene painter by avocation who founded the Meiningen Players, who became famous on tours throughout Europe from 1874 to 1890. The second was the British scenic designer Gordon Craig (1872–1966), whose stage designs and writings promoted the idea of the total production reflecting a single creative vision.

From its very start in postbellum America, the musical had seemed almost to invite the concept of a superdirector because of the centrifugal nature of its form. Music, book, lyrics, dance, spectacle, and effects fairly demanded something more than a mere traffic manager to keep it all from spilling over. Yet that is not what happened. Directors did not become marquee names; with perhaps the single exception of Arthur Voegtlin, between 1866 and 1927 American musical theater established itself without the guiding vision of conceptual superdirectors. How well does popular memory or even the professional historian recall who was responsible for stage movement and physical production in *The Black Crook* (1866), *Evangeline* (1874), *Adonis* (1883), *A Trip to Chinatown* (1891), *Babes in Toyland* (1903), *Naughty Marietta* (1910), *No, No, Nanette* (1922), or even *Show Boat* (1927)? Before about 1930, musical show directors were invisible journeymen, some of them stage managers like Zeke Colvan who no doubt would have become fine stage directors in another era. The gaudy names were the impresarios—Ziegfeld and Shubert—not the directors.

To the extent there was any distinctive style of directing American musicals in the late nineteenth century—an era noted for chaotic books, illogical scene changes, wild jumps of plot, and inorganic interpolations of songs—it seems to have been the emphasis on spectacle eventually perfected by Voegtlin. Practitioners of this approach included Ben Teal (1862–1917), Eugene Presbrey (1853–1921), and Voegtlin's Hippodrome colleague R. H. Burnside (1870–1952). Book-based direction could not have developed to any degree of sophistication with the uncultivated revuelike scripts of that era. Yet even in the early twentieth century, as book construction of musicals became progressively tighter from the operettas of Victor Herbert to the Princess Theatre shows of Jerome Kern, stage directors did not emerge from facelessness. Who now remembers Edward Royce (1870–1964), who directed the Kern-Wodehouse Princess Theatre shows, the Harry Tierney hit *Irene* (1919), and several *Ziegfeld Follies* in the 1920s; Frederick Latham (1853–1943), who directed Herbert's *Mlle. Modiste* (1905), *The Red Mill* (1906), and Friml's great hit *The Firefly* (1912); Alexander Leftwich (1884–1947), who directed Rodgers and Hart's *A Connecticut Yankee* (1927) and many of the Gershwin musical comedies of the 1920s; or J. C. Huffman (1869–1935), who directed Sigmund Romberg's most successful operetta, *The Student Prince* (1924), and more than two hundred other Broadway shows?

The Deft Deaf Director-Choreographer

Amid the prevailing directorial anonymity, one forerunner of the late-twentieth-century director-choreographer emerged. Although highly paid, he never became a marquee name like the producers, stars, or songwriters. Legend has it that the character Julian Marsh, played by Warner Baxter in the immortal 1933 Warner Brothers movie musical *42nd Street,* is based on this proto–Michael Bennett named Julian Mitchell (1852–1926). Certainly Mitchell's real-life career began and ended as cornily as any biopic: he started as a callboy at Niblo's Garden, and—like Gower Champion fifty-four years later—died right before opening night of the last show he worked on, *No Foolin'.* He was even afflicted with a Hollywoodesque disability: Mitchell grew increasingly deaf as he became more successful, and by the peak of his career had to resort to Beethovenian tricks like putting his ear on the rehearsal piano to hear the music he was choreographing. (Jerome Robbins also became significantly hearing impaired toward the end of his life, but he too continued choreographing.)

Mitchell danced in one of the first revivals of *The Black Crook* and by the age of twenty was dancing in shows he produced and toured. He hooked up with the writer-producer Charles Hoyt in the 1880s and became his principal co-director, notably for the great hit of 1891, *A Trip to Chinatown.* From 1895 to 1904 Mitchell was the staff director-choreographer for Weber and Fields's Music Hall shows; he also briefly worked as a director for Reginald De Koven. By the time he had directed the 1903 hits *The Wizard of Oz* and *Babes in Toyland* and the 1911 smash *The Pink Lady,* Mitchell was being singled out among the army of journeymen directors for his spectacular and swift-paced productions.

What made Mitchell different from the army of anonymous directors in his era was that he not only devised elaborate dances as a professional dancer could, but he also was the first hired specialist to supervise overall movement in musical shows. He usually did not direct the dialogue scenes, perhaps owing to his hearing impairment in later years, although as late as 1920 Cohan used him to block scenes. But Mitchell coordinated dancing, special scenic effects, and ensemble movement to a single-handed extent beyond his predecessors, excelling in supervising the scenic design of such spectacle-heavy shows as *The Wizard of Oz.* Surviving press accounts do not credit him with stamping an individual style or overall vision on the productions he director-choreographed; he was simply a slick, deft technical manager of complex stage movement. To the public the big name in *Babes in Toyland* was its composer, Victor Herbert, not Mitchell; the big name in *Little Nellie Kelly* was George M. Cohan.

Mitchell reached the pinnacle of his career when Ziegfeld made him the house director of the *Follies* from 1907 on (though "book" scenes were still usually directed by others). Mitchell quit the *Ziegfeld Follies* over an argument in 1915 but returned in 1924, meanwhile continuing to direct other shows. It is evident that during his *Follies* tenure, Julian Mitchell bequeathed his most lasting gift to the musical stage: by borrowing the chorus line idea from John Tiller and enlivening it with a director's imagination, he invented the "production number"—that ensemble dance genre that has ever after characterized Broadway musicals and revues, nightclubs, television variety shows, and movie musicals: "Mitchell discarded the English concept of a chorus girl as a lifeless ornament. Instead, he brought the showgirls to life through personable groupings and individual lights to their distinctive personalities. He made them smile and listen to the tenor. . . . For one of the production scenes he had them marching up and down the aisles with rattling snare drums."[18]

Ned Wayburn: Field Marshal of Stage Geometry

In the late nineteenth century the performers in dance ensembles could number anywhere from a dozen to 150 depending on the size of the stage. The dominant influence on Broadway dance numbers for some forty years continued to be the large chorus line. Until the advent of Broadway choreographers like Balanchine in the 1930s, the geometrical visual effect of mass movement onstage was more important than the solo, duet (Fred and Adele Astaire were an exception), or the narrative-based Broadway ballet. The dance director who did the most both to develop the chorus line and to codify the vocabulary of choreography used in subsequent book musicals was Ned Wayburn (1874–1942), who replaced Julian Mitchell in 1915 as supervising director of the *Ziegfeld Follies* and who was his legatee in every way.

Born Edward Weyburn in Pittsburgh (he adopted a playbill typo as his stage name), Wayburn grew up in Chicago. He learned mechanical drawing as a student and practiced it while working at a real estate firm and for the 1893 World's Columbian Exhibition in Chicago. He found his way into show business first as an opera house usher, later as a vaudeville piano player, then as a dancer and stage manager, and finally as a dance director working for all the top theatrical producers: the Hammersteins, Lew Fields, Klaw and Erlanger, and the Shuberts. Wayburn also was an entrepreneur—in 1905 in New York he founded the Ned Wayburn Institute of Dancing, a studio that was also the chief employment agency for chorus dancers—and thus even before becoming Ziegfeld's general director he held an enormous backstage influence on Broadway. Fred Astaire credited Wayburn with persuading him to give up ballet for tap dancing and to team with his sister Adele.

Like Mitchell, Wayburn put a premium on rapid pacing of staging and dance. But he went beyond Mitchell by implementing the geometrical thinking he had learned in mechanical draftsmanship, subdividing the stage floor into a twenty-four-square checkerboard (four deep upstage-downstage, six across left-right) coordinated like a grid for dance routines. Wayburn was so mathematical he even taught his dancers the exact degree of angle for different kinds of high kicks. As a teacher he approached chorus line instruction like a scientist, rigorously training dancers in five basic dance types—musical comedy dance, tap dancing, acrobatics, ballet, and ballroom—which subsequently became the lingua franca for all Broadway choreographers. In personal appearance, though, Wayburn was not, despite his eyeglasses, professorial; perpetually attired in a sweater with a whistle on a string (or sometimes a megaphone), he looked like a combination of large teddy bear and athletic coach.

Wayburn pioneered the aerial-formation geometric choreography later brought to its apogee by Busby Berkeley in the movies. It was also Wayburn who created the solemn processional of gaudily costumed showgirls in the *Ziegfeld Follies* (variously called the "Ziegfeld strut" and the "Wayburn walk"), famously parodied half a century later in the Sondheim musical *Follies* (1971). Some sources say the Ziegfeld strut was developed to enable the girls, bedecked in heavy costumes and headdresses, to negotiate steps and risers without falling. Others say Wayburn had the girls affect an attitude of calculated aloofness to discourage rowdy male patrons from jumping onstage in the tempting small confines of Ziegfeld's roof garden theater, where the "Midnight Frolics" were performed.

Wayburn also expanded the versatility of the packaged chorus lines that were imported as performing ensembles into many shows and revues. Previously, such chorus lines for hire could only do precision dancing like the Tiller Girls; after Wayburn, precision groups learned other skills as well. For instance, one of Wayburn's protégeés from his early years in vaudeville, an American dancer named Kitty Hayes (1898?–1955), assumed the stage name of Gertrude Hoffman and went on to present her Gertrude Hoffman Girls in imitation Russian ballet, acrobatic circus routines, fencing, risqué Tiller Girl–style choruses, and many other varieties of dance on Broadway. By the 1920s producers found that, by hiring pretrained ensembles like the Gertrude Hoffman Girls or the Chester Hale Dancers who required little rehearsal, they could save the rehearsal salaries required by Chorus Equity (the labor union). (Some shows featured both the Gertrude Hoffman Girls and the Tiller Girls.)

Certainly before 1920 the division of labor in a book musical had become quite specialized: there was a singing chorus and a dancing chorus; there was a book (dialogue) director and a dance director. The singing chorus didn't dance, and the dancing chorus didn't sing. (Even as late as the early 1960s, songs were usually directed by the choreographer, sometimes with the book director's collaboration.) There was little need to broker any differences of concept between the book director and dance director because the latter accepted his lot as a mere technician who served the former, and the few double-threat choreographer-stagers like Mitchell and Wayburn were not interested in organic auteurist concepts, only in maximizing the spectacle and quickening the pace for the audience. For musical revues, the directorial hierarchy was the inverse: there was a general director who was either a director-designer or a director-choreographer, and a book-scene director who was subservient to whoever was the general director.

Wayburn's geometric dancing was one-upped by the man who in retrospect might seem the most logical candidate for revolutionizing the direction of Broadway musicals: Busby Berkeley (1895–1976). Watching the kaleidoscopic astonishments of the dance numbers in Berkeley's Warner Brothers films is probably the closest one can come today to experiencing what the live *Ziegfeld Follies* actually looked like. But on Broadway Berkeley was merely a dance arranger, albeit a highly successful one in the late 1920s. His more notable book show credits included the dances for Rodgers and Hart's *A Connecticut Yankee* (1927) and *Present Arms* (1928) and for the Oscar Hammerstein–Vincent Youmans musical *Rainbow* (1928), and he also choreographed revues. The few nonmusical films Berkeley directed—such as *They Made Me a Criminal* (1939), a boxing saga film noir with John Garfield—are almost bereft of his visual daring (*They Made Me a Criminal* is shot through a sepia filter but has no unusual camera angles). But his musical movies' production numbers uniquely enhance the accumulated momentum of repeated choruses of songs by orchestrating a kaleidoscopic succession of danced tableaux-in-motion. He had done this first on Broadway: press accounts of Berkeley's 1925–30 stage choreography (for example, those written by the esteemed dance critic John Martin) describe in detail a very similar kind of dance-step coordination of the visual with the musical rhythm: apparently Berkeley would subdivide the rhythm of the song into different beats and have his dancers execute them, creating the kind of visual rhythmic polyphony we can see in the 1933 film of *42nd Street* (which the staging and choreography in the 2001 Broadway version, despite all its high tech, cannot equal). Perhaps Broadway did lose something when Berkeley found his métier in Hollywood.

The Riddle of Production Design in the Musical

Berkeley, whether onstage or in films, was, like Voegtlin, an exponent of the notion that moment-to-moment scenic production was more important than the underlying plot or dramatic through-line. Directors of musical revues were generally from this "production design drives stage movement" school. However, not all scenic designers of the time subscribed to this idea; some believed that the role of scenery in the musical theater was to serve the underlying unity of the plot or theme, thus better integrating the show as an expressive whole. These two competing philosophies—does one design for disconnected pictures or for the whole plot?—have vied ever since for dominant influence in our commercial musical theater. They gave rise to corollary dilemmas: Is less more? Or is more more? Is indirect suggestion better than graphic illustration (the latter also called, in actor's lingo, "indication")? Are impressionistic scenic backdrops more or less theatrically compelling than realistic three-dimensional architecture and theme-park gizmos?

One of the theater's most influential exponents of the notions that impressionism is more powerful than realism and that scenic design should embody the inner spirit and not the outer trappings of the play was the Austrian director-producer Max Reinhardt (1873–1943), whose productions both in Europe and on Broadway had a pervasive if indirect influence on many later designers and directors of Broadway musicals. Ironically, Reinhardt ultimately came to be known not for less-is-more scenic integration; many of his most successful productions were Hippodromal and Voegtlinesque in their battalion-like casts and outsized spectacle, such as his 1927 *A Midsummer Night's Dream* or the 1937 *The Eternal Road* (with music by Kurt Weill). But Reinhardt, like the later Rouben Mamoulian, was able to combine impressionistic suggestion with monumental pageantry.

Even when scene painting was combined with three-dimensional architecture and stage machinery, the subtle painterly qualities of the backdrops were still the uppermost element in the stage settings of the great designers for Ziegfeld and other spectacle-heavy musical revues. Ziegfeld's most important designer, the Austrian Joseph Urban (1872–1933), who had studied both painting and architecture in Vienna, was the signature stage designer for the *Follies*. He

> treated the stage as an architectural environment with many invisible planes
> rather than a flat stage floor surmounted by an expanse of space. He designed
> platforms and ramps and broke up space within the opening with narrow walls,
> sometimes altering the dimensions of the stage proscenium opening itself. . . .
> Urban's technique of painting scenery consisted of using strong colors as a base
> coat, then covering it with specks of different colored paint in built-up layers. . . .
> By playing different colored lights on the same surface, it was possible to make
> the scene change colors as if by magic.[19]

"Urban blue" (referring to the piercing hue of the sky in the designer's backdrops) became a household word in the 1920s, as did "Ben Ali Haggin tableau." James Ben Ali Haggin Jr. (1882?–1951), born in New York City to a wealthy family, studied art in Munich and returned to New York to become a leading society portrait painter. In 1917 Ziegfeld hired Haggin to create *tableaux vivants,* or "living pictures," for the *Follies.* These elaborate painted flats were copies of famous paintings of the masters or other iconic images (e.g., Lady Godiva riding) animated by chiffon-draped, nearly nude Ziegfeld girls standing immobile in front of the flats and, seen from the audience, merging with them. As with Urban's designs, Haggin's were greatly enhanced by subtle lighting effects. But for *Show Boat* (1927), Urban's scenic designs departed from what Jo Mielziner called his "candy-box-cover art" and combined vibrant color and a suggestion of fantasy with naturalistic detail—setting the stage for the design style used for most belle époque musicals.

Urban's and Haggin's use of strong primary colors repainted by lighting influenced director-designers such as Hassard Short, John Murray Anderson, and Vincente Minnelli to make color schemes—not plot, character, or subtext—a major element of their stagings. (It is a sad irony that the vast majority of surviving photographs of the *Ziegfeld Follies* are in black and white, leaving posterity only to imagine the colorist genius of Urban and Haggin.) Short, Murray Anderson, and Minnelli—not Mitchell, Wayburn, or George Abbott—were the first "name" directors of Broadway musicals to be given prominent display in advertisements and handbills, even though in most (maybe almost all) cases others directed their book scenes and set their dance numbers.

Hubert "Bobby" Hassard Short (1877–1956), a British-born ex-actor of stage and silent screen turned lighting and production designer, made copious use of stage platform elevators and such special effects as roller skating. But his real genius was creative lighting. Irving Berlin once wrote that when he asked the GIs in the audience at a wartime South Seas performance of *This Is the Army* to light their matches, seeing "an audience of 17,000 light up like so many flickering stars would even impress Hassard Short."[20] For the revue *Face the Music* (1932), Berlin made sure that Short was the supervisory director even though George S. Kaufman directed the dialogue scenes. In the 1930 revue *Three's a Crowd,* Short turned out the footlights and hung lights from the balcony—at the time unprecedented.

From the 1920s to the early 1950s Short stage-directed both revues—including several *Music Box Revues* of the 1920s, *The Band Wagon* (1930), Berlin's *As Thousands Cheer* (1932), Cole Porter's *7 Lively Arts* (1944)—and book shows. Among these were Jerome Kern's *Sunny* (1925), the Weill–Hart–Ira Gershwin *Lady in the Dark* (1941), the Duke-Latouche *Banjo Eyes* (1941), Hammerstein's *Carmen Jones* (1943), and the 1946 revival of *Show Boat.* But in most of the book shows, the dialogue direction was entrusted to someone else—Moss Hart in *Lady in the Dark,* Charles Friedman in *Carmen Jones,* Hammerstein in the 1946 *Show Boat.* As a stager of musicals, Short was one of the first to pioneer the pseudocinematic multiple scene changes common in post-1975 productions; for the revue *The Band Wagon* he designed and directed two stage turntables, considered revolutionary at the time; for *Lady in the Dark,* he mounted the show on four turntables devised by the set designer Harry Horner. He was also a color wizard. Taking a cue from Urban, Short discovered a way to use lights to change colors into black and white and back, and he designed all the scenes in *Carmen Jones* entirely in single hues. Hassard Short's legacy, while brilliant, is style, not content.

234

Like Short, John Murray Anderson (1886–1954) was noted more for production legerdemain than for unified dramatic statements. Canadian-born,
educated in Scotland and Switzerland, Murray Anderson began a career as an
accountant, then in the 1910s moved to New York's Greenwich Village and
quickly became an antiques dealer, ballroom dancer, and impresario of society
galas. Despite his early success as one of the preeminent ballroom dance
demonstrators, he never "director-choreographed" a Broadway show; he only
staged them, letting the dance director set the dance routines. Beginning with
his direction of the *Greenwich Village Follies* in 1919, he became known for
moving treadmills, dramatic scene changes, heightened use of color, and other
feats of technical virtuosity. He produced and directed revues, circuses, nightclubs, and even aquacades (and, like his fellow aquacade producer Billy Rose,
sometimes wrote lyrics), but he also staged a number of book musicals—
Rodgers and Hart's 1925 *Dearest Enemy* and 1935 *Jumbo* (at the Hippodrome),
the Romberg-Hammerstein *Sunny River* (1941), and Weill and Ira Gershwin's
1945 *Firebrand of Florence*. Like Short, Murray Anderson, although credited
with supervising the entire production, usually had a book-directing under-
ling (George Abbott on *Jumbo*). Of the two, Short, who had acted extensively,
had more of an instinct for dialogue and dramaturgy. For all his glittering reputation for stage magic, Murray Anderson never directed an important book
show. Richard Rodgers recalled:

> The official billing for *Jumbo* read: "Entire Production Staged by John Murray An-
> derson." Actually Murray, who had been so helpful ten years before in putting on
> *Dearest Enemy,* was primarily concerned with the physical aspects of the produc-
> tion—the scenery, lighting and costumes—and didn't really care much about the
> story or the way the songs fit in. I recall once just before the show's opening when
> he took me backstage to demonstrate the workings of a huge, complicated lighting
> switchboard. "Each one of the lights is controlled by its own special switch," he
> explained. "It's all pre-set. All you have to do is just touch a switch and you get ex-
> actly the lighting effect you want." Then he started to giggle. "See this little yellow
> one here?" he said, pointing to a tiny toggle switch at the far right of the board.
> "Do you know what that's for? That's for the book." A single light switch was all
> the plot of the musical meant to him.[21]

Vincente Minnelli (1903–86), initially a draftsman and painter, broke into
Broadway as a costume designer for the 1930 and 1931 editions of the revue *Earl
Carroll's Vanities.* For the 1932 *Vanities* he also designed sets and soon after be-
came general production designer for Radio City shows and for the Shubert

Brothers' 1930s retreads of the *Ziegfeld Follies*. By 1937, for the Shubert revue *The Show Is On*, Minnelli got a Voegtlin-style credit—"entire production conceived, staged, and designed by"—even though the program also stated that the well-known actor-producer-director Eddie Dowling "stage directed," Edward Clark Lilley directed "the sketches," and Robert Alton arranged the dances. Minnelli also was the designer and stager of *Hooray for What!* (1937), for which Alton also set the dances, and he designed and codirected *Very Warm for May* (1939) with Hammerstein before leaving for Hollywood, where he found lasting fame as a director of MGM movie musicals in the Arthur Freed unit. His Broadway career was brief but, like Berkeley's, notable for previewing the style that would become the signature of his films; in Minnelli's case, the signature was dazzling color and a high-toned elegance of production design. But in the theater this approach could be a formula for vacuity. In 1967, the producer David Merrick brought Minnelli back to direct an ambitious musical entitled *Mata Hari*. Minnelli "paid excessive attention to the scenery and costumes to the detriment of the whole. To compensate for the script's deficiencies, he ordered so much scenery that it could not fit in the theatre." The show's angered set designer, Jo Mielziner, told an associate that the result was "one third Minnelli, one third Mielziner, and one third shit."[22] *Mata Hari* closed out of town.

Short, Murray Anderson, and Minnelli were inheritors of the glittering production school of Voegtlin and Ziegfeld: the idea that the staged show should focus more on the scenic design than on the actors or human values, that a musical's entertainment value resides in production, not content. None of these directors is associated with the great book musicals that are revived for inherent strengths of book, music, or lyrics (though *Lady in the Dark* deserves to be). The first prominent scenic designer of musicals to sail against the prevailing winds of superimposed decoration and tack toward expressing the mood of the text was Jo Mielziner (1901–76). The son of a portrait painter, he was a precocious draftsman who was admitted to a leading art school at sixteen and won scholarships to study in Europe at twenty-one. Mielziner had originally intended to be an easel painter, but an experience with a Detroit summer stock production in 1921 as a gofer for his older brother, the actor Kenneth MacKenna, gave him the theater bug. In the summer of 1922 he apprenticed at Joseph Urban's scenery design studio in Yonkers, meeting and working with Urban. Later that year he attended productions in Berlin staged by Max Reinhardt and Leopold Jessner, spoke with Gordon Craig in Italy, and saw a production in Paris of *The Brothers Karamazov* acted by the Moscow Art Theatre without scenery, costumes, or lights and with only a bare table and chairs as props. Of this evening in the theater Mielziner's biographer Mary C. Henderson remarks, "The experience taught him that less was sometimes more in lighting the stage as long as the actors moved to speak within its range. He was convinced by this experience that simplicity had its own truth on the stage, an idea he would never forget but was only infrequently allowed to put into practice in his long career."

Starting in 1931 with the Gershwin brothers' musical satire *Of Thee I Sing*, Mielziner was the scenic designer (and sometimes the costume and lighting designer) for more than fifty musicals, including most of the canon of the golden age. In them he put into practice his aesthetic of selective realism, providing just the necessary three-dimensional physical properties while creating through painter's perspective and light—even with the labyrinthine sewer backdrop he painted for the crap-game scenes in *Guys and Dolls* (1950)—a boundless horizon of fantasy that helped establish the intangible feel of a show. He paved the path on Broadway for the style of text-driven design for musicals, the mode of such other superb scenic designers as Boris Aronson, Howard Bay, and Oliver Smith.

Mielziner was so highly regarded an artist that at times he unwittingly exerted the auteurist clout of a Voegtlin. During rehearsals for *South Pacific* his drawing of the island mountain Bali Ha'i led Hammerstein to rewrite the lyric for the song to fit Mielziner's conception. Early in the rehearsals for Rodgers and Hart's *Pal Joey*, the choreographer Robert Alton was conceptually at sea and threatened to quit. According to the show's director, George Abbott, it was Mielziner—not Rodgers, Hart, Alton, or Abbott—who conceived the idea of ending the first act with "a scene in which Joey envisions his future in the magnificent club which his new girl friend is going to buy him." This scene was acclaimed by dance critics and is now regarded as a forerunner of de Mille's and Robbins's ballets. Said Abbott, "I accepted the suggestion unhesitatingly. This is a perfect illustration of how many collaborators there really are in a musical comedy."[23]

Rouben Mamoulian: Stage Movement as Seamless Dramatic Integration

Before *Show Boat*, directors of Broadway book musicals were of three types. There were the aforementioned choreographers and designers who were the earliest superdirectors, all of whom began as and mostly remained revue directors. Then there were the anonymous stage managers like Zeke Colvan and journeyman directors like Alexander Leftwich whom theater history has largely forgotten. And there were the book writers who directed their own shows: George M. Cohan and Oscar Hammerstein before 1930; George S. Kaufman, Moss Hart, and Yip Harburg, among others, after 1930. Even *Show Boat* had no conceptually unifying stager, but rather a committee: the dances were by Sammy Lee, the sets by Joseph Urban, the book direction by Colvan and Hammerstein, who was only thirty-two at the time. Until the 1940s, dialogue direction and musical number direction of book musicals invariably were two separate jobs. The first important "total vision" director of Broadway musicals to break the mold of choreographers, designers, and writers staging a musical—arguably, the first director to bring a coherent directorial style to book musicals' direction, and the first to realize that the vulgar, lowly, vaudeville-derived Broadway musical was a theatrical form to which the full resources of high drama could be harnessed—was Rouben Mamoulian (1897–1987), familiarly known backstage as "Mamoo" or "the mad Armenian."

Born to well-to-do parents in czarist Russia, Mamoulian played the violin as a child and as a teenager studied at the Moscow Art Theatre under Evgeny Vakhtangov (who was known for his stylized or "fantastic" realism). Emigrating from revolution-embattled Russia to Britain, he directed a West End production when only twenty-five and in 1923 was recruited by the American philanthropist George Eastman to direct an opera theater lab at the Eastman School of Music in Rochester, New York. His school chum at Eastman, the then set designer and later novelist Paul Horgan, described the young Mamoulian as a wunderkind mixture of Leonardo and Orson Welles:

> He knew more about the various contributing elements of a stage production than any of the artists separately charged with creating each. His knowledge and taste in music were superior. . . . he was widely read in dramatic and operatic literature, as well as in other kinds. . . . He was an amusing draughtsman, and liked to draw . . . but beyond this, his love of the art of painting was nourished by a penetrating knowledge of the great visual art of the European past; and the authority of such taste made him immediately articulate in plans and criticism of stage decors.[24]

At Eastman, Mamoulian adopted Stanislavsky's method of directing opera singers as though they were method actors, with a concentration on inner dramatic truth. After three years he went to New York to work for the Theatre Guild, where he became an overnight sensation directing the Guild's 1927 production of DuBose Heyward's play *Porgy*. The following year he directed Eugene O'Neill's *Marco Millions;* in 1930 he directed the American premiere of

Arnold Schoenberg's one-act opera *Die glückliche Hand* in Philadelphia. After directing several more Guild attractions, Mamoulian turned to motion pictures, starting with *Applause* (1930) and proceeding to such innovative early sound films as *Dr. Jekyll and Mr. Hyde* with Fredric March, *Love Me Tonight* (arguably the first completely integrated musical comedy on stage or screen, with score and lyrics by Rodgers and Hart), *Queen Christina* with Greta Garbo, and *Becky Sharp,* the first Technicolor film. He directed most of *Laura* (1944) before he was pulled off the set by Darryl F. Zanuck and replaced by Otto Preminger, and he started filming *Cleopatra* (1963) before being replaced. Mamoulian periodically returned to Broadway to direct musicals, including the original production of the Gershwin-Heyward opera *Porgy and Bess* (1935), Rodgers and Hammerstein's *Oklahoma!* and *Carousel,* the Kurt Weill–Maxwell Anderson *Lost in the Stars* (1949), and a number of less successful musicals. His last major direction job was the 1957 film version of Cole Porter's last musical, *Silk Stockings;* after the humiliation of being fired from *Cleopatra,* he retired.

"Teamwork is impossible in directing a play," Mamoulian proclaimed in a 1964 book he wrote for children, neatly summing up his credo. He also told his young readers:

> In 1942, the Theatre Guild had a play script, "Green Grow the Lilacs," which they wanted to transform into a musical comedy. They offered me a contract just to direct.
>
> I refused. From the Rochester days, I'd dreamed of an integrated production— music, dancing, dialogue, action and singing—a truly American theatre. . . . In "Green Grow the Lilacs" I saw my opportunity. I persuaded the Guild to let me do the job my way. To my usual one-paragraph contract, another was added: I would "direct the whole production in all its elements."[25]

Mamoulian outdid Wayburn, Berkeley, and all other previous rhythmically savvy stage directors of musicals by holistically interweaving music, rhythm, blocking, and the "beats" of the scene (in actors', not musical, parlance) to create a sculpture-in-motion that was not merely superficially exciting but expressive of the psychological subtext. Where Wayburn had conducted his dance rehearsals like scrimmages with a whistle, the musically trained Mamoulian sometimes literally conducted: "with the script propped up on a music stand, keeping time with a conductor's baton, a metronome, and a whistle."[26] Where Berkeley orchestrated the image to embody the stomp of a song's beat, Mamoulian went one better by visualizing not only the song beat but blocking a visual rhythm that set the mood of the story and characters. Mamoulian described how he did this in directing *Porgy*'s opening scene to establish the teeming life of Catfish Row:

> All the activity, the pounding, tooting, shouting and laughing is done to count.
> First I use one/two time. Then beat three is a snore—zzz!—from a Negro who's
> asleep; beat four silent again. Then a woman starts sweeping the steps—whish!—
> and she takes up beats two and four, so you have Boom!—whish!—zzz!—
> whish!—and so on. A knife sharpener, a shoemaker, a woman beating rugs and
> so on, all join in. Then the rhythm changes: four: four to two: four, then to six:
> eight. All the natural rhythms of Charleston are syncopated.[27]

Seven years later Mamoulian staged the Catfish Row opening scene in Gershwin's opera in a similar manner: the drama critic John Mason Brown wrote that the production was "filled with a visual music of its own, unforgettable in the ever-changing beauty of its groupings, extraordinary in its invention, and amazing in the atmospheric details."[28] But Mamoulian's stagecraft wasn't only musically based: he was also a visual stylist, improving on the tableau idea of Ben Ali Haggin by animating and mobilizing the tableaux; he one-upped John Murray Anderson and Hassard Short by using chiaroscuro effects that highlighted emotions in the text. The producer Cheryl Crawford, who was Mamoulian's assistant stage manager at the time of *Porgy,* recalled of the funeral scene: "Mamoulian asked to have a lamp placed in front of the group of mourners. By accident, the main lights were brought down, and suddenly we saw the gigantic shadows of the mourners outlined against the back of the room. Everyone gasped at the effect, and of course Mamoulian kept it."[29]

Mamoulian built up massive pictorial compositions bit by bit from the psychological truth of each individual in the stage tableau. One of *Carousel*'s original cast members, Jan Clayton, recalled, "His direction is a very personal thing because to him each member of the cast is an individual performer. He handles large groups magnificently because he acknowledges no 'chorus' per se. Each performer, whose name he knows early on, is directed specifically to have a personality and purpose all his own."[30] The Hungarian playwright Ferenc Molnár, author of *Liliom,* the play upon which *Carousel* was based, sat in on a rehearsal of *Carousel* and told Mamoulian, "When you direct a large scene with a lot of people, you make it look as though there were twice as many people. You handle crowds better than any director I've ever known."[31]

Mamoulian had wanted to direct a musical version of *Liliom* ever since 1937, when his friend Kurt Weill had tried to get the rights from Molnár and asked

Mamoulian if he would direct. (Weill later wanted Mamoulian to direct his 1947 Broadway opera *Street Scene,* but Mamoulian was unavailable.) When Rodgers and Hammerstein obtained the rights to adapt *Liliom,* they reengaged Mamoulian and the rest of *Oklahoma!*'s creative team, including the choreographer Agnes de Mille. Molnár had opened his play with a carnival scene, without dialogue but with a crowd rhubarbing; Rodgers and Hammerstein decided to forgo a conventional overture and adapt Molnár's opening into an extended pantomime set to music (some of which Rodgers had composed years earlier but never used). Rodgers insisted on putting a real carousel onstage for the prologue, which left little room for de Mille to move dancers. But Mamoulian created a masterpiece, the seven-minute "Carousel Waltz" prologue:

> As "The Carousel Waltz" variously tootles, glides, and plows along, three principals emerge from the throng: heroine Julie, her friend Carrie, and hero Billy, the carousel barker who flirts, amiably, unconcernedly, with Julie. Other characters catch our notice—Mr. Bascombe, the pompous mill owner; Mrs. Mullin, the widow who runs the carousel and, apparently, Billy; a juggler; a dancing bear; an acrobat. But what draws us in is the intensity with which Julie regards Billy—the way she stands frozen, staring at him, while everyone else at the fair is swaying to the rhythm of Billy's spiel. . . . Julie and Billy ride together on the swirling carousel, and the stage picture surges with the excitement of the crowd, and the orchestra storms to a climax.[32]

The literature on *Carousel,* which generally focuses commentary on the songs "If I Loved You" and "Soliloquy," has not done justice to the cataclysmic opening of the show or the fact that, although de Mille had a hand in it, its concept and execution are pure Mamoulian. De Mille's biographer Carol Easton quotes the *Carousel* dancer Bambi Linn as recalling that the prologue wasn't working and that de Mille restaged it at Mamoulian's invitation shortly before the show's opening.[33] But in a July 25, 1973, interview, de Mille told a Mamoulian scholar, Bennett Oberstein, that the prologue was presented as Mamoulian staged it and that she didn't like it, referring to its staging as "flat and repetitious" and the music "tinkly and sentimental." De Mille also told Oberstein she would have preferred "additional rehearsal time to rewrite and restage the number" but that no such time was made available.[34]

The detailed stage action of *Carousel*'s pantomime prologue is carefully wrought beat by beat to create palpable excitement: that's Mamoulian. It is cinematic; that's also Mamoulian. It embodies narrative exposition, subtle dramatic characterization, visual éclat, suspense, haunting melody, and driving rhythm—all this, without a word being spoken or syllable sung. As a micro-cosmic *Gesamtkunstwerk,* it is arguably the greatest scene in American musi-cals. In a sense the rest of the show is almost an anticlimax, or at least a separate artistic entity. For all its undeniable pathos, *Carousel* never quite recaptures the compelling magic and momentum of its opening musical pantomime.

Yet the staging of the songs in *Carousel* also bore the director's signature; it was Mamoulian, shattering Broadway precedent, who directed the songs in *Oklahoma!* and *Carousel,* not the choreographer. His proportionate share in creating the stylistic revolution of the integrated musical epitomized by Rodgers and Hammerstein remains strangely unappreciated. Before Mamou-lian, the performance of songs in a revue or musical comedy was presenta-tional and extraneous: the singer would come to the footlights and sing, stop-ping the action and standing apart from it like a nightclub performer. Although *Show Boat* may have deviated somewhat from this, Kern's later mu-sicals like *Music in the Air* and *Very Warm for May* reverted to song presenta-tionalism, as did most Rodgers and Hart shows (*Pal Joey* excepted, although its action occurred mostly in a nightclub, mooting the point). In *Porgy and Bess, Oklahoma!,* and *Carousel,* Mamoulian took the downstage footlight out of the musical comedy song, integrating its performance within the total can-vas of narrative.

Mamoulian's imperious insistence on total control was both boon and bane. He feuded with the Theatre Guild during the runs of both *Oklahoma!* and *Carousel:* Mamoulian claimed the Guild gave his directorial credit insuffi-cient billing in advertising and playbills, while the Guild claimed he had taken too much credit for the shows' success in press interviews (perhaps that's why Rodgers and Hammerstein did not hire him again after *Carousel*). Some per-formers thought him indifferent to them, although many others, such as John Raitt and William Holden, gratefully credited him with forming them as young actors. His mastery of crowd scenes never abated. Recalled the actor William Greaves of Mamoulian's direction of the 1949 *Lost in the Stars:* "To show fear, he would place all the people in an aversive slant away from the source of danger. They weren't perpendicular to it, they were at about 75 de-grees so that, looked at from a distance, they would almost seem to be starting to run away."[35]

In his long retirement Mamoulian was something of a real-life version of Norma Desmond in *Sunset Boulevard*—a once-celebrated cultural icon who had survived too far beyond his glory days. He lived in the past, decrying post-1960 changes in film and theater in idealized paeans he would volunteer to anyone who would listen, but increasingly neglected his own day-to-day realities. He lived in seclusion in Beverly Hills with his unstable alcoholic wife and some forty cats. Mamoulian died thirty years after completing his last film, of "prolonged malnutrition and dehydration," according to the Los Angeles County Sheriff's office, which reported that the interior of the Schuyler Road mansion that was home to the one-time boy wonder and maestro of Broadway and Hollywood had been destroyed by "years of cat urination, defecation, and clawing. Everything in the house, including the Mamoulians themselves, was flea-infested."[36]

Pacemakers of Show Time: Cohan, Abbott, Logan, and Play Doctoring

After Mamoulian, the notion of what kind of stage direction artistically elevated the musical changed permanently. Although plenty of revuelike musical comedies—"tired-businessman specials"—continued to be presented on Broadway, shows written by the better composers and lyricists would henceforth be directed in a more thoughtful, nonpresentational style, as Elia Kazan recalled of Kurt Weill's *One Touch of Venus* (1943):

> I asked him [Weill] why they wanted me to direct the show. His response, spoken with the most persuasive conviction, was that they wanted the musical directed as if it was a drama, not in the old-fashioned, out-front staging tradition of our musical theatre. That style was dated now; *Oklahoma* had changed everything. After all, Kurt observed, songs were a continuation of the dialogue and should be so treated.[37]

But nonpresentationalism did not mean that the directorial function of maintaining a swift pace was obsolete. While cumbersome set changes may have retarded the action in the pre-1950 era and required "in-one" scenes to cover set changes behind the curtain, brisk scene pacing and dialogue timing had been characteristic of American musical comedy direction since Augustin Daly's nineteenth-century productions. But the artist who had lifted pep to its early Broadway apotheosis was "Yankee Doodle Dandy" George M. Cohan (1878–1942), in his long string of let's-out-jingo-Kipling, Horatio Alger-waves-the-Old Glory musicals such as *Little Johnny Jones* (1904), *Forty-five Minutes from Broadway* (1906), *George Washington Jr.* (1906), and many others from 1901 to the 1920s.

Certainly every moment of Cohan's shows—which he wrote, composed, directed, coproduced, and starred in—was stamped with his creed: "Speed! Speed! and lots of it; that's my idea of the thing. Perpetual motion."[38] Cecil

Smith called Cohan "the apostle of breeziness."[39] Brooks Atkinson wrote, "He invented a type of musical show in which everybody talked at the top of his voice, everybody sang full out and danced ferociously."[40] (However, one dance historian firmly believes that Cohan's own dancing was neither machine-gun tap-style nor acrobatic.)[41] The Cohan predilection for pell-mell pacing probably had as much to do with his shows' success with audiences as his hoofing and flag-waving ditties. In fact, Cohan's scripts, lyrics, and music were often panned by the drama critics. One critic wrote of Cohan's 1907 musical *The Honeymooners,* "It goes so fast that it almost bewilders and gives the impression of a great machine shooting out characters, choruses, songs, dances with rapid-fire quickness and precision." Ironically, this antique description could be lifted verbatim and applied to the directorial style of *Urinetown* (2001) and many other Broadway musicals post-1990. Of course, the subtle "beats" of a Stanislavsky or Mamoulian staging do not figure into the style of direction that puts speed and loudness above everything else.

The director often said to be the main inheritor of the Cohan style was George Abbott (1887–1995). Abbott was proverbial for cutting, streamlining, and energizing musicals—"Boredom is the enemy, and Abbott conquers it by keeping the show moving briskly"[42]—but the apparent similarity to Cohan is deceptive. Asked his secret, Abbott famously replied, "I make them say their final syllables," but then he added that

> the one thing a play should not have, is just simple uncontrolled speed. The director who thinks that pace is just hurry makes a tragic mistake and produces a noisy, violent hodgepodge devoid of any illusion. . . . The great actor knows that if the scene is good he is good and he does not have to be urged to pick up his cues, but there are other actors under the impression that the more time they can consume the better they will be—and so over and over they must be told to pick up their cue.[43]

In other words, pacing should be organic to the play, not pacing for pacing's sake, as Abbott's onetime stage manager, the director Harold Prince, observed of his mentor:

> There is never a dishonest moment on the stage. Characters are always consistent with their character. He never slams a door for the sake of slamming a door, he slams it for a reason. His shows are honest, peppy, energetic—*really* energetic, and that's another thing I learned from him. There's so much phony energy in the theatre: people think that by running around in circles like a crazed tiger, you're

244

displaying energy, and, in fact, you're not. You can have energy in the stillest place in the world, and he knew that.[44]

Raised in upstate New York and Wyoming, Abbott after college attended the famous dramatics course at Harvard taught by George Pierce Baker that also attracted Eugene O'Neill and other playwrights. Half a century later, Abbott wrote that Baker "gave you no nonsense about inner meanings and symbolisms; he turned your whole thoughts and energies into the practical matter of how to make a show." Abbott made his debut as an actor on Broadway in 1913 and by the 1920s had begun to get his plays produced; he then segued into directing. His first direction of a musical (assisting Murray Anderson) was *Jumbo* (1935); his last, at ninety-five, was the 1983 revival of *On Your Toes;* at age 106 he was working on a rewrite of the book of *Damn Yankees.* In fifty years he directed, cowrote, or coproduced more than two dozen hit musical comedies (*The Boys from Syracuse, On the Town, High Button Shoes, The Pajama Game, Fiorello!,* et al.), play-doctored many others, and became legendary as "Mr. Abbott." (In *On Your Toes* and *Where's Charley?*, the two reigning misters of theater and dance presided: "Mr. Abbott" directed and "Mr. B"—George Balanchine—choreographed.)

As a director Abbott was like a lofty military presence to many actors, some of whom were scared of him. Even the notoriously tough Jerome Robbins was deferential to Abbott when they collaborated on shows. The composer Jule Styne said of working with both men on *High Button Shoes* (1947), "I felt like a grape between two pieces of steel. Both Abbott and Robbins could chill you with a single look."[45] Abbott's direction "was all precision; you turn your head on this word, and all the sentences had to have an 'up' inflection," recalled Catherine Cox of the 1976 *Music Is.*[46] Gwen Verdon said, "I didn't much care for working with Mr. Abbott because he could never find a way to make me understand what I was doing. . . . he'd tell you where to go like he was a traffic cop."[47] Abbott even gave actors line readings (Cohan did, too). "He treated us like puppets," said David Holliday, another *Music Is* cast member,[48] and the songwriter Sammy Cahn called him "a rigid, robot-like man."[49]

Yet Abbott's autobiography gives the lie to these characterizations: it is introspective and astonishingly candid for 1963. The actor Joe Bova, who appeared in the 1959 Abbott show *Once Upon a Mattress,* said, "George Abbott worked on a musical as if it were a play. It wasn't just a question of putting a song here or there, with the right person to sing it. He really concentrated on the script; the reality of the script was what was important to him. He respected the character and the situation, and once he had those things established, the song and dance would grow out of that."[50] One writer, the ex-Broadway hoofer Denny Martin Flinn, even goes so far as to say that Abbott "was demanding the essence of the later Method school: truth."[51]

Pace or Truth? In musicals they may not be mutually exclusive. For certain aspects of staging a musical the Stanislavsky method may be inappropriate, although clearly Weill had wanted Kazan to direct *One Touch of Venus* because he knew that Kazan came from the Group Theatre, the 1930s repertory company whose alumni founded the Actors Studio in the 1940s and established the "Method" as the dominant style in American acting. Weill's first Broadway musical, *Johnny Johnson* (1936), had been a Group Theatre production directed by Lee Strasberg and with a cast including John Garfield, Robert Lewis, Sanford Meisner, Phoebe Brand, and Kazan himself. Group Theatre alumni, because of their emphasis on emotional truth, would indeed seem to have been likely choices to direct dramatically integrated musicals, yet over the years they had only equivocal success staging musicals. They did not redirect the course of the art form, as did Mamoulian and the later director-choreographers.

The Group's inability to lead the charge for a new kind of musical is also surprising because many of them had affinities for music, whether pop, jazz, or classical music and opera. Cheryl Crawford loved Gershwin tunes, and Robert Lewis was an opera buff. Strasberg and the Group Theatre playwright Clifford Odets were both rabid classical music listeners; years after he died, Strasberg's widow was still trying to have his vast record collection professionally cataloged. Harold Clurman also knew music well and was a close friend of Aaron Copland. Kazan appreciated music enough to use it sensitively later in his films; *East of Eden* (1955) opens with a five-minute overture by Leonard Rosenman to a blank screen, with no action or credits.

Strasberg's production of Weill's *Johnny Johnson* (1936) may well be one of Broadway's forgotten gems—during the opening-night performance Lorenz Hart tapped Weill on the shoulder and asked, "What are you trying to do, put people like me out of business?" But the show's lack not only of strong singing voices but also of a downstage, presentational vocal style, and Strasberg's overemphasis on naturalism, reduced its impact. The stylized naturalism of Mamoulian, the outright stylization of Hassard Short, or even the swift-paced pseudonaturalism of Abbott worked better for a Broadway musical. In his memoirs Elia Kazan—arguably American theater's greatest director of actors in the last sixty years—doesn't even mention the second (and last) musical he directed, the Weill-Lerner *Love Life* (1948). Cheryl Crawford, who hired him for that show, recalled that "his visual sense was not well developed." (Kazan turned down offers to direct both *Oklahoma!* and *On the Town.*)

The one Group Theatre alumnus who directed musicals prolifically and successfully combined fluid musical staging with dramatic truth was Robert "Bobby" Lewis (1909–97), a cofounder of the Actors Studio in 1947 and later a leading acting teacher. He directed Lerner and Loewe's *Brigadoon* (with Agnes de Mille's collaboration) (1947), Marc Blitzstein's *Regina* (1949) and his *Reuben, Reuben* (1955, closed in Boston), the Arlen-Harburg *Jamaica* (1957), *Kwamina* (1961), *Foxy* (1964), and *On a Clear Day You Can See Forever* (1965); he also directed the original London production of *Candide*. In *Brigadoon* Lewis implemented his own version of Mamoulian's nonpresentational singing style:

> Agnes and I collaborated on techniques to remove the intruding "seams" that come in the transitions from music to dialogue and vice versa. For example, when a number ends, often with a good "finish," the spoken dialogue that picks up then, being dynamically much lower, always invites a spate of coughing in the audience until the ears become adjusted. So at the start of the dialogue after a number (and applause?), I'd give the actors some strong intention to execute that would immediately grab the audience's attention, and then let the performers gradually slip into the ordinary dynamics of talking.[52]

A comically Pirandellian spoof of song-into-dialogue transition occurs in the 1966 musical *It's a Bird . . . It's a Plane . . . It's Superman.* In one scene, immediately after *Daily Planet* columnist Max Mencken finishes serenading Lois Lane with the last words of the song "You're the Woman for the Man," Lane's pickup line and walk-off cue is: "Agh, Max, that's six minutes out of my day shot to hell! [she exits]."

For Blitzstein's *Regina*—a "Broadway opera" adaptation of Lillian Hellman's play *The Little Foxes*—Lewis rehearsed the script first with the performers speaking their sung lines in dialogue, then speaking in dialogue with underscoring, and finally singing the dialogue. Lewis believed that "if the inner line of thinking has been set before, or along with, the learning of the music . . . the result was a *sung* play, with clear characterizations and confrontations."[53] Lewis also directed chorus members of musicals to play with the same "devotion to truthful detail" that Mamoulian had previously encouraged.

Joshua Logan (1908–88) came up with the University Players, a group of Ivy Leaguers (including the young Jimmy Stewart and Henry Fonda) who, like the Group Theatre, strove to base their approach on the Moscow Art Theatre. On a visit to the Soviet Union in the early 1930s, Logan had observed Stanislavsky directing opera scenes. The musicals Logan directed (he directed plays and films as well) included several later Rodgers and Hart shows, the Maxwell Anderson–Weill *Knickerbocker Holiday* (1938), *Annie Get Your Gun* (1946), *South Pacific* (1949), *Wish You Were Here* (1952), *Fanny* (1954), and various less successful shows in the 1960s and early 1970s. As a director of musicals Logan combined Abbott pace with cinematic fluidity and truthful acting. He staged the entire production of Rodgers and Hammerstein's *South Pacific* without a choreographer; the critic Cecil Smith commented that as a result of Logan's dramatically grounded staging the show "actually made some of the advance in the direction of seriousness which *Allegro* claimed to be making."[54] Logan's almost too-high energy level (his manic depression was untreated for years) was suited to musicals. Weill once told him, "Max [Maxwell Anderson] and I don't believe in the boom-boom-boom school of theatre the way you do, Josh. We believe an audience doesn't have to sit forward in their seats the whole evening. Once in a while they like to sit back and relax." To which Logan replied, "If it means never bore an audience, then I say boom-boom-boom forever!"[55]

Like Mamoulian, Logan complained that his direction never got the credit it deserved. But that was a paradox born of success, as the playwright-turned-director George S. Kaufman (1889–1961), who staged *Of Thee I Sing* (1931), *Guys and Dolls* (1950), and many other classic musicals, put it: "A play is supposed to simulate life, and the best direction is that which is so effortless and natural that it simply isn't noticed at all. Once it begins to call attention to itself, something is wrong."[56] The difficulty of discerning a directorial signature is also due to the widespread practice of play-doctoring—the hiring of a (frequently uncredited) new director to "fix" a show in preview or rehearsal trouble when, as Logan described, "there are no laughs at the funny lines and there is unrest rather than bated breath during the scenes of suspense, and they don't seem to care when the curtain comes down." Broadway musical stagings have often been nursed into life by multiple play doctors, and sometimes it's hard to tell the director from the play doctor or vice versa. This has been true since well before the 1940s. Cohan, Kaufman, Otto Harbach, Owen Davis, and Mamoulian were prime play doctors of their eras, as were Logan, George Abbott, Jerome Robbins, Abe Burrows, Kaufman's collaborator Moss Hart, Mike Nichols, Michael Bennett, and others. (Even Elia Kazan play-doctored the 1944 *Sing Out, Sweet Land*).

Surviving handbills and advertising tend to muddy the play-doctoring waters further. Posterity knows now that Rodgers and Hart's 1936 *On Your Toes* was directed by George Abbott. But Abbott was listed on the original playbill only as a co–book writer; the director he replaced, Worthington Miner, received the staging credit on the playbill. The story doesn't end there; the show's producer, Dwight Deere Wiman, fancied that he had also contributed and gave himself an "entire production under the supervision of" credit on the playbill (as did Lew Fields and other producers). Similar examples of multiple credits abound through decades of musicals, confounding theater historians. Sometimes a committee directed: the book writer here, the composer there, the star there. Sometimes the real director received no credit at all.

But the overall trends were clear: by the mid-1940s stage direction of musicals had evolved from an emphasis on style to an emphasis on content and had become a sophisticated craft without devolving into a cult of the director. The staging of a musical was an art that concealed art, as George Abbott said: "'Exactly what is the Abbott touch?' an interviewer asked me the other day. . . . [It is] artistic judgment—the decision as to just how much to do or not to do, at what point to leave one scene and get into another, and for the actor, how much to express and how much to imply."[57] In other words, timing—as singular to a musical's stage direction as to a comedian's delivery. But the doctrine that a stage director's effectiveness is in inverse proportion to his visibility would be upended in musicals from the 1960s, whereafter directing became a game of upstaging the very germinal impetus of musical theater—words and music.

The Transition from Hoofing to Choreography: From George White to George Balanchine

The change from using dances as disconnected numbers to using dances to forward the book happened far more rapidly—in less than twenty years— than the several decades it took to crystallize mature stage direction of musicals. The first faint stirrings of dramatically integrated dance in the 1920s, however, were drowned out by the persistence of the interpolated tap and precision dance routines of Mitchell, Wayburn, and Tiller, all of whom were still alive and working in mid-decade. Even well-plotted operettas like *The Student Prince* and *The Desert Song* used interpolation, mixing in extraneous dances like vaudeville numbers: fairy ballets, eighteenth-century gavottes, Spanish-flavored dances.

This vaudevillian mix of toe and tap held equally for musical comedies, many of which interpolated both ballets and tap dances. The 1924 hit *Rose Marie,* choreographed by David Bennett, is a case in point. Despite the fact that *Rose Marie* made a pretense of being dramatically integrated—its authors starchily wrote in the playbill, "The musical numbers of this play are such an integral part of the action that we do not think we should list them as separate episodes"—the show, nominally an operetta about a murder in the Canadian Rockies, included among its dances a Charleston, a black bottom, tap dancing, adagio ballet, and a gigantic precision chorus line number entitled "Totem Tom-Tom" featuring synchronized armies of female dancers dressed as totem poles.[58]

Before 1920 dance directors were usually uncredited in playbills. But after, just as pre-1940 book musicals frequently sported dual directorial credits—one for dialogue staging, one for song and dance staging—many musicals also often credited a musical comedy dance director, and a ballet director. But unlike most pre-1940 Broadway musical stage directors, almost all pre-1940 musical comedy dance directors also worked in Hollywood extensively, as did a few of the ballet directors. One or two even directed a few films. Of this group Busby Berkeley, Bobby Connolly (1896–1944), Seymour Felix (1892–1961), and Sammy Lee (born Samuel Levy, 1890–1968) have been dubbed the "Big Four"; all went on to Hollywood and on Broadway directed several shows. Berkeley's film work is proverbial, Connolly's choreography for the movie *The Wizard of Oz* is still watched by millions, while Sammy Lee in 1926 choreographed a ballet, *Skyscraper,* performed at the Metropolitan Opera House.

Yet none of this post-Wayburn generation—whether the Big Four or others such as David Bennett (1895?–1933?), George "Georgie" Hale (1900–1956), Leroy Prinz (1895–1983), Chester Hale (1897–1984), Robert Alton (1902–57), or Albertina Rasch (1891?–1967)—can honestly be said ever to have functioned as a Jerome Robbins–style conceptual director-choreographer. Rather, they were interchangeable cogs in the wheels of Broadway production: uncredited dance doctors were, then as now, as common as play doctors (for instance, Felix was called in to doctor Berkeley's dances for *A Connecticut Yankee*).

The tone for the post-Wayburn dance wave was set by the former burlesque and vaudeville hoofer and racetrack habitué George White (né Weitz, 1890?–1968), a turkey-trotting star of the 1915 *Ziegfeld Follies* who, instead of becoming a Broadway dance director, became a producer of revue. The annual *George White's Scandals,* which began in 1919 and premiered many great Gershwin songs, did much to set the tone for the show dancing of the era: shimmying, acrobatics, tap. Aspiring show dancers of the 1910s had had to study ballet as well as show steps at Ned Wayburn's school, but White shifted the emphasis to the latter. "When you got with Georgie White, you were doing some taps and some-soft shoe dancing and that sort of thing. He didn't have a ballet," said Dana O'Connell (1904–2000), who danced both for White and for Ziegfeld.

O'Connell also asserted that White, contrary to most biographical accounts, did stage his shows' dance routines: "Oh, he was there, all right, directing us, doing a lot of the rehearsing. He always wore his hat on the side of his head."[59] One dance authority characterized White's performance style as "machine-gun noneccentric tapper."[60]

With White and such other dance directors as Sammy Lee, tap dancing became the dominant mode of Broadway dance, supplemented by other flapper-era steps such as the Charleston, which outpaced Cohan's routines in ridiculous speed: "scrambled legs," in the words of Seymour Felix. Felix, who since 1918 had staged dances for both revues and book shows, was perhaps the first to try to break away from the prevailing interpolative production style. By the mid-1920s, according to Felix, "no longer are routines a matter of speed and noise. . . . The important thing today is the so-called 'book number.'"[61] He experimented with dances that pantomimed the plot. One reviewer said that in *Peggy-Ann* (1926) Felix had created "stage pictures, which supplemented the story of the play. His girls enter and listen to the principals as they sing the refrain of the Richard Rodgers–Lorenz Hart song quite as if they were overhearing a conversation."[62] Nevertheless, for years to come tap dance and other steps in musicals remained decorative, morphing into plot elements only in scenes where the script's characters were professional dancers, as with Sammy Lee's *Show Boat* choreography for the Cotton Blossom performers Frank (performed by Sammy "Funny-foot" White) and Ellie (played by White's wife, Eva Puck). In spite of this, Cecil Smith described Lee's *Show Boat* choreography as still mired in "precision dancing" conventions. A more successful attempt at using dancer-within-the-show characters to implement narrative choreography was Robert Alton's work for *Pal Joey* (1940), which takes place mostly in a nightclub.

Alton in fact ultimately became bigger than any of the Big Four, the last and most durable practitioner of the dance-as-decoration style of 1920s musical comedy choreography. Unlike Felix and most of the other dance directors who came up in the 1920s, Alton was trained in ballet. But he quickly turned commercial and stayed that way. He first made a big splash on Broadway in 1924, performing with his partner and wife, Marjorie Fielding, in the Marx Brothers' musical *I'll Say She Is*. He went on to stage live vaudeville prologues for movie theaters (called "presentation houses") for several years. From the early 1930s until the mid-1950s he was Broadway's busiest dance director for both book shows and revues, notably with Cole Porter and Rodgers and Hart shows. From 1936 he shuttled back and forth from Broadway to Hollywood, directing dances for many well-remembered movie musicals, including *Annie Get Your Gun, In the Good Old Summertime,* the 1951 (third) film version of *Show Boat, White Christmas,* and others. He made a rare cameo appearance as Greta Garbo's dancing partner in her last film, *Two-Faced Woman* (1941), and even directed two "B" features.

Alton essentially continued the old-fashioned frenetic style of the vaude-ville era, as surviving silent-film footage of his choreography for Rodgers and Hart's *Too Many Girls* (1939) and *Pal Joey* (from both the 1940 and 1952 pro-ductions) attests. The *Too Many Girls* footage displays a tap solo followed by ants-in-the-pants manic ensemble dancing, an athletic Latin number danced by Diosa Costello attired in formal dress and high heels, and a traditional cho-rus line. In *Pal Joey* (1952), Helen Gallagher does solo high kicks against a high-kicking chorus line in "You Musn't Kick It Around"; "Happy Hunting Horn" consists of ultraenergetic moves executed by different performers in counter-point against one another, and Harold Lang practically somersaults in "Joey Looks into the Future." Agnes de Mille said that Alton rehearsed "at a speed suggestive of a radio sports commentator, with a whistle between his teeth."[63]

Like George Abbott, Alton was the pro's pro, frequently doctoring other shows. Although he represented the highest standard of boilerplate profession-alism, he lacked conceptual imagination. Jerome Robbins was asked to doctor the dances in Rodgers and Hammerstein's *Me and Juliet* (1953) when Alton's choreography became confusing in rehearsals, but he declined out of respect for his senior colleague. Robbins undoubtedly would have made it a better show. On the two shows he "entirely supervised" late in his career (the 1952 re-vival of *Pal Joey* and the 1953 *Hazel Flagg*), Alton found it necessary to collabo-rate with a dialogue scene director, the noted acting teacher David Alexander.

Emerging at the same time as the Big Four were the first two important bal-let choreographers to work as Broadway dance arrangers: Chester Hale and Al-bertina Rasch. Though classical nineteenth-century ballet had developed a tradition of being built on strong narratives, neither Hale nor Rasch produced "story ballets" for musicals. Rather they, like Alton, went showbiz, creating dance "numbers," mongrelizing their ports de bras with jazzy pseudomodern moves and melding toe dancing with a modified Tiller precision style. In the 1920s and 1930s the Albertina Rasch Girls and the Chester Hale Girls were perennials in revues, book musicals, and presentation houses. Rasch, born in Vienna and trained at the Opera Ballet there (linguistically misplaced sobri-quets such as "Mademoiselle" and "Czarina of Broadway" were later attached to her) came to the United States to work as a Hippodrome dancer and then toured with Sarah Bernhardt. In 1923 she established her own New York dance studio, where Bill "Bojangles" Robinson later taught tap. Chester Hale (born Chester Chamberlain) was the first American man to dance with Diaghilev's Ballets Russes; he also danced with Anna Pavlova and studied with the legendary Enrico Cecchetti. Both Rasch and Hale also choreographed for the movies (Rasch married the film composer Dimitri Tiomkin), but of the two Rasch did more important Broadway musicals.

Rasch's Broadway work typifies the pre-Balanchine dualism of "hoofing" and "terping" on Broadway. A big musical like *Rio Rita* (1927) would feature "hoofed" numbers staged by Sammy Lee and "terped" (ballet) numbers staged by Rasch. They coexisted as parts of the same frothy evening, and there was no attempt to unify them. The Albertina Rasch Girls were eye diversions, "prancing on to cover a set change"[64] and evoking the *Black Crook* tradition of fairy dance interludes (the playbill to the 1931 Kern-Harbach show *The Cat and the Fiddle* lists a "Dance in Phantasy by Albertina Rasch Dancers"). By modern standards of taste the Rasch Girls would probably look silly, although there is evidence that some of Rasch's choreography by the 1930s became more substantive and ambitious. For the 1930 revue *The Band Wagon*, she set a dance for the classical ballerina Tilly Losch against a mirror on a raked stage to accompany the singing of the song "Dancing in the Dark." In 1998 the veteran theatergoing doyenne Mary Morse (1897–2000) recalled another Rasch number from the show: "The whole stage was blacked out, and so was Tilly Losch. All but her hands. Losch was on the stage alone, in front of the curtain, and her hands had fluorescent gloves against the lights, and she did sort of a port de bras with her hands, and all you saw was her hands."[65]

Rasch certainly played a role in establishing "Begin the Beguine" as a pop standard by setting an enchanting ethnic dance to it in the 1935 Cole Porter show *Jubilee*. But half of the newspaper reviews of *Lady in the Dark* (1941) didn't even mention Rasch's name when discussing the celebrated dream sequences she choreographed (stager Hassard Short and even costumer Irene Sharaff got more press), nor have later scholars said much about her contribution. Unlike Agnes de Mille, Rasch does not seem to have left an individual imprint on the stage musical as an art form, whether in dance steps, dramatic concept, or increased influence of the choreography on the total production.

Even so, Rasch's work may have nudged the public toward readiness for more artful integration of dance in musicals. Another trend that readied the public taste was the Depression-era influx of modern dancers and modern dance choreography into the commercial Broadway theater. Ever since the era of vaudeville began (circa 1880), modern dance practitioners had had to perform in less-than-elevating venues in order to appear at all before a paying public. Loie Fuller, Isadora Duncan, Ruth St. Denis, and Martha Graham all took turns in vaudeville or on Broadway, sometimes dancing in semiclassical numbers, sometimes doing showbiz hoofing. Ruth St. Denis (1877–1968) and her husband, Ted Shawn (1891–1972) (as a couple, known as "Denishawn"), toured for years cheek-by-jowl with performing seals to support their dance company; "Miss Ruth" and "Papa" Shawn were sometimes joined on their tours by the young Graham. The financial security of funded dance companies was decades away, and when the stock market crashed in 1929, terping on Broadway became a meal ticket for modern dancers more than ever.

At that time it was not uncommon for straight plays (usually historical dramas or revivals of classics) to include choreographed scenes supported by incidental music; Martha Graham choreographed such scenes for the 1934 Theatre Guild production of Maxwell Anderson's play *Valley Forge* and Katharine Cornell's 1934 production of *Romeo and Juliet,* as did the classical-turned-modern dancer Helen Tamiris (1905–66) for plays produced by the Group Theatre and the Works Progress Administration. Charles Weidman (1901–75) and Doris Humphrey (1895–1958) separately or together did the same for *Lysistrata* (1930), *Candide* (1933), and *The School for Husbands* (1933), dancing in them as well. Several others who trained with Denishawn or with Humphrey and Weidman also danced in 1930s musicals, including Jack Cole and José Limón.

Weidman was also the first dance director to interpolate modern dance elements into Broadway musicals, smuggling the Denishawn influence into such unlikely productions as the 1933 Moss Hart–Irving Berlin topical revue, *As Thousands Cheer,* and the 1934 revue *Life Begins at 8:40.* Weidman cochoreographed, with the show dance director Ned McGurn, the 1937 Rodgers and Hart musical satire on Franklin Delano Roosevelt (played by George M. Cohan), *I'd Rather Be Right,* and some of the bizarre results of this stylistic mélange survive on silent-film footage. The footage reveals a dadaistic fantasy ballet that spoofs FDR's then notorious scheme to pack the Supreme Court with his own justices. Sharing the stage with an aging but spry Cohan are several acrobatically gamboling Supreme Court justices and Folies Bergère–type chorines. They dance around a maypole; a male ballet dancer comes out of nowhere to do a dizzying pirouette. Cohan trots back and forth downstage in front of the chorus line, irreverently (in view of FDR's polio) high-kicking, flapping Ray Bolger–like loose-limbed eccentric moves while wagging his cane. The number is all at once showbiz hoofing, narrative ballet, and savagely barbed plot commentary hitherto unseen in Broadway musical comedy dancing.

Although his modern dance company became his principal career, Weidman, unlike Graham and Humphrey, continued occasionally to choreograph Broadway revues and book shows until 1958. Tamiris went Weidman one better: after leaving her own company in the mid-1940s she shifted primarily to Broadway dance work and became one of the Great White Way's most successful choreographers. Among her hit show credits were the 1946 revival of *Show Boat, Annie Get Your Gun,* and the 1954 *Fanny.* Hanya Holm (1893–1992) was another modern dancer who became a successful Broadway choreographer (*Kiss Me, Kate, My Fair Lady*).

Weidman's ballet for *I'd Rather Be Right* is forgotten; what *are* remembered as blazing the trail for advanced dance on Broadway are George Balanchine's "Princess Zenobia" and "Slaughter on Tenth Avenue" ballet sequences for the 1936 Rodgers and Hart musical *On Your Toes.* Balanchine (1904–83) was the first choreographer actually to receive billing as "choreographer" on a Broadway musical. But Balanchine—by almost universal consent the greatest ballet choreographer of the twentieth century—was, with one or two exceptions, not a great Broadway choreographer. Most of Balanchine's ballet oeuvre is nonnarrative, and his genius for abstract patterns did not always translate to Broadway structures. Unless he was setting a strong plot scenario like "Slaughter on Tenth Avenue," his Broadway choreography did not integrate with and push forward the narrative of the show as Jerome Robbins's did, nor did it probe character like Agnes de Mille's, though admittedly most of Balanchine's show assignments had inferior books.

Balanchine's years of Broadway choreography roughly corresponded with the interval between his arrival in the United States to become ballet master at the Metropolitan Opera (1934) and the founding of the New York City Ballet, his permanent home, in 1948. For the most part during these years on Broadway he was potboiling; he apparently did not regard his work there as building a new art form. (George Abbott commented that Balanchine "never liked musicals. He did it for the money."[66]) He designed a few dance numbers for the 1936 *Ziegfeld Follies* and then did four Rodgers and Hart musicals: *On Your Toes, Babes in Arms, The Boys from Syracuse,* and *I Married an Angel.* Except for "Slaughter on Tenth Avenue," his dances for these shows were either dream ballets tethered to their forgettable books or imaginative hoofing routines. He created Broadway ballets for two of his ballerina wives, Tamara Geva (*On Your*

Toes) and Vera Zorina (*I Married an Angel* and Irving Berlin's 1940 *Louisiana Purchase*), and despite his reputation as Broadway's designated choreographer he continued at times to share the choreography with show dance specialists (Carl Randall on *Louisiana Purchase,* Dick Andros on *What's Up?,* Fred Danielli on *Where's Charley?*).

A surprising amount of Balanchine's choreography for Broadway shows was poorly received by the drama critics (they often faulted him when his work was over their heads). There is also evidence that whenever he was in doubt about the material, he would dish up another dream ballet regardless of context. In 1948 John Chapman of the *Daily News* wrote of Balanchine's first act–ending ballet "Pernambuco" for *Where's Charley?*: "It is a fantasy not connected with the plot. In a musical I think it is wisest to advise the customers that a plot is at its thickest just before intermission, for this is the best way of getting them to come back in." The most cutting evaluation comes from Louis Kronenberger's review of the 1944 hit *Song of Norway* for *PM:* "[I am] disappointed that so fine a choreographer as George Balanchine, and such fine dancers as Danilova, Fredric Franklin, and the others of the Ballets Russes de Monte Carlo have left so little imprint on it. . . . Balanchine has not done his usual job by a long shot. . . . the ballet performers . . . are given no chance to infuse any distinction into their numbers."

The biographer Bernard Taper suggests that Balanchine's encounters with crude showbiz types in his Broadway gigs after the Rodgers and Hart shows turned him off creatively and led to hack work. But in 1940 Balanchine had his plummiest assignment, "entirely supervising" the succès d'estime *Cabin in the Sky,* a musical folk parable with a stellar all-black cast—Ethel Waters, Dooley Wilson, Rex Ingram, Katherine Dunham, and Todd Duncan—devised largely by a White Russian creative team: the director-choreographer Balanchine, the composer Vladimir Dukelsky (aka Vernon Duke), and the set designer Boris Aronson. (There were white non-Russians, too: the screenwriter Lynn Root wrote the book and John Latouche wrote the lyrics.) Photographs of the original production reveal a truly magical visual staging, surely Balanchine's. But the dialogue was directed by coproducer Albert Lewis and the dances were co-choreographed by Dunham. Late in life Balanchine admitted to an interviewer that he hadn't exactly "entirely" supervised *Cabin in the Sky:* "I did all this, the idea, how it looks, and, you know, the whole thing. Only I did not do the conversation. Also, the sound, you know, blacks talk a certain way. How can anybody . . . ? They do themselves very well without me. No, I was just placing people and dressing them."[67]

At rehearsals with the all-black cast, Dukelsky, Balanchine, and Aronson would speak Russian among themselves, leaving the players confused. Reviewers and backstage observers alike recall an arty hodgepodge of styles. One reviewer wrote that some of the show was "hotcha," some of it "dainty." Richard Watts in the *Herald Tribune* described it as a condescending "blackface *Liliom*"; dance observers such as the critic John Martin couldn't seem to agree on whether Balanchine had successfully balleticized African-American dance or had botched Dunham's dances by forcing them into musical comedy clichés. Four of the six daily newspaper reviewers used the same word to describe the dancing: "orgiastic." (In 1954 Balanchine was fired during out-of-town tryouts of the all-black Harold Arlen–Truman Capote musical *House of Flowers* and replaced by Herbert Ross. A young Alvin Ailey danced in the ensemble.) Balanchine's only other outing as a director-choreographer was a flop *sans estime*, Lerner and Loewe's first, forgotten musical, *What's Up?* (1943), a vehicle for the Chaplinesque vaudeville comedian Jimmy Savo. The show had jazz, tap, and jitterbug dancing together with dream ballets but no particular style, and it closed after sixty-three performances.

Without question Balanchine was one of the century's extraordinary artists. "Slaughter on Tenth Avenue" still shines as one of the handful of enduring show ballets. But with the transient exceptions of *On Your Toes* and *Cabin in the Sky,* he did not advance the evolution of the Broadway musical. Nor did he either inaugurate or add to the director-choreographer's role in Broadway musicals. The latter development was left to Agnes de Mille and Jerome Robbins.

Scene Two: *Apex: Agnes de Mille, Jerome Robbins, and Playwriting Choreography*

Agnes de Mille: The Choreographer as Playwright, Part 1

In the nineteenth century most ballets had been based on librettos solidly grounded in a story. Fokine, Massine, and Balanchine, as well as many modern dance practitioners, changed that with abstract, nonnarrative works. Despite occasional narrative ballets in Broadway musicals, such as Balanchine's "Slaughter on Tenth Avenue," most dancing in musicals prior to the early 1940s was divertissemental rather than dramaturgic or storytelling. Most of it in fact was Voegtlinesque, in that the typical Broadway dance number dressed the scenery and the songs while neither advancing plot nor probing character. This was true not just of the tap-dance school but even of most of Balanchine's work, and certainly of Rasch's. As Agnes de Mille noted of her early (1932) choreography assignment for *Flying Colors,* "There were conferences about costumes and scenery. . . . we were proceeding on the old-fashioned premise— costumes and scenery first; dance steps later, that would not interfere with the dress designs."[68]

In the early 1940s the British choreographer Antony Tudor (1909–87) created a new style of emotion-driven storytelling ballets in which the motivation of character, depth psychology, and other characteristics borrowed from drama and literature animated the steps. For Broadway Tudor choreo-

258

graphed only two minor 1945 musicals—the Gilbert and Sullivan parody *Hollywood Pinafore* and Lerner and Loewe's now forgotten *The Day Before Spring*—and his genius left no mark on the American musical as an art form. Tudor would choreograph *The Day Before Spring* only if Fritz Loewe provided him with a completely finished ballet score. Loewe complied, but this was and is not normal procedure for Broadway choreography, and Tudor could not or would not adjust. In her 1952 memoir, *Dance to the Piper,* de Mille lauded Tudor's Actors Studio–like exploration of character in his rehearsals, adding, "Contrast this with Massine's method, where the human bodies are used merely as units of design, grouped, lumped, and directed into predetermined masses. . . . [Sometimes] the performers could not have themselves explained what they were doing." She concluded, "Between Fokine and Tudor stand Proust and Freud."[69]

De Mille might well have said that between herself and virtually all her Broadway dance director predecessors also stood Proust and Freud—as well as Chekhov, the Moscow Art Theatre, O'Neill, and the rest of the High Drama pantheon. Agnes de Mille (1905–93) was in fact the single most important transitional figure in Broadway dance history. She was the choreographer most responsible for writers writing better books and composers more integrated scores for book musicals.

Despite pre-1940 harbingers, the integrated musical only really happened when de Mille's use of ballet transformed the art form. For the first time, movement assumed parity with book, music, and lyrics as a carrier of the dramatic through-line of a show. It was de Mille's discovery that tap, ballroom, and acrobatics were too expressively limited to open up the form, to convey subtext and character, to reveal that there could be meaty depths hidden under the entertaining surface of musical comedy. To achieve this, she refashioned ballet for Broadway into an eclectic theatrical language, narrative-driven and character-interpreting, that combined elements of classical ballet, interpretive modern dance, and occasional hoofing. She understood that tap couldn't subsume ballet, but ballet could subsume tap. Because of de Mille the typical Broadway hoofer changed from tapper to dancer trained in all forms; those who could only tap-dance were in effect thrown out of employment. She taught an "Acting for Dancers" class, and it was no doubt partly her influence that led many dancers in the 1940s to take acting classes, unheard of in the Ned Wayburn–George White chorus line era. The influence of de Mille's Broadway ballets was so potent that it stimulated the conception and writing of more dramatically ambitious musicals, not just the dancing of them.

De Mille's choreography also resulted in the permanent addition of dance music arrangers to the roster of musicals' creative teams. Prior to *Oklahoma!*, the music for dance numbers in musicals was extracted by the general orchestrator from song tunes elsewhere in the show. If there were ballets, they were dropped in, like Victor Herbert's "Butterfly Ballet" composed for *Sally* (1920), a show with Jerome Kern songs. For the pre-1943 dance director (even Balanchine), the music came first, the dance later. But when de Mille started choreographing integral ballets with their own internal dramatic scenarios, she demanded more than precomposed music: for her the show dance was independently important and had to be conceived concurrently with the music. "No musician would be required to hire orchestra players before his piece had been composed and scored. But composing, scoring and rehearsing occur simultaneously in dance composition," she wrote.[70] So she pressed her rehearsal pianists to improvise music that extended, recomposed, and added new material to the show composer's tunes. In *Oklahoma!* de Mille's rehearsal pianist was Morgan "Buddy" Lewis, best known to posterity as the composer of the song standard "How High the Moon." For the two decades onward from *One Touch of Venus* (1943), de Mille's rehearsal pianist and dance music arranger was Trude Rittmann, a superior musician and composer who would also work with Jerome Robbins and others, and forever after every show and every choreographer had a dance music arranger (Genevieve Pitot, Betty Walberg, John Kander, et al.). No previous composer, lyricist, or librettist had ever compelled such invention of a new job, and the course of how musicals actually are written was thus fundamentally altered.

Agnes de Mille—not Balanchine, Weidman, or even the later Robbins—is the person singularly responsible for elevating the role of choreographer in a musical to an authorial level. To a degree far beyond any previous Broadway dance director, she repeatedly forced songwriters, book writers, costume designers, set designers, and even directors to adapt their work to her notions of how the show should play (and this during a difficult era for strong women). It was de Mille who told Oscar Hammerstein to can his idea of ending *Oklahoma!*'s first act with a circus ballet. It was de Mille who forced her will over writer-director Yip Harburg and won the battle to have her tragedic Civil War ballet conclude *Bloomer Girl*. It was de Mille who pulled the strings on *One Touch of Venus,* as the show's director, Elia Kazan, recalled: "Kurt [Weill] may have once wanted the show directed as if it were a drama, not a musical, but Agnes would not have tolerated any such nonsense. She immediately gave orders (to me) to have the stage totally cleared of all scenery for her dances." "She was a Take Charge," said Jule Styne. It's poetic justice that de Mille was the first true director-choreographer, in 1947, for Rodgers and Hammerstein's *Allegro* (even if R & H did doctor the show themselves).

De Mille was the granddaughter of the nineteenth-century playwright and Belasco collaborator Henry de Mille, the daughter of the playwright and screenwriter William de Mille, the niece of the film director Cecil B. De Mille (the only family member to capitalize the "De"), and the granddaughter of Henry George, a celebrated nineteenth-century tax reformer and author of *Progress and Poverty* (early in her career she used her birth name, Agnes George de Mille). Both her parents were highly cultured, and she was encouraged to read great literature as a young child. Her father, William, a mediocre playwright, decided in 1914 to try his luck with his brother Cecil in the film industry and moved his family to Hollywood (he also directed films but never became as famous as his brother). There young Agnes was frequently taken to film sets during shootings, enflaming her already family-enkindled sense of theater. Then at thirteen she was taken to see Anna Pavlova perform, and from that moment she determined to become a dancer, even though she was the ugly duckling to her pretty sister, Margaret. Soon she was studying dance with Theodore Kosloff, a former member of Diaghilev's Ballets Russes. She also played the piano seriously as a teenager, practicing five hours a day during summers.

After graduating from UCLA in 1926, the short, stocky de Mille began to pursue (with family financial help that was unmunificent) an improbable career as a concert dancer. From her earliest solo recital pieces (*Harvest, Ouled Nail*) her choreography was narrative, theatrical, and humanistic. Seeing her work in 1929, the leading American dance critic, John Martin, dubbed it "choreographic acting."[71] Her legitimate theater debut (and first job choreographing more than two dancers) was a 1929 revival of *The Black Crook* staged in Hoboken, New Jersey. Her first Broadway choreography assignment was the 1932 revue *Flying Colors,* but she was fired during out-of-town previews and replaced by Albertina Rasch.

For the next ten years de Mille struggled, dividing her time between Europe and America and between concert work and abortive forays into Broadway and Hollywood dance directing. In London, where she studied with Marie Rambert and Antony Tudor, de Mille earned her first playbill credit, "Dances and Ensembles" for Cole Porter's 1933 West End musical, *Nymph Errant.* Even at this early juncture, she demonstrated her penchant for authorial collaboration: the twenty-eight-year-old de Mille boldly asked Porter to write a "Greek bacchanal" tune in 5/4 time for her, and he complied. Her uncle Cecil B., however, left her dances for his 1934 film *Cleopatra* on the cutting-room floor, nor did most of her dances survive for Irving Thalberg's film of *Romeo and Juliet* (1936) or Leslie Howard's 1936 Broadway production of *Hamlet*. Her hire by Vincente Minnelli as choreographer for the 1937 revue *Hooray for What!* seemed to signal an upturn in her fortunes until she was replaced by Robert Alton, although her "Hero Ballet" remained in the show; in 1939 her doctoring of Eugene Loring's dances for *Swingin' the Dream*, a short-lived all-black jazz version of *Midsummer Night's Dream*, received little notice.

Slowly but surely, de Mille's fortunes changed. She danced to acclaim in several Tudor ballets in London in the 1930s and in 1939 became one of the charter choreographers for Lucia Chase's newly formed Ballet Theatre (later called the American Ballet Theatre) in New York. Her ballet *Three Virgins and a Devil* for ABT in 1941 was a great success and became a perennial. The next year, her choreography of *Rodeo* to Aaron Copland's music was premiered by the Ballets Russes at the Metropolitan Opera House (de Mille herself danced in both *Three Virgins* and *Rodeo*) to twenty-one curtain calls. Among those in the audience were Richard Rodgers and Oscar Hammerstein. A few days later they hired her to create the dances for *Oklahoma!*

What de Mille did in *Oklahoma!*, far beyond merely introducing a new variation of dream ballet, was revise the psychological meaning of dance in musical comedy. For dream ballets were old hat, and not just *Lady in the Dark*'s and Balanchine's for Rodgers and Hart shows: *Dreams, or Fun in a Photograph Gallery*, a hit musical of 1880, had included an extended dream ballet in its first act, and shows such as *Tillie's Nightmare* (1910) and *Peggy-Ann* (1926) also featured staged dreams. No, what de Mille uncorked with the eighteen-minute "Laurey Makes Up Her Mind" dream ballet (really a nightmare ballet, wherein the feared Jud Fry murders good-guy Curly) was the heart of darkness in *Oklahoma!*, the missing piece of saturninity in the jigsaw that made it more than just square-dance calls and gingham. She thereby enlarged musical comedy itself from mere entertainment to a genre of drama. The Hammerstein script's Jud Fry is a cartoon: the de Mille ballet's Jud Fry is an elemental life-and-death matter. De Millean dance is musical comedy's choreographed version of the asides in Eugene O'Neill's *Strange Interlude*: a parallel unconscious level of dialogue. Dream ballets heretofore had been divertissements disconnected from the through-line, or connected only through humorous fantasies. Now they spoke the dark Freudian terrors of sunny worlds. (De Mille, like Moss Hart, *Lady in the Dark*'s librettist, had gone through psychoanalysis.) Suddenly musical comedy characters weren't cutouts: they had ids, egos, and superegos. Gone forever

262

were the pastoral sylphs of *The Black Crook*, the *Ziegfeld Follies*, and Albertina Rasch. De Mille discovered that psychologized ballet in dramatic musicals could function like Shakespearean soliloquy, illuminating not just the action but the consciousness of the characters.

Very late in life de Mille choreographed her last ballet for ABT, *The Other* (1992), a metaphysical parable of the eternal love triangle—the Lover, the Maiden, and the Other—in which the Other incarnates Death and snatches the Maiden from the seemingly sure grasp of the Lover, just as in *King Lear* Cordelia's life is snatched from her father. *The Other* was a reworking of earlier ballets de Mille had set in the 1970s, but much of the notion of "the Other" had long been implicit in her apparently sunny theatrical choreography. De Mille's use of dancers as doppelgängers of the actors in *Oklahoma!*, *Carousel*, and other works heightens the feeling of "otherness," which is why having the same performers play both the speaking characters and the dance characters loses something: otherness is enhanced by dual stage personas. (For *Ballet Ballads* [1948], John Latouche and Jerome Moross wrote a dancing alter ego into the script.) The jollity of community bonding rituals exists side-by-side with life-and-death otherness in de Mille shows, whether represented by Jud Fry in *Oklahoma!*, the renegade Harry Beaton, murdered in *Brigadoon*'s sword dance, or sexual predators like Starbuck in *110 in the Shade*. Earlier musical comedy dance could not convey any of this. Even the dances in *Show Boat*, despite the mixture of blacks and whites, did not explore otherness.

Although Mamoulian staged the songs in *Oklahoma!*, de Mille's dances—inclusively embracing ballet, folk dance, and tap—occupied twenty-six minutes of the show. She created all her ballets, whether for Broadway or for the concert stage, like a playwright (she herself called her Broadway dance creation "playwriting"), composing detailed prose scenarios that read like poetic stage directions. She insisted on hiring good dancers, not just good lookers who were girlfriends of the producer, and won her battles, making stars of Bambi Linn, Diana Adams, and Joan McCracken. Despite being relegated by Mamoulian to the men's lounge for her dance rehearsals, de Mille triumphed. When *Oklahoma!* became a hit of staggering dimensions and she bounded into choreographing *One Touch of Venus* (1943) and *Bloomer Girl* (1944), de Mille was suddenly the most powerful woman on Broadway. Balanchine was apparently jealous of her success and told his ex-wife Vera Zorina not to audition for the title role in *One Touch of Venus* because de Mille was choreographing it.

De Mille sometimes deliberately had her dancers stand still for dramaturgical reasons; most choreographers' bias is toward movement at all costs. As her biographer Carol Easton puts it, "her approach was a kind of Method Dancing";[72] her onetime dance partner Joseph Anthony said, "She was interested in much more than just the steps; they were a means of revealing the person's character and the quality of their life." Sybil Shearer, who danced in her ballets, added, "Most dancers don't see drama, they're just legsters. Agnes was a headster. . . . her subject was people, so that acting and dancing were combined into one whole." Bambi Linn agreed: "Until Agnes, dancers were fairies and dolls. Agnes asked us to be *people*. . . . She would say, 'It's snowing, feel the snow.'"[73] On the other hand, James Mitchell, her most frequent Broadway male dance lead, said, "She had a limited vocabulary and wasn't interested, for instance, in jazz. She didn't like anything abstract, didn't know what it was. There was no moving forward into new areas of dance or explorations of new kinds of movement."[74]

For *One Touch of Venus,* an urbanized pseudo–Pygmalion-Galatea fantasy written by S. J. Perelman with lyrics by Ogden Nash, de Mille choreographed two extended ballets, "Venus in Ozone Heights" and "Forty Minutes for Lunch." The show's director, Elia Kazan, later wrote, "Her dances were superb set pieces, beginning, middle, and end, with what any true artist gives his work: a most personal theme." For *Bloomer Girl,* a protofeminist musical set in the Civil War, de Mille's big set pieces were in the second act: the opening fifteen-minute "Sunday in Cicero Falls" and a twelve-minute tragic "Civil War" ballet near the end of the show. De Mille's choreography also significantly contributed to *Carousel:* there was a six-minute hornpipe in the first act, and de Mille's second-act dream ballet at twelve and a half minutes was twice the length of the "Carousel Waltz" prologue and usually brought a standing ovation for dancer Bambi Linn at each performance. (Balanchine's "Slaughter on Tenth Avenue" was seventeen and a half minutes long and "Princess Zenobia" twelve minutes.) For Lerner and Loewe's *Brigadoon* (1947), de Mille created so much dance so thoroughly integral to the action that it's impossible to give timings. *Brigadoon* was as much a dance musical as Jerome Robbins's *On the Town* or *West Side Story* and is arguably de Mille's greatest Broadway achievement.

It did not seem a leap for de Mille to graduate to supervising director. She always claimed to have been the de facto stager of most of *Bloomer Girl,* after the book director William Schorr was fired midway through rehearsals, although Yip Harburg retained the credit on the program. Rodgers and Hammerstein grabbed her to "entirely supervise" their next show, *Allegro* (1947), because Hammerstein's book was built on dance and movement as much as on story. *Allegro,* an uneasy bouillabaisse of *Our Town, Everyman,* Sinclair Lewis, and Dr. Kildare (with soupçons of Elmer Rice, Maxwell Anderson, and faux expressionism), was perhaps Hammerstein's unconscious bid for stature as an original playwright. When he showed de Mille an early first-act draft, she told him, "Oscar, you're writing several plays at once. You're all over the map." In ostensibly telling the story of a small-town boy turned big-city doctor who retreats to his roots, Hammerstein strove for cosmic statement, casting the action as a universal morality play complete with singing Greek chorus. Four days before rehearsals began, with the second act barely completed, de Mille still was confused about the play's meaning. "It's about a man not being allowed to do his own work because of wordly pressures," Hammerstein mustered. "That's not the play you've written," de Mille wisely replied.[75]

Hammerstein and Rodgers originally wanted a minimalist production design: no conventional sets, stage properties, or proscenium-bound geometry, but rather an open, fluid staging with cinematic transitions. The problem was that artily paring down production design paradoxically increased it: *Allegro* ended up with forty stagehands carrying on and off sixty mini-prop setups, five hundred Jo Mielziner lighting cues, platforms, treadmills, projections, and a "cast of thousands" (thirty-nine actors, twenty-two dancers, thirty-eight singers) more suited to a production of That Other De Mille. As new material was added during late rehearsals, it became logistically impossible for a single person to rehearse the dancers, teach the songs, and direct the new dialogue, so R & H stepped in to assist de Mille. Although there were several big ballets, they checked her attempt to go darker with the dance material. ("It will wound the audience," complained Rodgers of one ballet. "I hope so," replied de Mille. This time she lost the battle.)[76] Ultimately in the mixed reception accorded the show, only de Mille received consistently good notices. Cecil Smith hated the book, music, and lyrics but thought de Mille's contribution extraordinary, writing in *Theatre Arts,* "No previous musical has approached *Allegro* in consistency of movement, expertness of timing and shapeliness of visual patterns."

In the 1948–49 season de Mille staged Benjamin Britten's opera *The Rape of Lucretia* for an unusual Broadway run at the Ziegfeld Theatre. Kitty Carlisle Hart, one of eight singers in the cast, recalled that "Agnes used movement for dramatic effect so that every movement was timed with exact notes in the music. She asked us to do things that no opera director would ever ask us to do. She took no notice of singers' insistence on standing still to sing high notes. . . . We had to accommodate the singing to the acting. . . . We were *thrilled* to do these things!"[77] But the production closed after twenty-three performances.

After being fired as director from *Out of This World,* she choreographed musicals rather than directed them, notably *Paint Your Wagon* (1951), *Kwamina* (1961), and *110 in the Shade* (1963).

Throughout her Broadway career and beyond it—even after she suffered a devastating stroke in 1975—de Mille continued with her original métier of ballet choreography, creating such classics for American Ballet Theatre as *Fall River Legend* (1948) (about the Lizzie Borden murder case), *Sebastian* (1957), *The Four Marys* (1965), the various versions of *The Other,* and many more. She frequently reworked the ballets she had choreographed for Broadway into extended concert ballets, sometimes with different music: the Civil War ballet to Harold Arlen's music from *Bloomer Girl* became *The Harvest According* to Virgil Thomson's music (1952), dances from *Brigadoon* became *The Bitter Weird* (1962), dances from Marc Blitzstein's *Juno* (1959) became *The Informer* (1969). Many of her later shows were not box-office successes, but repeatedly de Mille received notices like Walter Kerr's for *Paint Your Wagon:* "[She] gives the show that honest and moving quality which the authors have everywhere aimed at and rarely achieved."[78] Time and again critics felt that the poetic visual language of her dances made a more powerful statement than the actual musical that contained them.

De Mille could be a tough cookie. "If we tried to cut one minute from one of her ballets all hell broke loose," recalled producer Cheryl Crawford.[79] Surveying all the theater people he knew in a fifty-year career, Elia Kazan said of her, "I know of no one more arrogant or estimable."[80] Stephen Sondheim, who worked as a gofer in 1947 on *Allegro,* thought her "a horror. She treated the actors and singers like dirt and treated the dancers like gods. . . . That was my first experience of bad behavior in the theatre."[81] Yet she was a generous colleague, remaining loyal even to friends who disagreed with her, disarming friend and foe alike with her famous wit. Upon meeting the dance critic Clive Barnes at a party, de Mille didn't miss a beat: "Mr. Barnes, do you expect me to kiss your axe?"[82]

De Mille was also an early, outspoken advocate for government support of the arts, and later she was one of the outstanding leaders in the cause of dance preservation. After her stroke she courageously continued to choreograph ballets for seventeen years while wheelchair-bound. And she is the finest nonplaywright writer in the American theater, publishing eleven books that form a uniquely personal chronicle of Broadway and the ballet world. No mere critic, biographer, or historian has ever touched her for novelistic evocation of theater personalities or could ever improve on her nuts-and-bolts accounts of how a musical is actually put together backstage. The richness of observation in her prose has preserved the golden age of Broadway for all time no less than have Al Hirschfeld's drawings.

Jerome Robbins: The Choreographer as Playwright, Part 2

> Musicals tend to be facetious. No one has ever
> used them as a medium to depict deep personal
> struggle, and I think this can be done.
> —Jerome Robbins, 1948[83]

Julian Mitchell and Ned Wayburn had been formed by nineteenth-century traditions of theater as amusement: farce-comedy, burlesque, and vaudeville, not Ibsen and Strindberg. Mitchell and Wayburn used whistles and megaphones, not character motivation, to make their stagings. Albertina Rasch, Chester Hale, and George Balanchine brought classical ballet into musical comedy to amuse, not to probe and deepen. Augustin Daly begat cue-biting pace as the director's imperative in a musical, which begat Cohan, George Abbott, and play doctors. For Arthur Voegtlin, Hassard Short, John Murray Anderson, and Vincente Minnelli, to direct a musical meant to interweave stage movement and production design: dances, book scenes, even pace were secondary. Directors of musicals from the Group Theatre did probe beneath the surface but tended to lack the necessary visual and kinetic sense. Until Mamoulian, there had been no consistent fusion of movement, acting, and subtext in musicals. Yet even for Mamoulian, a nonchoreographer, movement meant blocking and bits of business, not dancing. De Mille was the first to draw dance and subtext together so that dance itself was a parallel form of playwriting that fused with blocking and conarrated the book with the music and lyrics. Jerome Robbins (1918–98) was the second. He was also without a doubt the greatest director-choreographer ever, despite an almost universally detested rehearsal personality that led one personal assistant to dub him "Attila the Hitler."[84] (Choreographers seem to be viewed as Nazilike by their detractors. Producer David Merrick dubbed the director-choreographer Gower Champion "the Presbyterian Hitler.")

Robbins was a musical and creatively gifted child, raised in New Jersey by middle-class Russian Jewish immigrants named Rabinowitz (his father first ran a delicatessen, then a corset factory). His sister, Sonia (six years older), from the age of four was pushed by their mother into the life of a professional dancer. At first Jerome tagged along with Sonia, taking his first dance lessons from her. By 1936 he had emerged from Sonia's shadow to become a disciple of Senia Gluck-Sandor (born Samuel Gluck, 1899–1978) and his wife, Felicia Sorel. Gluck-Sandor, who like Robert Alton made a living choreographing presentation house shows, established the Dance Center, a combination ballet–modern dance workshop that also embodied elements of the Stanislavsky acting technique. (Thirty years later, Robbins would gratefully repay his one-time mentor by hiring him to play the Rabbi in *Fiddler on the Roof*.) Gluck-Sandor sent Robbins to study ballet with other teachers as well. During five summers (1937–41) at the adult arts camp Tamiment in the Poconos, Robbins grew further as a dancer and made fledgling efforts at choreography. He found work as a Broadway gypsy in *Great Lady* (1938), *Stars in Your Eyes* and *The Straw Hat Revue* (both 1939), and *Keep Off the Grass* (1940), choreographed by Balanchine. In 1940 he was hired for the corps de ballet at Ballet Theatre. Soon he was taking solo roles in de Mille's *Three Virgins and a Devil,* David Lichine's *Helen of Troy,* and the title role in Fokine's *Pétrouchka.* Like de Mille and Gluck-Sandor, he was not only a gifted dancer but a superb natural actor in his dancing.

Jerome Robbins was one of those rare artists whose gifts are fully formed from the outset. His apprentice effort as choreographer for the Ballet Theatre, *Fancy Free* (1944), about three sailors on shore leave in New York looking for girls, set to music by Leonard Bernstein, was an overnight sensation and entered the permanent repertory. Agnes de Mille called it the greatest first-time work she had ever seen in the theater. Later that year, Robbins's friends Adolph Green and Betty Comden expanded *Fancy Free*'s scenario into a full-length musical comedy book for which Bernstein composed a completely new score. The resulting show, *On the Town,* directed by George Abbott, contained about thirty minutes of dancing that was coconceived with Bernstein's music: the opening "New York, New York," the "Miss Turnstiles" ballet, the "Carnegie Hall Pavane," the act 1 finale "Times Square" ballet, and two Coney Island ballets, "Playground of the Rich" and "Coney Island Hep Cats." But they were ballets only in name, not steps: instead of de Mille's classical, Robbins used urban, jazz-based dance movements.

At twenty-six Robbins was already a star. He followed *On the Town* by choreographing a less successful Comden-Green-Abbott musical—*Billion Dollar Baby* (1945), a nostalgic 1920s spoof with music by Morton Gould—but then choreographed another hit, the nostalgic 1910s spoof *High Button Shoes* (1947), also directed by Abbott. Mack Sennett, the filmmaker whose Keystone Kops silent-film comedies Robbins spoofed in a ballet in *High Button Shoes,* won a lawsuit against the show for Robbins's unauthorized use of his and the "Keystone Kops" names. (The ballet was reprised anyway in the 1989 *Jerome Robbins' Broadway.*) Meanwhile, Robbins set two concert ballets, Morton Gould's *Interplay* and Bernstein's *Facsimile.* In 1948, following in de Mille's footsteps a few months earlier on *Allegro,* he codirected (with Abbott) and choreographed *Look Ma, I'm Dancin',* a farcical musical roman à clef on Lucia Chase and the Ballet Theatre; he also secretly cowrote it.

Later that year came his inevitable first assignment as director outright: a left-wing musical satire on the American presidency with an original book by Philip and Julius Epstein (coscenarists of the movie *Casablanca*) and music and lyrics by Harold Rome. Robbins spurned doing the choreography and hired Paul Godkin to create the dances. Called *That's the Ticket,* the show proved anything but. The twenty-nine-year-old Robbins cannily closed it in Philadelphia, turning what would have been a disaster for his career into a mere speed bump. "I was too young to direct then; it was a step I took too soon," he said ten years later.[85] Shortly after this, Robbins joined his permanent home, the New York City Ballet (NYCB), where he danced only for another few years but stayed for decades to choreograph the bulk of the ballet repertoire for which he is justly famous, becoming adjutant guru under Balanchine.

Though Robbins somewhat repudiated the Russian school of ballet in his choreography, he maintained a lifelong affinity for the Russian school of acting, which he first absorbed while training as a teenager under Gluck-Sandor in the 1930s. A few years later at Ballet Theatre, de Mille introduced Robbins to her childhood friend Mary Hunter, who was teaching acting at the American Actors Company; by 1941 Robbins was taking improvisation classes with Hunter. Already as a choreographer in the 1940s, he "went at dance almost as if you were at the Actors Studio, that type of approach," recalled the dancer Richard D'Arcy.[86] He prepared even for Broadway choreographing by deeply investigating historical background, character, and motivation in the Stanislavsky manner: "For three weeks preceding any big job Jerome Robbins works himself into a lather of excitement on studies, all of which, he explains, may very well be discarded once the dancers are assembled but without which he cannot begin. These preliminary exercises furnish him with momentum and conviction. They are a warming-up process," wrote de Mille.[87] By comparison, Robert Alton never researched and prepared; he came to dance rehearsal and winged it.

In 1947 Robbins joined the newly formed Actors Studio, taking classes there three times a week with its cofounder Robert Lewis. Among his fellow class members were Marlon Brando, Montgomery Clift, Eli Wallach, Maureen Stapleton, and Karl Malden. Lewis later recalled:

> He was a superb young dancer, now wishing to explore what the difference was in the source of expression for acting as opposed to dancing. We chose a completely realistic scene for him from Odets' *Waiting for Lefty*, with Jerry playing the young Jewish intern, a victim of anti-Semitism in a large hospital. I still remember the look on the future [*sic*] choreographer's face when, in my critical remarks after the scene, I complained that, fine as his emotional quality was, his physical movement was a bit awkward.[88]

When Lewis soon left the Studio, Robbins continued acting classes there with David Pressman, who recently recalled, "Jerry did some wonderful exercises, strictly acting exercises, because he was so interested in the class as related to his choreography. . . . [In one exercise] he gave himself a problem—that he had to reach the other side of the stage and the place was full of water. . . . He did an improvisation—he built himself a bridge. . . . his intensity and how he did it . . . was quite remarkable."[89] During rehearsals for *West Side Story* (1957), the original Maria, Carol Lawrence, recalled:

> Jerry wanted everything so thoroughly and so quickly that every fiber of your being had to be at his command. You had to justify every single word that you said, *with* a subtext and a basis in your own life. He was Stanislavsky reincarnated. He never called us anything but our character names when we were rehearsing. Once we came to rehearsal we were never allowed to even communicate with the opposition. It was a battleground.[90]

So Stanislavskyan was Robbins that when he directed a production of Brecht's play *Mother Courage* on Broadway in 1963, he consulted with Lee Strasberg, whose approach was absurdly unsuited to Brecht's "alienation effect." As late as 1995, when he re-created the *West Side Story Suite* for a new generation of City Ballet dancers, he asked the dancers to write biographies for their characters—an Actors Studio technique quite alien to most dancers' training. In 1984, he compared the current NYCB dancers to those of 1950 and concluded, "Before, there were people who were capable of dramatic presence. . . . Now I find that dancers are embarrassed if asked to act."[91] But choreographers are by nature authoritarian, and dancers are trained to do what they are told; actors, however, have to understand the whys in order to create the behavior of the character onstage, so there was often a dissonance between

Robbins's choreographic desire to command every onstage detail and the necessity for a good director to give way so that the actors could make their own emotional discoveries. His assistant director in the 1950s, Gerald Freedman, later recalled, "I went around repairing Jerry's damage with actors. . . . He didn't have the language, but he absolutely thought in terms of relationships and motivations."[92]

Robbins was what is now called a control freak: performers were mere objects, pawns in his design, even when he was trying to draw feeling out of them. He drove dancers to exhaustion in rehearsal by endlessly experimenting with different alternatives ("Jerome Robbins and his lack of decision are a byword in the dance profession," wrote de Mille).[93] Sondheim, who worked with him on *West Side Story* and *Gypsy*, went further: "Jerry's artistic ruthlessness was combined with real sadism."[94] James Mitchell called him "the most charming son-of-a-bitch I've ever known."[95] Maria Karnilova said, "Much of the time he was just mean . . . sometimes even evil."[96] Arthur Laurents, not only a collaborator but a onetime close friend, also called him "evil." The costume designer Miles White described him as "Miss de Mille with a beard. But not as witty, just vicious. He liked to rip things off costumes. . . . Jerry viciously tells you how terrible you are in front of the entire company at rehearsals. It's very demeaning; it takes you a long time to get over his vicious remarks."[97] During one rehearsal of *Billion Dollar Baby*, Robbins was so involved in yelling at dancers that he didn't realize where he was as he backed up over the apron of the stage and fell into the orchestra pit. "Nobody said, 'Watch it!' Nope. Off he went," recalled James Mitchell, who was present. "He could have killed himself. . . . Nobody went to his rescue."[98] Twenty years later, in *Fiddler on the Roof*, the sound man operated two different sound plots: one for when Robbins was in the theater, one for when he wasn't.

Nor did Robbins endear himself to the theatrical community when he named names at a House Un-American Activities Committee (HUAC) hearing in 1953. Some believed he ratted because he feared Ed Sullivan was going to expose him in his gossip column as a homosexual. Others, including Arthur Laurents and Nora Kaye, believed Robbins talked because he wanted to protect his future opportunities in motion pictures, for which informing was then a rite of passage (the Broadway theater was relatively immune to blacklisting). Ironically, he was fired for cost overruns midway through the filming of *West Side Story* and never worked in Hollywood again. In the early 1990s Robbins wrote and rehearsed an autobiographical play called *The Poppa Piece* in which he bared links between his behavior before HUAC and his early childhood traumas (Robbins, like many Broadway luminaries of his time, had been through much psychoanalysis). Perhaps *The Poppa Piece* was meant to be Attila the Hitler's apologia for being the monster that he was. But he ultimately abandoned the play; it never opened.

But people put up with Mr. Hyde Robbins because time and again Dr. Jekyll Robbins magically raised just about anyone's work to a higher level. In *Bells Are Ringing* (1956), which Robbins directed and cochoreographed with Bob Fosse, the subway number wasn't working in Fosse's choreography. Remembered one dancer, "Bobby had us all shaking hands on the subway, and Jerry would have us reach out and put our hands way over our heads in a big circle [and] bring them down to shake hands." It transformed the number. The same magic happened when Robbins rechoreographed his assistant Peter Gennaro's setting of "America" in *West Side Story*. When *A Funny Thing Happened on the Way to the Forum* was bombing in previews with the opening number "Love Is in the Air," it was Robbins who told Sondheim to replace it with a baggy-pants comedy number (which became "Comedy Tonight").

While Robbins had amply demonstrated his gifts for dramatically searing ballets in his concert works such as *Facsimile, The Age of Anxiety,* and *The Cage,* before 1951 he had not, despite his great theater success, been able to translate into Broadway terms the kind of dark subliminal scenarios for dance at which de Mille so excelled. But with his ballet "The Small House of Uncle Thomas" for Rodgers and Hammerstein's *The King and I* (1951), Robbins finally brought to Broadway his genius for choreographed psychodrama. "The Small House of Uncle Thomas" is a sixteen-minute Siamese dumb show (narrated by Tuptim in pidgin English) that cleverly collapses key scenes from Harriet Beecher Stowe's *Uncle Tom's Cabin* (a book new at the time of *The King and I*'s action, the early 1860s). In "Small House" the slave Eliza escapes from the slave master Simon Legree over the ice floes to Uncle Thomas's cabin. As the slave Tuptim narrates the pageant, it is clear that Eliza is meant as a metaphor for herself and Simon Legree as an embodiment of the King. Legree/King drowns in the chase, freeing Eliza/Tuptim to be with her lover, George, but after the ballet ends the enraged King tries to bullwhip Tuptim (Mrs. Anna prevents this).

"The Small House of Uncle Thomas" dumb show does not exist either in Margaret Landon's 1944 book, *Anna and the King of Siam,* or in the 1946 Rex Harrison–Irene Dunne film of the same title, the ostensible sources for *The King and I.* Hammerstein concocted it, in a none-too-veiled homage to the very similar play-within-a-play in act 3, scene 2 of *Hamlet,* in which Claudius watches the symbolic reenactment of his regicide. (Seven years earlier, the

Harburg-Arlen musical *Bloomer Girl* had also used *Uncle Tom's Cabin* as a play-within-the-play scene, though not with Hammerstein's allegorical elaboration.) Robbins contributed substantially to the dramatic effectiveness of Hammerstein's idea: he changed it from Hammerstein's original scripted notion of a production number into an ethnologically authentic dance that, through understated Asiatic gestures, paradoxically heightens the emotion. The published libretto (unlike the published play script) bears witness to the minutely detailed way in which Robbins orchestrated the stage movement for storytelling ("The chorus whenever speaking or singing in rhythm beat wood blocks and ancient cymbals on the downbeat. This applies through the entire ballet"). Robbins's visual playwriting added a power of symbolism to the dumb show well beyond Hammerstein's language. (The music was composed entirely by Trude Rittmann. Robbins, not the nominal director John van Druten, directed all the show's musical and dance numbers.)

Robbins's first credit as director-choreographer came with the 1954 Mary Martin musical *Peter Pan*, but it is *West Side Story* (1957) that is generally viewed as the first show both conceived and controlled by a commander-in-chief of movement. One reason such consolidation was possible was that in *West Side Story* the same performers acted, danced, and sang. But separate ensembles of singers and dancers continued to be the rule for years after *West Side Story*, nor were consolidated ensembles wholly new in 1957.

As Robbins moved from *The King and I* to the boxed highlighting of his name that marked his definitive command-and-control direction of *West Side Story, Gypsy,* and *Fiddler on the Roof,* he continued his Stanislavskyization of movement. "He choreographed for character. He choreographed the way a writer writes," said Rita Moreno.[99] Arthur Laurents has written of Robbins's "structuring a number like a play. . . . He would not choreograph a dance as a dance, he had to know what the dancing was about."[100] Jacques d'Amboise says even of Robbins's concert work, "He had a hard time choreographing ballets that didn't have a motivation. When you think of his great ballets—*Fancy Free, Interplay, The Cage, The Concert*—they're all theatrical, they're all motivated by character."[101]

Some of his collaborators were irked by his hogging the "conceived by" limelight on *West Side Story,* but Romeo and Juliet had been an idée fixe of Robbins's for years. In the early 1940s he had danced Benvolio and Mercutio in Antony Tudor's ballet *Romeo and Juliet,* and he had taken the role of Romeo-as-Jewish-boy to the dancer Janet Reed's Juliet-as-Catholic-girl in a Mary Hunter acting-class improvisation. In the late 1940s his ballet *The Guests,* to music by Marc Blitzstein, further explored the Romeo and Juliet theme. In *West Side Story,* dance was the primary storytelling mode: song and dialogue were secondary. Dialogue and stage directions that the librettist Arthur Laurents had written in verbose detail for the show's opening, for example, deliquesced into Robbins's prologue scene, a five-minute finger-snapping dance pantomime without music, more eloquent than any dialogue.

West Side Story raised Robbins's cachet to an exalted level; he soon left City Ballet to form his own short-lived dance company, Ballets U.S.A. (he returned to City Ballet in 1969). But while Robbins received the ego-inflating "box" again for *Gypsy* in 1959 and *Fiddler on the Roof* in 1964, he continued to be the uncredited director-choreographer doctor for such shows as *A Funny Thing Happened on the Way to the Forum* (1962) and *Funny Girl* (1964). He also directed two straight plays, Arthur Kopit's *Oh Dad, Poor Dad, Mama's Hung You in the Closet and I'm Feeling So Sad* (off-Broadway, 1962) and *Mother Courage* (1963). *Fiddler on the Roof* (1964) was the last original Broadway musical he director-choreographed. Perhaps no other director-choreographer could have so brilliantly devised sectarian communal ritual dances to express universal human truths.

Why did Robbins, who lived to seventy-nine and choreographed ballet well into his seventies, retire from Broadway at age forty-six? He told Clive Barnes that he left because he was "tired of interpreting other people in staging musicals, while when I choreograph a ballet I am myself the real creative artist, working with my collaborators on a quite different level."[102] Zero Mostel's costar in *Fiddler on the Roof,* Maria Karnilova, thought that Mostel deliberately and vindictively set out to dismantle Robbins's exquisite gem of direction with increasingly anarchic stage behavior after the show opened (Mostel had been a victim of blacklisting and had never forgiven Robbins's singing to Congress). The superperfectionist Robbins finally threw up his hands and quit the theater. For a few years thereafter he ran the American Theatre Laboratory, a nonprofit experimental music/theater workshop. Then he returned full bore to the New York City Ballet to create his late ballet masterpieces.

As the years passed, a different kind of Broadway musical seemed to be eclipsing the glorious era Robbins had helped shape: "I'm not crazy about what happened since they took the New Testament and made a musical out of it," he told a *New York Times* reporter in 1987. Lest the world forget him, he jump-started the Shubert Organization into producing *Jerome Robbins' Broadway* (1989), a spare-no-expense Ziegfeldian re-creation of his greatest dance numbers from a dozen of the musicals he choreographed from 1944 to

1964. Although the resurrection of the original dance steps and production designs was accomplished with extraordinary fidelity, there was a curious vacuum to the evening as a whole. For all Robbins's brilliance both as visual compositor and playwriting choreographer, his dances, when seen divorced from the matrix of their original shows, weren't nearly as dramatically compelling. No longer embedded within the characterization, suspense, or subtext of a particular play, they seemed oddly neutered. The show was a museum-in-performance rather than a cumulative theatrical wallop. *Jerome Robbins' Broadway* demonstrated that even for Broadway's greatest choreographer, removing the libretto guts the drama, turning playwriting dance back into mere decorative dance.

Perhaps that is why Robbins ultimately chose the concert ballet world: he knew that his ballets were whole, sealed units of intrinsic expression, even as they became more abstract and less story-oriented later in his career. Show dances and show ballets may be memorable in the mind, but you can't hum them with your eyes. But when Robbins's Broadway work is seen unexcerpted, in the contexts for which it was created, it is clear that, for all his gratuitously personal nastiness, he enlarged the expressive palette of musicals and elevated the medium. He spoke his own credo best: "Why couldn't we, in aspiration, try to bring our deepest talents together to the commercial theatre?"[103]

There was one other Broadway choreographer during the heyday of de Mille and Robbins who equaled them in originality but never quite left a mark on the medium of the musical. Jack Cole (1911–74), who began dancing on Broadway in the early 1930s and choreographing in the early 1940s, was the first choreographer to adapt jazz dance and ethnic "world music" dance forms for mainstream Broadway, nightclubs, and Hollywood. He influenced Bob Fosse enormously (Gwen Verdon was originally a Jack Cole dancer). The physical movements (including the upper body) he called for were unusually strenuous, his choreography often violent or frankly sexual, his personality as difficult and abusive as Robbins's. Unlike de Mille and Robbins, he never worked significantly in ballet. Many of the shows he choreographed for Broadway were potboilers, but his dances could stop the show with their fierce emotional power—such as the rape ballet in *Man of La Mancha* (1965)—or their astonishingly uncommercial exoticism. De Mille was so bowled over by Cole's dances for the tropically set *Magdalena* (1948, with score by Heitor Villa-Lobos) that she wrote him a fan letter. She later said, "Jerry Robbins advised me to see it. He'd gone *five* times."[104]

Why did such a powerful choreographer not leave his stamp on the art of the musical? Cole's two efforts as a director-choreographer, both in the year 1961—*Donnybrook* and *Kean*—were not even to be judged succès d'estimes. *Kean*'s star Alfred Drake later said, "Jack was not good with words. He was not articulate. So, perhaps as director of the book there were things lacking. His ideas—he *had* ideas, but his expression of them was not always clear. . . . He really didn't want to play around with the book, or discuss the book, or think about the book."[105] Cole's biographer expands this: "He knew how to explore and boldly project the movement and emotive potential of a dancer's body. But in most of his dances, there is little evidence of an overriding philosophy or an intriguing comment on human beings beyond the domain of satire."[106] In other words, Cole, a great and individual dance maker, lacked the writer's sensibility that de Mille and Robbins had. He was not a playwriting choreographer and thus could not endow a musical with a dramatic through-line.

But the same woefully obvious lack of a playwright's sensibility didn't deter the post-Robbins, post-Cole generation of director-choreographers from posing as godlike auteurs, as we'll next see.

Scene Three: *Decline: Directors and Choreographers as Conceptual Showmen*

The Theater of Spectacle-as-Content Returns: Conceptual Showmanship Ousts Playwriting Choreography

> For the first time a director, Tom O'Horgan, did more than merely present a play imaginatively. He simply ran riot. By so doing, he thrust the role of director into a position that others, less bizarre and genuinely theatrical, were to follow. In future years, producers and customary investors became more concerned with who would be directing than the play itself.
>
> — Alan Jay Lerner[107]

During the prime Broadway years of Agnes de Mille, Jerome Robbins, and Jack Cole, many other choreographers entered the ranks: Hanya Holm, Gower Champion, Bob Fosse, Michael Kidd, Peter Gennaro, Herbert Ross, Joe Layton, Onna White, Patricia Birch, Ron Field, Joe Layton. A few of these also served as director-choreographers; at least one (Kidd) even produced two shows he director-choreographed (*L'il Abner* in 1956, *Wildcat* in 1960). Yet the Broadway musicals that constitute the canon of the golden age almost entirely

predate this flowering of the director-choreographer. In fact, the more important director-choreographers became, the less important musicals became in
the general culture. Why?

Forgotten somewhere along the way from 1945 to 1975 was the reason the
choreographer gained artistic ascendancy in the first place: to enhance the
book, not to enhance the production values. When de Mille and Robbins came
up in the 1940s, the book drove the dance. As domineering as they were, they
still designed movement that served the book above all else. Now the dance
and the staging began to drive the book, to wag the dog. And yet the much-
heralded advent of the director-choreographer has never imprinted on theater
history a roll call of choreographers that are household names like those
of Kern, Berlin, Gershwin, or Rodgers. Even the universally praised Kidd
(b. 1919), who also choreographed ballet, and whose dances for *Finian's Rainbow* (1947), *Love Life* (1948), *Guys and Dolls* (1950), *Can-Can* (1953), *Destry Rides
Again* (1959), and other shows by all accounts enhanced those shows, did not
leave an authorial mark on Broadway. Was it because, for all his superb gifts,
he was not a conceptual visionary? A chorus member of the original 1947 production of *Finian's Rainbow* recently recalled that Kidd took over the direction
of the show when Bretaigne Windust was fired, and thus Kidd may indeed have
been somewhat authorial.[108] But isn't it apparent that the reason most of the
choreographers and director-choreographers of the post-Robbins era have
not lasted in memory is that they were not *playwriting* choreographers? Or is
Kidd's lamentable disappearance due to something more elemental: that a
choreographer, no matter how gifted, cannot offer the fundamental intelligence that creates musical theater which remains literature of the stage, and
that therefore the notion that the choreographer-director can somehow dis-
place the composer and librettist from authentic authorhood is absurd—an
absurdity that has perversely gained respectability.

Two of the post-Robbins director-choreographers—Gower Champion and
Bob Fosse—did have a profound, if devolutionary, impact. Certainly neither
was a playwriting choreographer, nor was either a conceptual visionary on the
order of Max Reinhardt. Both of them, however, could be termed modern
"conceptual showmen," as later at times could Tommy Tune and the directors
Tom O'Horgan (*Hair, Jesus Christ Superstar*), Trevor Nunn (*Les Misérables,* the
Lloyd Webber musicals, but not *Oklahoma!*), and Baz Luhrmann (*La Bohème*).
Conceptual showmanship became the guiding directorial ethos in Broadway
musicals after Robbins's retirement.

Conceptual showmanship poses as artistic statement but is essentially vacuous: its main aim is to engage the eye and amuse. There's nothing at all wrong with delivering entertainment. Entertainment is necessary for good theater. Good showmanship brings joy to audiences. But *conceptual* showmanship is aesthetic social climbing, entertainment with a wise-guy attitude: it tries to pawn off showmanship as auteurist commentary. It is faux serious. It proffers kitsch as art. The chichi Ben Ali Haggin *tableaux vivants* of the *Ziegfeld Follies* in the 1920s and the solemn-named pageants of the Kiralfy brothers, Voegtlin, and Burnside, only pretended to be delivering themes. They sold the audience on the illusion that it had digested "something more," when it had digested only window dressing. Busby Berkeley was a showman but not a conceptual showman, because he did not present his staging designs as containing significance beyond entertainment value.

Robbins's retirement from the Broadway stage with *Fiddler on the Roof* in 1964 was the watershed. The more powerful that directors and director-choreographers became after the watershed, the more they pursued the direction of conceptual showmanship and abandoned the playwriting choreography of de Mille and Robbins. Conceptual showman directors sit their concepts on top of the book like oil on water. They can be breathtaking virtuosos of staging, even though as auteurs they may merely be glorified graffitists. Ultimately the success of Champion, Fosse, Tune, and others loosened the hold of the integrated book show paradigm, the paradigm so often attributed exclusively to Rodgers and Hammerstein but in fact codeveloped by many writers and composers. After the mid-1960s not only did the book matter less but, pari passu, the music and lyrics also became less important. They became as incidental to a show's impact as the jerry-built songs of Manuel Klein had been to the Hippodrome extravaganzas of Arthur Voegtlin. With the exception of one great inheritor of the de Mille/Robbins mantle (Michael Bennett), the organic link between text and movement—which was what had made the high-water American musical different from the light musical theater of all other nations—was sundered for good.

The realities of the commercial theater have been and will always be that powerful directors sometimes insist on script changes, notwithstanding the Dramatists Guild. "'You don't like it?' I've warned playwrights," recalled Elia Kazan. "'Then don't work with me.' . . . When the plays were right at first reading, like *Death of a Salesman*, *A Streetcar Named Desire*, and *Tea and Sympathy*, I've asked for no changes."[109] The changes the director Joshua Logan wrought in first-time playwright Thomas Heggen's script for *Mister Roberts* (1948) left Heggen uncertain about his own talent; in early 1949 Heggen committed suicide. Post-Robbins director-choreographers, however, typically one-upped even Kazan and Logan: they held total control of the book because staging itself had replaced the script and score as the generator of the show; the staging *was* the driving idea. Respectful deference to the writer was dispensable. Thus the writers of *Pippin* (1972), the composer Stephen Schwartz and the playwright Roger Hirson, could not get their show produced unless they agreed to let Bob Fosse rework their concept from scratch for "Fosse-lizing." If Rouben Mamoulian had told Rodgers and Hammerstein to relocate *Carousel* to a "Bowery Boys" setting, they would have fired him. But by the early 1970s the director's power was greater than that of any writer. By 1980 most large Broadway musicals were "staged rather than written," according to the librettist Peter Stone—exactly as Voegtlin had staged rather than written his Hippodrome productions.[110]

Conceptual showmen have created a cult of the director without delivering a commensurate vision. As they have attained power and influence, they have weakened traditions of strong writing and the staging achievements of de Mille, Robbins, Mamoulian, Logan, and Robert Lewis. Post-1965 conceptual showmen returned the prevailing stage direction of musicals to presentation rather than integration, diminished the importance of the text (whether music, lyrics, or script), and paved the way for the Broadway takeover by Europop and Disney musicals, which are constructed entirely for spectacle-as-content. For conceptual showmen, physical production and machinery have assumed an importance equal to or greater than words and music: welcome back, *The Black Crook* and John Murray Anderson. Conceptual showmanship, ever seeking after physical grandiosity and kinetic sensation, has destroyed the intimate humanity that was at the core of even large-scale golden-age musicals. Even a more traditional director of musicals like Harold Prince began to take on aspects of conceptual showmanship.

Hello, Dolly; Good-bye, Text-Driven Staging

It is a widely held opinion that the post-1968 influx of British, European, and rock musicals administered the coup de grâce to the old-style Rodgers and Hammerstein musical. But the most important nails in the coffin were driven in earlier, by an apple-cheeked, midwestern, all-American boy who looked like an 8 by 10 glossy photograph. Gower Champion (1919–80) was an extraordinary master of staging qua staging. His greatest Broadway success, *Hello, Dolly!*, was the first megahit, long-running book musical that wasn't in the

R & H mold: that is to say, it was the first in which the production aspects were more important than the integration. *Hello, Dolly!* certainly has a plot and characters, but not only are they subordinate to gestures of staging, they are enveloped and overwhelmed by them. *The King and I* was also a show of exorbitant physical production; Irene Sharaff's wardrobe plot took up eight pages. Rodgers wrote Sharaff after the opening, "I still find myself overpowered by such visual beauty. . . . My doctor was talking to me about the show the other day. He said, 'I can't get it out of my eyes.'"[111] But *The King and I*'s intimate drama was never sacrificed to spectacle. *Hello, Dolly!* and other Champion shows reversed this balance, and, through an influence ingeniously sustained through a long run by the producer David Merrick, ultimately helped the Broadway musical to regress from a *Gesamtkunstwerk* to the equivalent of a pre-1920 song-and-dance show with a mere excuse for a plot.

Champion, born in Illinois, began dancing in nightclubs in Los Angeles as a teenager and moved in the late 1930s to Broadway, where he teamed with the dancer Jeanne Tyler in such shows as the 1939 Abbott and Costello revue *Streets of Paris* and in the 1942 *The Lady Comes Across* (choreographed by Balanchine). After the war he found a new dance partner, Marjorie Belcher, whom he soon married; as Marge and Gower Champion they became fixtures of movie musicals of the late 1940s and early 1950s, notably the 1951 film version of *Show Boat*. Gower's first important assignment as a de facto director-choreographer was the 1948 revue *Lend an Ear* with Carol Channing (ironically, years later Channing had to campaign hard to get him to cast her in *Hello, Dolly!*). He was the first choreographer offered *My Fair Lady,* but his fee was too high for the show's producer, Herman Levin. The book show that really cemented his reputation as a director-choreographer was the 1960 *Bye Bye Birdie,* which he followed with *Carnival!* (1961), *Hello, Dolly!* (1964), and *I Do! I Do!* (1966). Later came less successful shows—*The Happy Time, Sugar, Mack and Mabel*—until he capped his career with the triumph of *42nd Street* (1980). His death from a rare blood cancer on *42nd Street*'s opening night, August 25, 1980, was announced from the stage by the producer David Merrick and has become show-business legend. Champion also play-doctored, taking over from Noël Coward on *High Spirits* (1964), from John Gielgud on *Irene* (1973), and even from Martin Scorsese on *The Act* (1977).

From the beginning to the end Champion was a concept director, not a word or book director. "He didn't work very well with dialogue," recalled the actor Lee Roy Reams of *42nd Street*. "He was always saying, 'too many words.'"

He also didn't like actors to stand still while they were singing a song. He always had to have something going on. It was all very cinematic: scenery just moved on and off, and there was never any real break in the action."[112] Adds his fellow cast member Joe Bova, "The book kept getting shaved. . . . Practically all our rehearsal time went to the chorus. . . . I said to [the stage manager,] 'Ask Gower when he's going to rehearse the book.'"[113] Twenty years earlier, on *Bye Bye Birdie,* according to the composer Charles Strouse, Champion was much the same: "Flipping the set is a conventional idea today, but when Gower devised it in 1960, it was quite an innovative staging concept. He had the teenagers say good-bye to Birdie in New York, take off their coats, and turn them inside out—and the set flipped to Sweet Apple while they continued singing the same song. *We wrote to the concept* [emphasis added]. That was typical of Gower."[114]

The late playwright-librettist Peter Stone characterized directors like Champion and Michael Bennett as aliterate: "lacking literary background, as Stone sees them, they are acutely uncomfortable in the presence of ideas and the words that express them: 'I don't mean they're dumb. They are like abstract painters except their forte is movement.' They have no use for words 'that can be directed but can't be *staged.* . . . You want to preserve ideas through words and the choreographer's trying to get them out.'"[115] Michael Bennett, who unlike Champion was a true playwriting director-choreographer, "never finished high school and had few interests outside the theatre. Except for an occasional thriller, he did not read books or, perhaps, even newspapers."[116] Even Jerome Robbins was verbally challenged, according to Arthur Laurents: "Words were his enemy; he often mispronounced them and he wasn't articulate."[117] Compare this with the vast cultural groundings of Rouben Mamoulian or Agnes de Mille.

Or compare the director's book contribution on *My Fair Lady* (1956) to that of Champion's on *Dolly.* Alan Jay Lerner based his libretto on Shaw's own screenplay for *Pygmalion,* preserving at least half of Shaw's original dialogue. Lerner took the familiarity-breeds-tepid-affection bond that joins Eliza and Professor Higgins at the end of the 1938 film and tweaked it into a more overtly romantinc finale for *My Fair Lady. My Fair Lady's* director, Moss Hart, "contributed very little to the book," according to Hart's friend Stone Widney.[118] But a similarly critical alteration of the original source (Thornton Wilder's play *The Matchmaker*) in *Hello, Dolly!* was entirely authored by Champion, not by its librettist Michael Stewart, according to Stone, who believed that "Wilder distilled the whole philosophy of his play in one scene that takes place at a garden on 14th Street where key characters engage in their most revelatory discussion" and that Champion had violated the pith of the play: "Gower put a curtain around the tables and staged a big splashy number, the waiters' dance. David Hartman was the head waiter. You could hardly miss him and the other dancers running around with trays. All you missed were matters of the utmost consequence—happening off-set behind a curtain."[119]

The waiter/Dolly scene was staged on a ramp. According to Champion's wife, Marge, "Until he got the idea for the ramp, Gower wasn't even interested in doing *Hello, Dolly!* . . . The ramp was used to track through the show— where Dolly could talk to her husband, where the people came out when Dolly came back from retirement."[120] The waiters' dance (actually called "The Waiters' Gallop") became the setup for the title number:

> The head waiter . . . is so awed by her imminent return to their establishment that he puts his staff of waiters through their paces in a dress rehearsal meant to demonstrate the phenomenal alacrity of their service. In this number, "The Waiters' Gallop," the movement of the characters undergoes an almost unreal acceleration. The choreography is complex, with breathtaking acrobatic displays and seemingly unavoidable yet narrowly averted collisions of rushing and interweaving waiters balancing large silver trays on upraised arms. The exhilaration of "The Waiters' Gallop" has barely subsided when the "Hello Dolly!" number begins. The waiters form groups on either side of the grand staircase leading down from a curtained entrance upstage center. Dolly appears at the top of the staircase in a red dress, pauses for an instant, and begins her slow descent to the accompaniment of music and applause. The upsurge of music is punctuated, improbably, by a sassy, bump-and-grind burlesque beat.[121]

The trouble is, exciting as Dolly's entrance down the stairway is, there's no real warrant for the number's hysteria anywhere in the scripted character or the original play. Merrick originally had offered the direction of *Hello, Dolly!* to Harold Prince, who in the fall of 1962 had directed a production of *The Matchmaker*. Prince declined, saying, "I couldn't for the life of me see why those waiters were singing how glad they were to have her back where she belonged, when she'd never been there in the first place."[122]

Champion detached from the story line and cleverly superimposed on the audience a manufactured excitement. That's more than mere showmanship. Champion inaugurated the divorce of sense from style as a style in itself. *That's* conceptual showmanship: staging that exalts a director's visual composition but does not psychologically investigate the text.

Bob Fosse, Swami of the Bookless Book Musical

> Congratulations. You finally did it. You got rid of
> the author.
>
> —Alan Jay Lerner's telegram to Bob Fosse
> on the opening of *Dancin'*, 1978[123]

Bob Fosse (1927–87) performed in burlesque houses as a child, later danced in nightclubs, became a hoofer on Broadway (first show: *Call Me Mister* in 1946), and soon began dancing in movie musicals. He understudied Harold Lang and went on tour in the title role for the 1952 revival of *Pal Joey*. In 1954 he choreographed his first Broadway musical, *The Pajama Game*, making a splash with his finger-snapping dance for the number "Steam Heat." He next choreographed *Damn Yankees* (1955), *Bells Are Ringing* (1956), and *New Girl in Town* (1957), but the first *echt* Fosse show was *Redhead* (1959), which he director-choreographed and which starred his future wife, Gwen Verdon. A murder mystery set in a London wax museum, *Redhead* had a book and songs slight enough to enable the visual éclat (Fosse's dances and the production design of Rouben Ter-Arutunian) to emerge as the main player. In the 1960s Fosse continued ascending the superdirector path, going from musically staging *How to Succeed in Business without Really Trying* (1961) to directing and choreographing *Little Me* (1962), to "conceiving, directing, and choreographing" *Sweet Charity* (1966).

From early on, Fosse had the most recognizable visual signature of any show choreographer past or present with the possible exception of Busby Berkeley: the derby hats, the white gloves; the black costumes and black backgrounds upon which he'd throw trompe l'oeil lighting effects; the bent knees, turned-in feet, and hunched shoulders; the pelvic thrusts; the small group of dancers slithering across the stage in a synchronized movement known as the "Fosse amoeba." As his dance style further evolved from the 1950s to the 1970s, every dancer in a Fosse ensemble became a replica of Fosse himself, a Fosse homunculus, a clone of the Pierrot character Fosse had made his self-caricature. In his late shows Fosse's dances became metaphysical distillations of vaudeville, as if each dancer were a Beckett clown and each number were recapitulating the entire history of show dancers as a race—an arresting conceit, but one unrelated to underlying text, plot, or character. Certainly after *Sweet Charity,* Fosse's dances were about dance, not about the narrative or through-line of the librettos they purportedly illustrated. Fosse was a brilliant and original choreographer, but his work, like Champion's, did incalculable damage to the integrated Broadway musical's previous ability to create moving and coherent drama.

It is an interesting fact that plugging a Broadway musical on a television commercial, for the last thirty years a standard practice, was originally the brainchild not of a Madison Avenue adman but of Fosse. Fosse made the suggestion to Fred Golden of the Blaine-Thompson ad agency to put a snippet from *Pippin* (1973) on a television commercial, followed by the voice-over: "You've just seen sixty seconds of *Pippin*. If you want to see the other 119 minutes, go to the Imperial Theatre." "The curious thing was that the beautiful little moment Fosse staged for the commercial wasn't even in the show," recalls American Theatre Wing's Roy Somlyo. "It became so popular that ultimately he did put it in, and whenever that moment came up, the audience broke out in wild applause." Fosse was thus responsible not only for helping to make musicals a primarily visual medium, but for selling them to the public as a visual, not a storytelling, medium.[124] *Pippin*'s producer, Stuart Ostrow, wrote: "I have mixed emotions about having created the *Pippin* commercial that I put on television in 1973. The commercial was the first of its kind, a minute of lightning in a bottle, but it never occurred to me that it would change the way theatre was to be produced. From that moment on hucksters could sell shows as commodities so long as their spot had glitter and hype. Never mind producing a great show, produce a great commercial!"[125]

Pippin at least had a narrative concept and some decent songs. *Chicago* (1975), which Fosse directed, choreographed, cowrote, and called "A Musical Vaudeville," ruptured the template of the book musical and turned it into a Fosse amoeba. The show was adapted from a 1926 play described by Brooks Atkinson as a "shrill, breezy cartoon about the travesty of justice. A murderess won the sympathies of a male jury by pretending to be an expectant mother"; Atkinson added that melodramas of *Chicago*'s type "were not realistic, they were not iconoclastic, they were not polemical: they were romantic in the happy mood of the twenties. Their motive was no more serious than a conspiracy between the authors and the audience to have a good time."[126] In other words, the 1926 *Chicago* was featherlight escapism, as even the playwright thought: "I had tried to get to Maurine Watkins, who wrote the original play, for years," recalled Gwen Verdon, "and I finally contacted her in Florida during the Cuban missile crisis. She said, 'How can we talk about that piece of fluff when I have guns aimed right at me?'"[127]

Unlike Champion, who on *Dolly* was working with a Thornton Wilder play of some substance, Fosse attempted to make a "piece of fluff" into a statement, and to render the production numbers as textual, substantive commentary. With *Chicago*, Fosse sought to create "Brecht Lite." But the vaudeville turns essayed by the two murderesses in *Chicago* seem to come from nowhere, unlike the vaudeville turns in Jerome Robbins's *Gypsy*, which are firmly planted in discernible characters and story. Attempting to create a *Mahagonny*-like commentary on tabloid crime by vaudevillizing it in Brecht-Weill fashion, Fosse's treatment lost all grounding in text. His visual legerdemain for *Chicago* was not specific—it would have made just as much or as little sense illustrating happy nuns who had just left the convent so they could smoke and wear fishnet stockings.

Director-choreographers choose weak books for the same reasons that some presidential candidates choose weak vice-presidential running mates: so as not to be upstaged. For his second-to-last musical, *Dancin'* (1978), Fosse used only music and songs from the past and no book. His final show, the unsuccessful *Big Deal* (1986), also used only already existing songs. Sharing creation with a strong composer's new music, as the monomaniacal Robbins had managed to do with Bernstein, or as Fokine did with Stravinsky, was not Fosse's modus operandi.

Fosse thus owed more to Ned Wayburn, Julian Mitchell, and even John Tiller than to Jerome Robbins or Agnes de Mille. He revived the most antique precursors of modern Broadway musicals—the girlie show, the leg show—put bowler hats on them, repackaged them with neoprecision formations à la the Gertrude Hoffman Girls, and proffered the results as a new form of authorship in musical theater.

The most baffling contradiction about this undeniably gifted man is that as a film director, he was not only a visual magician but also strongly story-oriented and dramatically brilliant. The few motion pictures he directed, despite some divergences in style, have all the depth and emotional truth his stage work lacked. Fosse, more than any other single director, brought the hollow revue style to the Broadway book show with the pretense that it bestowed vision on narrative material.

The Scenery Steals the Show

In the golden-age days of the Broadway musical, striking production values were considered a de rigueur element of revues but not of book shows. Among book shows, the Ziegfeld superproduction of *Show Boat* was the exception: the modest production values of the Princess Theatre shows of the 1910s were more typical. Even *Oklahoma!* and *South Pacific* in the 1940s were not physical superproductions. But with the advent of the conceptual-showman director-choreographer, physical production began to recover the lopsided importance it had enjoyed in the late-nineteenth- and early-twentieth-centuries era of *The Black Crook* and *The Wizard of Oz*. Yet even fifty years before *Starlight Express* and *The Lion King,* there were occasional book shows that were written to the "concept" of a specific production design. A few were created by writers of the canon: Cole Porter wrote the songs for *Around the World* (1946), and Rodgers and Hammerstein wrote *Me and Juliet* (1953). Let's look at what happened with these shows.

It is not well remembered that the French science fiction novelist Jules Verne (1828–1905) also wrote librettos for operettas, or that some of his novels were adapted for stage productions almost immediately after they were published. Verne's novel *Around the World in Eighty Days,* published in 1873, was given a stage production in Paris in 1874 and in New York in 1875 by the Kiralfy Brothers; in 1911 Arthur Voegtlin designed a Hippodrome production. On October 23, 1938—one week before he broadcast his notorious "War of the Worlds" radio adaptation on CBS radio—Orson Welles broadcast his adaptation of *Around the World in Eighty Days* on *The Mercury Theatre of the Air.* In 1945 Welles decided to try to revive his sagging wunderkind reputation by adapting the Verne novel as a Broadway stage extravaganza, and he interested Mike Todd in producing it and Porter in writing the songs (Welles was to write and direct). During rehearsals early in 1946, Todd abruptly withdrew from the project, leaving Welles to keep the production afloat with his own money. Inevitably, Welles even stepped into the cast as Dick Fix. (Ten years later, Todd did produce a hugely successful film version with an international all-star cast.)

The show, Welles's baby although billed on posters as "Orson Welles in Cole Porter's *Around the World,*" opened May 31, 1946, to scathing reviews, not just for the below-par Porter songs but because "there was too much staging," in the words of Cecil Smith. "Porter's songs were . . . obliterated by too elaborate a superstructure. . . . Robert Davison provided a resourceful stage setting equipped with panels at right and left, in which miniature scenes were enacted while the bigger ones among the thirty-two different settings were prepared on the main stage—which, in turn, was so planned that the front and back halves could be used either separately or together."[128] Welles even included filmed sequences as part of the live action (as did Gower Champion twenty years later in *The Happy Time*). The staging *was* the show; there was a circus scene complete with acrobats and tightrope walkers (a 1,600-pound mechanical elephant was dispensed with in previews), a magic show, and an elaborate special effect of a railroad train "falling through a trestle." The *Journal American*'s drama critic, Robert Garland, in a wink at Welles's 1936 *Macbeth,* wrote of *Around the World,* "It is a show shown by a show-off, full of sets and costumes, signifying nothing." Another critic dubbed it *Wellesapoppin'.* (Alan Jay Lerner, dissenting from the naysayers, thought *Around the World* "an uproarious, mad piece of theatre . . . a treat" and claimed Mike Todd stole much of his movie version from Welles's staging ideas.[129])

Forty years later, Andrew Lloyd Webber's *Starlight Express*—a show built entirely on a reproduction of a railroad train on roller skates—ran ten times as long as *Around the World* had in 1946. Surely Welles's *Around the World,* produced in 1986 or 2003, would also have enjoyed a long run. In 1946, however, Welles's diverting visual magic was dismissed by critics and audiences alike as infra dig for Broadway. The prevailing taste then did not permit the scenery to steal the show.

In 1952 Rodgers and Hammerstein were at the peak of their power and influence. With *South Pacific* and *The King and I* still running, they began work on an original script, a backstage story about the human relationships between the cast and crew of a fictional show in production: the show, called *Me and Juliet* (the name of the fictional show-within-the-show), was to be mounted with state-of-the-art stagecraft. The main plot involved a love triangle between the stage manager of the show-within-a-show, the female lead of the show-within-the-show, and her jealous, bullying boyfriend, who is the show's lighting designer. A backstage drama built around a show-within-a-show was no innovation (*Show Boat, Pal Joey*); in fact, Cole Porter's then-recent hit *Kiss Me, Kate* was entirely built on this conceit. The innovation of *Me and Juliet* was the way the show was staged. For *Me and Juliet,* the production design simultaneously displayed to the audience the proscenium of the show-within-the-show and the wings and flies of its backstage, where the "human drama" took place. The designer Jo Mielziner told the press that "as the scenery moves, the audience will get the sensation that the auditorium is turning while the stage is standing still."[130] When the real audience returned to their seats after intermission, act 2 opened with a scene worthy of Pirandello: the audience of the show-within-the-show appeared onstage having drinks and smoking cigarettes at the lounge talking about "Me and Juliet," the show within *Me and Juliet.* But as Hammerstein's biographer notes, "It was in fact the [actual] audience's talk about the sets as they left the theater that confirmed Dick and Oscar's doubts about the play itself."[131]

If *Around the World* was the granddaddy of *Starlight Express, Me and Juliet* was certainly a granddaddy of the self-conscious *Grand Hotel* (1989). But *Grand Hotel* ran for more than a thousand performances; in 1953, *Me and Juliet* flopped. The critics George Jean Nathan and Walter Kerr said virtually the same thing: "A show without a show with all the necessary externals for a good show but missing the internals" (Nathan); "Mechanically, the show is pure magic. . . . [but it comes] perilously close to . . . a show-without-a-show" (Kerr).[132] Mielziner's set got the best reviews. Today *Me and Juliet* is only a footnote for theater scholars or trivia pursuers (it featured the Broadway debut of Shirley MacLaine, albeit in an ensemble role). But its pioneering use of metal machinery for production design was fateful. According to the veteran set designer Oliver Smith, the architectural approach of Mielziner's forgotten *Me and Juliet* design eventually resurfaced and overtook everything. "Rather than use delicately painted sets, designers and their directors want to do iron and steel movable structures or just redo the theatre for large effects. Now there is also motorization to move massive props or sets in perfect timing with computerized lights."[133]

By the 1980s it was considered okay for the scenery to steal the show if the show was a box-office success (*Cats, Starlight Express*). By the late 1990s it was not only okay, it was considered aesthetically upscale for the production design to take over (*The Lion King*). The Broadway orchestrator Michael Starobin believes that "the producers today invest in the set, not the talent. Today, the talent is secondary. The set is the star. They don't develop the songwriting talent the way they used to. Arrangements have gotten smaller in number of players, especially fewer strings, because of cost; producers don't want to pay for it, they want to pay for sets."[134] The veteran costume designer Miles White remembered the charm of the low-tech set design prevalent early in his career:

In *Jerome Robbins' Broadway,* we didn't have a singing chorus like in the original show. The opening business in the Atlantic City ballet [from *High Button Shoes*] is supposed to start with showgirls, singers, and men as whole separate groups, and he couldn't afford that in this one. In 1947 the beginning of that was done in one; that is, in front of the curtain with the singers in their elaborate costumes. They stripped on the stage and opened into the set of Atlantic City in bathing suits. Now you don't do that anymore. You turn the scenery around in front of the public. And everybody applauds the scene change. Before, we used to close the curtain, have something in one, or a drop, so that they could change everything to a marvelous big set, instead of just turning it around. Scenery now is very inventive in movement; it's often fascinating to watch things change. Before, we never showed how things changed, and that's mostly because people had to push it. Now it's moved by pushing a button someplace.[135]

Even the dean of contemporary lighting designers on Broadway, Jules Fisher, thinks that production for the sake of production has displaced text-driven production design:

> Commercial values on Broadway have given us the money to get anything we want—the best actors, the best scenery, the best lighting. If I need a lot of gold fabric I can afford it. On the other hand, we could make the same complaint that everyone makes of television. The audience is less demanding. With super-commercialism, less of the audience uses its brain. More and more, it's lulled into going to a musical just to see something very splashy and to be happy with nothing but glitz.[136]

This new doctrine of stagecraft-before-braincraft has resulted at times in some reinterpretations of classic musicals. In 1999 the first major revival of Cole Porter's *Kiss Me, Kate* since the original 1948 production opened for an 881-performance run. In the second act the character Bill Calhoun sings to his girlfriend, Lois, the song "Bianca," which Porter wrote to order for the original Bill, Harold Lang, who had wanted a solo. The director, Michael Blakemore, or the choreographer, Kathleen Marshall (or perhaps both), bizarrely staged this entire number with the muscular, tank-topped actor playing Bill Calhoun ascending the metal bars of the two-flight stage set like Tarzan swinging on tree vines, focusing the audience's attention on an irrelevant display of gymnastics. The song became the accompaniment to the action, not vice versa. "Bianca" is admittedly not one of Porter's most scintillating lyrics. But why was the audience treated as though it were a hyperactive child, fidgety unless chewing gum for the eyes was provided? The veteran Actors Studio director David Pressman still scratches his head over this. He recalls the staging of the song in the 1948 original: "They didn't do it that way at all. He just sang the song to her and she reacted." (Gerald Bordman recalls Lang doing a tap dance between verses of the song.)

In the old days, character-exposition songs like "Bianca" were considered interesting enough to be presented without any kinetic stage enhancement beyond a tap-dance interlude. A silent film survives of a live performance of Mary Martin singing the ballad "That's Him" in the 1943 *One Touch of Venus:* the staging is simplicity itself, with Martin mostly sitting in a bare chair in front of a single backdrop that does not revolve or flip. Despite the lack of soundtrack and the performer's largely sedentary position, any viewer of this silent clip can palpably sense the song's liveliness and charm. But then, as we now know, Agnes de Mille, choreographer of *One Touch of Venus,* sometimes wanted her dancers and players *not* to move. Gower Champion and his artistic heirs never wanted movement to cease, and the result has often been a manic but emotionally impoverished theatrical experience.

The theme-park set design of the Disney musicals of the 1990s and 2000s is another throwback to the Hippodrome, when most shows were built on production design themes and directors like Arthur Voegtlin and R. H. Burnside doubled as actual amusement park designers when their theatrical careers ebbed. Theme-park production design tends to push the already sped-up pace of modern musicals into overdrive, but the current stage direction of even underproduced musical shows such as *Urinetown* now tends to offer energy in lieu of sense.

Even revivals of intimate musicals have lately evidenced the "speed creep" of contemporary stage direction. The original 1963 production of the musical *She Loves Me* was the second show to be directed by Harold Prince. The show, a charmingly Old World lonely-hearts tale, was based on the play *Parfumerie* by the Hungarian playwright Miklos Laszlo and its 1940 film adaptation directed by Ernst Lubitsch, *The Shop around the Corner.* (The play also was the basis of the 1949 Judy Garland film musical *In the Good Old Summertime,* and some believe that the 1998 film *You've Got Mail* was also suggested by it.) In 1993 the Roundabout Theatre produced the first major revival of *She Loves Me,* directed by Scott Ellis. I saw both the 1963 and the 1993 productions and recently recalled in a conversation with the show's composer, Jerry Bock, that the pace of the 1963 show was much gentler, the 1993 version hectic by comparison. Bock confirmed my childhood memory as fact.

At times conceptual showmanship has led not only to text-challenged overproduction but to the evacuation of dramatic meaning from dancing and stage movement. The gifted young tap dancer Savion Glover, after appearing in *Black and Blue* (1989) and *Jelly's Last Jam* (1992), coconceived, choreographed, and danced in *Bring in 'Da Noise, Bring in 'Da Funk* (1996). But Glover, unlike Gene Kelly, Bill Robinson, or Gregory Hines, does not play to the audience from his waist up. He even looks at his feet while he's dancing. He does not act, or even use his eyes to project. As exciting and kinetic as he can be, he never conveys character or narrative with his performance style; rather, he resembles a kind of postmodern vaudeville dancer, onstage only to display his own virtuosity. Compare this to Robert Alton's dances for *Pal Joey,* in which Alton

made tap dance the illustrator of a complex scenario, the dramatizer of detailed levels of character, simply by directing Gene Kelly to use his upper body
and face as much as his legs. To eliminate the upper body in a theatrical dancer
is not only to constrict his expressive range as a performer, but to stultify the
playwriting aspect of theater dance. *Bring in 'Da Noise, Bring in 'Da Funk* has
been hailed by the librettist-lyricist Tom Jones (*The Fantasticks, I Do! I Do!*) as
"an actual breakthrough into a new kind of musical theatre," though he adds,
"despite the pleasures of the serious sub-text . . . an enormous part of the success of the show is based solidly on . . . old verities of vaudeville."[137]

The Director as Überscenarist: Harold Prince and Michael Bennett

> Devising stage business and analyzing character,
> however vital to the success of a play, cannot be
> placed on the same creative plane as composing—
> either musical or choreographic.
>
> — Agnes de Mille, 1956

The Champion-Fosse style of conceptual showmanship was not the only directorial approach practiced post-Robbins, but its influence carried to the
styles of even the two great modern standard-bearers of traditional text-driven
direction: the choreographer-director Michael Bennett (1943–87) and the
nonchoreographer director Harold Prince (b. 1928). For Champion and Fosse,
the staging became the show; for Michael Bennett and sometimes for Hal
Prince (especially later in his career), the staging became the book. Bennett (*A
Chorus Line, Dreamgirls*) and Prince (*Evita, The Phantom of the Opera*) were,
in effect, director-scenarists: they constructed the continuity and emotional
meaning of musicals by assembling undeveloped fragments (taped life histories of Broadway dancers, record albums) into coherent narratives that the
physical production propelled as much as the script and the songs. Because
both directors' approaches, unlike Champion and Fosse's, were grounded in
the emotional through-line, their work was often powerful, even inspired, yet
because they adopted the conceptual showmanship ethic of the director as
auteur, their work at times overwhelmed the competing creative contributions
of the book, music, and lyrics. Since both directors were wont to dominate any
production they directed, the unintended byproduct of their überscenarist
style was to further diminish writers and composers in the conceptual scheme
of creation. George Abbott, Moss Hart, and George S. Kaufman were all playwrights, but when they directed material written by others, they merely re-

wrote lines or at most asked for book rewrites; they did not substitute for the book the equivalent of a cinematic shooting script of their own making, as Bennett and Prince would often do.

Bennett (born Michael DiFiglia in Buffalo, New York) started as a Broadway gypsy in three forgettable musicals of the early 1960s. A charismatic individual with born instincts for musical staging, he advanced so quickly that by the age twenty-six he was not only choreographing Broadway musicals but also winning the confidence of no less than Katharine Hepburn to direct her in the 1969 musical *Coco* when Hepburn's handpicked director, Michael Benthall, couldn't handle the assignment. Bennett next choreographed Sondheim's *Company,* which Harold Prince directed in 1970, and then choreographed and codirected with Prince Sondheim's 1971 *Follies.* After that, with *Seesaw* (1973), Bennett was not only director-choreographer but "he made it absolutely clear to management that he had total, dictatorial control," recalled the show's musical director, Donald Pippin. "No one could question him; neither Cy Coleman nor Dorothy Fields, who wrote the score, had to approve anything he did."[138] The original book writer, Michael Stewart, quit *Seesaw* when the Bennett style made him superfluous.

Bennett achieved showbiz apotheosis with the *succès fou* of *A Chorus Line* in 1975, which he "conceived, directed, and choreographed," although its true author was the workshop, a form of open-ended exploratory rehearsal that Bennett arguably invented with this show. Oral histories of actual Broadway dancers were harvested during the workshops and then hammered into material by Bennett and his team of songwriters and scriptwriters. Bennett forever after used the workshop process to develop (read: to maintain authorial control over) both his produced and his unproduced musicals (there were eight in development after *Dreamgirls,* his last show to open on Broadway). He produced *Ballroom* in 1978 completely out of his own pocket and lost his $3 million investment, but the brilliant 1981 *Dreamgirls* was a hit.

Bennett's environmentally conceived stagings always spoke the emotional subtext of the characters and the story because he intuitively understood, as conceptual showmen do not, that production should not supplant story. "In *Follies,*" Bennett remarked, "the idea and the visual metaphor became stronger than the material, or more interesting. That's why it was not successful."[139] With *A Chorus Line* and *Dreamgirls* he achieved a complete fusion of visual presentation and emotional connection. Elsewhere his production design veered into giantism (which worked with *Follies*) or a Championesque tendency to dwarf emotional intimacy (particularly with *Ballroom,* of which its lighting designer, Tharon Musser, commented, "If any show ever proved that scenery, lights, costumes, and staging can't do the whole thing, that was it"[140]). Notwithstanding these tendencies, Bennett was the truest (and maybe only) inheritor of Robbins's movement-has-deep-meaning style; as Prince put it, "He works very much from character and isn't interested in steps per se."[141] Unlike Robbins, however, Bennett was supportive of his performers and as a result was well liked by almost everybody he worked with, although he could also manipulate people like a Svengali.

Bennett was the de facto author of his musicals even though he didn't pen them, because he coached the creative team to implement his own visual scenarios, just as the musically untrained Irving Berlin coaxed composer Russell Bennett to midwife his musical fragments into full Broadway scores. Indeed, by the standards of the legitimate theater, Bennett, a high school dropout, was illiterate: "I'm really surprised I can write at all, because I can't spell," he once admitted, while *Chorus Line*'s coauthor James Kirkwood said Bennett's "attention span was too short" for a real writer's.[142] *Company*'s company manager, Charles Willard, said, "Michael was not an intellectual. . . . I don't think he ever stood back and intellectualized it, or had discussions about concept musicals,"[143] and Joseph Papp added, "He was not a literary-type person. He was a street person."[144] Perhaps, then, it is not surprising that Bennett weakened the role of the librettist in musical theater, and that such an intuitive stage genius as his demanded control as a condition of its efficacy. "I think Michael was not totally comfortable with a person who has strong ideas about how they want to do something," said Donald Pippin. "He liked people who weren't quite that developed, who he could mold and manipulate."[145] *Chorus Line* cowriter Nicholas Dante agreed: "With Michael, you were out the door if you were a threat."[146]

The music theater scholar Ken Mandelbaum notes that *A Chorus Line* was the first (but not the last) musical ever to be cast and put into rehearsal before it was even written.[147] That is another way of saying that the writer's vision doesn't count. (None of the other musicals that traded on the *Chorus Line* oral history model—*Runaways, Working*—were nearly as successful.) Bennett's modus operandi ("He called in his group of writers, he guided the ideas to a theme, they discussed the outline—the beginning, middle, and end—then he continued in the driver's seat throughout the development of the script, and ultimately, the production itself"[148]) was more in the style of television or film creation than of the legitimate theater. His very success was a symptom of a playwright's theater in decline.

Michael Bennett was a brief candle, a meteor who shot from strip-joint dancing to anonymous gypsy chorus to choreographer to the whole ball of wax in a few short years. Harold Prince is still with us and has had the most remarkably durable career of any director in the Broadway theater since George Abbott. Prince started as gofer for Abbott in 1949, progressed to assistant stage manager by 1950, and then with *The Pajama Game* in 1954 to boy-wonder coproducer (he was famous enough by 1958 to be impersonated by Robert Morse in that year's musical backstage roman à clef, *Say, Darling*). Beginning with *A Family Affair* in 1962, even as he continued producing through the 1980s, Prince has been the Broadway musical's preeminent director, a stylistic eclectic who at his best is perhaps the true inheritor of Rouben Mamoulian, a postmodern master of through-line–based stage tableaux. Unlike many producers who try the switch to director, Prince developed into a true creative artist. Certainly his ingenious musical staging of the courtroom scene in *Parade* (1998)—in which the eventually lynched Leo Frank is depicted enacting multiple characters' conceptions of him like the multiply retold rape scene in Kurosawa's film *Rashomon*—was far beyond the compass and conceit of any younger American director currently working in the Broadway theater.

Prince's reputation as a director who could fuse integrative emotion with a quasi-Brechtian presentational style really took off with *Cabaret* (1967). With the Stephen Sondheim shows he directed (*Company, Follies, A Little Night Music, Pacific Overtures, Sweeney Todd, Merrily We Roll Along*), his stagings began to strike some as more Brechtian alienation than Robbinsian integration (Prince himself has denied being influenced by Brecht, pointing to directors Vsevolod Meyerhold and Erwin Piscator as greater influences). With Andrew Lloyd Webber's libretto-deficient musicals *Evita* (1979)and *The Phantom of the Opera* (1988), Prince's latent überscenarism found the perfect chrysalis. "When they sent me the lyrics for *Evita* I wrote a three-thousand word response about how to transform a group of songs into a dramatic script with tension. . . . taking lyrics from the album, I turned each song into a scene, describing to Lloyd Webber and Rice what I felt the action should be. . . . I created a script from lyrics. . . . it's a short script—it's like a series of telegrams."[149] The music producer Freddie Gershon further described how Prince "scenarized" *Evita*:

We had recorded the score for *Evita,* and the album soared. It was a huge, huge hit. As a musical play, however, it had no form or substance. It was just this record album.

And then Hal Prince got involved, and *Evita* was invented. It was Hal who transformed a four-hour concert piece into a coherent two-hour musical play. How do you tell the story of the five-year rise of Juan Perón from colonel to general to dictator? Hal Prince told it in two minutes, in a number with a group of men playing musical chairs. The last man in the chair is Perón.

How do you tell the story of the five-year rise of Evita, who screwed her way to the top? Hal Prince told it in two minutes, in a number with a revolving door. A cheap-looking woman goes through a revolving door on the arm of an undistinguished man. When she comes around, she's better dressed and on the arm of a more important-looking man. She keeps going through the revolving door, each time emerging better dressed, better coiffured, with bigger jewels and more glamorous furs. On the last go-around, she emerges on the arm of a general, who introduces her to Perón.[150]

Later, with *The Phantom of the Opera,* Prince said, "I felt the story could be told primarily through images and music; you don't need words. . . . I wanted to stress the rudimentary psychology that is at the core of the material." *Phantom* is a kind of masterpiece of visual storytelling, worthy of comparison with the silent films of D. W. Griffith; Lloyd Webber tunes or no, the show would never have had half the success it enjoyed without Prince's transformation. *Phantom* was truly *written* by Prince.

Prince originally had set out to become a playwright: fresh out of college in 1948, he sent his scripts around to producers and in 1950 his play *A Perfect Scream* (coauthored with Ted Luce) almost made it into production. In recent decades Prince has been a virtual writer more important than the actual writers on most of his shows. "My needs as an artist require involvement at an early time. That can be exceedingly annoying to certain writers. . . . Sure I liked being part author."[151] But Prince's notion of authorship is not playwriting: "For me, set design is a form of co-authorship," he has said.[152] Like the late Michael Bennett, he won't work on a show unless he can exert authorial control. "I must have the final word. People have walked away from that over the past twenty-five years, which is their prerogative. Choreographers can leave or accept the finality of my word. There's no halfway house."[153]

As his success grew, some concurred with the theater historian Denny Martin Flinn that Prince "began to take himself and his concepts too seriously. They began to overwhelm his material, and the production as well" with "directorial diddling" that "distracted from, rather than supported, the material."[154] The antiauthorism of conceptual showmanship began to creep in.

Prince's staging of the song "I Have the Room Above Her" in his 1994 revival of *Show Boat* was, in the opinion of theater critic Mark Steyn,

> not remotely convincing as an expression of the riverboat gambler's emotions at this point in the drama; it is there purely as a pretext for a staging gimmick. . . . [Prince's direction] sets itself up in active opposition to the qualities that make the show worth reviving in the first place. . . . The stage pictures are cluttered, with too many elements jostling for attention. . . . Hammerstein is the man who made sense of musicals; at times, Prince's revival seems determined to undo his life's work.[155]

Prince even rewrote Hammerstein's libretto so that the romantic duet "Why Do I Love You?" originally written for Gaylord Ravenal and Magnolia could be given to Parthy (Elaine Stritch) to sing to Magnolia's newborn daughter. "To reorient *Show Boat* so that a non-singing character can get a solo," continued Steyn, "returns us to the theatrical dark ages—to the world Kern and Hammerstein set out to alter forever. . . . This revival is alarming because it suggests that America's most distinguished director can no longer hear the words. Before *Show Boat*, we had star vehicles; after *Show Boat*, we had shows; now, even the greatest show is no more than a star vehicle for the director."

As George S. Kaufman noted, a strong director can still be strong by choosing to give way, to be the artist who conceals his art. But Prince sees his role as that of driver, not server. He has said, "You hear about novelists, star novelists who don't know where novels are going to end? Well, there must be playwrights who do that, too. And there must be lousy musical books that have been written that way and have gone on to be very successful; but the truth is it's not a good rule. You really ought to know where you're going. Where you're going implies you had a reason to get there."[156] Compare Elia Kazan's view: "I began to learn not to try to pin a play's meaning down to a didactic theme. . . . I preferred . . . to tell a story that was as human and, therefore, as ambivalent and unresolved as life itself, so that the audience would leave the theatre asking, 'I wonder what the hell all that means.' Which is the same experience one has in life, isn't it? Or when reading a great novel."[157] Perhaps the cult of directorial authorship and its modus operandi of filling every vacuum has taken away some of the mystery Kazan refers to, poaching on the rightful creative zone of the librettist and composer. Alan Jay Lerner said of Moss Hart that his "objective as a director was to produce what the author had written, tastefully, theatrically, and truthfully. He did not intrude—he guided. The most difficult thing to find in the theatre today is a director who will not make a contribution, that is, force the author to make unnecessary change to suit a directorial concept. Being a writer himself, Moss had profound respect for the written word of others."[158]

Harold Prince is the last great active practitioner of the glories of the Broadway musical's past. Yet one may fairly ask: if they were alive today, would the Gershwin brothers, Hammerstein, Rodgers, Hart, Weill, Loesser, Harburg, and the other creators of the canon acquiesce to his Princely demand: "I must have the final word. . . . There's no halfway house"?

Authentic Concept and Faux Concept Musicals—or Is the Concept of "Concept" Faux?

The success and notoriety of the post-1966 superdirectors—director-choreographers and director-scenarists alike—exploded the paradigm of the integrated book musical and blew a Bronx cheer at the writer in musical theater. When the primary language of theater is no longer word, character, or music but rather gesture, movement, and staging, the power and legitimacy of language and music are undermined. The musicals of the Broadway golden age had great language and music enhanced by gesture and movement; after about 1980 most new Broadway musicals featured crowd-pleasing gesture and movement with language and music as secondary elements—very much like the musicals before 1900.

Often touted as the new wave in post–golden-age musicals and cited as the raison d'être of the new superdirectors is the "concept" musical. Concept has been held by some to have become a paradigm superior to that of the integrated book musical of yesteryear. At times, when movement-based concept is presented in lieu of skilled writing (*Bring in 'Da Noise, Bring in 'Da Funk*), it is even regarded as aesthetically superior to skilled writing. Often concept is faux playwriting by the director, signaling that he or she has dressed the script with a production that gives the appearance of making a statement. But *A Chorus Line* is not a concept show; it is a narrative show, brilliantly staged to enhance the story's emotional power. *Company* is not a concept show; it is a narrative show with brilliant songs. *Sunday in the Park with George* deals with ideas but remains a narrative show with one extraordinary moment of staging: the *tableau vivant* of Seurat's famous Grande Jatte painting (an effect all but stolen outright from Ben Ali Haggin of the *Ziegfeld Follies*). Neither is *Allegro* a concept show; rather, it is a laudably ambitious but muddled narrative show with a concept of physical staging written by the playwright into the script's stage directions.

298

Today when a musical show is sufficiently diffuse in its writing to ask to be taken for its intentions rather than for its achievement, it is accorded the cachet of "concept." Sometimes the concept musical label is used to airbrush the illusion of a unifying theme over a show that doesn't really have one. Of course concept was not just discovered yesterday in world theater. Are not great narrative dramas like *The Master Builder, Man and Superman, The Iceman Cometh,* or *Othello* largely built on concepts? Yet they are not called "concept dramas," and their perennial power is independent of directorial jiggery. Operas aren't concept-based either; they're libretto-based, and their music's power is libretto-driven, even when the libretto is as execrable as *Il trovatore's.*

With diffuse theatrical concepts, it is more difficult for composers and lyricists to create memorable material, because they are called upon to musicalize and lyricize atomized moments or disincarnate ideas instead of an emotional through-line or a developed characterization. Cheryl Crawford, producer of one of the earliest concept musicals, the Weill-Lerner *Love Life* (1948), wrote that "because Kurt's score served the style of the writing, it didn't have the warmth of his best ballads. . . . its theme was fresh but it had no heart, no passion. The audience couldn't get emotionally involved in the marital problems of the couple."[159] (Even Sondheim agrees, remarking that *Love Life* failed "because it started out with an idea rather than a character.")

Yet somehow songwriters in the 1900–1940 period created memorable songs for revues without through-line or plot or character. How so? Because the lyricists of that time had a genius for playwriting, just as choreographers like de Mille and Robbins had a genius for playwriting—they dramatized the universality of human situations within the confines of a thirty-two-bar song, thus compensating for the lack of a supporting through-line. Today's concept musical songs, with the exception of Sondheim's, rest neither on universal observation nor on dramatic through-line and thus fall between two stools. The concept musical—often directed by a conceptual showman—is in fact a fancy term for a musical revue, many of which were directed by the precursors of today's conceptual showmen, Hassard Short and John Murray Anderson. One is also reminded that the Kiralfy brothers' revues of the 1870s and 1880s were heavy on grand-sounding interlinking themes that could also be called concepts. Modern concept musicals take the presentation style of the revue and foist it onto the template of the book show. The only arena where concept musicals may be legitimately so termed is the avant-garde theater: the plotless Martha Clarke–Richard Peaslee theater piece *Vienna Lusthaus* (1986) is a genuine concept musical.

The current respectability of the concept musical is an indication that Broadway has abandoned any hope that strong writing and composing could ever again mean what they used to in the commercial musical theater. Calling director-diddled Broadway shows concept musicals is no less false packaging than calling used cars preowned automobiles.

Wagging the Musical into Mediocrity

> A director's theatre is a theatre in decline.
>
> — George Pierce Baker

The Broadway musical theater lost its magic at exactly the point when stagers replaced writers as the preeminent players in the creation of the product. Compare the books of *Chicago* and *The Phantom of the Opera* with those of *Carousel, My Fair Lady,* and *The Music Man.* Compare the songs of *Ragtime, City of Angels,* and *Side Show* with those of *Show Boat, Porgy and Bess,* and *Guys and Dolls.* Is it merely a coincidence that one group was written in the wake of conceptual director-choreographers, and the other in the age before?

In the last ten years on Broadway, there has been a return to dividing the work of director and choreographer between two people. But the text-driven dance of Robbins and de Mille is usually missing from newer choreographers' work. There are also a few gifted newer director-choreographers such as Kathleen Marshall and Susan Stroman, who have shown respect for the text. In *Contact* (2000), Stroman, working from original librettos provided by John Weidman, crafted three original one-act dance musicals entirely to preexisting music. Some musicals are "through-sung"; *Contact* was a creative "through-danced" musical, only partly expressed in dialogue and pantomime. Stroman was doing playwriting choreography, although she did so with canned music à la Fosse.

Yet although most of the showman director-choreographers are dead, their legacy of a musical theater of diminished words and music abides with their successors. The legendary choreographer-directors reversed history and brought the Broadway musical back to the nineteenth century's emphasis on physical production and indifference to writing. Making the hypervisual director the star broke the compact of the integrated book show whereby composers, lyricists, and choreographers synergized. It also emasculated not only strong-voiced writers and composers, but the very tradition of strong writing. Though the Euro-poperas are indifferently choreographed, they are massively staged and they usually embody style over substance, the same disconnect between the visual noise and the textual sense pioneered by Champion, Fosse, and others. Energy and sensation are now prized over nuance, as if to suggest that if the direction is loud and fast enough, no one will notice the essential mediocrity of the material.

Various phenomena outside the theater share responsibility for the rise of the hypervisual director. The rise of visual culture and aliteracy, the predominance of oral over written culture, arguably even the abstractionist and anti-narrative tendencies of modernism, all favor a more frontal role for virtuoso visual staging. Certainly the work of Julie Taymor, a truly individual visual stage artist, for *The Lion King,* is cause for celebration. But the foundational Western dramatic literature from Shakespeare and Ibsen to Gilbert and Sullivan and Rodgers and Hammerstein is nonvisual, grounded in words, narrative, and character. Although non-Western theatrical forms like Kabuki or Chinese opera may be based on physical gesture (Robert Wilson has said that all Asian drama is based on a "visual book"), the Western legitimate theater uniquely subsumes both visual and verbal, and therein lies its peculiar power. In the hands of Jerome Robbins, the mixture of the non-Western visual style with the Western verbal style in *The King and I* was a thrilling theatrical marriage. In lesser hands, the appropriation of non-Western gestural theater for commercial purposes is vacuous, superficial, and circuslike. The cult of the visual leads to the manic, soullessly kinetic direction seen today in most musicals. Our current musical theater focuses on outer vision; the golden age's focused on inner vision. It's the integrationists like Mamoulian, de Mille, and Robbins who advanced the artistic possibilities of musicals, not the visualists like Champion, Voegtlin, and Ziegfeld. Baz Luhrmann is neither Jerome Robbins nor Rouben Mamoulian; he is Arthur Voegtlin with digital technology and an MTV sensibility.

Musicals have always been created collaboratively, but in the golden age how often did the director demand and get book changes? The strong writers of the past—Porter, Rodgers, Hart, Hammerstein, Harburg, the Gershwin brothers, Lerner and Loewe, et al.—exerted pressure on their directors, not the other way around. Surviving promptbooks of Rodgers and Hammerstein musicals spell out how exactly Richard Rodgers—not the directors John van Druten or Joshua Logan—insisted that lines be read. Similar evidence shows that Kurt Weill did the same. As for Kern and Hammerstein, Hammerstein's biographer writes:

They liked to have every detail worked out, even the stage business, which is why they preferred not to have an outside director for their shows. . . . They mapped out the staging so that when one actor began to sing, others continued actions on-stage and life would not seem to stop on the downbeat. . . . They had written detailed stage directions into the script, down to the smallest production detail.[160]

Would *Show Boat, My Fair Lady, Porgy and Bess, Oklahoma!* have been written the way they were written if directors like Michael Bennett and Harold Prince had been permitted to muscle them into their conceptions? Any more than the playwrights of *Right You Are If You Think So* or *Waiting for Godot* would have allowed their directors to rewrite them from the get-go? How is it that the American musical established itself before 1940 as a unique popular art form without any significant manipulation from above-the-marquee directors? And if the greatest ballet choreographer of the twentieth century, George Balanchine, could not and did not provide an integrated conceptual approach to directing musicals, how can lesser mortals? "I am not a director, really," said Balanchine late in life. "It is not my business to direct words."[161] The few ballet or modern dance choreographers who have recently tried Broadway—Peter Martins in Lloyd Webber's *Song and Dance,* Twyla Tharp in Billy Joel's *Movin' Out,* Mark Morris in Paul Simon's *Capeman* (before he was fired)—have not been able to fuse their creative visions synergistically with writers in the manner that marked the great theater collaborations of de Mille, Robbins, Jack Cole, and Balanchine.

There's no analogy between the choreographer as the auteur of a musical and the choreographer as author of a ballet; that is why Robbins ultimately spent more of his working life in the ballet. Broadway director-choreographers are not Fokine or Petipa. Nor are they film directors with the total control provided by the camera. Composers, lyricists, and book writers are Broadway's legitimate authors.

A harbinger of hope for the restoration of text-rooted stage direction was Trevor Nunn's recent (London, 1999; New York, 2002) revival of *Oklahoma!,* which revealed fascinating new depths in the original Hammerstein book. Could not this approach be applied to new musicals? (The heightened realism of the direction was slightly marred by sound design that made Curly's offstage singing of "Oh, What a Beautiful Morning" hit the ear as if he were onstage before his entrance.)

More often, however, the exaltation of the director, of movement for the sake of movement, of technological scenic design, has brought the outer trappings of the cinema to the musical theater without the cinema's inner psychological eye. Literal illustration in the Broadway musical has taken over the power of suggestion and imagination, which is the essence of the art of the theater. It is not Cyrano's makeup that is remembered when we recall Cyrano's nose; rather, it is his poignant character and his unrequited love for Roxanne that are remembered.

Literal illustration is forgotten by theater history. Imaginative suggestion is remembered and becomes permanent literature.

Rideout. *The Age of McMusicals: Vaudeville Redux*

> Only commercial success counts on Broadway:
> Musicals cater to the market, not necessarily to
> posterity or any loftier artistic ideals. . . . The liter-
> ary theater leads more and more of a shadowy ex-
> istence, with serious works only attracting a good
> house by featuring movie and television stars. In-
> deed, the so-called legitimate theatre in America
> may well be considered decentralized with Broad-
> way not really its home any more. . . . With main-
> stream Broadway and West End productions com-
> peting in a theatreland version of "Can You Top
> This?," many creative theatre artists can't possibly
> enter the fray—and therefore don't even try. Where
> once a show produced off Broadway, say, at Joe
> Papp's Public Theatre, or even at regional festivals
> around the country or around the world, might
> just "make it" to Broadway, and then might just
> become a hit and make a name for all involved,
> many just might not. Then what happens? They do
> not get recorded; they do not get popularized;
> often they are not remembered.
>
> —Rudiger Bering[1]

The biggest smash hit on Broadway in recent years has been *The Producers* (2001). Mel Brooks's savage backstage parody of the folklore of raising money for shows is wildly funny, but it touches a nerve. All too much of it is accurate. In fact, much of the character Max Bialystock is based on Arthur J. Beckhard, an actual Broadway producer of the 1930s and 1940s (in the 1968 movie *The*

Producers, "Beckhard" is the name of one of the actors who auditions for the part of Hitler).

It is impossible to ignore the impact that Broadway producers have had on the art form, or the effect on creativity of astronomically rising production costs. After all, the persons who ultimately decide what Broadway theatergoers see are the producers. "The American musical theater industry is dominated by a handful of Broadway business leaders whose center is the Executive Committee of the League of American Theatres and Producers," write Bernard Rosenberg and Ernest Harburg. "Overwhelmingly, members of that committee shape the musical theater business. It bargains collectively with seventeen craft unions, guilds, and associations that speak for freelance labor. Its members, and other nonmembers, independent entrepreneurs like Harold Prince, endlessly seek new projects."[2]

The late Al Hirschfeld characterized producers then and now:

The producers then produced their own shows. Nobody put up money for them except the producer. And he was a producer. He *produced,* in short. It is now a corporate thing. It's like organizing U.S. Steel to put on a show now. I mean, it's a lot of people who don't know each other. There's no continuity, there's no flow of that kind. Belasco had a staff that worked seven days a week, fifty-two weeks a year, and consequently, you would see the Lunts, you would see Cornell, Helen Hayes, and it was a continuous thing. These people worked together, they knew their limitations, and they pushed it about as far as you could go with individual talents. But now it's different. I don't know if it's worse or better, it's just different.

The producers then all were theatrical in themselves. Frohman used to wear a collar that was about six inches high, a tremendous collar. Belasco, of course, had the clerical collar. Billy Rose also invented himself. They all did, you know. Max Gordon. Dillingham. Brady. They were all part of the theater, really, and they didn't just go into it to make a lot of money, although some of them did do very well. But it was a different aim. Now it's a question of committees getting together deciding what—I don't know how playwrights exist today, really. And actually the playwright is the mainstay of the theater. Without him, there's no theater. But today the playwright has a much tougher time than the scenic designer— all of those things that have made tremendous strides technologically and scientifically.[3]

Morton Gottlieb, one of the last independent producers, now retired, told me:

I won't produce a show anymore. It was altogether different then. I would read a script, finish it, call the agent and say, "Okay, I would like to do this play," and maybe six months later it would open out of town. Life was a cinch then. Of course, when I was coproducing with Helen Bonfils she put up all the money, but you know what I used to do after that? I'd get ten stagehands to take one unit, ten people on the *Daily News* to take one unit, and things like that. I thought that it's marvelous to have all kinds of people who care about the theater investing together and putting up little bits. One show had two hundred people. . . . You can't do that any more. The costs are too high.[4]

Since the 1940s, limited partnerships, with shares divided among many different investors, have provided the capital for Broadway musicals. Before that, theater owners and independent one-man operations were both major producers of shows. While independents sometimes put up all their own money to capitalize musicals, they were even then frequently assisted by investor backers—"angels"—well before the advent of limited partnerships. John Murray Anderson writes in his memoirs of many angels who helped him produce shows in the 1920s, among them the banker and Metropolitan Opera magnate Otto Kahn. Back in the 1910s and 1920s, the contracts between theatrical producers and the talent (composers, lyricists, book writers) were simple letter agreements that made no mention of how the money was raised, only of how royalties were to be split.

As recently as the 1950s and 1960s it was still commonplace for a single name to appear above the title as producer: David Merrick, Alexander Cohen, Herman Levin, Cheryl Crawford, Kermit Bloomgarden, Leland Hayward. In the 1970s production costs began to skyrocket, and theater owners once again became major producers. By that time the Shuberts, in the opinion of Stuart Ostrow, one of Broadway's last independent producers,

> crowned themselves heads of the theatre chain. Their reign has lasted for nearly three decades, during which the amount of new musicals produced for Broadway has been drastically reduced. Coincidence? I think not. As landlords, they succeeded in changing the terms of a producer's theatre rental contract, in demanding a larger share of the proceeds, and in many cases, in insisting on being a coproducer. If you can't join 'em, enjoin 'em. The Shubert Foundation prospered, and the ranks of the independent producers thinned. . . . I produced *Pippin* in 1972 for $500,000. I was recently offered a budget of $10 million to produce the Broadway revival.[5]

Today, with budgets of seven and eight figures, it requires armies of co-producers to mount a single show. Ostrow writes that the new Broadway establishment

> prefers to buy the future rather than undertake the labor of making it. . . . Today the theatre is ruled by bottom-line thinking. Who's the star? What does it cost? When will it recoup? Where is the profit-earnings ratio? . . . The individual entrepreneur, the lone gun, the stubborn independent, has always been our best hope. . . . To be present at the creation of an original musical is what interests me most . . . and it is of little interest to the current crop of Broadway wise guys. They are only end-game players.[6]

Harold Prince, who is also an independent and not a member of the League of American Theatres and Producers, addressed the league on November 12, 1999, bemoaning the corporatized production system prevalent on Broadway today:

> I am concerned . . . about the paucity of creativity in the commercial theatre. . . . It's not just our epidemic, but an epidemic in all forms of art, significantly influenced by corporate dictatorship. . . . I note that in introducing me someone referring to audiences said, "What it is THEY want." I would propose that THEY do not always know what they want. The shows that established my reputation are those that nobody knew they wanted until they wanted them. . . . You would really rather have a new equivalent *West Side Story* or *Fiddler on the Roof* than one of the McShows you are so busy trying to book. Everything is imitative, smaller, and a sense of occasion is lost. . . . Why don't you raise the money and collaborate with the advertising agencies, forgetting the playwrights, the composers, the directors, the choreographers, the designers? They just get in your way. . . . We've all witnessed the disappearance of the mom-and-pop business in our country. The theatre is not a grocery store. It is the theatre and it needs mom-and-pop businesses.[7]

In the past, Arthur Hopkins, Cheryl Crawford, the Theatre Guild, Kermit Bloomgarden, and in our time, Prince, Ostrow, and Philip Rose actually brought some artistic discernment to the musicals they produced as independents. Some highly successful independent producers, however, have not advanced the art form aesthetically: David Merrick, for example. Stories of the tasteless judgments of old-time producers like Max Gordon, Billy Rose, and Mike Todd are legion, yet even Cheryl Crawford turned down *West Side Story*. People of taste are not clairvoyant, much less those of cruder sensibilities. According to Florenz Ziegfeld's secretary, Goldie Stanton Clough, although Ziegfeld agreed to produce *Show Boat,* he didn't like it, and he especially disliked Jules Bledsoe's singing of "Ol' Man River":

> He swore every time that they played it. He'd sit next to me and mumble under his breath. I think he changed his mind later, but during rehearsals he was very unhappy with it. He used to squirm in his seat and swear and swear. . . . The first night was a disaster for us. I mean, we thought it was, because nobody applauded. . . . Mr. Ziegfeld and I sat on the steps leading up to the balcony, and he was actually crying. "The show's a flop. I knew it would be. I never wanted to do it."[8]

But more often than not, the composers, lyricists, and book writers of the golden age benefited from unusually enlightened producing. They also benefited from the far lower producing costs and shorter recoupment times of that era. Artistic daring was less of a financial risk for the Broadway producer and investor at that time. Today Broadway musicals are conceived and produced by the Shuberts, Cameron MacKintosh, Hyperion/Disney, Dodger, Nederlander, Jujamcyn, and other conglomerate-like operations, and despite all the lip service they put up, these organizations do not foster artistic exploration by individual writers. They do not treat the book writers, lyricists, and composers of musicals as creative writers, but rather as providers of commodities for an increasingly stultified audience.

When the producers of the golden age mounted the shows of Gershwin, Porter, Rodgers, Hammerstein, Hart, Weill, Lerner and Loewe, Bernstein, Blitzstein, and Loesser, the writers who were cultural icons included Eugene O'Neill, Ernest Hemingway, and F. Scott Fitzgerald. Today both the producers and the creative talent operate in an era in which the writers who are cultural icons are John Waters, Stephen King, Steven Bochco, and David E. Kelley. When Ben Ali Haggin created his *tableaux vivants* and Jo Mielziner created his imagination-kindling backdrops, they reflected a living visual tradition of fine painting. When sets are designed on Broadway today, they reflect the prevailing design aesthetic of the high-tech theme park. Hammerstein, Hart, and Ira Gershwin drew on the slow nuances of fine language; today's producers and writers draw on a cultural fund of cartoons, sitcoms, action movies, television commercials, music videos, rock music, and computer games—all media of high speed, not slow nuance. Neither the writers nor the producers on today's Broadway, unlike the canonical writers of the golden era, are grounded in a culture that knows and respects literature, painting, classical music, and the tradition of the great playwrights. One seasoned Broadway production designer of thirty-five years' experience told me, "Are the people of taste in charge? Broadway producers were smarter in 1956." One might well ask the same question of the contemporary theater audience, whose routine standing ovations have become so indiscriminate that they have lost all meaning.

The result on the Broadway of the 2000s is an Age of McMusicals: corporately franchised staged happenings that are actually music videos packaged for theatre. Says a leading Broadway sound designer, "Striving for a live performance is absolutely gone in the theater." Sound design and the microphone may have liberated physical staging, but they have also erected an invisible psychological barrier between the stage and the audience that is the opposite of theater.

Throughout history there has been a duel between the theater of cheap thrills and the theater of higher aspiration. During the 1866–1920 era, most of American theater was of the cheap thrills variety. The belle époque Broadway musical comedy evolved during an era when the Theatre Guild, the Group Theatre, and the Playwrights Company strove to present challenging plays, not fluff, to a commercial audience. The postmodern Broadway musical is a reversion to cheap thrills. It has abandoned literacy as a benchmark of theatricality and substitutes visual saturation. As in the superproductions of a century ago, the ear and the eye are assaulted while the brain is numbed and narcotized. You can't make people appreciate great paintings by shining blinding lights in their faces as they look at the paintings. Likewise with high decibels and eye candy in the theater: all subtlety is removed. Such shows tell us that contemporary musical theater is a medium, not one that suspends disbelief, but one that suspends thinking. This is a devolution in theater, counter to centuries of practice of the art.

In opera, Wagner's concept of the music drama affected almost all his successors; nearly all subsequent opera composers wrote more dramatically integrated operas, including Verdi's later works. Forty years ago, it was thought that the artistic innovation of the book-driven integrated musical would have a similar cascade of effects on future musicals. But Rodgers and Hammerstein's and Bernstein's and Robbins's adaptations of music drama have failed to exert the lasting influence on Broadway that Wagner did on opera. It seems perverse that this happened, because to substitute mere kinetic design for a base in good playwriting is to remove a fundamental dimension of the theatrical experience. You can have both.

In fact, the book-driven integration of the best musicals of the golden age was a *Gesamtkunst* rendering of the Stanislavsky/Boleslavsky acting concept variously termed the superobjective, spine, or through-line. The composers composed for the through-line; the lyricists wrote words to the through-line; the choreographers set dances to the through-line; the designers designed to the through-line; even the orchestrators arranged instrumentation to the through-line. In the pre-1927 first age of Broadway, this convergence of creators had been unknown. Now, once again, in recent decades intensely wrought, centripetal through-lines have vanished from the creation of Broadway musicals.

The empire of contemporary pop has engineered a giant takeover of the Broadway musical and vaudevillized Broadway's product, suspending the critical faculty. As did old-time vaudeville, contemporary pop embodies performance but not drama. As did old-time vaudeville singers, contemporary pop singers use an abundance of vocal ornamentation that has little to do with the text. And like old-time vaudeville, rock-based musical theatre has a permeable fourth wall. Vaudeville performers like Blanche Ring and Al Jolson famously interacted with their audiences. Actor confederates—stooges—were deliberately planted in vaudeville audiences as part of the act. Modern nightclub performance and stand-up comedy are the inheritors of this aspect of vaudeville. When Al Jolson bantered with the audience in *Hold onto Your Hats* (1940) and Eddie Cantor did the same in *Banjo Eyes* (1941), that was thought to be the last gasp of vaudeville's breach of the fourth wall and corruption of the Broadway musical theater. *Oklahoma!* put an end to that; actors were required to stay on book and behave.

Forty years later, the actress Liliane Montevecchi, in the original production of *Nine* (1983), broke the fourth wall by ad-libbing with audience members during the show's book portions, returning vaudeville to the Broadway musical perhaps for the first time since the early 1940s. This was not a Pirandellian commentary; it was nightclub entertainer–style interruption of the script. The book of *Nine,* ostensibly of some integrity, was at that moment instantaneously jettisoned and deconstructed.

What followed in the coming years were shows embodying pop culture's equation of seriousness in art with exaltation of the trivial. During the belle époque there had been a sense of professional craft, almost an unspoken guild mentality, among the writers and composers of musicals. Today it's assumed that anyone who has an idea that can be backed by ten million dollars can turn that something into a McMusical. Then these McMusicals are produced, written, and staged to equate physical and sensory sensation with substance—an equation that is postmodernism's version of the pathetic fallacy.

Choreographer-directors, the rock groove, and overdriven sound design have been accidental conspirators in the dilution of a once great popular art. Because choreographer-directors wanted their dancers to be able to hear the drums during their numbers, they had drums play constantly, and sound levels got louder. But sound levels also moved up not only because choreographer-directors started to move performers facing upstage or sideways, making body mike amplification a necessity, but because rock idioms entered theater and forced the grafting of a studio sound onto live performance. When sound design became overdriven, visual logic and stage directionality started to get lost. When technological advances in set design made scenes "in one" before a traveler curtain unnecessary, the sophisticated craft of writing song lyrics, situation, and character that would carry the action forward without computer push-buttons was also made unnecessary. Lest we forget, in Shakespeare, language does it all: scene changes, special effects.

In the canonical era of Broadway, popular music and the theater had an equal cachet and cultural reach. Contemporary pop is now a phenomenon larger than the theater, and therefore not only are pop songwriters jury-rigged into the theater before they can learn theater writing, but the very notion that there is a craft of theater writing is nonchalantly dismissed. The composer Irwin Bazelon (1922–95), who wrote music for commercial television and films as well as for the concert hall, observed that

> the talents of songwriters like George Gershwin, Cole Porter, Harold Arlen, Jerome Kern, and Richard Rodgers shined through and raised the craft to an art of great sophistication. . . . [Today's pop composers,] having no set cultural values, . . . set up a raucous, rhythmic, ostinato beat on percussion and bass guitars, add a melodic line on top, play around with the electric guitars until you hit on "something," and—look ma, I'm a composer! It is this kind of simplistic, homophonic ineptness, ingeniously spiced with exotic sound augmentation and special recording gimmickry, that is passing for serious composition today.

Bazelon ascribed this to

> a deep-rooted pop-tune mentality . . . that has conditioned millions of people to accept each generation's pop culture as a valid barometer of musical excellence, creativity, and full value for the dollar. . . .
>
> To comprehend what makes people susceptible to the musical message and massage of its pop culture, it must be understood that at heart America is a great songwriting-happy country. More prestigious attention is paid the pop songwriter in the mirror of public recognition than all the other representatives of fine arts

put together. Make no mistake: in the minds of most people, a composer *is* a writer of pop songs. The mass media have encouraged the public to accept this fallacy by elevating songwriting to the status of an institution. Respect and admiration are such that the pop-music-song-and-dance ambassadors of show biz outnumber genuine artists 10,000 to 1 in receiving invitations from the President to the White House, where, along with professional athletes, actors, and actresses, they accept official accolades for giving a grateful nation its beloved music and entertainment.[9]

The manifest destiny of contemporary pop has also decimated songwriting language, as the music critic Gene Lees insinuated in his preface to Alec Wilder's *American Popular Song:*

Alec restrains himself in this book. He says that the age of the professional songwriter was ended. He once put it to me more bluntly: "After 1955, the amateurs took over." And he meant it: the kids with the guitars, who knew three or four chords and were devoid of literate sensibilities. They in turn affected not only the quality of the work of the next generation of "composers" but that of the lyricists, who weren't exposed to the words of Johnny Mercer and Yip Harburg and Howard Dietz but only to those of the songwriters who supplied Elvis Presley. The use of language itself deteriorated.[10]

As the love affair with the written and spoken word has died, "jukeboxicals" have stepped into the breach—desperate attempts to salvage the songs of Gershwin, Porter, Kern, and even Burt Bacharach by interpolating them into new, artificial librettos. The shows that result are visualized record players, uncompelling and unmemorable. With volume levels ever increasing, the jukeboxicals are becoming boom-boxicals.

What, if anything, can be done? Elizabeth Swados, herself a composer of musicals, argues that the historical moment for the golden-age Broadway musical cannot be replicated:

The American musical was conceived for a historical time quite different from the present. The popular culture of the 1930s and the 1940s and early 1950s was a relatively naive, idealistic, and romantic one (though the times themselves were brutal). The characters in musicals, with a few exceptions like Rose in *Gypsy,* had an aura of innocent "Aw, shucks" about them, and their conflicts and resolution were simplistic. . . . Today, in a society that has come a long way from "Aw, shucks," writers don't believe the simplicities and clichés of their conventions, the audience knows instinctively it's being handed something bogus, and so more money, more elaborate gimmicks, more spectacular costumes, and flashier orchestrations are required to cover up the essential emptiness of the undertaking.[11]

But when have sociocultural changes ever stopped people from reading Jane Austen novels? The sex, drugs, and rock-and-roll generation didn't give up on musicals because of their romanticized content; they gave up on the notion that structure, narrative, and words have meaning. It wasn't the message or the content of "Oh, What a Beautiful Morning" they rejected, it was the art and the craft of musical theater, which can be equally applied to sordid, cynical, and even violent content (see *The Cradle Will Rock*, *The Threepenny Opera*, and yes, Sondheim).

The international opera conductor John Mauceri is today's leading champion of great Hollywood film and Broadway show music as a genre of classical music that needs to be perennially performed. He was both the conductor and a coproducer of the 1983 Broadway revival of *On Your Toes*. He believes there should be a national company that mounts classic musicals fully staged, just as the Metropolitan Opera performs the classic operas. "I hate the word 'revival' and I object to it and still object to it. In opera, we call it 'a new production of.' You don't say, 'We're reviving' *Aida*." He continues:

> But when you are playing the masterpieces that are central to an American phenomenon of cultural expression, which is musical theater, it's truly sad that there's no place where you can actually sit in a theater and see a show which begins at the beginning and ends at the end and has some kind of acoustical and musical reference to what it originally was. When I was a consultant for musical theater at the Kennedy Center, I said to Roger Stevens, "There's this entire corpus of American musicals that no one has seen, and we should be producing them," and we were working on it. There still should be a national musical theater where we do two of these a year and take them to the arts centers of the country. This is what Roger and I were planning to do. They come out of someplace, wherever they want to start, probably the New York area or L.A., where there's the most concentrated talents, where you can actually put together a company. And you make it a limited run.
>
> Right now we have only two choices. Either we see *Annie Get Your Gun* in the *Encores!* series, and we have Patti LuPone or somebody standing with a book in her hand, wearing an evening gown, with the orchestra upstage, or we get to see a completely rewritten version of it, where it's playing eight times a week, all the orchestrations are new, and the story has been changed.[12]

Many new musicals of quality that might be pointing vital new directions for the theater either go unproduced or get at best limited local attention in regional or fringe venues, do not get national distribution, and evaporate with no effect on the overall culture. Joseph Papp deplored this situation when he wrote:

> It has become quite apparent that serious and meaningful American playwrights are being produced off-Broadway only—which means that our most important playwrights cannot make a living in the commercial theatre. They are forced to write for a limited audience, which not only means limited income, but limited distribution of significant ideas. This latter loss is the most devastating and it is a loss to the nation. . . . Without a significant national platform, the serious writer will turn to other means for his living.[13]

The McMusical "studio" system is like designer clothing lines taking over what a lone artisan produced and mass producing and commercializing it beyond recognition. Is the musical as an art form played out in the Spenglerian sense? Was the Broadway belle époque a unique accident of history, like Flemish painting, or is it renewable?

The acting, singing, and dancing talent today is as good as it ever was. But, culturally, the legitimate theater today is a niche, not a cynosure, and as it has forsaken strong writers, strong writers have forsaken it. The only way American musical theater can regerminate is if vital and inspired writers, motivated to write for the sake of the theater, turn to it rather than to movies or television, and only if new production approaches are undertaken—a paradox, since high cost and musical theater production are inextricably linked. Real orchestras are more expensive than virtual orchestras.

Adaptations have played out their string. They are now killing the musical and foreclosing its further artistic development. There must be more attempts at dramatically sound original librettos.

The best works of the belle époque occurred either because the writers themselves were fortunate enough to be the producers and hence were the "muscle" (Rodgers and Hammerstein), or because creative producers who respected writers turned a messy, untidy collaborative form into enlightened collectivism. On today's Broadway only a megamillionaire pop musician like Paul Simon can afford to be his own writer-producer. Whether the bête noire is the labor unions, the producers, the five-hundred-channel satellite television, the music video, the DVD, or the download, there has to be a workable new economic model somewhere, somehow, to support creative new musical theater. It is very possible that such a new economic model may not emerge on Broadway.

American popular music has always driven the commercial Broadway musical. The theater now has to drive, somehow. It has to take the reins and rediscover a way to seize the public imagination without waiting to mirror whatever is going on in the nation's popular music culture. Is it too late for this to happen?

Meanwhile, droves of tourists from all over the world still flock to Disney theater productions, just as they came one hundred years ago to Arthur Voegtlin's Hippodrome. Some things never change.

Which song is to be our rideout? "The Party's Over"? Or "Something's Coming"?

NOTES

Full citations appear in the bibliography for all sources that are mentioned in the following notes with abbreviated references (author and title only).

Curtain Raiser

1. John Mauceri, author interview, April 1, 1999.
2. Murray Anderson, *Out without My Rubbers*, p. 5.
3. Foster Hirsch, *Harold Prince and the American Musical Theatre*, p. 4.
4. Miles White, author interview, May 22, 1998.
5. Bethel Leslie, author interview, July 15, 1998.
6. Aaron Frankel, author interview, May 15, 1998.
7. Cecil Smith and Glenn Litton, *Musical Comedy in America*, p. 201.
8. Letter from Friedrich Luft to Kurt Weill, May 14, 1949, quoted in *Street Scene: A Sourcebook* (New York: Kurt Weill Foundation for Music, 1996), p. 61.
9. Jacques Barzun, *From Dawn to Decadence: 500 Years of Western Cultural Life, 1500 to the Present* (New York: HarperCollins, 2000), p. 735.
10. Carroll O'Conner obituary, *New York Times*, June 22, 2001, section B, p. 8.

Act One

1. David Craig, *On Singing Onstage*, pp. 96, 250.
2. *Richard Rodgers: The Sweetest Sounds*, "American Masters" PBS television documentary, 2001.
3. Lehman Engel, *Getting Started in the Theater*, pp. 85–86.
4. Gene Brown, *Show Time*, p. 62.
5. Henry Pleasants, "Crosby, Bing (Harry Lillis)," in Hitchcock and Sadie, eds., *New Grove Dictionary of American Music*, Vol. 1, p. 547.
6. Stanley Green, *The World of Musical Comedy*, p. 12.
7. Nikolay Rimsky-Korsakov, *Principles of Orchestration*, p. 134

8. Robert Russell Bennett, "*The Broadway Sound*," p. 254.

9. Engel, *Getting Started in the Theater*, p. 86.

10. Ibid., p. 87.

11. Max Morath, *The NPR Curious Listener's Guide to Popular Standards*, p. 211.

12. Sigmund Spaeth, *A History of Popular Music in America*, p. 299.

13. Craig, *On Singing Onstage*, p. 2.

14. Warren Hoge, "400 Years Later, Play Goes Hip-Hop," *New York Times*, May 29, 2003, pp. E1, E5.

Act Two

1. Harold Clurman, *On Directing*, p. 10.

2. Ira Weitzman, author interview, January 28, 1999.

3. Bernard Rosenberg and Ernest Harburg, *The Broadway Musical*, pp. 219–20.

4. Ibid., p. 109.

5. Lehman Engel, *This Bright Day*, pp. 188–89.

6. Otis L. Guernsey Jr., ed., *Playwrights, Lyricists, Composers on Theater*, p. 38.

7. Cheryl Crawford, *One Naked Individual*, p. 180.

8. Charles H. Hoyt, *Five Plays*, ed. Douglas L. Hunt, pp. xii–xiv.

9. Nicholas E. Tawa, *The Way to Tin Pan Alley*, pp. 58–59.

10. Hugh Fordin, *Getting to Know Him*, p. 63.

11. Laurence Bergreen, *As Thousands Cheer*, pp. 100–101.

12. Ibid., p. 105.

13. Alan Jay Lerner, *The Musical Theatre*, pp. 63–64.

14. Cecil Smith and Glenn Litton, *Musical Comedy in America*, p. 158.

15. Ethan Mordden, *Rodgers and Hammerstein*, pp. 83–84.

16. Robert Russell Bennett, "*The Broadway Sound*," ed. George J. Ferencz, p. 124.

17. Ibid., pp. 99–100.

18. Meryle Secrest, *Somewhere for Me*, p. 361.

19. Meryle Secrest, *Stephen Sondheim: A Life*, p. 56.

20. Lerner, *The Musical Theater*, p. 162.

21. Brooks Atkinson, *Broadway*, p. 313.

22. Stanley Green, *The World of Musical Comedy*, p. 215.

23. Ibid., p. 215.

24. Trude Rittmann, author interview, November 6, 1998.

25. Souvenir program, *Street Scene*, Adelphi Theatre, New York, January 1947.

26. Weill's production notes, December 21, 1946, reprinted in *Street Scene: A Sourcebook*, 2d ed. (New York: Kurt Weill Foundation for Music, 1996), p. 17.

27. Elia Kazan, *Elia Kazan: A Life*, p. 72.

28. John Mauceri, author interview, April 1, 1999.

29. Engel, *This Bright Day*, p. 78.

30. Lehman Engel, *Words with Music*, p. 246.

31. Lehman Engel, *The American Musical Theater*, pp. 39, 44.

32. Engel, *Words with Music*, p. 293.

33. Ibid., p. 291.

34. Ibid., p. 300.

35. Tawa, *The Way to Tin Pan Alley*, p. 164.

36. Charles Hamm, *Yesterdays*, p. 290.

37. Lehman Engel, *Their Words Are Music*, p. 5.

38. Ernie Harburg and Harold Meyerson, *Who Put the Rainbow in* The Wizard of Oz?, pp. 17–18.

39. Ibid.

40. Philip Furia, *The Poets of Tin Pan Alley*, p. 7.

41. Harburg and Meyerson, *Who Put the Rainbow in* The Wizard of Oz?, pp. 75–76.

42. Ibid., p. 349.

43. Kurt Gänzl, *The Encyclopedia of the Musical Theatre*, vol. 3, p. 1704.

44. Jonathan Mantle, *Fanfare: The Unauthorized Biography of Andrew Lloyd Webber* (London: Michael Joseph, 1989), p. 31.

45. Bennett, *"The Broadway Sound,"* p. 303.

46. Elizabeth Swados, *Listening Out Loud*, pp. 115–18.

47. Mark C. Carnes, ed., *Invisible Giants: Fifty Americans Who Shaped the Nation but Missed the History Books* (New York: Oxford, 2002), pp. 150–51.

48. Lerner, *The Musical Theatre*, p. 228.

49. Rosenberg and Harburg, *The Broadway Musical*, p. 169.

50. Michiko Kakutani, "Portrait of the Artist as a Focus Group," *New York Times*, March 1, 1998, Section 6, p. 26.

51. Harburg and Meyerson, *Who Put the Rainbow in* The Wizard of Oz?, p. 25.

52. Ibid., p. 30.

53. Hugh Fordin, *Getting to Know Him*, p. 190.

54. Michael John LaChiusa, "I Sing of America's Mongrel Culture," *New York Times*, November 14, 1999, Section 2, p. 1.

55. Lehman Engel, *Words with Music*, p. 198.

56. Frank Rich, "Conversations with Sondheim," *New York Times Magazine*, March 12, 2000, p. 38.

57. Steven C. Smith, *A Heart at Fire's Center*, p. 126.

58. Peter W. Goodman, *Morton Gould*, pp. 198–99.

59. Engel, *This Bright Day*, p. 81.

60. Aaron Copland, *The New Music, 1900–1960* (New York: Norton, 1968), p. 141.

61. Wilfrid Howard Mellers, *Music in a New Found Land: Themes and Developments in the History of American Music* (New York: Stonehill, 1975), p. 420.

62. Eric Gordon, *Mark the Music*, p. 338.

63. Frank Loesser, liner notes for Marc Blitzstein, *Regina*, Columbia Records LP recording O3S202, released in 1958, p. 3.

64. Vernon Duke, *Passport to Paris,* p. 386.

65. Sam Kashner and Nancy Schoenberger, *A Talent for Genius,* p. 59.

66. Nicolas Slonimsky, *Perfect Pitch* (New York: Oxford, 1988), p. 79.

67. Harlow Robinson, *Sergei Prokofiev* (Boston: Northeastern University Press, 2002), p. 314.

68. Al Hirschfeld, author interview, June 17, 1998.

69. Nicolas Slonimsky, *Music since 1900* (New York: Schirmer Books, 1994), pp. 537–38.

70. Dawn Powell, *The Diaries of Dawn Powell,* p. 361.

71. Robert Emmet Long, *Broadway, the Golden Years,* p. 107.

Act Three

1. Ira Gershwin, *Lyrics on Several Occasions,* p. 111.

2. Tyler Anbinder, *Five Points,* p. 175.

3. James J. Fuld, *The Book of World-Famous Music,* p. 333.

4. Nicholas E. Tawa, *The Way to Tin Pan Alley,* p. 111.

5. Sigmund Spaeth, *A History of Popular Music in America,* p. 369.

6. Paul Bierley, *John Philip Sousa,* p. 123.

7. Robert Russell Bennett, *Instrumentally Speaking,* p. 8.

8. Irene Castle, *Castles in the Air,* p. 118.

9. Reid Badger, *A Life in Ragtime,* p. 116.

10. Harry Fox scrapbook, Theater Collection, Research Division, New York Public Library for the Performing Arts.

11. Joan Peyser, *The Memory of All That,* p. 52.

12. Rudi Blesh and Harriet Janis, *They All Played Ragtime,* p. 193.

13. Abel Green and Joe Laurie Jr., *Show Biz from Vaude to Video,* p. 36.

14. Tawa, *The Way to Tin Pan Alley,* p. 74.

15. Laurence Bergreen, *As Thousands Cheer,* p. 104.

16. Gerald Bordman, *Jerome Kern,* p. 138.

17. Robert Russell Bennett, *"The Broadway Sound,"* p. 288.

18. Rudi Blesh, ed., *Scott Joplin: Collected Piano Works* (New York: New York Public Library and Belwin-Mills Publishing, 1971), p. xv.

19. Lehman Engel, *Words with Music,* pp. 127–28.

20. Elizabeth Swados, *Listening Out Loud,* pp. 115–17.

21. Tawa, *The Way to Tin Pan Alley,* p. 201.

22. John McWhorter, *Doing Our Own Thing,* pp. 212–20.

Act Four

1. John Murray Anderson, *Out without My Rubbers,* p. 5.

2. Stanley Green, *The World of Musical Comedy,* p. 23.

3. Geoffrey Block, ed., *The Richard Rodgers Reader,* pp. 201–5.

4. Agnes de Mille, *And Promenade Home*, p. 62.

5. Cecil Smith and Glenn Litton, *Musical Comedy in America*, p. 24.

6. Nicholas E. Tawa, *The Way to Tin Pan Alley*, p. 28.

7. Sigmund Spaeth, *A History of Popular Music in America*, pp. 320–21.

8. Glenn Loney, ed., *Musical Theatre in America*, p. 120.

9. de Mille, *And Promenade Home*, p. 78.

10. *Street Scene: A Sourcebook*, 2d ed. (New York: Kurt Weill Foundation for Music, 1996), p. 16.

11. Ibid., p. 28.

12. Herbert Warren Wind, "Another Opening, Another Show," *New Yorker*, November 17, 1951, p. 48.

13. Ibid., p. 60.

14. Robert Russell Bennett, *"The Broadway Sound,"* p. 66.

15. Ibid., p. 95.

16. Ibid., p. 65.

17. Ibid., p. 71.

18. Ibid., pp. 98–99.

19. Ibid., p. 2.

20. William McBrien, *Cole Porter*, p. 151.

21. Ibid., pp. 247–48.

22. Alan Jay Lerner, *The Musical Theatre*, p. 71.

23. Laurence Bergreen, *As Thousands Cheer*, pp. 314–15.

24. Mary Ellin Barrett, *Irving Berlin*, p. 292.

25. Edward Jablonski, *Irving Berlin*, p. 42.

26. John McCabe, *George M. Cohan*, p. 259.

27. Joshua Logan, *Josh*, pp. 284–85.

28. Susan Loesser, *A Most Remarkable Fella*, pp. 155–56.

29. Trude Rittmann, author interview, November 6, 1998.

30. William G. Hyland, *Richard Rodgers*, p. 295.

31. Bergreen, *As Thousands Cheer*, p. 456.

32. Bennett, *"The Broadway Sound,"* p. 226. See also McBrien, *Cole Porter*, p. 317.

33. Bennett, *"The Broadway Sound,"* p. 254.

34. Wind, "Another Opening," p. 48.

35. Ibid., p. 68.

36. Ibid., p. 70.

37. Lehman Engel, *Getting Started in the Theater*, pp. 147–48, 151, 158.

38. John Mauceri author interview, April 1, 1999.

39. Bennett, *"The Broadway Sound,"* p. 197.

40. Mary C. Henderson, author interview, April 29, 2003.

41. Harold Prince, *Contradictions: Notes on Twenty-six Years in the Theatre* (New York: Dodd, Mead, 1974), p. 165.

42. "Direct from Broadway, Inc.," seminar at the Bruno Walter Auditorium, New York Public Library for the Performing Arts, New York, March 15, 1990.

43. Howard Whitfield, author interview, June 3, 1998.

44. Bethel Leslie, author interview, July 15, 1998.

45. George Izenour, letter to author, May 16, 2003.

46. Gerald Bordman, *The American Musical Theatre*, p. 210.

47. Robert Baral, *Revue*, p. 165.

48. "An Interview with Sound Designer Tony Meola," www.meyersound.com/markets/theatre/meola.htm, 2002 (accessed May 7, 2003).

49. "Direct from Broadway" seminar.

50. Sam Kashner and Nancy Schoenberger, *A Talent for Genius*, p. 216.

51. Charles Cooke and E. J. Kahn Jr., "Distant Music," *New Yorker*, April 1, 1939, p. 14.

52. David Farneth, with Elmar Juchem and Dave Stein, *Kurt Weill*, p. 171.

53. Ronald Sanders, *The Days Grow Short*, pp. 257–58.

54. Farneth, *Kurt Weill*, p. 171.

55. Lehman Engel, *The American Musical Theater*, p. 154.

56. Rittmann, author interview.

57. Block, *Richard Rodgers Reader*, p. 304.

58. Ethan Mordden, *Rodgers and Hammerstein*, p. 174.

59. "Direct from Broadway" seminar.

60. Engel, *The American Musical Theater*, pp. 154–55.

61. Bennett, *"The Broadway Sound,"* p. 289.

62. Robert Russell Bennett, *Instrumentally Speaking*, pp. 12–13.

63. "Direct from Broadway" seminar.

64. Otts Munderloh, author interview, April 28, 2003.

65. John A. Leonard, *Theatre Sound*, pp. 111–14.

66. Munderloh, author interview.

67. David Chase, author interview, May 19, 2003.

68. Munderloh, author interview.

69. "A Conversation with Jonathan Deans," www.meyersound.com/markets/theatre/deans.htm, 2002 (last accessed May 8, 2003).

70. "An Interview with Sound Designer Tony Meola."

71. Ibid.

72. "Direct from Broadway" seminar.

73. Munderloh, author interview.

74. Izenour, letter to author.

75. Craig Zadan, *Sondheim and Company*, p. 177.

76. Eric Stern, author interview, January 27, 1999.

77. David Budries, author interview, May 7, 2003.

78. Mauceri, author interview.

79. Leonard, *Theatre Sound*, p. 8.

80. Mauceri, author interview.

81. Stuart Ostrow, *A Producer's Broadway Journey*, p. 112.

82. Bill Dennison, "Machine vs. Musicians: The Virtual Pit Orchestra Scam," *Allegro* (newspaper of Local 802 of the American Federation of Musicians) 103, no. 1 (January 2003), http://www.local802afm.org (last accessed May 7, 2003).

83. Leonard, *Theatre Sound*, p. 8.

Act Five

1. Alan Jay Lerner, *The Musical Theatre*, p. 236.

2. Robert Lewis, *Slings and Arrows*, pp. 122–23.

3. Kurt Gänzl, *The Encyclopedia of the Musical Theatre*, vol. 1, p. 184.

4. Cecil Smith and Glenn Litton, *Musical Comedy in America*, p. 10.

5. Ibid., p. 15.

6. Gerald Bordman, *American Musical Comedy*, pp. 85–91.

7. Arthur Voegtlin clippings in the Robinson Jeffers scrapbooks, New York Public Library for the Performing Arts; Voegtlin obituary in the *New York Times,* January 20, 1948.

8. Norman Clarke, *The Mighty Hippodrome*, pp. 76–77.

9. Brooks Atkinson, *Broadway*, p. 47.

10. Ibid., pp. 45–47.

11. Howard Bay, *Stage Design*, p. 105.

12. Harold Clurman, *On Directing*, p. 7.

13. DeWolf Hopper, *Once a Clown, Always a Clown*, p. 14.

14. Foster Hirsch, *Harold Prince and the American Musical Theatre*, p. 25.

15. John McCabe, *George M. Cohan*, p. 205.

16. Agnes de Mille, *And Promenade Home*, pp. 256–57.

17. Carol Ilson, *Harold Prince*, p. 423.

18. Robert Baral, *Revue*, pp. 45–46.

19. Mary C. Henderson, *Mielziner*, pp. 19–20.

20. Mary Ellin Barrett, *Irving Berlin*, p. 220.

21. Richard Rodgers, *Musical Stages*, pp. 172–73.

22. Henderson, *Mielziner*, pp. 263–64.

23. George Abbott, *Mister Abbott*, p. 195.

24. Mark Spergel, *Reinventing Reality*, p. 42.

25. Ibid., pp. 22–23.

26. Ibid., p. 63.

27. Ibid., p. 62.

28. Hollis Alpert, *The Life and Times of Porgy and Bess*, pp. 116–18.

29. Cheryl Crawford, *One Naked Individual*, p. 39.

30. Samuel Marx and Jan Clayton, *Rodgers and Hart*, p. 152.

31. Rodgers, *Musical Stages*, p. 241.

32. Ethan Mordden, *Rodgers and Hammerstein*, pp. 74–75.

33. Carol Easton, *No Intermissions*, p. 245.

34. Bennett Thomas Oberstein, "The Broadway Directing Career of Rouben Mamoulian," p. 298.

35. William Stott with Jane Stott, *On Broadway*, p. 150.

36. Spergel, *Reinventing Reality*, p. 243.

37. Elia Kazan, *Elia Kazan*, pp. 233–34.

38. Julian Mates, *America's Musical Stage*, p. 178.

39. Smith and Litton, *Musical Comedy in America*, p. 85.

40. Atkinson, *Broadway*, p. 112.

41. Barbara Naomi Cohen-Stratyner, *Biographical Dictionary of Dance*, p. 19.

42. Mary C. Henderson, *Theater in America*, p. 111.

43. Abbott, *Mister Abbott*, pp. 264–65.

44. Mark Steyn, *Broadway Babies Say Goodnight*, p. 315.

45. Greg Lawrence, *Dance with Demons*, p. 116.

46. Dennis McGovern and Deborah Grace Winer, *Sing Out, Louise!*, p. 147.

47. Ibid., p. 142.

48. Ibid., p. 146.

49. Al Kasha and Joel Hirschhorn, *Notes on Broadway*, p. 41.

50. McGovern and Winer, *Sing Out Louise!*, p. 141.

51. Denny Martin Flinn, *Musical!*, p. 295.

52. Lewis, *Slings and Arrows*, p. 170.

53. Ibid., p. 204.

54. Smith and Litton, *Musical Comedy in America.*, p. 200.

55. Joshua Logan, *Josh*, p. 169.

56. Henderson, *Theater in America*, p. 110.

57. Abbott, *Mister Abbott*, pp. 263–64.

58. Camille Hardy, "United States of America—Musical Theater," *International Encyclopedia of Dance*, ed. Selma Jeanne Cohen et al. (New York: Oxford University Press, 1998), vol. 6, p. 273.

59. Dana O'Connell, author interview, May 19, 1998.

60. Cohen-Stratyner, *Biographical Dictionary of Dance*, pp. 940–41.

61. Richard Kislan, *Hoofing on Broadway*, p. 57.

62. Ibid., p. 58.

63. Agnes de Mille, *Dance to the Piper*, pp. 239–40.

64. Ethan Mordden, *Make Believe*, p. 155.

65. Mary Morse, author interview, May 15, 1998.

66. Steyn, *Broadway Babies*, p. 180.

67. Samuel Leiter, *The Encyclopedia of the New York Stage*, pp. 94–95.

68. de Mille, *Dance to the Piper*, pp. 163–64.

69. Ibid., pp. 308–9.

70. de Mille, *And Promenade Home,* p. 62.

71. Easton, *No Intermissions,* p. 70.

72. Ibid., p. 205.

73. Ibid., pp. 161, 163–64, 248.

74. Robert Emmet Long, *Broadway, the Golden Years,* p. 59.

75. Hugh Fordin, *Getting to Know Him,* pp. 253–54.

76. Easton, *No Intermissions,* pp. 269–70.

77. Ibid., pp. 287–88.

78. Ibid., p. 316.

79. Crawford, *One Naked Individual,* p. 129.

80. Kazan, *Elia Kazan,* p. 300.

81. Meryle Secrest, *Stephen Sondheim,* p. 54.

82. Easton, *No Intermissions,* p. 427.

83. Lawrence, *Dance with Demons,* p. 31.

84. Ibid., p. 476.

85. Ibid., p. 135.

86. Ibid., p. 130.

87. de Mille, *And Promenade Home,* p. 190.

88. Lewis, *Slings and Arrows,* p. 186.

89. Lawrence, *Dance with Demons,* p. 122.

90. William Westbrook Burton, *Conversations about Bernstein* (New York: Oxford, 1995), p. 177.

91. Lawrence, *Dance with Demons,* p. 464.

92. Ibid., p. 243.

93. Agnes de Mille, *Speak to Me, Dance with Me,* p. 253.

94. Lawrence, *Dance with Demons,* p. 247.

95. Ibid., p. 175.

96. Ibid., p. 49.

97. Miles White, author interview, May 22, 1998.

98. Lawrence, *Dance with Demons,* p. 101.

99. Ibid., p. 288.

100. Arthur Laurents, *Original Story,* p. 357.

101. Lawrence, *Dance with Demons,* p. 425.

102. Clive Barnes, "Jerome Robbins: An Appreciation," *Dance,* October 1, 1998, p. 56.

103. Amanda Vaill, "Jerome Robbins," in *The Scribner Encyclopedia of American Lives,* ed. Kenneth T. Jackson et al., vol. 5 (New York: Charles Scribner's Sons, 2002), pp. 484–87.

104. Glenn Loney, *Unsung Genius,* p. 237.

105. Ibid., p. 268.

106. Ibid., p. 317.

107. Lerner, *The Musical Theatre,* p. 215.

108. Arlene Anderson Skutch, author interview, February 22, 2003.

109. Kazan, *Elia Kazan*, p. 301.

110. Bernard Rosenberg and Ernest Harburg, *The Broadway Musical*, p. 131.

111. Irene Sharaff, *Broadway and Hollywood*, dust-jacket flap.

112. McGovern and Winer, *Sing Out, Louise!*, p. 130.

113. Ibid.

114. Harvey Frommer and Myrna Katz, *It Happened on Broadway*, p. 141.

115. Rosenberg and Harburg, *The Broadway Musical*, p. 134.

116. Long, *Broadway, the Golden Years*, p. 244.

117. Laurents, *Original Story*, p. 347.

118. Steven Bach, *Dazzler*, p. 342.

119. Rosenberg and Harburg, *The Broadway Musical*, pp. 134–36.

120. Frommer and Katz, *It Happened on Broadway*, p. 144.

121. Long, *Broadway, the Golden Years*, pp. 200–201.

122. Ilson, *Harold Prince*, p. 83.

123. Steyn, *Broadway Babies*, p. 179.

124. Frommer and Katz, *It Happened on Broadway*, pp. 150–51.

125. Stuart Ostrow, *A Producer's Broadway Journey*, p. xvi.

126. Atkinson, *Broadway*, p. 244.

127. McGovern and Winer, *Sing Out Louise!*, p. 136.

128. Smith and Litton, *Musical Comedy in America*, pp. 183–84.

129. Lerner, *The Musical Theatre*, p. 163.

130. Mordden, *Rodgers and Hammerstein*, p. 157.

131. Fordin, *Getting to Know Him*, p. 310.

132. Mordden, *Rodgers and Hammerstein*, p. 158.

133. Rosenberg and Harburg, *The Broadway Musical*, p. 27.

134. Michael Starobin, author interview, December 30, 1998.

135. White, author interview, May 22, 1998.

136. Rosenberg and Harburg, *The Broadway Musical*, p. 174.

137. Tom Jones, *Making Musicals*, p. 81.

138. Ken Mandelbaum, *A Chorus Line and the Musicals of Michael Bennett*, p. 81.

139. Ibid., p. 75.

140. Ibid., p. 209.

141. Ibid., p. 60.

142. Ibid., pp. 124–25.

143. Ibid., p. 61.

144. Ibid., p. 267.

145. Ibid., p. 138.

146. Ibid., p. 146.

147. Ibid., p. 111.

148. Rosenberg and Harburg, *The Broadway Musical*, p. 137.

149. Foster Hirsch, *Harold Prince and the American Musical Theatre*, p. 159.

150. Frommer and Katz, *It Happened on Broadway*, p. 260.

151. Rosenberg and Harburg, *The Broadway Musical*, p. 137.

152. Hirsch, *Harold Prince*, p. 40.

153. Rosenberg and Harburg, *The Broadway Musical*, p. 103.

154. Flinn, *Musical!*, pp. 471–73.

155. Steyn, *Broadway Babies*, pp. 246–50.

156. Rosenberg and Harburg, *The Broadway Musical*, p. 112.

157. Kazan, *Elia Kazan*, p. 505.

158. Alan Jay Lerner, *The Street Where I Live*, p. 76.

159. Crawford, *One Naked Individual*, p. 77.

160. Fordin, *Getting to Know Him*, pp. 101, 122.

161. Stott with Stott, *On Broadway*, p. 60.

Rideout

1. Rudiger Bering, *Musicals*, pp. 37–38, 164.

2. Bernard Rosenberg and Ernest Harburg, *The Broadway Musical*, p. 81.

3. Al Hirschfeld, author interview, June 17, 1998.

4. Morton Gottlieb, author interview, March 31, 1998.

5. Stuart Ostrow, *A Producer's Broadway Journey*, pp. 105–6.

6. Ibid., pp. xv, xvi–xviii, 161.

7. Carol Ilson, *Harold Prince*, pp. 427–29.

8. Goldie Stanton Clough, interview with Miles Kreuger, April 30, 1988, in liner notes to *Show Boat* recording, Angel A23–49108.

9. Irwin Bazelon, *Knowing the Score*, pp. 30–32.

10. Alec Wilder, *American Popular Song*, p. xvi.

11. Elizabeth Swados, *Listening Out Loud*, pp. 119–20.

12. John Mauceri, author interview, April 1, 1999.

13. Helen Epstein, *Joe Papp*, p. 307.

BIBLIOGRAPHY

Books

Abbott, George. *Mister Abbott.* New York: Random House, 1963.

Alpert, Hollis. *The Life and Times of* Porgy and Bess: *The Story of an American Classic.* New York: Knopf, 1990.

Anbinder, Tyler. *Five Points: The Nineteenth-Century New York City Neighborhood That Invented Tap Dance, Stole Elections, and Became the World's Most Notorious Slum.* New York: Free Press, 2001.

Anderson, John Murray, as told to and written by Hugh Abercrombie Anderson. *Out without My Rubbers: The Memoirs of John Murray Anderson.* New York: Library Publishers, 1954.

Applebaum, Stanley, ed. *Show Songs from* The Black Crook *to* The Red Mill: *Original Sheet Music for Sixty Songs from Fifty Shows, 1866–1906.* New York: Dover Publications, 1974.

Atkinson, Brooks. *Broadway.* New York: Macmillan, 1970.

Bach, Steven. *Dazzler: The Life and Times of Moss Hart.* New York: Knopf, 2001.

Badger, Reid. *A Life in Ragtime: A Biography of James Reese Europe.* New York: Oxford University Press, 1995.

Banfield, Stephen. *Sondheim's Broadway Musicals.* Ann Arbor: University of Michigan Press, 1993.

Baral, Robert. *Revue: A Nostalgic Reprise of the Great Broadway Period.* New York: Fleet Publishing, 1962.

Barnes, Djuna. *Interviews.* Edited by Alyce Barry. Washington, D.C.: Sun and Moon Press, 1985.

Barrett, Mary Ellin. *Irving Berlin: A Daughter's Memoir.* New York: Simon and Schuster, 1994.

Bay, Howard. *Stage Design.* New York: Drama Book Specialists, 1974.

Bazelon, Irwin. *Knowing the Score: Notes on Film Music.* New York: Arco, 1975.

Bennett, Robert Russell. *"The Broadway Sound": The Autobiography and Selected Essays of Robert Russell Bennett.* Edited by George J. Ferencz. Rochester, N.Y.: University of Rochester Press, 1999.

———. *Instrumentally Speaking.* Melville, N.Y.: Belwin-Mills Publishing, 1975.

Bergreen, Laurence. *As Thousands Cheer: The Life of Irving Berlin.* New York: Viking, 1990.

Bering, Rudiger. *Musicals.* New York: Barron's, 1998.

Bierley, Paul. *John Philip Sousa: American Phenomenon.* Columbus, Ohio: Integrity Press, 1973.

Blesh, Rudi, and Harriet Janis. *They All Played Ragtime.* New York: Knopf, 1950.

Block, Geoffrey, ed. *The Richard Rodgers Reader.* New York: Oxford University Press, 2002.

Bloom, Ken. *American Song: The Complete Musical Theatre Companion.* 4 vols. New York: Schirmer Books, 1996.

Blum, Daniel. *A Pictorial History of the American Theatre, 100 Years: 1860–1960.* New York: Bonanza Books, 1960.

Bordman, Gerald. *American Musical Comedy: From* Adonis *to* Dreamgirls. New York: Oxford University Press, 1982.

———. *American Musical Revue: From* The Passing Show *to* Sugar Babies. New York: Oxford University Press, 1985.

———. *The American Musical Theatre: A Chronicle.* New York: Oxford University Press, 1978.

———. *American Operetta: From* H.M.S. Pinafore *to* Sweeney Todd. New York: Oxford University Press, 1981.

———. *Jerome Kern: His Life and Music.* New York: Oxford University Press, 1980.

———. *Oxford Companion to the American Theatre.* New York: Oxford University Press, 1984.

Brown, Gene. *Show Time: A Chronology of Broadway and the Theatre from Its Beginnings to the Present.* New York: Macmillan, 1997.

Castle, Irene. *Castles in the Air.* New York: Da Capo Press, 1958.

Clarke, Norman. *The Mighty Hippodrome.* South Brunswick, N.J. and New York: A. S. Barnes and Company, 1968.

Clurman, Harold. *On Directing.* New York: Macmillan, 1972.

Cohen, Selma Jeanne, ed. *International Encyclopedia of Dance.* 6 vols. New York: Oxford University Press, 1998.

Cohen-Stratyner, Barbara Naomi. *Biographical Dictionary of Dance.* New York: Schirmer Books, 1982.

Colvan, E. B. (Zeke). *Face the Footlights! A New and Practical Approach to Acting.* New York: Whittlesey House, McGraw Hill, 1940.

330

Conrad, Christine. *Jerome Robbins: That Broadway Man, That Ballet Man*. London: Booth-Clibborn Editions, 2000.

Craig, David. *On Singing Onstage*. New York: Schirmer Books, 1978.

Crawford, Cheryl. *One Naked Individual: My Fifty Years in the Theatre*. Indianapolis: Bobbs-Merrill, 1977.

Crawford, Richard. *America's Musical Life: A History*. New York: W. W. Norton, 2000.

Csida, Joseph, and June Bundy Csida. *American Entertainment: A Unique History of Popular Show Business*. New York: Watson-Guptill, 1978.

de Mille, Agnes. *And Promenade Home*. Boston: Little, Brown, 1958.

———. *Dance to the Piper*. Boston: Little, Brown, 1952.

———. *Speak to Me, Dance with Me*. Boston: Little, Brown, 1973.

DeVenney, David P. *The Broadway Song Companion: An Annotated Guide to Musical Theatre Literature by Song Type and Song Style*. Lanham, Md.: Scarecrow Press, 1998.

Duke, Vernon. *Passport to Paris*. Boston: Little, Brown, 1955.

Easton, Carol. *No Intermissions: The Life of Agnes de Mille*. Boston: Little, Brown, 1996.

Engel, Lehman. *The American Musical Theater: A Consideration*. New York: Macmillan, 1967.

———. *Getting Started in the Theater: A Handbook for Breaking into Show Business*. New York: Macmillan, 1973.

———. *The Making of a Musical*. New York: Limelight Editions, 1977.

———. *Their Words Are Music: The Great Theatre Lyricists and Their Lyrics*. New York: Crown, 1975.

———. *This Bright Day*. New York: Macmillan, 1974.

———. *Words with Music*. New York: Macmillan, 1972.

Epstein, Helen. *Joe Papp: An American Life*. Boston: Little, Brown, 1994.

Farneth, David, with Elmar Juchem and Dave Stein. *Kurt Weill: A Life in Pictures and Documents*. Woodstock, N.Y.: Overlook Press, 2000.

Ferencz, George J. *Robert Russell Bennett: A Bio-Bibliography*. Westport, Conn: Greenwood Press, 1990.

Flinn, Denny Martin. *Musical! A Grand Tour: The Rise, Glory, and Fall of an American Institution*. New York: Schirmer Books, 1997.

Fordin, Hugh. *Getting to Know Him: A Biography of Oscar Hammerstein II*. New York: Random House, 1977.

Frankel, Aaron. *Writing the Broadway Musical*. New York: Drama Book Specialists, 1977.

Friedwald, Will. *Stardust Melodies: The Biography of Twelve of America's Most Popular Songs*. New York: Pantheon, 2002.

Frommer, Harvey, and Myrna Katz. *It Happened on Broadway: An Oral History of the Great White Way*. New York: Harcourt Brace, 1998.

Fuld, James J. *The Book of World-Famous Music: Classical, Popular, and Folk.* 5th ed. New York: Dover Publications, 2000.

Furia, Philip. *The Poets of Tin Pan Alley: A History of America's Great Lyricists.* New York: Oxford University Press, 1990.

Gänzl, Kurt. *The Encyclopedia of the Musical Theatre.* 2d ed., 3 vols. New York: Schirmer Books, 2001.

———. *The Musical: A Concise History.* Boston: Northeastern University Press, 1997.

Gershwin, Ira. *Lyrics on Several Occasions.* New York: Knopf, 1959.

Giddins, Gary. *Bing Crosby: A Pocketful of Dreams—The Early Years: 1903–1940.* Boston: Little, Brown, 2001.

Gioia, Ted. *The History of Jazz.* New York: Oxford University Press, 1997.

Goldman, William. *The Season: A Candid Look at Broadway.* New York: Harcourt, Brace, and World, 1969.

Goodman, Peter W. *Morton Gould: American Salute.* Portland, Ore.: Amadeus Press, 2000.

Gordon, Eric. *Mark the Music: The Life and Work of Marc Blitzstein.* New York: St. Martin's Press, 1989.

Green, Abel, and Joe Laurie Jr. *Show Biz from Vaude to Video.* New York: Henry Holt, 1951.

Green, Stanley. *Broadway Musicals Show by Show.* 2d ed. Milwaukee: Hal Leonard, 1987.

———. *Encyclopedia of the Musical Theatre.* New York: Dodd, Mead, 1976.

———. *The World of Musical Comedy.* New York: Grosset and Dunlap, 1962.

Guernsey, Otis L., Jr., ed. *Playwrights, Lyricists, Composers on Theater.* New York: Dodd, Mead, 1974.

Hamm, Charles. *Yesterdays: Popular Song in America.* New York: W. W. Norton, 1979.

Harburg, Ernie, and Harold Meyerson, with the assistance of Arthur Perlman. *Who Put the Rainbow in* The Wizard of Oz? *Yip Harburg, Lyricist.* Ann Arbor: University of Michigan Press, 1993.

Henderson, Mary C. *Mielziner: Master of Modern Stage Design.* New York: Watson-Guptill, 2001.

———. *Theater in America: 250 Years of Plays, Players, and Productions.* 2d ed. New York: Harry N. Abrams, 1996.

Hirsch, Foster. *Harold Prince and the American Musical Theatre.* Cambridge: Cambridge University Press, 1989.

———. *Kurt Weill on Stage: From Berlin to Broadway.* New York: Knopf, 2002.

Hischak, Thomas. *The American Musical Theatre Song Encyclopedia.* Westport, Conn: Greenwood Press, 1995.

Hitchcock, H. Wiley, and Stanley Sadie, eds. *The New Grove Dictionary of American Music.* New York: Grove's Dictionaries of Music, 1986.

Hopper, DeWolf, in collaboration with Wesley Winans Stout. *Once a Clown, Always a Clown: Reminiscences of DeWolf Hopper.* Boston: Little, Brown, 1927.

Horowitz, Mark Eden. *Sondheim on Music: Minor Details and Major Decisions*. Lanham, Md.: Scarecrow Press in association with the Library of Congress, 2003.

Hoyt, Charles H. *Five Plays*. Edited by Douglas L. Hunt. Bloomington: Indiana University Press, 1940.

Hummel, David. *The Collector's Guide to the American Musical Theatre*. 2 vols. Metuchen, N.J.: Scarecrow Press, 1984.

Hyland, William G. *Richard Rodgers*. New Haven: Yale University Press, 1998.

Ilson, Carol. *Harold Prince: A Director's Journey*. New York: Limelight Editions, 2000.

Jablonski, Edward. *Harold Arlen*. Boston: Northeastern University Press, 1996.

————. *Irving Berlin: American Troubadour*. New York: Henry Holt, 1999.

Jasen, David A. *Tin Pan Alley: The Composers, the Songs, the Performers, and Their Times—The Golden Age of American Popular Music from 1886 to 1956*. New York: Donald I. Fine, 1988.

Jones, Tom. *Making Musicals: An Informal Introduction to the World of Musical Theatre*. New York: Limelight Editions, 1998.

Kasha, Al, and Joel Hirschhorn. *Notes on Broadway: Intimate Conversations with Broadway's Greatest Songwriters*. New York: Simon and Schuster, 1985.

Kashner, Sam, and Nancy Schoenberger. *A Talent for Genius: The Life and Times of Oscar Levant*. New York: Villard, 1994.

Kaye, Deena, and James LeBrecht. *Sound and Music for the Theatre*. New York: Watson-Guptill, 1992.

Kazan, Elia. *Elia Kazan: A Life*. New York: Knopf, 1988.

Kimball, Robert, and Tommy Krasker. *Catalog of the American Musical: Musicals of Irving Berlin, George and Ira Gershwin, Cole Porter, Richard Rodgers, and Lorenz Hart*. Washington, D.C.: National Institute for Opera and Musical Theater, 1988.

Kinney, Troy. *Social Dancing of Today*. New York: F. A. Stokes, 1914.

Kislan, Richard. *Hoofing on Broadway: A History of Show Dancing*. New York: Prentice Hall Press, 1987.

Kowalke, Kim H., and Lys Symonette, eds. and trans. *Speak Low (When You Speak of Love): The Letters of Kurt Weill and Lotte Lenya*. Berkeley: University of California Press, 1996.

Kreuger, Miles. *Show Boat: The Story of a Classic American Musical*. New York: Oxford University Press, 1977.

Laufe, Abe. *Broadway's Greatest Musicals*. Rev. ed. New York: Funk and Wagnalls, 1977.

Laurents, Arthur. *Original Story: A Memoir of Broadway and Hollywood*. New York: Knopf, 2000.

Laurie, Joe, Jr. *Vaudeville: From the Honky-tonks to the Palace*. New York: Henry Holt, 1953.

Lawrence, Greg. *Dance with Demons: The Life of Jerome Robbins*. New York: Putnam, 2001.

Lees, Gene. *Inventing Champagne: The Worlds of Lerner and Loewe.* New York: St. Martin's Press, 1990.

Leiter, Samuel L. *The Encyclopedia of the New York Stage.* 3 vols. Westport, Conn.: Greenwood Press, 1985–92.

Leonard, John A. *Theatre Sound.* New York: Routledge, 2001.

Lerner, Alan Jay. *The Musical Theatre: A Celebration.* London: Collins, 1986.

———. *The Street Where I Live.* New York: W. W. Norton, 1978.

Levant, Oscar. *A Smattering of Ignorance.* Garden City, N.Y.: Garden City Publishing, 1942.

Lewis, Robert. *Slings and Arrows: Theater in My Life.* New York: Stein and Day, 1984.

Loesser, Susan. *A Most Remarkable Fella: Frank Loesser and the Guys and Dolls in His Life, A Portrait by His Daughter.* New York: Donald I. Fine, 1993.

Logan, Joshua. *Josh: My Up and Down, In and Out Life.* New York: Delacorte Press, 1976.

———. *Movie Stars, Real People, and Me.* New York: Delacorte Press, 1978.

Loney, Glenn. *Unsung Genius: The Passion of Dancer-Choreographer Jack Cole.* New York: Franklin Watts, 1984.

Long, Robert Emmet. *Broadway, the Golden Years: Jerome Robbins and the Great Choreographer-Directors, 1940 to the Present.* New York: Continuum, 2001.

Mandelbaum, Ken. *A Chorus Line and the Musicals of Michael Bennett.* New York: St. Martin's Press, 1989.

———. *Not Since Carrie: Forty Years of Broadway Musical Flops.* New York: St. Martin's Press, 1991.

Marx, Samuel, and Jan Clayton, *Rodgers and Hart: Bewitched, Bothered, and Bedeviled—An Anecdotal Account.* New York: Putnam, 1976.

Mates, Julian. *America's Musical Stage: Two Hundred Years of Musical Theatre.* Westport, Conn.: Greenwood Press, 1985.

McBrien, William. *Cole Porter: A Biography.* New York: Knopf, 1998.

McCabe, John. *George M. Cohan: The Man Who Owned Broadway.* New York: Doubleday, 1973.

McCarthy, Albert J. *The Dance Band Era: The Dancing Decades from Ragtime to Swing, 1910–1950.* Radnor, Pa.: Chilton Books, 1971.

McGovern, Dennis, and Deborah Grace Winer. *Sing Out, Louise! 150 Stars of the Musical Theatre Remember 50 Years on Broadway.* New York: Schirmer Books, 1993.

McWhorter, John. *Doing Our Own Thing: The Degradation of Language and Music and Why We Should, Like, Care.* New York: Gotham Books, 2003.

Morath, Max. *The NPR Curious Listener's Guide to Popular Standards.* New York: Grand Central Press/Perigee, 2002.

Mordden, Ethan. *Beautiful Mornin': The Broadway Musical in the 1940s.* New York: Oxford University Press, 1999.

————. *Coming Up Roses: The Broadway Musical in the 1950s.* New York: Oxford University Press, 1998.

————. *Make Believe: The Broadway Musical in the 1920s.* New York: Oxford University Press, 1997.

————. *Rodgers and Hammerstein.* New York: Harry N. Abrams, 1992.

Newsom, Jon, ed. *Perspectives on John Philip Sousa.* Washington, D.C.: Library of Congress, 1983.

Nolan, Frederick. *The Sound of Their Music: The Story of Rodgers and Hammerstein.* New York: Walker and Company, 1978.

Norton, Richard. *A Chronology of American Musical Theatre.* New York: Oxford University Press, 2002.

Ostrow, Stuart. *A Producer's Broadway Journey.* Westport, Conn.: Praeger, 1999.

Peyser, Joan. *The Memory of All That: The Life of George Gershwin.* New York: Simon and Schuster, 1993.

Potter, John, ed. *The Cambridge Companion to Singing.* Cambridge: Cambridge University Press, 2000.

Powell, Dawn. *The Diaries of Dawn Powell, 1931–1965.* Edited by Tim Page. South Royalton, Vt.: Steerforth Press, 1995.

Raymond, Jack. *Show Music on Record: The First 100 Years.* New rev. ed. Falls Church, Va.: Jack Raymond, 1998.

Rigdon, Walter, ed. *Who's Who of the American Theatre.* New York: James H. Heineman, 1965.

Rimsky-Korsakov, Nikolay. *Principles of Orchestration.* 1922. Reprint, New York: Dover Publications, 1964.

Rodgers, Richard. *Musical Stages: An Autobiography.* New York: Random House, 1975.

Rosenberg, Bernard, and Ernest Harburg. *The Broadway Musical: Collaboration in Commerce and Art.* New York: New York University Press, 1993.

Rubin, Martin. *Showstoppers: Busby Berkeley and the Tradition of Spectacle.* New York: Columbia University Press, 1993.

Sadie, Stanley, and Christina Bashford, eds. *The New Grove Dictionary of Opera.* 4 vols. New York: Grove's Dictionaries of Music, 1992.

Sadie, Stanley, and John Tyrrell, eds. *The New Grove Dictionary of Music and Musicians.* New York: Grove's Dictionaries, 2000.

Sanders, Ronald. *The Days Grow Short: The Life and Music of Kurt Weill.* New York: Holt, Rinehart, and Winston, 1980.

Schuller, Gunther. *Early Jazz: Its Roots and Musical Development.* New York: Oxford University Press, 1968.

Secrest, Meryle. *Somewhere for Me: A Biography of Richard Rodgers.* New York: Knopf, 2001.

————. *Stephen Sondheim: A Life.* New York: Knopf, 1998.

Sharaff, Irene. *Broadway and Hollywood.* New York: Van Nostrand Reinhold, 1976.

Slide, Anthony. *The Encyclopedia of Vaudeville.* Westport, Conn.: Greenwood Press, 1994.

Smith, Cecil, and Glenn Litton. *Musical Comedy in America.* 1950. Reprint, New York: Routledge/Theatre Arts Books, 1996.

Smith, Steven C. *A Heart at Fire's Center: The Life and Music of Bernard Herrmann.* Berkeley: University of California Press, 1991.

Snyder, Robert W. *The Voice of the City: Vaudeville and Popular Culture in New York.* New York: Oxford University Press, 1989.

Spaeth, Sigmund. *A History of Popular Music in America.* New York: Random House, 1948.

Spergel, Mark. *Reinventing Reality: The Art and Life of Rouben Mamoulian.* Metuchen, N.J.: Scarecrow Press, 1993.

Spoto, Donald. *Lenya: A Life.* Boston: Little, Brown, 1989.

Steyn, Mark. *Broadway Babies Say Goodnight: Musicals Then and Now.* New York: Routledge, 1997.

Stott, William, with Jane Stott. *On Broadway: Performance Photographs by Fred Fehl.* Austin: University of Texas Press, 1978.

Swados, Elizabeth. *Listening Out Loud.* New York: Harper and Row, 1988.

Taper, Bernard. *Balanchine: A Biography.* New York: Times Books, 1984.

Tawa, Nicholas E. *The Way to Tin Pan Alley: American Popular Song, 1866–1910.* New York: Schirmer Books, 1990.

Traubner, Richard. *Operetta: A Theatrical History.* Garden City, N.Y.: Doubleday, 1983.

Walker, Leo. *The Wonderful Era of the Great Dance Bands.* Berkeley, Calif.: Howell-North Books, 1964.

Waters, Edward N. *Victor Herbert: A Life in Music.* New York: Macmillan, 1955.

Wilder, Alec. *American Popular Song: The Great Innovators, 1900–1950.* Edited by James T. Maher. New York: Oxford University Press, 1972.

Zadan, Craig. *Sondheim and Company.* New York: Macmillan, 1974.

Ziegfeld, Richard, and Paulette Ziegfeld. *The Ziegfeld Touch: The Life and Times of Florenz Ziegfeld, Jr.* New York: Harry N. Abrams, 1993.

Zinsser, William. *Easy to Remember: The Great American Songwriters and Their Songs.* Jaffrey, N.H.: David R. Godine, 2000.

Selected Articles, Theses, and Festschrifts

Finson, Jon. "Realism in Late Nineteenth-Century American Musical Theater: The Songs of Edward Harrigan and David Braham." In Edward Harrigan and David Braham, *Collected Songs,* edited by Jon Finson. Madison, Wis.: A-R Editions, 1997.

Kurt Weill Foundation for Music. Study guides for: *Lady in the Dark,* 2d ed., and *Street Scene,* 2d ed. New York: Kurt Weill Foundation for Music, 1996, 1997.

Loney, Glenn, ed. *Musical Theatre in America: Papers and Proceedings of the Conference on the Musical Theatre in America.* No. 8, *Contributions in Drama and Theatre Studies.* Westport, Conn.: Greenwood Press, 1984.

Mitchell, Jon Ceander. "John Philip Sousa: A Comparative Instrumentation Study of the Manuscripts and Published Orchestral Scores of Selected Works." *Journal of the Conductors Guild* 21, nos. 1 and 2 (2000).

Oberstein, Bennett Thomas. "The Broadway Directing Career of Rouben Mamoulian." Ph.D. diss., Indiana University, 1977.

Sagolla, Lisa Jo. "The Influence of Modern Dance on American Musical Theatre Choreography of the 1940s." *Dance: Current Selected Research* 2 (1990): 47–68.

Stratyner, Barbara. *Ned Wayburn and the Dance Routine: From Vaudeville to the Ziegfeld Follies.* No. 13, *Studies in Dance History.* Madison: University of Wisconsin Press, 1996.

Wind, Herbert Warren. "Another Opening, Another Show." *New Yorker,* November 17, 1951, pp. 48–71.

PERMISSIONS ACKNOWLEDGMENTS

INDEX

For references to individual musicals, see under titles of works.

Abba, 45
Abbott and Costello, 85, 281
Abbott, George: Anderson (Murray) and, 235; on Balanchine, 255; on Belasco, 224; as director, 107, 244–46, 267, 268, 292–93; on Mielziner, 237; as play doctor, 248–49; on the "Abbott touch," 249
acoustics: orchestrators and, 185–87; sound design and, 198–99; theater design and, 191
actor-managers, 223–24
Actors' Equity, 208
Actors Studio, 246, 247, 269–70, 290
Adams, Diana, 263
Adams, Franklin P., 54
adaptations as responsible for decline of musicals, 80, 309
African-Americans: all-black Broadway shows, 132; and ostinato, 152; and vocal style, 19–21, 36
African Suite (Bledsoe), 60
Age of Anxiety, The, 272
Agee, James, 112
agogic accents, 153–54, 160. *See also* back-phrasing
Ahrens, Lynn, 89, 95–96
Aida (2000): lyrics in, 92; sound design in, 196; vocal deformation and, 42; vocal style in, 46
Ailey, Alvin, 257
Albertina Rasch Girls, 252–53
Alexander, David, 252

Alexander's Ragtime Band (film), 38
aliteracy, as sign of cultural decline and decline of musicals, 185, 282, 301, 308–9
Allegro: directorship of, 260–61, 264–65; fox-trot song in, 149; influence of, 64; as narrative show, 298; song recycling in, 33
Allen, Gracie, 59
Alton, Robert: as choreographer, 251–52, 262, 269, 291–92; as dance arranger, 236; as dance doctor, 250; and *Pal Joey,* 237
American Ballet Theatre, 262, 263, 266
American Federation of Musicians, labor disputes, 192, 207–9
American Popular Song (Wilder), 11, 312
American Society of Composers, Authors, and Publishers (ASCAP), 101, 117
American Theatre Laboratory, 274
American Theatre Wing, 285
American Way, The, 192
Americana, 67, 68
Anderson, John Murray, 240; as conceptual showman, 299; as director, 108, 235, 245, 248, 267; on Harbach, 59; and nostalgia, 2; on production backers, 306; on vocal projection, 167
Anderson, Leroy, 112
Anderson, Maxwell, 54, 60, 74–75, 92
Andrews, Julie, 43, 203
Andros, Dick, 256
Angell, Roger, 2–3, 4

341